# *The Vinson Court*

# ABC-CLIO SUPREME COURT HANDBOOKS

**Peter G. Renstrom, Series Editor**

ABC-CLIO SUPREME COURT HANDBOOKS

# *The Vinson Court*

## Justices, Rulings, and Legacy

### Michal R. Belknap

ABC-CLIO

Santa Barbara, California • Denver, Colorado • Oxford, England

Library of Congress Cataloging-in-Publication Data

Belknap, Michal R.
    The Vinson Court: justices, rulings, and legacy / Michal R. Belknap.
        p.  cm. — (ABC-CLIO Supreme Court handbooks)
    Includes bibliographical references and index.
    ISBN 1-57607-201-0 (hardcopy: alk. paper)   ISBN 1-85109-542-X (e-book)
1. Vinson, Fred M., 1890–1953.  2. United States.  Supreme Court —History—20th century.  3. Constitutional history—United States. I. Title. II. Series

    KF8742.B43  2004
    342.7302'9—dc22                                              2004011690

08  07  06  05  04     10  9  8  7  6  5  4  3  2  1

This book is also available on the World Wide Web as an e-book. Visit abc-clio.com for details.

ABC-CLIO, Inc.
130 Cremona Drive, P.O. Box 1911
Santa Barbara, California 93116-1911

This book is printed on acid-free paper ∞.
Manufactured in the United States of America

# *Contents*

# *Series Foreword*

There is an extensive literature on the U.S. Supreme Court, but it contains discussion familiar largely to the academic community and the legal profession. The ABC-CLIO Supreme Court series is designed to have value to the academic and legal communities also, but each volume is intended as well for the general reader who does not possess an extensive background on the Court or American constitutional law. The series is intended to effectively represent each of fourteen periods in the history of the Supreme Court with each of these fourteen eras defined by the chief justice, beginning with John Jay in 1789. Each Court confronted constitutional and statutory questions that were of major importance to and influenced by the historical period. The Court's decisions were also influenced by the values of each of the individual justices sitting at the time. The issues, the historical period, the justices, and the Courts' decisions in the most significant cases will be examined in the volumes of this series.

ABC-CLIO's Supreme Court series provides scholarly examinations of the Court as it functioned in different historical periods and with different justices. Each volume contains information necessary to understand each particular Court and an interpretative analysis by the author of each Court's record and legacy. In addition to representing the major decisions of each Court, institutional linkages are examined as well—the political connections among the Court, Congress, and the executive branch. These relationships are important for several reasons. Although the Supreme Court retains some institutional autonomy, all the Court's justices are selected by a process that involves the other two branches. Many of the significant decisions of the Court involve the review of actions of Congress or the president. In addition, the Court frequently depends on the other two branches to secure compliance with its rulings.

The authors for the volumes in this series were selected with great care. Each author has worked extensively with the Court, the period, and the personalities about which he or she has written. ABC-CLIO wanted each of the volumes to examine several common themes, and each author agreed to work within certain guidelines. Each author was free, however, to develop the content of each volume, and many of the volumes advance new or distinctive conclusions about the Court under examination.

Each volume contains four substantive chapters. The first chapter introduces the Court and the historical period in which it served. The second chapter examines each of the justices who sat on the particular Court. The third chapter represents the most significant decisions rendered by the particular Court. Among other things, the impact of the historical period and the value orientations of the individual justices are developed. A fourth and final chapter addresses the impact of each particular Court on American constitutional law—its doctrinal legacy.

Each volume contains several features designed to make it more valuable to those whose previous exposure to the Supreme Court and American constitutional law is limited. Each volume has a reference section that contains brief entries on some of the people, statutes, events, and concepts introduced in the four substantive chapters. Entries in this section are arranged alphabetically. Each volume also contains a glossary of selected legal terms used in the text. Following each of the four chapters, a list of sources used in the chapter and suggestions for further reading appears. Each volume also has a comprehensive annotated bibliography. A listing of Internet sources is presented at the end of the bibliography. Finally, there is a comprehensive subject index and a list of cases (with citation numbers) discussed in each volume. ABC-CLIO is delighted with the quality of scholarship represented in each volume and is proud to offer this series to the reading public.

Permit me to conclude with a personal note. This project has been an extraordinarily rewarding undertaking for me as series editor. Misgivings about serving in this capacity were plentiful at the outset of the project. After tending to some administrative business pertaining to the series, securing authors for each volume was the first major task. I developed a list of possible authors after reviewing previous work and obtaining valuable counsel from several recognized experts in American constitutional history. In virtually every instance, the first person on my list agreed to participate in the project. The high quality of the series was assured and enhanced as each author signed on. I could not have been more pleased. My interactions with each author have been most pleasant, and the excellence of their work will be immediately apparent to the reader. I sincerely thank each author.

Finally, a word about ABC-CLIO and its staff. ABC-CLIO was enthusiastic about the project from the beginning and has done everything necessary to make this series successful. I am very appreciative of the level of support I have received from ABC-CLIO. Alicia Merritt, senior acquisitions editor, deserves special recognition. She has held my hand throughout the project. She has facilitated making this project a reality in every conceivable way. She has encouraged me from the beginning, provided invaluable counsel, and given me latitude to operate as I wished while keeping me on track at the same time. This project would not have gotten off the ground without Alicia, and I cannot thank her enough.

—*Peter G. Renstrom*

# *Preface*

F red Vinson was not a great chief justice. Nor was the Supreme Court he headed from 1946 to 1953 a great Court. Indeed, both were at most mediocre. The Vinson Court was a product of an anxious era after World War II, when the euphoria inspired by the greatest military triumph of the United States gave way to uncertainty and fear aroused by a developing Cold War between this country and the Soviet Union.

During Vinson's chief justiceship, the Supreme Court had to deal with difficult issues, especially in the field of civil liberties. In the opinion of most legal scholars and historians, it did not handle these very well. Rather than protecting individual rights from the ravages of McCarthyism, the Vinson Court gave judicial support to the anti-Communist hysteria that swept the nation during the early years of the Cold War. Besides compiling an antilibertarian record, it seethed with internal conflict. Appointed to unify a collection of strong-willed justices, whose public feuding had embarrassed the Court, Vinson failed to accomplish his mission. The inadequate leadership he provided exacerbated the divisions within his Court and contributed to its disappointing record.

That record needs to be put into perspective, however. Just as the reputation of President Herbert Hoover has suffered from frequent comparisons with his successor, Franklin Roosevelt, so that of the Vinson Court suffered when its performance was contrasted with that of the Warren Court, headed by Vinson's successor. Earl Warren's Court revolutionized many aspects of constitutional law and vastly expanded civil rights and civil liberties. Vinson's Court achieved far less. Comparing it with Warren's is not entirely fair, however. In the first place, it lasted less than half as long. Secondly, many of the Warren Court's accomplishments actually represent the flowering of developments that began during the Vinson era. Fred Vinson headed what was in many respects a transition Court.

That there should have been continuity between Vinson's Court and Warren's is hardly surprising, for many of the same men served on both. Justices Felix Frankfurter and Hugo Black, whose jurisprudential and personal rivalry dominated the Court until 1961, continued under Warren a struggle they had waged while Vinson was chief justice. Like Black, William O. Douglas served throughout the entire history of both Courts. Along with Stanley Reed and Robert Jackson, whose judicial careers also lasted into the Warren era, Douglas, Black, and Frankfurter were Roosevelt appointees.

The core of the Vinson Court, however, consisted of four men named to the high tribunal by President Harry Truman. This group included the chief justice and Associate Justices Harold Burton, Tom Clark, and Sherman Minton. All owed their appointments primarily to the fact that they were the president's buddies. None was the intellectual equal of Black, Douglas, Frankfurter, or Jackson. It was the Truman appointees who gave the Vinson Court its well-deserved reputation for mediocrity. They also made it a more conservative body than the Stone Court had been or than the Warren Court would be. After the appointments of Clark and Minton in 1949, the four Truman appointees provided the core of a conservative majority that determined the outcome of important cases and the jurisprudential direction of the Vinson Court.

That direction was generally conservative, but the reason was not the political conservatism of the judges who composed the Court. Indeed, Burton was the only Republican on it. He was a moderate, and like all of his colleagues, had been appointed by a liberal Democratic president. Some members of the Vinson Court, such as Frankfurter and Minton, had once been regarded in conservative circles as left-wing extremists. That they now rendered decisions pleasing to those who had once criticized them was perhaps due in part to the fact that they, like many Americans, had drifted to the right during and after World War II. Even more likely, though, their judicial conservatism was due to a strong commitment to two tenets of Roosevelt's New Deal. Most of the justices who served on the Vinson Court believed in the goodness of government, and they also believed that unelected judges should not use their power to thwart the initiatives of politically responsible legislators and executive officials. Their commitment to judicial restraint was even stronger when they passed on actions of the national government than when they reviewed those of state and local authorities. Their restraint was also firmer when the issue they confronted was the constitutionality of a congressional initiative rather than the validity of some administrative action. Their devotion to supporting whatever the government did was particularly powerful when national security was at stake.

Because of their concern for national security and their tendency to uphold whatever actions the government considered necessary to protect it, the Vinson Court affirmed the constitutionality of a host of measures designed to safeguard the United States from communism, many of which severely restricted freedom of speech. These decisions earned it a reputation as an enemy of the First Amendment. Although deserved, that reputation was exaggerated, for it ignored the fact that this Court sometimes held unconstitutional the actions of local governments that interfered with freedom of expression, especially when those took the form of prior restraints. Likewise, while generally supporting actions the executive branch considered necessary to ensure national security, it did not always do so. Although refusing to interfere with U.S. military trials of former members of the German and Japanese armed forces after World War II, or to become involved in the case of Russian spies Julius and Ethel Rosenberg, the Vinson Court prohibited President Truman from seizing the nation's steel mills in order to maintain production of a militarily vital commodity during the Korean War. The reason for that decision was that, although Truman considered his action necessary to safeguard national security, in taking it he had defied the will of Congress, which was the authority to which the old New Dealers who comprised the Vinson Court deferred above all others.

The justices' challenge to presidential authority in the steel seizure case, *Youngstown Sheet and Tube Company v. Sawyer* (1952), was the most important decision rendered by the Vinson Court. It was far from representative of the jurisprudence of that tribunal, however. Generally, the Vinson Court upheld governmental action. In an increasingly conservative era, the result of doing that was a generally conservative jurisprudence. The conservatism of Vinson Court rulings was evident in areas as diverse as labor law, criminal procedure, and the relationship between church and state.

Yet, the conservative trend of the Vinson Court's decisions tends to obscure the fact that during the period 1946 to 1953, seeds were germinating that would flower into the liberal jurisprudence of the Warren Court. For example, although Vinson and a majority of his colleagues rejected the contention that the Fourteenth Amendment had made the Bill of Rights applicable to the states, Black's unsuccessful argument for that proposition in *Adamson v. California* (1949) initiated a debate among the justices that led eventually to the Warren Court's selective incorporation of most of its criminal justice provisions into that amendment's Due Process Clause Although the Vinson Court more often upheld governmental assistance to religion than found it unconstitutional, it was the Court that incorporated the First Amendment's Establishment Clause into the Due Process Clause. It was also the first Court (in striking down a program under which clergymen provided instruction to public school students on school property during school hours) to find something a government had done that violated this constitutional prohibition. The Vinson Court's rulings in this area paved the way for the far better-known decisions of the Warren Court that held prayer and Bible reading in public schools unconstitutional. It was, of course, the Warren Court that decided *Brown v. Board of Education* (1954), the case that held school segregation unconstitutional and banished racial apartheid from U.S. constitutional law. But the Vinson Court had been chipping away at the separate-but-equal rule that *Brown* rejected for several years prior to that landmark decision. Its more limited rulings outlawing segregation in interstate transportation, prohibiting judicial enforcement of racially restrictive covenants in real estate deeds, and especially insisting that African Americans be afforded graduate education equal to that which whites received, made the *Brown* decision, by the time that the Warren Court ruled a year after Vinson died, all but inevitable.

Thus, the Vinson Court, despite its shortcomings and the damage it did to civil liberties, deserves more credit than it has received. Conversely, I deserve less credit than ABC-CLIO has given me by placing my name on the cover of this book. While working on it, I was stricken with what was originally diagnosed as a fatal brain tumor. Thank God, my illness eventually proved to be only a brain abscess, but even that left me so incapacitated that for a time I could not respond to simple commands, dial a telephone, or read more than a couple of sentences. It took more than a year for me to recover completely. Because my illness severely restricted my ability to work on this book, Peter Renstrom and Melvin Urofsky generously volunteered to help me with it. Although I wrote all of Chapter 2 and about half of Chapter 3, Pete roughed out the rest of Chapter 3 and all of Chapter 1, and Mel drafted Chapter 4. They gave me the opportunity to go over everything they wrote and make whatever changes I wanted, so responsibility for what appears in the pages that follow rests squarely on my shoulders. I could not have completed this book without their *very substantial* assistance, however, and I want to take this opportunity to express my sincere gratitude to both Pete and Mel and to give them all the credit they so richly deserve. I also wish to thank my wife Patricia, without whose love, support, and prodding I could not have regained my health, let alone written *The Vinson Court*.

—*Michal R. Belknap*

# PART ONE

## *Justices, Rulings, and Legacy*

# *The Vinson Court and the Period*

T he Vinson Court was the product of the troubled era just after World War II, during which euphoria inspired by the greatest military triumph in U.S. history gave way to anxiety, caused by the development of a bitter Cold War with the Soviet Union and the outbreak of a shooting conflict in Korea. The man who headed that Court, Frederick Moore Vinson, was nominated for chief justice on June 6, 1946. He took his seat on the Court less than three weeks later, and the Vinson Court era had begun.

The Court Fred Vinson joined was of Franklin D. Roosevelt's (FDR) making. Roosevelt was seeking justices who were committed to the political and economic principles underlying the New Deal. He got economic liberals and justices dedicated to protecting constitutional liberties as well. Between 1937 and 1943, FDR was able to nominate nine justices, including his promotion of Justice Harlan Fiske Stone to the chief justiceship. The Court of this era is often called the Roosevelt Court. Roosevelt died in April 1945 and was succeeded by Harry S. Truman. Chief Justice Stone passed away a year later. Before Stone's death, the Court was moving toward fully developing the "preferred position" doctrine he articulated in *United States v. Carolene Products Company* (1938). That doctrine directs the Court to scrutinize closely any government act that impinges on fundamental constitutional protections.

President Truman replaced not only Stone, but also Justices Owen Roberts, Frank Murphy, and Wiley Rutledge. The replacement of Roberts, a conservative appointee of Herbert Hoover, with Harold Burton did not really change the ideological composition of the Court; both Roberts and Burton were judicial conservatives. Murphy and Rutledge, on the other hand, were the most enthusiastic advocates of a more protective civil liberties jurisprudence. Truman replaced Stone, Murphy, and Rutledge with justices who did not share that view—Vinson, Sherman Minton, and Tom Clark. It is not clear that Truman had a definite plan in mind for the Court, but his nominees changed the Court's direction, especially in the area of constitutional protections. In fact, the Truman appointees so changed the emerging jurisprudence of the Stone

Court that the Court under Vinson can be accurately called the Truman Court. His appointees interrupted whatever continuity might have developed between the Stone and Warren Courts and delayed by more than a decade the so-called rights revolution begun by the Stone Court and finished by the Warren Court.

## Truman Succeeds Roosevelt

Franklin Delano Roosevelt died of a cerebral hemorrhage less than three months after being inaugurated for his fourth term as president. His vice president, Harry S. Truman of Missouri, had served only eighty-three days in that position before succeeding to the presidency. Truman had governmental experience and brought personal strengths to the office. Nonetheless, his first months as president consisted of "on-the-job training." Although he had been an attentive second in command, his work had chiefly involved him in the operations of the Senate and in making speeches. The task facing Truman was daunting. Among other things, he had to preside over the end of World War II. From the moment of his succession, Truman felt enormous pressure. When informed of Roosevelt's death, he said he felt as though "the moon, the stars, and all the planets had fallen on me." The day following Roosevelt's death, the new president said at his first press conference, "Boys, if you ever pray, pray for me now" (McCoy 1984, 1).

Much of the public wondered just who Harry Truman was. He was not well known and lacked the charisma of a Roosevelt. At the same time, he came to the presidency with more political experience than Theodore Roosevelt, Woodrow Wilson, or Herbert Hoover had, when they began their respective presidential terms. Truman was the product of the Pendergast political machine in Kansas City, Missouri. After holding office at the local level, he was elected to the U.S. Senate in 1934. Truman won reelection in 1940, and with his second term came an opportunity for leadership. He was made chairman of the Senate Committee to Investigate the National Defense Program. Known as the Truman Committee, it did an "admirable job in promoting economy, efficiency and effectiveness in defense production" (McCoy 1984, 7). As a result of the committee's work, Truman's personal influence in Washington increased, as did his reputation among Democratic leaders. The unexpected by-product was the U.S. vice presidency.

Important as he had become in Washington, Truman was certainly not a national figure in 1944. The better-known prospects for the Democratic vice presidential nomination were the incumbent, Henry A. Wallace, War Mobilization Director James F. Byrnes, and Supreme Court Justice William O. Douglas. None of them was able to gain, or in Wallace's case retain, Roosevelt's endorsement, however. Each was considered by the Democratic convention delegates to have flaws too serious to warrant nomination as Roosevelt's running mate. After much political maneuvering, the convention delegates found Truman an acceptable compromise. Few Democrats attending the convention "thought to ask what he might be like as president," but he "excited no fear in the various quarters that opposed the possibility of having a strong-willed Wallace, Byrnes, or Douglas succeed to the White House." Truman did little to boost the electoral strength of the ticket, but he did what was expected of him, giving his share of speeches and shaking the hands of prospective supporters. Following his nomination, Truman was "catapulted from the lower circles of senatorial leadership to take office as the nation's second-ranking official" (McCoy 1984, 7–8).

When Roosevelt's death thrust Truman into the top spot, Truman was aware that he had become president only because his predecessor had chosen him as his running mate over others who were greater liabilities. Truman had no national political base, and his personality was very different from that of his predecessor. For some time after his succession, "he walked in the long shadow of the dead president" (Milkis and Nelson 1994, 295). Truman's situation was made more difficult by his having no time to work on or compensate for his "actual or perceived deficiencies." He had become president at the moment of Roosevelt's death and "would be held accountable if he did not immediately act the part, especially with World War II yet to be concluded." Truman's character enabled him to make the most of his "on-the-job training" as president—he was "brisk, decisive, industrious, practical and tough" (McCoy 1984, 15). On balance, Truman was a "solid successor" to Roosevelt. Although Roosevelt's strongest supporters were often frustrated with him, he "deeply believed in the changes that the New Deal had made." Try as he might, however, he was a "poor speaker who was awkward in the presence of reporters," and he "suffered persistently low popularity"—his public approval rating was less than 50 percent for the majority of his tenure as president (Milkis and Nelson 1994, 295).

## Ending the War

Bringing the war against the Axis to a speedy conclusion was obviously Truman's most pressing priority. He addressed a joint session of Congress on April 16, 1945, where he pledged himself to "achiev[ing] a speedy victory" over Germany and Japan and reaffirmed that the United States would demand the "unconditional surrender" of both. The war in the European theater was progressing toward a victorious conclusion when Truman succeeded to the presidency. In fact, Truman was able to announce the complete surrender of Germany less than a month after taking office (McCoy 1984, 20–21). As for the Pacific theater, American objectives were similar—win as quickly as possible with as few Allied casualties and at as little cost as possible. How to accomplish these objectives was not so clear. The possibilities for a strike against Japan included naval and air blockades and a full invasion of the Japanese home islands. The blockade, however, would be a long-term and costly process. Such a strategy would be "unacceptable to the war-weary and victory-expectant American leaders and people." The invasion was also long-term and might exact at least half a million casualties. That left one possibility for an immediate end to the war—the atomic bomb (McCoy 1984, 22–24). After extended discussion with his principal advisers at the Potsdam Conference near Berlin in July 1945, Truman made his decision to use the bomb. An ultimatum was issued to Japan, demanding immediate and unconditional surrender, with total destruction as the alternative. Speed was imperative—both to save lives and resources, and to lessen the chances of Russian intervention in the Asian war. When Japan did not reply affirmatively to the surrender ultimatum, an atomic bomb was dropped on the city of Hiroshima on August 6. A second one was dropped on Nagasaki three days later. The following day, Truman received word that Japan would surrender on Allied terms. Formal announcement of Japan's unconditional surrender came from Truman on August 14.

The Allies faced difficult decisions once the war had ended. They had to determine what to do with Germany. They had to remove the vestiges of the Nazi regime, deal with the millions of prisoners of war, set up a transitional military government, and establish a temporary civil government. Truman, Stalin, and Clement Attlee worked out the details—East Germany was assigned to Russia, northwestern Germany to Britain, and southwestern Germany to the United States, with France receiving two smaller areas. Treating Germany as a single economic entity was not a viable option, and there were even sharper differences on how to govern the respective assigned territories. The Russians wanted to communize all of Central Europe; the Soviet Union took over not only the Baltic states (seized during the war), but East Prussia, Poland, and eastern Germany as well. Less than two years after the defeat of Hitler, Germany was partitioned into two nations, and its capital, Berlin, was divided as well.

## The United Nations

President Franklin Roosevelt and Prime Minister Winston Churchill issued a joint statement in August 1941 known as the Atlantic Charter. The charter contained a number of principles upon which U.S. and British foreign policy would be based. Among other things, the charter called for world peace and disarmament following the war and the creation of a permanent system for world security. The wartime alliance between Russia and her Western allies was artificial. It was based on mutual need and the fact that they faced a common enemy. Nonetheless, the Allies were hopeful that the Soviet Union might cooperate with the West in fashioning a new international order. The first steps in establishing the United Nations began in January 1942. For the next two and one-half years, representatives of the Allies drafted proposals for a postwar international organization. In August 1944 the delegates met at Dumbarton Oaks, in suburban

Washington, D.C., to prepare language for the United Nations Charter. Invitations had already gone out for a United Nations conference to meet in San Francisco to finalize a charter for the new international organization when Roosevelt died on April 12.

Delegates from fifty nations assembled in San Francisco and formally established the United Nations. The UN Charter provided for a General Assembly with representatives from all member nations and a Security Council with five permanent members and six other rotating ones. The key component was the Security Council, which was charged to "maintain international peace and security." In addition, the charter established an International Court of Justice and a number of other agencies. With the wholehearted support of the Truman administration, the Senate ratified the UN Charter with only two dissenting votes. Truman then turned to the issues of reconverting the U.S. economy and reconstructing the European economy.

## *Reconversion*

As the war came to a close, Truman had to guide the country through the transition back to peace. The task of converting from a wartime to a peacetime economy caused a number of concerns for the administration. The principal worry for the Truman administration was that without the stimulus provided by the war, the country would return to the unemployment levels of the 1930s. Many feared a postwar depression as defense contracts were cancelled and military contractors laid employees off. Indeed, forecasts of 8 million unemployed seemed likely to come true. Assisted by the return of many veterans to school under the GI Bill, however, the economy swiftly absorbed the millions of returning servicemen. In a remarkably short time, American industry changed over to a peacetime footing, and the feared depression never materialized. Unlike the experience following World War I, the Truman years featured an expansion of wartime prosperity.

Franklin Roosevelt had indicated that he had "ambitious plans to expand New Deal reforms after the war." Roosevelt's followers were more than apprehensive about the fate of his plans with Truman in the White House. Truman, however, called for a "Fair Deal," intended to follow through on Roosevelt's plans. This greatly relieved those supporting a continuation of the Roosevelt reforms. Nonetheless, there was substantial concern about the conservatives Truman brought into his administration.

Fortunately, the Truman administration's policies spurred economic expansion. Less than a year after the surrender of the Japanese, 75 percent of the American armed forces had been demobilized. The impact of transitioning that many service personnel from military to civilian life was mitigated by a package of programs, including compensation for mustering-out of the military and unemployment, job reinstatement, veterans' preference for civil service positions, subsidies for education and training, and funding for health and medical care. As good as all this was, there was one serious problem—inflation. American producers, both manufacturers and farmers, had been stringently controlled throughout the war. Now free of price regulations, all sought to take advantage of pent-up consumer demand for products that had been unavailable during the war. Truman was expected both to terminate the wartime controls and to head off inflation, and he faced political consequences for failing to do either.

When the new president took measures to address inflation, he ran into conflicts with organized labor. John L. Lewis led almost half a million members of the United Mine Workers (UMW) out on strike in April 1946. The forty-day strike threatened the nation's energy supply and also threatened to weaken a U.S. economy robust enough to help resuscitate the European economy. The government took control of the mines, and the UMW essentially secured the wage increases Lewis sought. At the same time, the strike fostered antiunion sentiment. A threatened railroad walkout followed, and once again Truman resorted to seizure to forestall a strike. He intended to seek congressional authorization to draft strikers into the army, but the labor conflict was resolved before the president could take that step. Nonetheless, even considering it cost him the support of Roosevelt liberals and union leaders.

The politics of inflation hurt Truman at both ends of the political spectrum. Shortly after threatening to draft striking railroad workers, he battled Congress over the issue of price controls. Consumer demand threatened to undermine the otherwise healthy national economy. The Truman administration had to limit wages, prices, and profits and restrain the growing expectations of a number of interest groups. He was put in the position of trying to restrain not only business demands but the demands of farmers and workers as well. This was particularly difficult because farmers and workers were part of the traditional Democratic coalition. The statutory authority for the Office of Price Administration, the wartime price control agency, was set to expire. Truman wished to extend its authority, but Congress delayed. As the price control controversy played out, the midterm election of 1946 took place. Exasperated by inflated prices and shortages of certain commodities, among other things, voters put the Republicans in control of Congress for the first time since 1930.

## The Cold War Begins

One problem with the emerging U.S. foreign policy was that the principle of self-determination sometimes became compromised. There was "no doubt the Truman administration, which was impatient in its quest for world peace and harmony, considered Soviet expansionism to be a grave threat" (McCoy 1984, 78). In a speech in early February 1946, Stalin indicated that long-term peace among nations was impossible so long as capitalist forces controlled the noncommunist world. Two weeks later, Iran went to the UN complaining that the Soviet Union was preventing it from dealing with its own internal conflicts. In addition, the Soviets tried to force their influence on strategic areas in Turkey. All of this was "spiritually reinforced" by Winston Churchill's visit to the United States, where in a speech at Westminster College in Fulton, Missouri, on March 5, he declared that from the Baltic to the Adriatic "an iron curtain has descended across Europe, basically with police states to the east and free nations to the west" (McCoy 1984, 80).

The term *Cold War* describes the struggle that developed between the so-called Eastern bloc of nations, headed by the Soviet Union, and the Western bloc, led by the United States. The conflict was called the Cold War because it did not involve actual fighting. The Cold War was the product of mutual distrust and suspicion by the United States, the Soviet Union, and their respective allies. It manifested itself at the end of World War II as the Western bloc adopted a "get tough" policy toward the Soviet Union in response to its expansionism in Eastern Europe. The Soviets in turn accused the United States and its capitalist allies of seeking to encircle it and overthrow its Communist economy and government.

Relations between the Eastern and Western blocs deteriorated quickly after the Yalta Conference in February 1945. During the remainder of 1945 and early 1946, the Soviets expanded into much of Eastern Europe. Truman responded by announcing that the United States would aid any nation resisting Communist aggression. His Truman Doctrine evolved into a broad policy of containing international communism. Secretary of State George Marshall then proposed giving economic aid to European nations to stimulate economic recovery. His proposal, called the European Recovery Program, became better known as the Marshall Plan. In June 1948, the Western Allies announced plans to unify their German occupation zones and to establish in them a Federal Republic of Germany. The Soviets answered with a blockade of Berlin. For the next eleven months, West Berlin was supplied with food and fuel entirely by plane. The U.S.S.R. lifted the blockade in May 1949, and the Allies ended the airlift the following September. During the blockade, the United States pledged continuing military aid to Western Europe. For this purpose, the United States and its allies developed the North Atlantic Treaty Organization (NATO), a mutual defense treaty linking the United States, Canada, and ten West European nations. The final and most serious manifestation of the Cold War during Truman's presidency was the Korean War, which broke out in 1950.

## The Fair Deal and the 80th Congress

The 1946 midterm elections focused on all of Truman's shortcomings as Roosevelt's successor. His popularity, as measured by the Gallup poll, had dropped to 32 percent. Indeed, Truman's support levels had fallen so badly that the Democratic national chairman, Robert Hannegan, suggested that he maintain a low profile while the national party used recordings of Roosevelt's speeches to recapture FDR and party loyalists. The strategy failed, and Truman, playing second fiddle to a dead man, got the blame for the outcome of an election in which Republicans won control of Congress for the first time in sixteen years. In the aftermath of the midterm elections of 1946, the 80th Congress set out to dismantle Roosevelt's New Deal programs, and Democrats sought to blame everything on Truman.

Yet, Truman was trying to expand on Roosevelt's policies. The Fair Deal was his attempt to codify FDR's vision of "a complete economic constitutional order." The domestic program Truman presented to Congress in 1945, though not yet called the Fair Deal, accepted the Roosevelt view that the country needed a "Second Bill of Rights under which a new basis of security and prosperity can be established for all." To secure this vision, the federal government should guarantee a "useful and remunerative job, adequate medical care, a decent home, and a good education." The program Truman presented to Congress was an appeal "to make the attainment of those rights the essence of post-war economic life." Among the twenty points he called for were extension of Social Security to more workers, an increase in the minimum wage, national health insurance, and full employment (Milkis and Nelson 1994, 296). Congress failed to support most of these proposals, however. That turned the midterm elections of 1946 into an opportunity for extended debate on Truman's domestic agenda.

The midterm election went badly for Truman and the Democrats, and the results were interpreted as a vote of no confidence in his administration. Indeed, there were people, including some Democrats, who called for the president's resignation. In addition, labor problems began to plague Truman. In October 1946 John L. Lewis had taken advantage of Congress being out of session and public preoccupation with the election to demand higher wages for the country's mine workers. After negotiations broke down and Lewis decided to take the United Mine Workers out on strike, the government secured a contempt citation and substantial fines against him. (The next March, the Vinson Court upheld the fines against Lewis but reduced the union's liability to $700,000.) Having prevailed in this showdown, Truman slowly began to improve his political position.

He approached 1947 with some confidence, even though his party no longer had control of the Congress. Truman's standing in Gallup polls improved to a 48 percent approval rating by January. In addition, the postwar economy was performing reasonably well, notwithstanding inflationary concerns. Most agricultural commodities were available in sufficient quantities, and other consumer goods were in plentiful supply. When Truman delivered his State of the Union message to Congress on January 6, 1947, he focused on five points in particular: the "promotion of harmonious relations between management and labor," aggressive regulation against monopoly and other restraints on fair competition, subsidization of home construction, a balanced federal budget, and achievement of a reasonable return for the country's farmers (McCoy 1984, 93–94).

Truman's Republican opponents were in agreement on what they did not want. Foremost was maintenance of Roosevelt's New Deal policies, no matter how those policies might be softened or camouflaged. Another GOP priority, and one of the first actions of the 80th Congress, was to adopt language for the Twenty-Second Amendment. The amendment, although exempting Truman, would limit future presidents to two terms in office. Although it was not ratified by the states until 1951, it was an "overt Republican rebuff to Franklin Roosevelt's scrapping of the two-term tradition." More substantial was GOP "eagerness . . . to reduce income taxes, contrary to Truman's wishes" (McCoy 1984, 95–96).

Congress and the president agreed on almost no domestic issues. Inflation was the leading and most important example. In dispute were economic controls—Truman wanted to retain and ever extend the wartime ones, and the Republican Congress wanted to reduce if not eliminate them. This was just one example of the unwillingness of Congress and the administration to cooperate on domestic legislation in 1947. It was "repeated again and again, on questions dealing with monopoly, health, housing, agriculture, education, Social Security, and natural resources." The conflict was not just a matter of Congress's blocking administration initiatives. Truman considered most issues to be nonnegotiable and vetoed many Republican measures, killing thirty-two in 1947 alone. Some of his vetoes came on relatively minor legislation and were produced by the institutional contest between the executive and legislative branches. He vetoed a number of extremely significant measures, however, including bills aimed at reducing the income tax, weakening the Interstate Commerce Act, exempting newspaper and magazine vendors from Social Security, and subsidizing the production of copper, lead, manganese, and zinc. The "most important and highly publicized case," and the only one in which the Congress overrode the president's veto, "concerned the rewriting of the National Labor Relations Act of 1935" by the Taft-Hartley Act (McCoy 1984, 97).

Senator Robert Taft had some differences with the most conservative Republican members in Congress, but they agreed that restricting organized labor was essential. Republicans, as well as some conservative Democrats, had opposed the National Labor Relations (Wagner) Act. The "series of disruptive strikes strengthened their case for imposing restrictions on labor unions." The Taft-Hartley Act of 1947, which Taft cosponsored, was "certainly the most important piece of conservative legislation after the war" (Urofsky and Finkelman 2002, 754). The act outlawed the closed shop, and the secondary boycott required a sixty-day cooling-off period for strikes and authorized an eighty-day injunction against strikes that might affect the national health or safety. Like other postwar statutes, Taft-Hartley "had little regard for civil liberties"

(Urofsky and Finkelman 2002, 755). It prohibited political contributions from unions, and, among other provisions, required union leaders to take a noncommunist oath.

Truman vetoed Taft-Hartley because, in his view, the law was incompatible with national labor policy that had been in place since the 1930s. It can be argued that the president was both right and wrong in his action. He was correct in his judgment that the Taft-Hartley Act was divisive and discriminated against unions. His veto was a significant part of Truman's effort to regain the support of liberals and organized labor before the 1948 election campaign. Congress, however, overrode his veto by a large margin. There is no doubt that the Taft-Hartley Act was the most important domestic legislation of the Truman presidency (McCoy 1984, 99).

Although Truman's objections to it were valid, what he was unwilling to acknowledge was that Taft-Hartley did correct some abuses by organized labor. The changes in the authority of the National Labor Relations Board (NLRB) did not produce substantial changes in the regulatory activities of the NLRB and did ensure that the board would follow even more closely the legal models and procedures that had been part of its operations since its inception. Only in refusing to enforce a closed shop could Taft-Hartley be said to be a retreat from the Wagner Act. Truman gained politically by his opposition to it, while the Republicans suffered political damage from their support of the new law; the act "drove organized labor back into Truman's arms." In the 1948 election, union members turned many Republican supporters of Taft-Hartley out of office, including Representative Fred Hartley Jr.

Taft-Hartley, like many postwar statutes, had little regard for civil liberties, and it required union officials to file affidavits that they were not members of the Communist Party or any other subversive organizations. In many ways, this provision marked the beginning of the postwar Red Scare, and it was among the first to reach the Supreme Court. In 1950, the Court upheld Section 9(h), denying access to the NLRB to those unions whose officers had refused to swear that they were not Communists. In *American Communications Association v. Douds* (1950), Chief Justice Vinson admitted that the statute discouraged the lawful exercise of political freedom by requiring oaths related to individual political beliefs. This abridgement of free speech, however, had to be weighed against the government's power to regulate commerce.

Besides alienating organized labor, the 80th Congress mishandled a promising opportunity to capitalize on Democratic vulnerability when it failed to enact civil rights legislation and chose instead to coalesce with Southern Democrats to block reforms. In response to protest about a number of racial murders in the South, Truman appointed a Committee on Civil Rights, which issued its report, entitled *To Secure These Rights*, in October 1947. The following February, Truman asked Congress to implement the report's recommendations and approve a program that would create a permanent Civil Rights Commission, a federal Fair Employment Practices Act, and legislation to protect the right to vote, do away with poll taxes, and prevent lynching.

Following the wishes of Southern Democrats, the 80th Congress categorically rejected the initiative. Truman refused to alter his position and benefited politically from his sincere advocacy of civil rights.

Another Republican success pleasing to Southern Democrats was the Twenty-Second Amendment. It was one of the "political aftershocks" of the New Deal. The amendment was proposed by the 80th Congress in 1947 and completed the ratification process four years later. It prohibits any person from being elected president more than twice. It limits vice presidents who succeed to the presidency from being elected more than once, if they served more than half of their predecessors' four-year term. The amendment, which exempted Truman from its provisions, was a "posthumous slap at Franklin Roosevelt, who had challenged the 'two-term tradition' by being elected president four times" (Milkis and Nelson 1994, 303). Support for it came, of course, from Republicans, whose "hatred of Franklin Roosevelt . . . unif[ied] the party more than anything else that year." Southern Democrats joined the "feeding frenzy, especially after Truman's Committee on Civil Rights issued its report." Determined to "protect Jim Crow," Southern leaders saw the amendment as a "tool to reduce presidential power." Truman, of course, opposed the amendment, recognizing its potential "for making a 'lame duck' out of every second-term President for all time in the future" (Urofsky and Finkelman 2002, 753–754).

Throughout the election year of 1948, Truman pressed vigorously for what he believed was necessary for the good of the country. If he could generate support from the Republican Congress, he would advance his own agenda. If Congress refused to join him, he could paint the Republican Congress with the brush of obstructionism, which of course, would serve him well in the November election. Truman reiterated the need for congressional action to subsidize new rental housing and to promote private investment in home building. In this case, his persistence was rewarded as Congress, albeit reluctantly, extended rent control for another year. Vetoes figured prominently throughout Truman's presidency, but in 1948 his conflict with Congress was reflected in his veto of forty-three bills (McCoy 1984, 105).

Truman was essentially accurate in saying "most of the business of the 80th Congress was left unfinished." The Republican Congress had often "trumpeted how it would put things right for the nation." With the exceptions of the Commission on the Organization of the Executive Branch (the Hoover Commission), Taft-Hartley, and income tax reduction, there was little major domestic legislation to show for the Congress's efforts during 1947 and 1948 (McCoy 1984, 112). On balance, Congress had given Truman little of what he requested on domestic matters. Instead, Republican legislators had handed him an effective theme for appealing to the voters in 1948. The 80th Congress's record on foreign policy and military affairs was somewhat more positive, but that was a double-edged sword; Truman had initiated most of what the Congress had done (McCoy 1984, 112–113).

The 80th Congress rejected Truman's proposals for new social legislation and instead set out to repeal the New Deal. For almost a decade, a bipartisan conservative coalition had sought to block liberal initiatives. After the election of 1946, it achieved success. Its ranks swelled by such Republican newcomers as Senator Joseph McCarthy of Wisconsin and Congressman Richard Nixon of California; it also voted to enacted a regressive tax proposal and cut funds for such programs as rural electrification and crop storage.

## The 1948 Election

The Democratic convention in July 1948 opened with most delegates fearful that the White House would be lost. The loss of Congress two years earlier and serious intraparty conflicts had virtually every political observer believing that Truman would lose. The Democrats even tried to talk General Dwight Eisenhower into making the run and had Truman's blessing to do so; the president had agreed to drop back to the vice presidential slot, if Eisenhower could be persuaded to head the ticket. When he declined, Truman was nominated by default. The administration sought to keep the party together by moderating its position on civil rights, but Minneapolis Mayor Hubert Humphrey pressed for a stronger commitment. Truman's political advisers counseled that it was vital to have high turnout among racial and ethnic minorities and that an aggressive civil rights platform would be helpful. Besides, Southern voters had voted Democratic for decades, and it was not expected that they would defect. When the convention adopted the Humphrey proposal, however, delegates from Mississippi and Alabama left the convention. It soon became clear that politicians in the Deep South were bitterly disaffected. Within a week, the States Rights Party—the so-called Dixiecrat Party—was organized by Southerners, who bolted from the party. Governor J. Strom Thurmond of South Carolina was chosen as the Dixiecrat's presidential candidate.

As the Dixiecrats were cutting off Truman's support on the right, those opposed to his foreign policy were cutting him off on the left. Truman had removed Henry Wallace from his cabinet in September 1946, because Wallace had been too critical of the Truman administration's Cold War policies. At the end of 1947, Wallace left the Democrats. In his view, there was no real difference between Truman and a Republican—both advocated a foreign policy with a "get tough" approach to the Soviet Union, which, in turn, greatly elevated the prospect of war. Wallace's followers broke from the Democrats and organized the Progressive Party, with Wallace as their standard-bearer. Wallace appealed to big-city voters, who believed that Truman was betraying Roosevelt's priorities. Polls taken early in 1948 indicated that Wallace had jeopardized Truman's chances of winning those states where a large urban vote would decide the outcome.

These developments seemed to all but foreclose Truman's chances. Indeed, the Republicans were so confident that they nominated Thomas E. Dewey, who had lost to Roosevelt in 1944. The second place on the ballot was given to Governor Earl Warren of California. The Dewey-Warren campaign was cautious to say the least. The election was theirs to lose, and they intended to make no mistakes. Given the split in the Democratic ranks, everyone knew Dewey would win easily. The GOP candidate was so certain of victory that he revealed his cabinet choices to reporters.

Truman was forced to embark on a most aggressive campaign if he wanted to remain in the White House. He used the power of his incumbency in an effort to revive the Roosevelt coalition. He challenged the Republican Congress to enact a number of reform proposals and even called Congress into special session in July 1948. When Congress did nothing, Truman had his issue—not only Dewey and his record but also the performance of the "do-nothing" Republican Congress. Truman concentrated his campaign on the metropolitan areas that had given Roosevelt success. He embarked on a transcontinental "give 'em hell Harry" tour, during which he relentlessly targeted the 80th Congress.

To the surprise of everyone, Truman was able to achieve one of the biggest political upsets in the history of U.S. elections. He took advantage of strong Democratic candidates below him on the ballot to increase voter support—a kind of reverse coattail. He was also able to revive the Roosevelt coalition when many thought that impossible. Truman rolled up 24.1 million votes (49.5 percent) to Dewey's 22 million (45.1 percent) and a 303 to 189 margin in the Electoral College. Thurmond's 1.2 million votes enabled him to win 39 electoral votes, all in the South. The election results were a tribute to Truman's tenaciousness, but they also reflected the durability of the New Deal coalition. Truman won by turning out enough of the old Roosevelt following in the minority and blue-collar precincts in industrial cities, also capturing the farm vote, which was unhappy at the failures of the 80th Congress.

The election marked the emergence of Truman from the shadow of Roosevelt. He immediately tried to assert his newfound standing by pronouncing to Congress that every American should be able to expect a "fair deal" from the government. Present the Fair Deal as he might, the program looked like little more than a warmed over version of the New Deal. Indeed, his domestic program was regarded as Roosevelt's "fifth term." The 81st Congress met for the first time in January 1949 and adopted more progressive legislation than any Congress since 1938. It increased Social Security benefits and extended its coverage to 10 million more people. In addition, Congress raised the minimum wage and expanded public power, rural electrification, and flood control projects. The National Housing Act of 1949 provided for the construction of 810,000 units to provide subsidized housing for low-income families. The act also provided funds for urban renewal and rural housing. With few exceptions, however, the new enactments were no more than extensions of New Deal programs. The only significant difference between Truman's Fair Deal and Roosevelt's New Deal was that the former dealt with a relatively robust economy rather than the Great Depression. When Truman tried to break new ground with initiatives in his "Fair Deal" program, he had little success. He proposed a national health insurance program, but Congress lost its nerve in the face of concerted opposition by the American Medical Association. Although the 81st Congress was more receptive to Truman's proposals than the Republican-controlled 80th Congress had been, it provided problems for Truman, nonetheless. His difficulties with Congress were certainly a product of a tumultuous period, but they resulted as well from his own shortcomings as a legislative leader. Although genuinely interested in achieving change, he never could arouse the kind of popular enthusiasm for his proposals that Roosevelt had. Nor did Truman take pains to cultivate goodwill among members of Congress.

## *Foreign Policy, the Truman Doctrine, and the Marshall Plan*

Truman's "most daring and politically costly initiatives came in the realm of international relations." These included his decisions to "use atomic weapons against Japan . . . and, in 1950, to commit troops to combat in Korea" (Milkis and Nelson 1994, 298). In addition, during Truman's first term, Congress acted to change the institutional presidency, an initiative that had significant consequences for the conduct of foreign policy. A 1947 statute unified the armed services, creating a single National Defense Establishment under a secretary of defense. Two years later this was reorganized as the Department of Defense. The National Security Act also set up a National Security Council, a Central Intelligence Agency, and a National Security Resources Board, and gave legal status to the Joint Chiefs of Staff. The Truman years thus marked a transition from the informal personal presidency of the Roosevelt era to the institutionalized White House of the Eisenhower years. By 1947 the president was also statutorily obligated to present to Congress the State of the Union address, the budget message, and an economic report (as required by the Employment Act of 1946, which mandated a Council of Economic Advisers).

Truman came to power just as Soviet-American distrust was congealing, and he was "determined to prove himself a strong president who would brook no nonsense from the Kremlin" (Morison, Commager, and Leuchtenburg 1980, 665). Much of the disagreement between the Soviets and the West centered on policy concerning their defeated enemy, despite elaborate efforts to agree on a common course. Wartime meetings of the Allies had worked out the basics for dealing with Germany after the war. Paramount were the destruction of German militarism, dissolution of the Nazi Party, and the punishment of war criminals. Partitioning Germany into occupation zones, adjustments of Germany's eastern border to compensate Poland for territory lost to Russia, and resolving the matter of reparation payments were also high priorities.

Truman implemented a foreign policy that featured something called the Truman Doctrine. This doctrine represented a major reorientation in U.S. foreign policy and was designed to contain the Soviet Union by aiding countries that requested assistance in resisting Soviet expansion or subversion. Truman announced his doctrine to a joint session of Congress on March 12, 1947. The president declared, "it must be the policy of the United States to support free people who are resisting subjection by armed minorities or outside pressures" (McCoy 1984, 121–122). The Truman Doctrine was an outgrowth of Great Britain's inability to respond unilaterally to the expansionist initiatives of the Soviet Union in Europe and in Asia. Churchill proposed a coordinated Anglo-American response. The first locus of conflict between Russia and the West took place in the Mediterranean. At Truman's request, Congress appropriated $400 million to help both Greece and Turkey resist Communist-led attacks against their governments. By doing so, the United States thereby assumed a commitment in the eastern Mediterranean that the British, for economic reasons, felt compelled to relinquish.

The United States also made an economic commitment to war-torn Western Europe. The United States was the only Allied country to emerge from the war largely in tact economically. As a result, it assumed broad responsibility for extending assistance to other Allied countries in need of relief and reconstruction. Rebuilding the war-ravaged economies of Western Europe called for bold and expensive new initiatives. Europe needed virtually everything, but had no money to buy anything. The United States, by contrast, desperately needed to sell—if the European economy did not improve, it could adversely impact the otherwise healthy U.S. one. The United States moved on many fronts to ease restrictions on trade, stabilize currencies, and encourage investments. Secretary of State George Marshall invited European governments to send representatives to Paris for the purpose of developing a European recovery plan. This program set new production targets, sought financial stability, and called for the abandonment of trade barriers. It also provided grants and loans for all European nations that agreed to participate. On December 19, 1947, President Truman submitted the European Recovery Program, known as the Marshall Plan, to Congress, together with his own recommendations for an appropriation of $17 billion over a four-year period. The proposal received widespread support from American business, farm, and labor organizations and was easily approved by Congress.

The sixteen European countries that agreed to participate in the program established a regional Organization for European Economic Cooperation to facilitate cooperation in economic reconstruction projects. Over the next four years, the United States provided more than $15 billion in loans and grants-in-aid under the Marshall Plan. The Cold War tensions defined virtually everything that happened during this period. As the United States was providing financial aid to Western Europe, the Soviet Union was attempting to revolutionize the economies of Eastern Europe. The United States also endeavored to establish defense alliances, and so did the Soviet Union.

The Marshall Plan, in which Russia's allies declined to participate, succeeded in reviving Western Europe, but it also served to deepen Cold War tensions between the United States and the U.S.S.R. Economic aid became the primary weapon in the contest between East and West. Within three years from the advent of the Marshall Plan, all U.S. aid was being directed toward strengthening Western defenses. On June 24, 1948, the Russians cut off all surface access to the partitioned city of Berlin, by blockading it. When Berlin was divided between the Soviets and the Allies, access to the American and British areas had not been guaranteed, so technically the Soviets could cut off access to them by erecting roadblocks and stopping trains. Although tempted to confront their blockade with force, the Americans and British instead undertook an airlift operation to supply West Berlin with food, fuel, and other necessities. The West successfully sustained this airlift for almost a year, and on May 12, 1949, the Russians abandoned the blockade.

The Berlin crisis and the ousting of the democratic regime in Czechoslovakia prompted negotiations for a military defense alliance between North American and Western European nations. The North Atlantic Treaty of April 4, 1949, formally joined the United States and Canada with ten nations of Western Europe in an alliance against aggression. The alliance was ultimately enlarged to include several Mediterranean nations as well. Joining it involved a substantial relinquishment of sovereignty. Equally important, it reflected recognition by all treaty members that their respective borders were effectively located along the line dividing the noncommunist West from the Communist East. The Truman administration then proposed a military assistance program, giving the North Atlantic Treaty Organization (NATO) authority to acquire weapons and other military necessities, as well as providing additional aid to Greece and Turkey, which soon thereafter joined NATO. Establishment of NATO was viewed by the Soviet Union as a threatening development and resulted in the establishment of the Warsaw Pact, a defense alliance designed to counter NATO.

The Truman administration did far more to resist Communist expansion in Europe than in Asia. When Truman became president, he continued in the Far East Roosevelt's "China first" policy. Under it China was viewed as the central focus of U.S. interests. The policy committed the United States to support of the Chinese Nationalists against the Chinese Communists. By the end of 1949, however, the Communists had pushed Nationalist leader Chiang Kai-shek and his followers from the Chinese mainland to the island of Formosa. The "fall" of China to the Communists had a number of consequences. Through the ideology of communism, the "revolution" in China created something approaching an alliance between one-half billion Chinese and the Soviet Union. It dramatically shifted the Cold War balance of power. When World War

II ended, the objective of the Allies was to ensure that the Japanese would not constitute a military threat in Asia. In pursuit of this objective, the occupation authorities sought to democratize Japan and reduce its capacity to rebuild its military. Almost immediately after the Japanese surrender, General Douglas MacArthur began the process of altering Japan's governance and economic structure. When the Communists drove the Nationalists from the Chinese mainland, U.S. policymakers changed their minds about Japan. They began to view it as capable of striking a military balance with Red China. The "loss of China" saddled the Truman administration with a huge political liability.

## The Korean War

Going into 1950, the most pressing foreign policy problems seemed to be in Europe. The so-called fall of China to the Communists required Truman to expand his focus to Asia. Absent from the U.S. foreign policy calculus at the time was Korea. That would soon change. When the Soviet Union entered the war against Japan, it also established a military presence in Korea. The Korean peninsula was divided into occupation zones along the 38th parallel. The United States then aligned itself with the conservative regime in South Korea, led by Syngman Rhee. The Communist victory in China, coupled with the establishment of a Communist regime in North Korea, left South Korea extremely vulnerable.

On June 25, 1950, North Korean troops launched an all-out attack on South Korea. The South Korean capital of Seoul was captured within a matter of hours, and the entire country seemed on the verge of being overrun. On June 27, Truman announced that he was sending U.S. forces to the aid of the South Koreans. The same day the United Nations Security Council decided to create an international force to intervene in Korea. The Security Council then asked Truman to create a unified command for U.S. and UN forces. He selected General Douglas MacArthur to head it. Although the military force aiding South Korea could be characterized as an international or a UN police force, the large majority of the troops came from the United States. As a result, most Americans viewed the Korean engagement as a U.S. war. Truman insisted all along that the Korean intervention would be of limited duration. He clearly wished to avoid having it expand into a shooting war with either the Soviet Union or Communist China.

The UN forces stabilized the military situation. MacArthur then surprised the enemy by landing troops in their rear at Inchon and began pushing the North Koreans back across the 38th parallel. He was not satisfied with simply driving them out of South Korea, however. Rather, he was convinced that the only way to end the war satisfactorily—best serving U.S. interests and uniting Korea—was to take control of the entire Korean peninsula. MacArthur drove north and approached the Manchurian border. He was met by a massive force of Chinese "volunteers," which entered Korea and threw back MacArthur and the UN forces. MacArthur was censured for miscalculating both China's intentions and the ferocity of its invasion. Wanting a chance to redeem himself, he sought to launch another push north. Although Truman initially had considered the "liberation" strategy favored by MacArthur, he became concerned that such an approach might lead to all-out war with Communist China. Instead, the president sought an end to the fighting as soon as possible. Once South Korea had been freed of Chinese troops, Truman and the UN pressed for negotiations to end the conflict. MacArthur was outraged by the change of policy in Washington, and although he had been warned not to make statements to the contrary, in late March 1951 he threatened China with an attack. Truman felt his remarks diminished chances of an early end to the war. In an unmitigated challenge to Truman's authority, MacArthur insisted to House Republicans that all-out victory should be the only objective. After consulting with his military and foreign policy advisers, Truman relieved the general of his command. With the situation in Korea stalemated, the Soviets suggested an armistice, with each side withdrawing to its respective side of the 38th parallel. The United States quickly agreed.

The Korean War greatly eroded Truman's authority in his last two years as president. The public had grown disenchanted with the price the United States was paying for "Harry's War." Equally important, Truman's unilateral decision to intervene in Korea was viewed by many Washington insiders as a usurpation of congressional authority to declare war. As the North Koreans and Red Chinese were killing young Americans defending Korea, those who warned of the Communist threat at home found a receptive audience. The media was more than willing to focus on the accusation that the Truman administration had been "soft on communism." The issue served the Republicans extremely well in the midterm elections of 1950. When the votes were tallied, the Republicans had won enough seats to destroy all chances of Truman's Fair Deal proposals being enacted.

## The Communist Issue

Communism had largely been removed as an issue from the 1948 election when Henry Wallace, who received support from American Communists, bolted from the Democratic Party. It was not clear what course the defeated and humiliated Republicans would take after the election, but events defined the future. First, Chiang Kai-shek and the Nationalists took refuge on the island of Formosa, placing the huge Chinese mainland under the control of the Communists. Second, the Soviet Union developed an atomic bomb. Third, of course, there was the Korean War. As serious as all of these were, there were some who believed that strategically placed Americans were in league with the enemy. Fingers were pointed at the intellectuals, "one-worlders," and others who sympathized with the Soviet Union or other Communists. The case of Alger Hiss gave this a surreal focus.

Former *Time* magazine editor Whittaker Chambers accused Hiss of having been a Communist. Hiss had been a State Department official before becoming president of the Carnegie Endowment for International Peace. Truman was initially dismissive of the allegations against Hiss, viewing the matter as something designed by the Republicans to divert attention from the 80th Congress. Chambers, however, substantiated his original allegation and went on to accuse Hiss of having been a Soviet agent. Hiss, of course, denied the charges, but he was indicted for perjury, the only charge possible because the statute of limitations had run out on any espionage he might have committed, immunizing him from prosecution for that offense. After a mistrial, Hiss was retried, found guilty, and sentenced to five years imprisonment. China, Korea, Alger Hiss, and other similar factors set the stage for Senator Joseph McCarthy.

Although the Cold War with Russia and the hot war in Korea provided much of the impetus for McCarthyism, the concerns over subversion that McCarthy exploited predated World War II. During the 1930s in particular, there was suspicion that political radicals had infiltrated government, unions, and the country's schools. In 1938 the House created a committee on un-American activities. Since its establishment in 1938, the House Un-American Activities Committee (HUAC) had been largely composed of members who believed that the New Deal was a manifestation of communism. In the Cold War period following World War II concerns became widespread that political subversives, in conjunction with radical political movements from abroad, had become a serious threat to the country. When the State Department announced that Soviet Russia possessed the atomic bomb, Republicans charged that those developing the U.S. Eastern European and Asian policies were to blame.

All of this prompted Truman to issue Executive Order 9835 to investigate the loyalty of civil servants. Like the congressional inquiries, Truman's loyalty-security program relied on guilt by intention and association. Unlike the congressional investigations, the inquiry initiated by Truman provided at least some procedural safeguards. Despite its initiatives to root out subversives, his administration was still accused of being "soft on communism." In response, the Truman Justice Department obtained indictments of a dozen top Communists for violations of the Smith Act. These defendants were eventually convicted of conspiring to teach and advocate the violent overthrow of the government, convictions that the Vinson Court upheld in *Dennis v. United States* (1951).

Senator McCarthy arrived in Wheeling, West Virginia, on February 12, 1950, to address the Republican Women's Club. By that time in the fourth year of his first Senate term, McCarthy had done nothing of legislative consequence. He had established a reputation as a bully and was known for his reckless and vicious verbal assaults on those with whom he disagreed. His speech was a composite of sound bites from speeches of Richard Nixon and others. McCarthy claimed that he had the names of more than 200 subversive State Department employees. He plugged in to the "anti-communist" predisposition of the country—an attitude that radical political conspiracies had taken hold of the country. The Hiss trial could not have better served the purposes of McCarthy and other anticommunists. Hiss had been a New Deal official and political affairs specialist in the State Department and had participated in the San Francisco Conference that produced the United Nation's Charter. McCarthy's speech carried him from relative obscurity to center stage. In July 1950 a Senate committee under Senator Millard Tydings of Maryland reported that McCarthy's charges were a "fraud and a hoax perpetrated on the Senate and the American people" (Morison, Commager, and Leuchtenberg 1980, 634).

McCarthy appealed to a deep-seated distrust of political liberals. He had a rather easy sell on the matter of Communist infiltration of the State Department. In the 1952 presidential campaign, Republican vice presidential candidate Richard Nixon made extensive use of McCarthy-like invective, referring to Democratic presidential nominee Adlai Stevenson as "Adlai the appeaser," who "carries a Ph.D. from Dean Acheson's cowardly college of Communist containment" (Cochran 1973, 383). Eisenhower's victory propelled McCarthy for the first time to chairmanship of the Senate Committee on Government Operations, and "the Grand Inquisitor" used his new power to rampage through the foreign affairs agencies of the new Republican administration. When McCarthy chose to assault the military establishment, however, he overstepped himself. The televised portions of the Army-McCarthy hearings, which lasted from April 22 to June 17, 1954, gave many Americans their first close glimpse of McCarthy—his bullying, his rasping intrusions, his unshaven face like that of a Hollywood "heavy." Thereafter McCarthy went rapidly downhill, carrying this latter-day Red Scare with him. On December 2, 1954, the Senate voted 67–22 (with no negative Democratic votes and the Republicans dividing evenly), to "condemn" McCarthy for various affronts to the dignity of the Senate. As a self-advertised gladiator against communism, McCarthy proved to be a charlatan. He first gained the limelight by piecing together a set of fabrications and innuendoes. When a Senate subcommittee investigated his charges, it concluded that McCarthy was waging a nefarious campaign of half-truths and untruths.

For a period of five years the smear campaign that came to be called McCarthyism dominated the U.S. political landscape. Truman tried to free himself from the issue of Communist subversion, but he was never able to do so. His Justice Department secured indictments against the top leaders of the American Communist Party under the Smith Act. That statute, passed in 1940, outlawed advocacy of the violent overthrow of any government in the United States, among other things. The Truman administration was in a no-win situation—its actions both troubled liberals and failed to satisfy Congress. Out of the sense of panic aroused by McCarthy came the McCarran Internal Security Act of 1950. This law required all Communist and Communist-front organizations to register with the attorney general, excluded Communists from employment in defense plants, made it illegal to conspire to perform any act that would substantially contribute to the establishment of a dictatorship in the United States, debarred from this country anyone ever affiliated with a totalitarian organization, or with organizations looking to the revolutionary overthrow of government, authorized deportation of aliens involved in suspect organizations, denied passports to Communists, provided for the internment of subversives in the event of war, and set up a Subversive Activities Control Board. Truman vetoed the bill, alleging that it was worse than the Sedition Acts of 1798. Congress passed it over his veto by acclamation, however. The subversion issue highlighted the 1950 elections in which the Republicans picked up five seats in the Senate and twenty-eight in the House. In California, Richard Nixon won a Senate seat by exploiting McCarthyite issues. The 1950 elections not only sealed the fate of the Fair Deal but also encouraged the Republicans to anticipate that the same tactics would win them the White House in 1952.

## The Steel Seizure Case

Although hammered on Capitol Hill, Truman continued to exercise vigorously the powers of the presidential office. A year after dismissing General MacArthur, he took another bold action. The Korean conflict was, in the eyes of the Truman administration, a war that permitted the exercise of the same kind of power the government had used during World War II. When the United Steel Workers threatened to strike after the Wage Stabilization Board was unable to resolve a wage dispute, Truman issued Executive Order 10340, directing Charles Sawyer, his secretary of commerce, to seize and operate the steel mills in order to maintain production levels of steel for defense needs. Truman could have forestalled the strike by invoking the Taft-Hartley Act's provision for an eighty-day "cooling off" period if a strike would adversely affect the public interest. Truman had vetoed Taft-Hartley, however, and was loathe to use it. Instead, he "seized the mills, informed Congress of what he had done, and invited its astounded members to take legislative action if they thought it was necessary" (Urofsky and Finkelman 2002, 770).

Truman's lawyers later argued that he had acted "solely on inherent executive power, without the need for statutory support." Although this was an "unparalleled action," most observers believed the steel companies would ultimately lose their legal challenge to it in the Supreme Court; after all, the Court was "composed entirely of men appointed by either Roosevelt or Truman" (Urofsky and Finkelman 2002, 770). Also, the companies conceded that the government could seize industries during a national emergency; they objected only to the fact that the president rather than Congress had taken this action. Nonetheless, by a vote of 6–3 in *Youngstown Sheet and Tube Company v. Sawyer*, the justices ruled that the president had acted unlawfully.

Justice Black delivered the opinion of the Court, which denied that the president "had authority under any statute, under any express provision of the Constitution, or even by any implied power as commander-in-chief to seize the steel mills." Without explicit constitutional mandate, the president could only act with express or clearly implied authorization from Congress. If Congress "remains silent, then no power is granted." Justice Frankfurter's concurring opinion saw somewhat more leeway for the executive, but concurred with the majority view. The president could act, Frankfurter argued, "even in the face of congressional silence, if it could be shown that historically, the legislative branch had acquiesced in similar actions." Justice Jackson argued that Congress had not been silent about this situation, but in its debates on the Taft-Hartley and Defense Production Acts "had considered giving the president such power and had decided not to do so." The Court, looking at such recent legislative history, concluded that Congress "did not want the president to have this power" (Urofsky and Finkelman 2002, 770).

Chief Justice Vinson had privately assured Truman that if its legality were challenged, the seizure would be upheld. When the case actually reached the Supreme Court, Vinson could deliver only two votes beyond his own (Reed and Minton). The chief executive, he maintained, "could act in every instance except where limited by express constitutional refusal." The chief's dissenting opinion "implied a practically unlimited executive power, a position Truman had not even asserted." The *Youngstown* decision triggered a fifty-three-day strike in the steel industry. Although the Court had determined that Congress and the president had "ample statutory means to avert the strike, the political sensitivities of an election year prevented either from acting." *Youngstown* remains one of the "great" modern cases because it "helped redress the balance of power among the three branches," a balance that had been "severely distorted by the enormous growth of executive authority first in the New Deal and then during the war and the postwar search for global security" (Urofsky and Finkelman 2002, 771).

## The 1952 Election

By 1952, Americans were ready to listen to the Republicans' contention that it was time for a change after twenty years of Democratic administrations. The conservative wing of the GOP contended that Republicans had failed to capture the presidency in recent elections because they had "offered no real alternative to the policies of liberal Democrats, and they called now for a return to rugged individualism and isolationism." Party moderates were convinced that nominating a conservative would be a disaster and looked to General Eisenhower to provide more progressive and internationally oriented leadership (Morison, Commager, and Leuchtenberg 1980, 637). Two-time presidential nominee Thomas Dewey "marshaled the Eisenhower cohorts" and undecided delegates "fell in line under a convention that only Ike could win." Senator Richard Nixon, "who had distinguished himself only by his zeal in exploiting the issue of subversion was nominated for Vice-President." The Democratic Convention selected Governor Adlai Stevenson of Illinois on the third ballot (Morison, Commager, and Leuchtenberg 1980, 636).

Eisenhower was initially unwilling to take on the policies of the Truman administration. After a "momentous meeting with Taft," however, he began to give "aid and comfort to the right wing of his party." Ike eventually accepted support from the likes of Joe McCarthy, denounced the Truman administration for harboring subversives, charged Acheson with responsibility for the Communist attack in Korea, "and poured scorn on the 'eggheads' who had rallied to the support of Stevenson." The Republicans had sufficient financial resources to exploit fully television, which, for the first time, played an important part in a presidential campaign. However, the greatest advantage the GOP enjoyed was Eisenhower himself. The election returns provided an "accurate index of the General's popularity." He won more than 55 percent of the popular vote and secured 442 electoral votes to Stevenson's 89 (Morison, Commager, and Leuchtenberg 1980, 637). By January 1953, Truman was gone from the national political stage, and, eight months later, death removed Chief Justice Vinson, thus ending the Vinson (Truman) Court era.

## Assembling the Vinson Court

Eleven justices sat on the Vinson Court, a Court that spanned a seven-year period. The members of the Vinson Court were nominated by only two presidents—Franklin D. Roosevelt and Harry S. Truman. Roosevelt took office in March 1933. Benjamin Cardozo had joined the Court in March 1932. The next vacancy would not occur until June 1937, when Justice Willis Van Devanter left the Court. This period between Supreme Court vacancies spanned Roosevelt's entire first term. At a time when he needed the Court's support, Roosevelt was unable to make the personnel changes necessary to obtain it. This was perhaps the most important factor prompting him to pursue his scheme to "pack" the Court, a plan he unveiled following his reelection in 1936. The plan he submitted to Congress was not adopted, but it signaled the beginning of a so-called revolution in constitutional doctrine.

Once Van Devanter retired, Roosevelt was given more than ample opportunity to reshape the Court. Following Hugo L. Black's nomination in August 1937, Roosevelt nominated three additional justices in the next nineteen months. By June 1941, the number of nominations had increased to seven, including Associate Justice Harlan Fiske Stone's elevation to chief justice. In other words, there was a period of almost five and one-half years when no new justices were appointed (1932–1937), followed immediately by a period of less than four years when eight changes were made to the Court (1937–1941). Only George Washington nominated more people to the Court than Roosevelt did during these four years. Unlike the nominees of presidents from other periods, almost all of Roosevelt's appointees neither stirred much controversy nor were politically troublesome; the exception was Hugo Black, whose association with the Ku Klux Klan did produce a brief furor. Furthermore, the Democrats controlled the Senate, ensuring that virtually any Roosevelt nominee for the Court would be confirmed. Truman would not enjoy the same political circumstances. The Roosevelt nominees were distinguished by anyone's standards: Black and Felix Frankfurter have been ranked as "great" by Court experts, and William O. Douglas, Robert H. Jackson, and Wiley B. Rutledge as "near great"—a record of professional approbation attained by no other president. Seven Roosevelt-nominated justices carried over to the Vinson Court. The remaining four justices, including Chief Justice Vinson, were nominated by Truman.

The most senior justice when Vinson became chief justice was Black, Roosevelt's first nominee. Roosevelt was seeking justices who embraced libertarian objectives, but his highest priority was to find ones who were committed to the political and economic principles underlying the New Deal. When Justice Willis Van Devanter retired, the leading candidate to replace him was Senator Joseph T. Robinson of Arkansas, Democratic majority leader of the Senate. Robinson faithfully supported every New Deal proposal and was the point man in the attempt to pass Roosevelt's "Court-packing" plan. While that proposal was still pending before the Senate, Robinson was stricken with a fatal heart attack. Roosevelt's attorney general, Homer Cummings, was then instructed to come up with a list of other possibilities. The list that emerged contained the names of several persons who would eventually join the Court—Solicitor General Stanley Forman Reed, Senator Sherman Minton, Senator Hugo Black, and Assistant Attorney General Robert Jackson.

The need to appoint an economic liberal was the most urgent consideration in the selection of Roosevelt's first nominee. The Hughes Court had begun in 1937 to take a new direction on issues relating to federal economic regulation, but the new majority contained only five votes, including Hughes and Roberts. The difficulty facing Roosevelt was securing Senate confirmation for his selection. Even though the Democrats controlled the Senate, many of them were Southern conservatives. There were also a number of Democrats who remained bitter over Roosevelt's "Court-packing" proposal. Not only did some of them see the proposal as an attempt to "strong-arm" the Court, but they were also bothered that Roosevelt had introduced his proposal without consulting any of the Senate Democrats. Roosevelt and his political advisers hoped that the nomination of one of the Senate's own members might help reduce some of the problems of securing confirmation. Nonetheless, the nomination was viewed in some quarters as Roosevelt's "revenge" for the defeat of the "Court-packing" proposal.

Black did not possess obvious judicial qualifications. There were some who were put off by his limited legal experience and his politics—he was seen as too partisan, too liberal, and too much a populist. In addition, Black brought "Klan baggage" to the table, which prompted concerns among political liberals. Finally, there were some in the Senate who felt his nomination was nothing but a reward for his support on the Court-packing bill. Although support on this particular measure may have been important to Roosevelt, it was more important that Black had clearly demonstrated his wholehearted support of the New Deal programs.

Black was the only Roosevelt nominee to generate an unusual level of controversy, although he was eventually confirmed by a 63–16 vote. The issue of his former membership in the KKK did not go away, however. He eventually took to national radio to explain the circumstances of his membership and the subsequent abandonment of his association with the Klan. This strategy was effective, and the issue then faded from public consciousness. Black replaced one of the New Deal's staunchest opponents in Justice Van Devanter, and his vote was the first step in solidifying a more dependable, Roosevelt-friendly majority on the Court—Black added a solid vote to the pro–New Deal trio of Cardozo, Stone, and Brandeis.

Roosevelt's second opportunity to nominate a justice came only six months after Black was confirmed. George Sutherland, another of the laissez-faire Four Horsemen, retired from the Court in January 1938. Roosevelt's choice to fill the Sutherland seat was Stanley F. Reed, who, as solicitor general, had argued many of the New Deal cases before the Supreme Court on behalf of the Roosevelt administration. Reed had been considered for the nomination that went to Black, and his unswerving commitment to Roosevelt's political agenda made him the immediate front-runner for the Sutherland seat.

Although Roosevelt had not sought counsel prior to submitting his Court-packing proposal and Hugo Black's nomination to the Senate, he did before deciding on a nominee to replace Sutherland. The president consulted many advisers and members of the Senate, and he heeded the recommendations of those he consulted. Reed emerged as the consensus choice. He was an attractive candidate for several reasons. Reed was young, had a solid legal reputation, was not controversial, and was from the state of Kentucky. He was confirmed by voice vote in the Senate on January 25, 1938. Reed's confirmation marked the second time in six months that Roosevelt was able to replace one of the principal foes of the New Deal. He now had a solid liberal majority on the Court.

Felix Frankfurter joined the Court a year after Reed, filling a vacancy created by the death of Benjamin Cardozo. Frankfurter did not produce an immediate gain for

Roosevelt, in that he replaced a man who had generally supported New Deal proposals before 1937. Roosevelt had known Frankfurter for a number of years and had long
considered him an exceptionally well-qualified candidate for the Court. The possibility of nominating him was seriously affected by political constituency considerations,
however. Roosevelt told Frankfurter that he would have to nominate someone from
the West. The president also thought it impossible to nominate Frankfurter, who was
Jewish, to a Court that already contained two Jewish justices (Brandeis and Cardozo).
Frankfurter understood and began to prepare a list of viable candidates on Roosevelt's
behalf. Substantial support was generated for him following Cardozo's death, however. Some of this was orchestrated by Frankfurter himself and by his protégés in Roosevelt's "brain trust." The pressure on Roosevelt to nominate Frankfurter "became
intense," and many, including Stone, Jackson, Harold Ickes, Harry Hopkins, and Senator George Norris, urged the president to set aside constituency considerations and
nominate him anyway. Attorney General Jackson urged naming Frankfurter if for no
other reason than that he could interpret the Constitution with scholarship and with
sufficient assurance to hold his own with Hughes in conference discussions. Finally,
Roosevelt yielded, indicating to his advisers that there "isn't anybody in the West . . .
who is of sufficient stature" (Abraham 1999, 221).

Frankfurter was the first nominee since Harlan Fiske Stone to appear before the
Senate Judiciary Committee. Despite some opposition from those who tried to represent him as a political radical, he was confirmed by a unanimous voice vote in the Senate. Frankfurter brought his academic background to the Court, and it was evident
during the Stone years: The Chief Justice chose not to limit conference debate, and as
a result, Frankfurter would often monopolize the discussion, usually to the annoyance
of his colleagues. In his first term (1938) on the Court, Frankfurter voted with the
other Roosevelt appointees, but by the time Stone became chief justice in 1941, he and
Reed had repositioned themselves and become part of a more conservative bloc,
which also included Stone and Associate Justices Jackson and Roberts. Although five
judges made up this centrist bloc, one or another of them would frequently break off
to join the Court's more liberal members. Although Frankfurter occasionally left the
centrist bloc, he shared little common ground with the liberal-activist bloc during the
Stone Court period.

Four weeks after the Frankfurter nomination, Justice Brandeis retired. His
departure created the fourth vacancy on the Court in less than four years. Roosevelt
was still interested in nominating a Westerner for political reasons. William O. Douglas, then chair of the Securities and Exchange Commission, had been born in Minnesota and raised in Washington, although he had completed law school at Columbia
and taught at Yale Law School. Hence, he was in Roosevelt's eyes a "two-thirds East-
erner." Douglas was an FDR favorite, however, and an "insider." Roosevelt was lobbied
hard by a number of people to make him his nominee, among them the outgoing Jus-

tice Brandeis, who wanted Douglas "[t]here in his place." Douglas's chances were enhanced by Idaho Senator William Borah, who claimed him as one of the West's own, but he himself felt it was Brandeis's support that was "ultimately decisive" with Roosevelt. The Senate confirmed Douglas four weeks after his nomination by a 62–4 margin. The four opposition votes were all from Republicans, but they were progressive Republicans who characterized Douglas as a "reactionary tool of Wall Street," something he never was. At forty, he was the youngest man nominated to the Court since Joseph Story, who was confirmed in 1811 at the age of thirty-two. During the first two terms of Douglas's tenure, the Roosevelt appointees generally voted together. By the 1940 term, however, Stone, Reed, and Frankfurter had begun to vote less often with Black and Douglas. In that 1940 term, Black and Douglas voted together in every nonunanimous decision of the Court. After the appointment of Wiley Rutledge, a four-justice liberal cluster of Black, Douglas, Murphy, and Rutledge was evident for the duration of the Stone Court (Abraham 1999, 170–171).

There was no hesitation by Roosevelt when Pierce Butler died on November 16, 1939. The day Butler died, Roosevelt told Attorney General Frank Murphy of his intentions to place him on the Court, although the official nomination did not come until six weeks later. Senate confirmation occurred by voice vote on January 15, 1940. Murphy was at first reluctant to accept the nomination feeling "utterly inadequate" to join the Court. He was known as a crusading New Deal liberal and had served as an assistant U.S. attorney, a Michigan judge, and mayor of Detroit. Roosevelt sent Murphy to the Philippines as governor general, but in 1936 he gave up that post both to assist with Roosevelt's reelection and to be elected governor of Michigan. He lost in his bid for reelection two years later, however, and was appointed U.S. attorney general by Roosevelt. Murphy's priorities while heading the Justice Department did not always coincide with those of FDR or some of his key advisers. Some suggested that Murphy's appointment to the Court was a "kick upstairs"—a promotion to get him out of the Justice Department. He soon became the most liberal of the Stone Court justices.

By the time Roosevelt won his third term, the Supreme Court's post-1937 doctrinal "revolution" was firmly cemented. Roosevelt had nominated five new justices during his second term. The replacements of Cardozo and Brandeis did not affect decisional outcomes, as these two justices had supported most of the components of the New Deal program and demonstrated sensitivity to individual liberties issues. The other three appointments—Black, Reed, and Murphy—all represented net gains for Roosevelt, as they replaced three of the four unyielding opponents of the New Deal. The last of the Four Horsemen, and maybe their most tenacious and reactionary member, James McReynolds, retired in 1941. Given the personnel changes, McReynolds correctly concluded there was no point in fighting a fight that had been settled for several years.

Most Court observers thought the McReynolds seat would go to Attorney General Robert Jackson. Jackson had been attorney general for only a year, however, and

Roosevelt did not want to replace him so soon. There was also substantial political pressure from influential Southern Senate members for Senator James Byrnes of South Carolina to receive the nomination. Byrnes was considerably more conservative than the other Roosevelt nominees, but with the Court heavily committed to Roosevelt's priorities already, it really did not matter.

Jackson's nomination to the Court finally came in June 1941, but he was not offered the chief justiceship he wanted. Although Chief Justice Hughes gave Jackson a favorable recommendation, Hughes argued that Stone's record should give him "first claim" on the chief justiceship. Roosevelt also sought counsel from Frankfurter, who said he preferred Jackson on "personal grounds," but from a "national interest" standpoint, he saw no reason to prefer Jackson to Stone. When Roosevelt discussed the matter with Jackson, he deferred to the "persuasiveness of Frankfurter's logic" (Abraham 1999, 234). Jackson also anticipated that the sixty-nine-year-old Stone would be chief justice for only a short time and that the position would be his eventually. Confirmation of Jackson took a little longer than expected because of opposition from Senator Millard Tydings of Maryland, who was unhappy with Jackson for not prosecuting columnist Drew Pearson for alleged libel against Tydings. The Senate Judiciary Committee unanimously recommended him after only a few moments debate, however, and Jackson was confirmed with only Tydings voting against him. Controversy developed around Jackson at the end rather than the beginning of the Stone Court period. He retained his wish to be chief justice, and he had a second opportunity when Stone died in 1946. However, Jackson's feud with Justice Black, which was both doctrinal and personal, prompted Truman to go outside the Court for a new chief justice—Fred Vinson. When Jackson returned from the Nazi war crimes trials, he separated himself from the liberal activists (Black, Douglas, Murphy, and Rutledge), aligned himself with Frankfurter, and voted in a more conservative manner on national security and state criminal process issues.

Including the Jackson and Stone nominations, Roosevelt had appointed eight justices in four years. In October 1942, Byrnes resigned to take a more active administrative role in the conduct of the war. His resignation brought Roosevelt his ninth and last opportunity to nominate a justice to the Supreme Court. Many solid New Deal supporters were already on the Court, and Attorney General Francis Biddle was not interested in becoming a justice. Widely mentioned possibilities were Senator Alben Barkley, Solicitor General Charles Fahy, Judge John J. Parker, and Dean Acheson. This vacancy, however, gave Roosevelt an opportunity finally to nominate someone from west of the Mississippi, and he instructed Biddle to find him a suitable candidate. The attorney general's recommendation was Wiley B. Rutledge Jr. Rutledge, a former law professor, had been considered earlier, but it was decided that he should be groomed for later nomination by serving for a time on the U.S. Court of Appeals for the District of Columbia. Rutledge was only a marginal Westerner, although he had more claim to the region than did Douglas. Roosevelt had never met him, but a White House conversation satisfied the president that Rutledge was solidly committed to his philosophy. Confirmation of Rutledge, Roosevelt's only Supreme Court nominee with federal judicial experience, came on a unanimous Senate vote.

Harry Truman's first opportunity to nominate someone to the Supreme Court was created by the resignation of Justice Owen Roberts. He chose Harold H. Burton of Ohio, who had served in the Senate with Truman and was a member of his War Investigation Committee. This committee's work catapulted Truman to national prominence. There were political reasons for Burton's selection: Truman felt national unity was best served by designating a Republican to replace Roberts, a GOP justice from Pennsylvania. In Truman's view, Burton demonstrated the appropriate temperament for a judge. Truman also expected that the Democratic governor of Ohio would replace the Republican Burton with a Democrat (which he did). In addition to the political factors, another reason factored into Truman's decision to nominate Burton; Truman was prone to reward loyalty and Burton was the first of four "crony" appointments to the Court. Burton was unanimously confirmed by the Senate on the day Truman nominated him.

The cerebral hemorrhage that killed Chief Justice Stone on April 22, 1946, created a vacancy that presented Truman with a particularly difficult problem—he had to not only replace Stone but also find someone who could handle the extensive philosophical and personal differences among the justices. Citing these intra-Court conflicts, former Chief Justice Hughes and Associate Justice Roberts counseled Truman not to promote any of the sitting justices. In an effort to achieve greater harmony on the Court, Truman decided to nominate his secretary of the treasury, Frederick Moore Vinson. Vinson had previously served fourteen years in Congress and five years on the U.S. Court of Appeals. In addition to their common political values, Truman saw in Vinson a consensus-builder capable of unifying a conflicted Court. He nominated Vinson on June 6, 1946, and the Senate unanimously confirmed him two weeks later. With his confirmation, the Vinson Court era began.

Although there was a new chief justice, the Roosevelt Court majority remained. That situation came to an end in 1949 with the deaths of Murphy and Rutledge. Truman's choice to replace Murphy was his attorney general, Tom C. Clark of Texas. A prosecuting attorney in Dallas, Clark went to Washington to serve as head of the Justice Department's Antitrust Division and later as head of the Criminal Division. When Truman succeeded to the presidency on the death of Franklin Roosevelt, Clark was named to succeed Francis Biddle as attorney general. He was one of Truman's closest political advisers on domestic issues and was heavily involved in the president's campaign for reelection in 1948.

Clark's nomination to the Court was not universally popular. Some saw it as a political reward; it looked to them like "blatant cronyism" and Clark "cashing in . . .

political IOUs." Others had ideological concerns. Clark had overseen the relocation of Japanese Americans from the West Coast following the attack on Pearl Harbor. In addition, he was seen as a conservative attorney general, "especially regarding procedural safeguards in criminal justice and toward minority groups" (Abraham 1999, 185). There were also allegations of scandal stemming from his time as a private practitioner in Texas and from his role in the parole of organized crime figures. Investigation of these allegations during the confirmation process, however, did not conclusively demonstrate impropriety on Clark's part, and he eventually won Senate confirmation by a 73–8 vote.

Justice Rutledge died two months after Murphy and provided Truman with his fourth and final opportunity to nominate someone to the Supreme Court. Once again, Truman chose a former Senate colleague and close friend. His choice was Sherman Minton of Indiana. Like Truman, Minton had come to the Senate in 1934. Unlike him, he lost in his bid for reelection in 1940. An ardent New Dealer, Minton was given a White House position after losing his Senate seat. Shortly thereafter, Roosevelt nominated him to the U.S. Court of Appeals, where he served for eight years. It was "clear that loyal political and personal dedication was once again rewarded" with Truman's selection of Minton (Abraham 1999, 188). Despite Minton's previous service in the Senate, there were questions about him. He was requested to appear before the Senate Judiciary Committee, but declined to do so. He was confirmed nonetheless by a 48–16 vote. After Clark and Minton joined the Court in 1949, its composition did not change until Earl Warren replaced Vinson as chief Justice in 1953. Their appointments completed the Vinson Court.

## References and Further Reading

Abraham, Henry J. 1999. *Justices, Presidents, and Senators: A History of the U.S. Supreme Court Appointments from Washington to Clinton.* Rev. ed. Lanham, MD: Rowman and Littlefield.

Belknap, Michal R. 1977. *Cold War Political Justice: The Smith Act, the Communist Party, and American Civil Liberties.* Westport, CT: Greenwood.

Cochran, Bert. 1973. *Harry Truman and the Crisis Presidency.* New York: Funk & Wagnalls.

Lacey, Michael J., ed. 1989. *The Truman Presidency.* New York: Cambridge University Press.

Leuchtenberg, William E. 2001. *In the Shadow of FDR: From Harry Truman to George W. Bush.* 3d ed. Ithaca, NY: Cornell University Press.

Lukacs, John. 1961. *A History of the Cold War.* Garden City, NY: Doubleday and Company.

McCoy, Donald R. 1984. *The Presidency of Harry S. Truman.* Lawrence: University Press of Kansas.

Milkis, Sidney M., and Michael Nelson. 1994. *The American Presidency: Origins and Development, 1776–1993.* 2d ed. Washington, DC: CQ Press.

Morison, Samuel Eliot, Henry Steele Commager, and William Leuchtenberg. 1980. *The Growth of the American Republic.* 7th ed., vol. II. New York: Oxford University Press.

Phillips, Cabell. 1966. *The Truman Presidency: The History of a Triumphant Succession.* New York: Macmillan.

Urofsky, Melvin I. 1997. *Division and Discord: The Supreme Court under Stone and Vinson, 1941–1953.* Columbia: University of South Carolina Press.

Urofsky, Melvin I., and Paul Finkelman. 2002. *A March of Liberty: A Constitutional History of the United States.* 2d ed., vol. II. New York: Oxford University Press.

White, G. Edward. 1988. *The American Judicial Tradition: Profiles of Leading American Judges.* Expanded ed. New York: Oxford University Press.

# *The Justices*

Eleven men served on the Supreme Court during the brief seven-year period that Frederick Moore Vinson presided over it. Several of these held their seats far longer than Vinson did. Hugo L. Black, for example, joined the Court in 1937 and did not retire until 1971. Felix Frankfurter sat with Black from 1939 until 1962, and William O. Douglas, the longest-serving justice in the history of the Court, joined it the same year as Frankfurter and did not retire until 1975. Black, Frankfurter, and Douglas all towered over Vinson intellectually, and a clash between judicial philosophies for which Black and Frankfurter were the leading spokesmen preoccupied what was supposedly the Vinson Court.

Yet, it did matter that Fred Vinson occupied the Court's center seat. Like his colleagues, the chief justice has only one vote. But he has the prerogative, if in the majority, to decide who writes the opinion in a case. He also controls the clerks, marshals, and other members of the Court's support staff and is the head of the entire federal judiciary. As Melvin Urofsky points out, "A strong chief justice—such as John Marshall, William Howard Taft, or Charles Evans Hughes—can have a major impact on the Court's work, not only defining its agenda but influencing the general jurisprudential direction that the Court takes" (Urofsky 2001, 29). Even a weak one can affect the Court's course. Fred Vinson is proof of that.

When Vinson became chief justice in 1946, the Court's most powerful bloc consisted of four liberal activist judges: Black, Douglas, Frank Murphy, and Wiley Rutledge. All they had to do to determine the outcome of a case was attract one vote. While Harlan Fiske Stone was chief justice, the four liberals could generally count on his support, but Vinson was vastly more conservative than his predecessor. Stone's death and Vinson's appointment meant that the liberal bloc immediately lost its assured majority. Its position weakened further when, during the Court's summer recess in 1949, both Murphy and Rutledge died unexpectedly. Their replacements, Tom Clark and Sherman Minton, shared many of Vinson's views, as did Stanley Reed, a longtime member of the Stone Court, and Harold Burton, who like Vinson, had been appointed by President Harry Truman. From 1949 to 1953 this group comprised a majority of the Supreme Court. There was not a real leader among them. Simply by virtue of his position, however, Vinson became the one around whom the others rallied. From 1949 to 1953 there was something that actually deserved to be called the Vinson Court.

## *Frederick Moore Vinson*

Vinson, however, did not supply the Court with the strong and effective leadership that it desperately needed when he was appointed chief justice on June 6, 1946. Nor did he write great opinions of lasting significance. A pragmatic problem solver with an administrator's mentality, Vinson cared far more about resolving the disputes that had given rise to cases than about shaping the development of legal doctrine. Highly supportive of public officials, and especially of Congress and the president, he hardly ever interpreted the Constitution in a way that seriously restricted governmental authority. As Melvin Urofsky observes, during his tenure on the Court, which ended with his death on September 9, 1953, "Vinson's decisions . . . nearly always favored the power of the federal government over that of the states and the power of government in general over that of the individual" (Urofsky 1997, 150). Vinson's decisions earned him a reputation as an enemy of civil liberties and a jurist of rather modest ability.

Although an undistinguished chief justice, Vinson had compiled a distinguished record in all three branches of government before his appointment to the Supreme Court. The son of an eastern Kentucky jailer, he was born in the small town of Louisa on January 22, 1890, and grew up poor, selling and delivering newspapers to help his family financially. After graduating from Louisa High School, where he quarterbacked the football team, Vinson continued his education at Kentucky Normal College, an unaccredited teacher training institution, where he was valedictorian of his class. He moved on to Centre College, earning the highest grade point average any student had compiled there, while also playing basketball and baseball. After completing his undergraduate degree, Vinson attended Centre's law school, where he again finished at the top of his class. He financed his legal education in part by playing professional baseball and also participated in a wide range of extracurricular activities.

After receiving his law degree in 1911, Vinson returned to Louisa. Except for a year in the appointive position of city attorney and a few months in the army during World War I, he devoted the next decade to private practice. Then in 1921 he launched a political career, winning election as the commonwealth's attorney. Two years later he won a special election for the Ninth District congressional seat. Vinson was reelected in 1924. In the House he quickly established a reputation as a tax expert, devoting his first speech to attacking Secretary of the Treasury Andrew Mellon's plans to reduce taxation of the wealthy. He easily won reelection in 1926 but, handicapped by his party's call for repeal of Prohibition, he was swept out of office in the Republican

*Frederick Moore Vinson (Harris and Ewing, Collection of the Supreme Court of the United States*

landslide of 1928. After practicing law in Ashland, Kentucky, for two years, Vinson returned to the House in 1930.

He won an effortless reelection in 1932, the same year Franklin Roosevelt captured the presidency. Soon, "Vinson was in the front lines battling for the President's New Deal Revolution" (St. Clair and Gurgin 2002, 66). The financial demands of Roosevelt's programs were enormous, and as a member of the Ways and Means Committee, a taxation subcommittee, and a joint House-Senate panel on tax evasion and avoidance, Vinson spearheaded the administration's efforts to plug loopholes and tap new sources of revenue. In the process he earned "a lasting and deserved reputation as the preeminent tax authority in the House" (St. Clair and Gurgin 2002, 82). He also played a key role in the development of the legislation that became the Social Security Act. Vinson loyally supported almost all of FDR's policies, even introducing the House version of his controversial 1937 proposal to "pack" the Supreme Court. Except for championing bonus payments to veterans, which the president opposed, "He was in lockstep with Roosevelt on just about everything that came before Congress from the spring of 1933 until his departure more than five years later for the federal bench" (St. Clair and Gurgin 2002, 64).

Virtually all observers viewed Vinson's 1938 elevation to the U.S. Court of Appeals for the District of Columbia as a reward for his strong support of the president's legislative agenda. Even after his appointment to the bench, he continued to work for the New Deal, delaying his swearing in until more than five months after his confirmation, so he could steer an administration tax bill to passage. His legislative experience set Vinson apart from most of the men Roosevelt appointed to appellate judgeships, who tended to be judges or law professors.

The court he joined was a quite cohesive one. Vinson wrote five dissenting opinions in five years, and that was about average. Most of the 107 cases in which he spoke for the majority addressed rather routine issues, involving the application of laws, rather than their constitutionality. Vinson especially relished the 18 percent that dealt with tax matters, which allowed him to draw on his own expertise in that field. Taxation was about the only area in which he did not give unquestioning deference to administrators and to Congress. Judge Vinson also almost always affirmed the rulings of lower federal courts. His tendency to side with the government was especially evident in criminal cases, where he held against the defendant in nine of twelve majority opinions. He decided very few civil liberties issues, but those, too, he resolved in favor of the government. In his only race case, he followed Supreme Court precedent in holding that the Fourteenth Amendment did not prohibit private discrimination. Although the Supreme Court reversed him in three out of the four appeals, it reviewed one of his decisions. "As a member of the circuit court, Vinson . . . established a reputation as a competent but cautious judge" (St. Clair and Gurgin 2002, 123).

He impressed Chief Justice Stone enough that in 1942 Stone appointed him to serve as chief judge of the Emergency Court of Appeals, which Congress had created to hear complaints about price ceilings for commodities and rents imposed under the Emergency Price Control Act. His work on that tribunal was excellent preparation for the job of director of the Office of Economic Stabilization (OES) to which Roosevelt appointed him in May 1943. Giving up life tenure on the bench because he felt he was not making enough of a sacrifice in World War II, Vinson took on the task of presiding over practically every facet of the home front economy. As the government's chief inflation fighter, he earned a reputation as a tough-minded and able administrator. "Available Vinson" also came to be viewed as a reliable troubleshooter, who could be counted on to handle any task. After nearly two years at OES, he moved on to the Federal Loan Agency, where he supervised war lending activity for less than a month before succeeding James Byrnes as director of the Office of War Mobilization and Reconversion. That made him the "assistant president" for domestic affairs and put him in charge of postwar planning. After three months in that position, Truman, who had become president when Roosevelt died on April 12, 1945, asked Vinson to become secretary of the treasury.

On June 24, 1946, he switched jobs again, this time becoming the chief justice of the United States. Vinson might have been recommended for that job by retired Chief Justice Charles Evans Hughes or retired Associate Justice Owen Roberts. Truman admired his record in government and agreed with his political philosophy, but the president's most important reason for selecting Vinson was his personality. The Supreme Court was riven by infighting, which had engendered a nasty public conflict between Associate Justices Robert Jackson and Hugo Black. This internal strife, and the diminution in popular respect for the Court it had caused, convinced Truman that, rather than elevating a sitting justice, he should choose an outsider. The new chief would have to be a peacemaker, and Vinson seemed ideally suited to that role. "His sociability and friendliness, his calm, patient, and relaxed manner, his sense of humor, his respect for the views of others, his popularity with the representatives of many factions, and his ability to conciliate conflicting views and clashing personalities" all commended him to Truman (Kirkendall 1995, 1345). Senators liked the president's choice. Although one Republican voted against him in the Judiciary Committee, the full Senate confirmed Vinson unanimously.

Truman had so much confidence in his nominee that he continued to use him as a policy adviser even after he joined the Supreme Court. The president often consulted the chief justice during late-night telephone conversations. In 1948 Truman tried to send Vinson to Moscow to negotiate with Soviet leader Joseph Stalin, abandoning that idea only because the secretary of state objected. He even wanted Vinson to succeed him in the presidency. Although Truman vigorously urged the chief justice to run in

1952, he declined to do so, telling the president he did not think he should use the Supreme Court as a stepping-stone to the White House.

Vinson retained Truman's confidence despite his failure to fuse together the fractured Court the president had wanted him to unify. Neither lack of effort nor lack of personality explains his failure as a judicial leader. Felix Frankfurter had little respect for Vinson's legal abilities or his intellect, and considerable personal rancor developed between the two of them. Most members of the Court, however, liked the congenial chief justice. He was affable and worked hard at fostering good relations with his colleagues. Vinson went out of his way to accommodate their personal needs, rescheduling Court business when one of them had a personal conflict and encouraging those with health problems to recover fully before returning to work. He also drastically reduced the Court's workload. Convinced that the justices were overworked and believing this had contributed to the untimely death of Wiley Rutledge, Vinson cut down the number of cases the Court decided with full written opinions from more than 200 per term, where it had been in 1930, to barely 100. He also showed consideration for his colleagues in the way he assigned opinions. Vinson maintained tight control over opinion assignments by bending to the will of the majority so he would be part of it, aligning with the winning side 86 percent of the time. He did not, however, grab the most important cases for himself. His sole motivation in making assignments was to attain an equitable distribution of the workload. He gave the most cases to those justices who wrote the most quickly, even though their views differed markedly from his own.

Although Vinson was congenial and solicitous of his colleagues' needs and feelings, he lacked the intellect required to command the esteem of several brilliant associate justices. Nor did he have the leadership skills needed to bridge the deep personal and philosophical divisions within his Court. Its members, all appointed by Presidents Roosevelt and Truman, shared a common commitment to the economic policies of the New Deal but disagreed on the new issues (mostly involving civil liberties and civil rights) that became the focus of the Court's attention during and after World War II. The kind of pragmatic compromising that Vinson favored could not erase the sharp philosophical disagreements and intense personal rivalries that divided them. In his first term as chief justice, the Court decided only 36 percent of its cases with unanimous opinions. By his third term, that figure had dropped to 26 percent, and by his final one, it was down to 19 percent, then the lowest in the Court's history. Many decisions were made by 5–4 votes, and often the members of the majority could not agree on a rationale. As Urofsky observes, "Given another lineup at a different time, Vinson might well have been considered a good chief, but he proved unable to control or guide his colleagues" (Urofsky 1997, 151). Lacking any real power over the associate justices, a chief justice can lead them only to the extent that they defer to him. Regarding Vinson as an intellectual inferior and a Johnny-come-lately, some of his colleagues would not even treat him as a first among equals.

He did eventually gain some influence over "his" Court, but that was due mainly to changes in its membership affected by death and Truman. Initially the Vinson Court fragmented into three blocs. The largest one, led by Black, also included Douglas, Murphy, and Rutledge. All of them tended to favor the active use of judicial power to implement their liberal values, especially those embodied in the Bill of Rights. At the other end of the spectrum were the Court's most conservative members, Reed and Burton. The third bloc, which often voted with the second, consisted of Frankfurter and Robert Jackson. Although disagreeing with Black on a number of issues, they were most critical of what they considered his result-oriented activism. Frankfurter maintained that the Supreme Court should exercise great restraint in the use of its power to declare laws unconstitutional, generally deferring to the popularly elected branches of the government. Because of his long career in elected office, Vinson "naturally inclined toward this view" (St. Clair and Gurgin 2002, 170). Frankfurter tried hard to lure the chief justice into his camp with flattery and instruction on the Supreme Court's operations, and during his first year on the Court, Vinson frequently sought Frankfurter's advice. Eventually, the relationship between them deteriorated, however, becoming so bad that Frankfurter would not sign any opinion Vinson wrote. What alienated him was that the chief justice would no longer consistently vote his way.

Vinson's independence increased, and Frankfurter's stature declined because of the deaths of Murphy and Rutledge in the summer of 1949. Clark and Minton, whom Truman named to replace them, both held views similar to those of his earlier appointees, Burton and Vinson. The four Truman justices joined Reed to form a voting bloc that controlled the Court. Because Frankfurter and Jackson held views that were closer to theirs than to those of Black and Douglas, they often voted with these five. As long as Vinson and his allies stuck together, however, they had a majority without them. The chief, who had dissented in 18 percent of the cases decided in the 1948–1949 term, dissented in only 2 percent of those decided the following year, dramatic evidence of how much the replacement of Rutledge and Murphy by Clark and Minton had improved his position. Vinson's Court came, despite his ineffective leadership, to render decisions that reflected his views.

Preeminent among those views was his belief in the need for a powerful national government that could solve the country's problems the way he and other federal officials had done during World War II. The fact that President Truman was a personal friend enhanced Vinson's propensity toward supporting whatever the administration did. Thus, in *United States v. United Mine Workers* (1947), a case generated by a Truman legal initiative to halt a coal strike, the chief justice wrote a majority opinion upholding the government's position on every issue. On the other hand, when the Court ruled in *Youngstown Sheet and Tube Company v. Sawyer* (1952) that the president had acted unlawfully in seizing the nation's steel mills in order to prevent a work stoppage that threatened to disrupt production during the Korean War, Vinson filed a lengthy dissent.

His dedication to supporting the government made him a nemesis of civil liberties. As Richard Kirkendall observes, "Vinson's civil liberties record was characterized by an overwhelming tendency to uphold governmental power as opposed to individual claims" (Kirkendall 1995, 1343). He supported the federal government more than 90 percent of the time in civil liberties cases and backed states more than 80 percent of the time. He almost always voted to deny rights to aliens.

Although his record in the criminal justice field was somewhat ambivalent, there, too, Vinson generally favored governmental interests over individual rights in both federal and state cases. A persistent theme in his opinions was that officials should not be left helpless to respond to threats against order. Vinson resisted Black's efforts to require the states to afford defendants all of the procedural safeguards the Bill of Rights required the federal government to give them. He also consistently rejected claims that defendants had been denied the right to counsel. Although he had written a strong defense of the Fourth Amendment while on the Court of Appeals, as a justice he proved unsympathetic to claims that convictions should be reversed because of unreasonable searches or seizures.

Vinson's determination to preserve governmental power made him resistant not only to Fourth Amendment claims but also to First Amendment ones. Although he did generally oppose licensing schemes that could interfere with the dissemination of ideas, when local authorities claimed a prior restraint was necessary to prevent a breach of the peace, he would uphold it. If the federal government maintained that national security required restricting freedom of expression, Vinson would support its position. Thus, he backed its initiatives to combat domestic communism. In *American Communications Association v. Douds* (1950), Vinson upheld a section of the Taft-Hartley Act that required labor union officials to take an oath that they were not affiliated with the Communist Party and did not believe in the violent overthrow of the government. It was, he maintained, a valid exercise of the congressional power to regulate interstate commerce that did not violate the First Amendment. In probably his most famous opinion, *Dennis v. United States* (1951), he rejected a challenge to the Smith Act, a statute that made it a crime to teach and advocate the violent overthrow of the government or create an organization to engage in such teaching and advocacy. That law did not violate the First Amendment, he insisted. In the same year that he wrote *Dennis*, Vinson did rule that the government had violated the Eighth Amendment by setting unusually high bail for some Smith Act defendants, but usually he saw no constitutional problems with the way the government went about combating communism.

Decisions such as *Dennis* and *Douds* earned Vinson a well-deserved reputation as a menace to civil liberties. Often overlooked are the positive contributions he made to the expansion of African American civil rights. In 1948 Vinson held illegal in the District of Columbia the restrictive covenants by which homeowners bound themselves not to sell their property to nonwhites. Although these were legal elsewhere, he declared, courts could not enforce them, because doing so would violate the Equal Protection Clause of the Fourteenth Amendment. In 1950 Vinson ruled that the Interstate Commerce Act prohibited segregating railroad dining cars. That same year in *Sweatt v. Painter* (1950) and *McLaurin v. Oklahoma State Board of Regents* (1950) he held that a law school Texas had created for African Americans and an internally segregated education graduate program at the University of Oklahoma both violated the "separate-but-equal" rule that had governed interpretation of the Equal Protection Clause since 1896. Vinson's opinions, which focused on intangible differences between the educations Texas and Oklahoma were affording to whites and African Americans, suggested that no state could possibly comply with that doctrine as the Court was now interpreting it. His opinions encouraged the National Association for the Advancement of Colored People to seek a ruling holding separate-but-equal education itself unconstitutional.

The Court did that in *Brown v. Board of Education* (1954). What would have happened had Vinson not died while that case was before the Court is uncertain. He had dissented from a decision extending his own restrictive-covenant ruling and was clearly not enthusiastic about the idea of simply repudiating the separate-but-equal rule. Vinson liked whenever possible to resolve cases on the basis of precedent, and he thought change should be evolutionary rather than revolutionary. On the other hand, he had spoken for a nearly united bench on racial issues, and pressure to maintain that unity, along with desire to write for the Court in such an important case, might have led him to join the majority in *Brown*.

Had he done so, he could have enhanced a less than outstanding historical reputation. As it is, despite his numerous contributions to the development of civil rights law, Vinson is remembered mainly as an almost dogmatic supporter of the government who damaged civil liberties while failing to unify his badly divided Court.

## Hugo Lafayette Black

When the Court took the bench, Hugo Black (1886–1971) occupied the seat to Vinson's right. That is ironic, for he was one of the Vinson Court's most liberal members. During thirty-four years on the bench, Black compiled one of the most distinguished records in U.S. judicial history. Because his views commanded the support of only a minority of the Vinson Court, however, he registered his most notable achievements during other eras.

Black, who was born on February 27, 1886, rose to judicial eminence from rural Clay County, Alabama, where his father ran a general merchandise store. His mother

*Hugo Lafayette Black (Harris and Ewing, Collection of the Supreme Court of the United States)*

wanted him to become a doctor, but he abandoned medical education after one year to attend the University of Alabama Law School, from which he graduated near the top of his class in 1906. He built a successful private practice in Birmingham, achieving financial success, despite handling mostly personal injury cases and representing mainly middle- and lower-class clients. He also took a part-time position as a police court judge. In 1914 Black was elected county solicitor. As a prosecutor he attacked Jefferson County's corrupt fee system, prosecuted coal companies for unfair wage practices, and initiated a grand jury investigation of police interrogation tactics. He quit to enter military service in World War I.

In 1926, after joining the Ku Klux Klan and mounting a campaign that emphasized populist themes, Black defeated two better-known candidates to win election to the U.S. Senate. Alabama voters reelected him in 1932. In the Senate he sponsored a bill to limit the workweek to thirty hours, supported legislation benefiting consumers and labor and higher taxes on corporate profits, and investigated shipping firms, airlines, and public utility holding companies. He also championed Roosevelt's controversial "Court-packing" plan.

Although Roosevelt's plan failed to win enactment, Justice Willis Van Devanter's retirement in the spring of 1937 made it possible for Roosevelt to appoint a justice. On August 1, he nominated Black. Despite rumors about the Alabaman's Ku Klux Klan connections, his fellow senators quickly confirmed him by a vote of 63–16. On August 19 Black took the seat he would occupy until eight days before his death on September 25, 1971. A month after his confirmation, the press reported that he had been a Klansman, igniting a furor that subsided only after the new justice responded to the allegations against him in an unprecedented national radio broadcast. He acknowledged past affiliation with the KKK, but insisted he had long since severed his connections with that controversial organization.

Although Black outgrew the Klan, he retained the populist suspicion of governmental authority he had learned in rural Alabama. This made him distrustful of all public officials, including judges. What constrained judicial power, Black believed, was the Constitution. "I cherish every word of it," he declared in a 1968 lecture, "and I personally deplore even the slightest deviation from its commands" (Yarbrough 1988, 20). Black believed that judges had a responsibility to follow the Constitution literally and had no authority to put their own gloss on it. Thus, as far as he was concerned, the First Amendment's declaration that Congress might "make no law" restricting freedom of speech was a prohibition of all governmental restrictions on expression, not just those judges found unacceptable. Black's First Amendment absolutism became "the centerpiece of his thought" (Newman 1994, 413). It was one facet of what Tinsley E. Yarbrough characterizes as his constitutional positivism. Black believed that when a judge construed the Constitution, its language should be his primary guide. When it yielded no answer to the question before him, he might look to the history of the provision in question. Only if that failed to clarify the intent of the framers was it proper for a judge to give a constitutional provision the interpretation that seemed best to him. Black realized that even the Constitution's most specific provisions were not self-executing and that their language and history had to be interpreted. But he found far more clear-cut meanings in the language and history than did his critics.

Viewing the words of the Constitution as a barrier against dangerous judicial innovating, Black sought to use those in the Bill of Rights to confine the vague and potentially expansive Due Process Clause of the Fourteenth Amendment. He rejected the view that this clause prohibited states from denying people whatever rights were implicit in the concept of ordered liberty and the notion that it guaranteed criminal defendants nothing more specific than fundamental fairness. In his opinion, such vague standards left too much room for judicial subjectivity. As early as 1939, Black concluded that the framers of the Fourteenth Amendment had intended to incorporate within its first section all of the specific guarantees of the Bill of Rights. Thus, the Due Process Clause imposed on the states precisely the same limitations that the Bill of Rights itself imposed on the national government—nothing less, but also nothing more. Black's theory both enlarged and restricted the ability of judges to protect individual freedom. "If under the due process clause the judge was bound to apply the Bill of Rights to the states, his power was increased," Tony Freyer explains. "At the same time," however, "this authority could not exceed what was literally prescribed in those same provisions" (Freyer 1990, 101).

In other words, incorporation would reconcile judicial activism with judicial restraint. Black shared with all of the justices appointed by Roosevelt and Truman a revulsion for the way the pre–1937 Supreme Court had invalidated economic regulatory and social welfare legislation of which its members disapproved. In reviewing such laws, he believed, judges should practice self-restraint, accepting the policy judgments of legislators, rather than overriding them, while purporting to enforce the Constitution. To Black the notion that some forms of liberty were so fundamental that government could not abridge them without violating due process was dangerous. It allowed judges to convert their personal values into standards for determining constitutionality and to employ an "accordion-like method of expanding or deflating due process, including or excluding rights with each case" (Newman 1994, 349). This was true even when a judge was seeking to protect civil liberties. Yet, while committed to judicial restraint in the economic realm, Black believed courts had an obligation to enforce personal rights vigorously. Incorporation would enable them to do that while avoiding the abuses of judicial discretion associated with economic substantive due process, for the language of the Bill of Rights would provide clear limits to what judges might do in giving meaning to the Due Process Clause.

Black saw nothing wrong with treating civil liberties differently than economic rights. Judges had an obligation to enforce the clear commands of the Constitution, even if that meant thwarting the legislative will. His jurisprudence assigned a preferred constitutional status to certain civil liberties, especially the First Amendment's guarantees of freedom of expression.

That jurisprudence made him the natural ally of Douglas, with whom he voted more consistently than any other justice during their more than three decades together on the Supreme Court. Murphy and Rutledge also quickly aligned themselves with Black. Between their appointments and 1946, when Vinson became chief justice, both generally voted with him more than 70 percent of the time. Black became the recognized leader of a liberal bloc. The significance of that declined after the deaths of Murphy and Rutledge, and the appointments of Clark and Minton halved the size of that bloc. During most of the Vinson era, Black shared the bench with four Truman appointees, whose views were far more conservative than his own, and with Frankfurter and Jackson, with whom he had both sharp intellectual disagreements and testy personal relations.

Consequently, he did not often speak for the Vinson Court in important cases. The most notable exception was *Youngstown Sheet and Tube Company v. Sawyer*. Douglas was the only other member of the majority who supported his rationale for that ruling, however. Black's most influential decisions came after Earl Warren replaced Vinson in 1953. During the period 1946–1953 his most memorable opinions were dissents. Black repeatedly protested decisions upholding anticommunist measures that interfered with freedom of expression and other individual rights. In *American Communications Association v. Douds*, for example, he dissented from Vinson's ruling that Section 9(h) of the Taft-Hartley Act was constitutional. In an unforgettable dissent in *Dennis v. United States*, Black expressed hope "that in calmer times, when present pressures, passions and fears subside, this or some later Court will restore the First Amendment liberties to the high preferred place where they belong in a free society" (*Dennis* 1951, 581).

That happened after Warren became chief justice. So did the incorporation of the Bill of Rights into the Due Process Clause that Black had advocated in his landmark dissenting opinion in *Adamson v. California* (1947). A law professor established that Black was wrong when he contended in *Adamson* that the framers of the Fourteenth Amendment had intended it to make the Bill of Rights applicable to the states, and he could not persuade a majority of his Vinson Court colleagues to accept his thesis. The Warren Court never adopted his "total incorporation" theory either, but it did incorporate piecemeal almost all of the guarantees in the Bill of Rights that had not previously been held to be protected by the Due Process Clause.

Although they were perhaps less memorable than his *Adamson* and *Dennis* dissents, Black did write a few important majority opinions while Vinson was chief justice. One of these held that, because a company town performed public functions, the fact that it was privately owned did not exempt it from the constitutional rules with which other municipalities had to comply. Black's most significant opinion for a majority of the Vinson Court was *Everson v. Board of Education* (1947), in which the Supreme Court for the first time interpreted the clause in the First Amendment prohibiting the "establishment of religion." Black maintained that the Establishment Clause had been intended to create a "wall of separation" between church and state. He then held, however, that New Jersey had not breached this wall when it authorized townships to reimburse parents for the bus fare they paid to transport their children to parochial schools. The following year, Black accepted the absolutist implications of his own reading of the Establishment Clause, this time writing for the Court that "released-time" programs, under which members of the clergy provided on-campus religious instruction to public school students during school hours, were unconstitutional.

That opinion excited widespread public criticism. In putting Black out of step with prevailing sentiment it was hardly unique. During the Vinson years he was best known as a dissenter, who repeatedly challenged the prevailing antilibertarian orthodoxy. His fertile mind generated many provocative ideas but far less constitutional law.

## Stanley Forman Reed

Black's career as a whole was considerably more illustrious than that of Stanley Reed (1884–1980), but Reed achieved greater success during the Vinson years. The reason was not his intellectual power or judicial craftsmanship, but simply the fact that he was in the right place at the right time. Because he shared many of Vinson's views, Reed aligned himself with the chief justice and the other Truman appointees. Since the five of them constituted a majority of the Court, he was assured of being on the winning side in most cases.

Reed shared not only Vinson's views but also his Kentucky roots. Born into a locally prominent family in the small town of Minerva on December 31, 1884, he earned B.A. degrees from both Wesleyan College and Yale University. Although Reed studied law at the University of Virginia, Columbia, and the Sorbonne, he never graduated from any of these institutions. Instead, he completed his legal education by reading law in the office of a Kentucky attorney. Soon after entering practice, he plunged into politics. A Wilsonian Progressive, Reed won election to the Kentucky legislature in 1912, serving there for four years. After military service in World War I, he built a successful practice in Maysville, representing wealthy corporate clients, which included the Burley Tobacco Growers Cooperative Association. That connection led the Republican Hoover administration to appoint him counsel to the Federal Farm Board, despite the fact that Reed was a Democratic partisan who had managed one

*Stanley Forman Reed (Harris and Ewing, Collection of the Supreme Court of the United States)*

of Vinson's congressional campaigns. He held the Farm Board position from 1929 to 1932, when he moved over to the new Reconstruction Finance Corporation (RFC).

Hoover left office in 1933, but Reed did not. He stayed on in Washington to head the RFC for the new Roosevelt administration. Among the ways it sought to raise the prices of agricultural commodities was by nullifying clauses in private contracts that required payment in gold. So that he could champion the legality of this policy before the Supreme Court, Reed was made a special assistant to the attorney general. The government won the *Gold Clause Cases* (1935), and soon thereafter, Roosevelt made Reed solicitor general. He defended controversial New Deal measures before the Court for the next three years, and although he lost several major cases, his loyal service and strong commitment to a broad interpretation of congressional power under the Commerce Clause obviously impressed the president. On January 15, 1938, following the retirement of Justice George Sutherland, Roosevelt nominated Reed to take Sutherland's seat. He held it until his own retirement in 1957, twenty-three years before his death at the age of ninety-five, as the longest-lived Supreme Court justice ever.

When Reed joined the Stone Court in 1938, he aligned himself with its more liberal members. By the time Vinson became chief justice, however, the composition of the Court had changed sufficiently that he found himself on its right wing. There he joined forces with the chief and the recently appointed Harold Burton. When Clark and Minton replaced Murphy and Rutledge, this group became a majority. Although liberal by the standards of the early 1930s, by those of the late 1940s it was a conservative group.

Like its nominal leader, Reed retained the expansive view of governmental power that had made both him and Vinson enthusiastic New Dealers. As Daniel L. Breen has written, "Few justices were as dependable a friend of governmental intervention in the economy as Reed" (Breen 1994, 368). Even though a federal tax on gamblers seemed designed to force gamblers to reveal information that states could use to prosecute them, he upheld it in *United States v. Kahriger* (1953), saying he could not see why its indirect effects should raise any doubts about the validity of such an exercise of the federal taxing power. In *United Public Workers v. Mitchell* (1947) Reed validated the Hatch Act's prohibition on federal employees engaging in certain kinds of political activity. If Congress and the president, who were responsible for maintaining an efficient public service, considered such a measure necessary, Reed could see no constitutional objection to it.

As far as he was concerned, there were few if any limits to what Congress or the president might do, especially in the interests of national security. Thus, he voted to uphold the exclusion of Japanese Americans from the West Coast during World War II and signed Vinson's *Youngstown* dissent, supporting the chief's contention that the Constitution authorized Truman's seizure of the nation's steel mills during the Korean conflict. Reed wrote for the Court when it ruled that the government could hold Communist aliens without bail, pending a determination of their deportability, but he dissented when it ruled that the attorney general could not designate an organization as "Communist" for purposes of determining the loyalty of federal employees without providing some way for the group to contest its designation.

The strong commitment of this buoyant New Dealer to supporting virtually all actions of Congress and the president goes a long way toward explaining his rather negative record in civil liberties cases. It is not the full explanation, however, for Reed endorsed many state and local restrictions on individual rights as well. He spoke for the Court in *Kovacs v. Cooper* (1949), when it upheld a municipal ordinance prohibiting "loud and raucous" messages broadcast by sound trucks. Reed joined majorities that permitted local governments to ban door-to-door solicitation and to arrest a rabble-rousing speaker for disorderly conduct. He also consistently supported communities that imposed license fees and other restrictions on the distribution of religious literature, and dissented from the Court's invalidation of released-time programs in *McCollum v. Board of Education*. The strong communitarian tendencies that he exhibited in these cases also explain why he responded less favorably than did many of his colleagues to claims by convicted criminals that their rights had been violated. It was Reed who wrote the majority opinion in *Adamson v. California*, rejecting, in order to uphold a California law that allowed judges and attorneys to comment on a defendant's failure to testify, the contention that states were required to comply with the Fifth Amendment's prohibition of compulsory self-incrimination.

Yet, his civil liberties record was not an entirely negative one. Reed was a vigorous opponent of censorship, who wrote the opinion in *Winters v. New York* (1948) striking down a law prohibiting the distribution of publications that featured stories about violent crime. He concurred when the Court brought motion pictures within the protection of the First Amendment and took the position that judges might not employ their contempt power to punish press criticism of the courts. Also, for a Kentuckian, Reed was surprisingly supportive of civil rights for African Americans. In 1944 he wrote an opinion holding unconstitutional the Texas Democratic Party's whites-only primary, and in 1946 he authored one invalidating a Virginia statute requiring segregated seating on buses passing through the state. Both employed narrow rationales, however, and when the NAACP asked the Court to declare that school segregation violated the Equal Protection Clause, Reed balked. He went along with the majority in *Brown v. Board of Education* only after Vinson's death left him as the lone defender of separate-but-equal and Warren persuaded him that for the good of the Court and the country the inevitable judicial rejection of segregated schools must be unanimous.

His colleague Felix Frankfurter praised this selfless act as Reed's most lasting service to his country. Fittingly, it involved simply going along with the majority. That was the secret of Reed's success on the Vinson Court.

## *Felix Frankfurter*

Unlike Reed, Felix Frankfurter (1882–1965) was a leader rather than a follower. At least he tried to be. Much of the history of the mid-twentieth-century Supreme Court is the story of Frankfurter's tireless crusade to convert other justices, the legal profession, and the country to his views about how the Supreme Court should do its job. It is a story with an unhappy ending, for a flawed judicial philosophy and an inability to get along with colleagues who would not accept his direction combined to reduce his influence and minimize his accomplishments.

Unlike the judges he tried to dominate, Frankfurter was an immigrant. He did not come to this country from Austria until he was eight, but by the time he was nineteen, he was graduated third in his class from City College of New York. After briefly attending two local law schools at night and working for the city's Tenement House Commission, this brilliant young man entered Harvard Law School, where he ranked at the top of his class for three years and won a position on the law review. Because he was Jewish, however, anti-Semitism hindered his quest for employment. It took an unusually strong recommendation from Dean James Barr Ames to land him a position with a New York law firm.

Having gotten the job, Frankfurter quickly tired of representing corporate clients. He soon abandoned private practice for public service, taking a position in the office of U.S. Attorney Henry L. Stimson. When Stimson became secretary of war, Frankfurter accompanied him to Washington, becoming a legal advisor to the War Department's Bureau of Insular Affairs and the center of a group of young bureaucrats and writers (which included Herbert Croly and Walter Lippman), who shared quarters they dubbed "The House of Truth." After a change of administration forced Stimson out of office in 1913, he raised money to create a position for Frankfurter at Harvard. The young lawyer returned to public service during World War I, serving as legal advisor to the president's Mediation Commission, chairing the War Labor Policies Board, investigating the deportation of miners from Bisbee, Arizona, and the controversial prosecution of a California labor activist, taking part in a diplomatic mission to Turkey, and attending the Versailles Peace Conference.

In 1919 Frankfurter rejoined the Harvard faculty. A talented teacher, over the next two decades he "trained a whole generation of lawyers in administrative law" (Urofsky 2001, 42). He also established a reputation as one of the leading academic authorities on the Supreme Court. Frankfurter maintained close personal relationships with Justices Oliver Wendell Holmes Jr. and Louis Brandeis. Idolizing Holmes, whose commitment to judicial self-restraint became a central feature of his own jurisprudence, he assumed responsibility for selecting his clerks. Frankfurter was even closer to Brandeis. Both were Jewish, and they shared commitments to Progressive reform and Zionism. For many years the wealthy Brandeis provided Frankfurter

*Felix Frankfurter (Harris and Ewing, Collection of the Supreme Court of the United States)*

with a financial subsidy, which enabled him to devote considerable time to the causes about which both of them cared. "During the 1920s Frankfurter, through his defense of Sacco and Vanzetti and his writings for the *New Republic*, became a leading reformer in his own right" (Urofsky 2001, 42). He also censured the Justice Department for its conduct during the Palmer raids. Outraged by his supposed radicalism, conservative alumni demanded that Harvard fire him.

Actually Frankfurter was not a radical at all, but a Progressive, who became a New Dealer. Having met Franklin Roosevelt sometime around 1906, he began actively courting his friendship after Roosevelt was elected governor of New York in 1928. When FDR became president, he offered to make his friend solicitor general. After consulting Holmes and Brandeis, Frankfurter decided to remain at Harvard, but he continued to advise the president. Although never exercising quite as much influence on the New Deal as his enemies claimed, he did assist in drafting important legislation and sent a bevy of former students down to Washington to do its legal work. Even after his elevation to the bench, Frankfurter continued to advise the Roosevelt administration on major public policy issues.

In 1938 the president rewarded Frankfurter's loyal service with a seat on the Supreme Court. His liberalism, his internationalism, and his religion, almost kept him from getting the nomination, but several people Roosevelt consulted, including Justice Stone, insisted Frankfurter was the best-qualified candidate. His friendship with the president and intense lobbying by many loyal supporters ultimately got him the appointment. Ecstatic New Dealers gathered in the office of Secretary of the Interior Harold Ickes to celebrate. They expected Frankfurter to become a liberal justice. Civil libertarians, who considered him one of their own, were also enthusiastic. It was widely expected that, because of his expertise on the operations of the Supreme Court, Frankfurter would become one of its leaders. Solicitor General Robert Jackson considered him the only man capable of taking on Chief Justice Hughes in conference discussions and holding his own. Expected to become both a liberal justice and a great one, he did neither. According to his biographer Melvin Urofsky, "Frankfurter ranks as one of the great disappointments in modern times" (Urofsky 2001, 40).

One reason for his failure to live up to expectations was his rigid adherence to a jurisprudential principle. "The tragedy of Mr. Justice Frankfurter," Urofsky writes, "is that he became the prisoner of an idea—judicial restraint" (Urofsky 1991, 149). Frankfurter believed that the Constitution permitted social experimentation and government that was vigorous and active. During Frankfurter's first twenty years out of law school, however, the Supreme Court often used the Constitution to thwart the sort of experimental humanitarian legislation that he and his fellow Progressives favored. As Frankfurter watched judges repeatedly cite the vague Due Process Clause to justify invalidating such laws, he grew skeptical about judicial review. When the Supreme Court employed its power to veto laws enacted by the people's elected representatives, Frankfurter became convinced it stunted the democratic process, thwarting the will of the people and encouraging a dangerous dependence on black-robed guardians to save society from foolish measures and tyranny. Frankfurter came to venerate Holmes and Brandeis for insisting that judges should refrain from imposing their economic prejudices on the public by overruling the policymaking of elected officials. "The correct judicial posture," he concluded, "ought to be one of deference to the legislature's judgment, unless that choice 'passe[d] the bounds of reason and assume[d] the character of merely arbitrary fiat'" (Parrish 1982, 168).

The judicial self-restraint that Frankfurter advocated required jurists not only to defer to legislative judgments but also to avoid deciding constitutional questions whenever possible. He was a strong proponent of the political question doctrine, which holds that some issues are not amenable to judicial resolution and thus should be left to the elected branches of government. Frankfurter applied this doctrine in *Colegrove v. Green* (1946) to decline to rule on the constitutionality of legislative malapportionment, which, he held, was a nonjusticiable political question. During the Vinson years, when the Court confronted issues that were especially divisive, Frankfurter often urged colleagues to dispose of these by deciding not to decide them.

His emphasis on the "passive virtues" set Frankfurter apart from colleagues such as Black. All of the Roosevelt and Truman appointees shared his belief that the Supreme Court should defer to the popularly elected branches of government when passing on the constitutionality of regulatory legislation. But in contrast to Black and his allies, Frankfurter "failed to distinguish between the regulation of economic and property rights and limitations upon individual liberties" (Urofsky 1991, 58). Unlike his mentor, Brandeis, he never accepted the idea that judges should be more active—and hold legislatures to higher standards of necessity—when passing on governmental actions affecting the freedoms of speech, press, religion, and political association. Thus, Frankfurter used judicial self-restraint to rationalize concurring in *Dennis v. United States*, despite his obvious distaste for the Smith Act. "While he believed in civil liberties," James F. Simon explains, "he also believed that the people—under the enlightened leadership of the legislative and executive branches—must defend those liberties for themselves and not leave defense of them to the courts" (Simon 1989, 108).

Unlike Black, who viewed the First Amendment as an absolute, Frankfurter balanced freedom of expression against other values. Often the other values prevailed. During World War II, for example, the need to promote national unity seemed more important to the extremely patriotic Frankfurter than did the free speech rights of a small religious sect, so he took the position that children of the Jehovah's Witnesses faith could be forced to salute the flag. In the 1950s he developed the concept of group libel in order to uphold the conviction of a white racist for distributing antiblack leaflets that attributed criminality to African Americans. To his credit Frankfurter did not succumb to the anticommunist hysteria of the McCarthy era. He tried unsuccessfully to get the Court to hear the case of convicted atomic spies Julius and Ethel Rosenberg, and he worked behind the scenes to rein in the Smith Act. Despite his earlier reputation as a civil libertarian, however, he generally failed to join Black in condemning on First Amendment grounds restraints on freedom of expression adopted in response to anticommunist hysteria. When he resisted such restrictions at all, it was likely to be because of what he viewed as violations of procedural due process.

Although Frankfurter was prepared to sacrifice First Amendment rights on the altar of judicial self-restraint, where the Fourth Amendment's prohibition of unreasonable searches and seizures was concerned, he was more of an activist than Black. This limitation on governmental authority seemed different to him, in part because it was very specific and rooted in and clearly defined by a particular historical controversy. Also, the Fourth Amendment needed more judicial protection than did the First. Although freedom of expression enjoyed strong support from organized interest groups (such as the press, publishers, and the motion picture industry), the prohibition of unreasonable searches and seizures did not. Regarding it as basic to a free society, Frankfurter spoke for the Court in *Wolf v. Colorado* (1949), when it held that this restriction was one of those the Due Process Clause imposed on the states.

*Wolf* did not, however, require the states to comply with the exclusionary rule, which had long made evidence obtained in violation of the Fourth Amendment inadmissible in federal courts. Frankfurter maintained that the states should be allowed to develop their own methods of ensuring compliance with the constitutional prohibition of unreasonable searches and seizures, rather than being forced to do what the national judiciary commanded. A believer in robust state-centered federalism, he resisted the economic nationalism that produced interpretations of federal statutes and the Commerce Clause that threatened to sweep away the states' regulatory authority. He also sought to protect from a federal judiciary imposing national legal principles the autonomy of state judges to decide cases on the basis of state law.

Frankfurter strongly opposed Black's incorporation theory, for if accepted by the Supreme Court, it would impose on the states national rules of criminal procedure derived from the Bill of Rights. That, in his opinion, would destroy the federal system. Frankfurter believed strongly that the Fourteenth Amendment had not been intended to make the Supreme Court a tribunal for the revision of state criminal convictions. It obligated the Court only to ensure that the states respected basic standards of decency, widely recognized in Anglo-Saxon jurisdictions. Justices should refuse to tolerate police practices that offended community standards of fair play and decency, but so long as the states avoided procedures that were unfair, the Supreme Court should allow them to adopt those they wanted. "Frankfurter thus equated due process with fundamental fairness" (Urofsky 1991, 151). The problem with his approach, as Urofsky points out, is that it provided few, if any, objective standards. "[F]or Frankfurter, those practices that shocked his conscience violated due process" (Urofsky 1991, 152). He believed that their legal expertise gave judges both the capacity and the responsibility to confirm society's moral progress by giving content to the Fourteenth Amendment. Black considered that approach too subjective. He wanted to constrain the seemingly limitless judicial discretion it could allow by equating "due process" with the commandments of the Bill of Rights. When he advanced his interpretation of the Fourteenth Amendment in the Court's internal discussions of *Adamson v. California*, however, Frankfurter maintained that it had already been rejected in *Twining v. New Jersey* (1908). The majority supported Frankfurter. Their debate did not end with the 1948 *Adamson* decision, however. Indeed, it continued until Frankfurter retired from the Court in 1962. As James F. Simon observes, "Whenever Frankfurter lectured on the due process clause of the Fourteenth Amendment, Black rejoined" (Simon 1989, 175).

Their debate on that subject was one facet of a larger dispute between the two men that was one of the major sources of division within the Vinson Court. Black and Frankfurter shared a common goal: preventing the abuse of judicial discretion that had so often resulted in the invalidation of liberal economic and social welfare legislation during the 1920s and 1930s. Frankfurter sought to achieve this objective through judicial self-restraint, whereas Black thought the solution to the problem lay in strict adherence to the letter of the Constitution. Frankfurter could not accept Black's contention that judicial discretion itself (rather than just its abuse) was a threat to democratic principles and considered mischievous the idea that judges could ever merely announce the law they discovered without engaging in some lawmaking themselves. Black, on the other hand, "became increasingly impatient with what he considered Frankfurter's 'natural law framework,' which did not tie the Court to an explicit set of constitutional rules" (Simon 1989, 173). His adversary countered that incorporation would give the judges who carried it out awesome power and that much of the language of the Bill of Rights was insufficiently specific to ensure that they would exercise it objectively. Black's constitutional views infuriated Frankfurter. As the debate between the two men grew increasingly heated, both lost sight of the fact that they were straying from their original common goal.

Contrasting personal styles exacerbated conflict-rooted jurisprudential differences. Black was diplomatic, even toward colleagues with whom he had strong disagreements. Frankfurter, on the other hand, tended to be feisty, contentious, and even petty in his dealings with coworkers. He "did not believe in consensus or compromise until an issue had been thoroughly articulated and explored" (White 1988, 330). When Black first joined the Court, Frankfurter offered him guidance on the workings of the judicial process, but during the 1940s, the relationship between them deteriorated badly. Writing in his diary, Frankfurter described Black's judicial behavior in deprecating terms, characterizing him as "a politician on the Court without professional integrity" (Simon 1989, 140). The relationship between the two men was complex, however. Even in the 1940s, when it was particularly tense, Frankfurter remained quite friendly with Black's children, and the two men grew closer following the death of Black's first wife in the early 1950s and again near the end of Frankfurter's life in the early 1960s.

Although not always as bitter as it appeared to outsiders, the conflict between them was real, intense, and divisive. Frankfurter constantly sought allies in his ongoing struggle with Black. He would lavish attention on new appointees, flattering them and offering them assistance. If one began to assert independence, however, and to adopt positions on legal issues of which he disapproved, Frankfurter would turn on him, criticizing him behind his back and eventually deeming him an enemy. With the exception of James McReynolds, no justice ever had worse relations with his colleagues. Frankfurter's personalization of issues had particularly disastrous effects during World War II, but it continued to divide the Court in the Vinson years.

Initially, the Vinson Court split into Frankfurter supporters and Black backers. In its early years Black could generally count on the support of Douglas, Murphy, and Rutledge. During the 1946–1948 terms, Douglas voted with him in 71 percent of nonunanimous cases, Rutledge in 76 percent, and Murphy in 78 percent. Frankfurter's most consistent supporter was Jackson, who voted with him in 74 percent of nonunanimous cases during those terms. Also backing him more than half the time were Vinson (62 percent), Burton (61 percent), and Reed (57 percent). The deaths of Rutledge and Murphy weakened Black's position in this internal struggle for power and influence, while strengthening Frankfurter's. During the 1949–1952 terms Clark voted with Frankfurter 59 percent of the time and Minton joined him 51 percent of the time. Clark aligned with Black in only 47 percent of nonunanimous cases, and Minton did so in only 41 percent. One measure of the decline in Black's influence is the percentage of cases in which he dissented, which was between 21 and 24 percent during the 1946–1948 terms, but rose to between 33 and 42 percent during the last four years of the Vinson Court.

Frankfurter's influence did not rise as much as Black's fell. Clark, Minton, Reed, and Burton all voted more frequently with the chief justice than they did with Frankfurter. Only Jackson aligned himself more often with Frankfurter than with the Court's inadequate titular leader. The progovernment pragmatism of the Truman appointees made them more likely to vote with Frankfurter than with Black, especially in civil liberties cases, and that tipped the balance of power within the Court in Frankfurter's favor. But they did not really care much about judicial philosophy, and most found irritating the former professor's loquaciousness, arrogance, and habit of lecturing less-learned colleagues on the law. Burton liked Frankfurter's flattery, but after initially responding positively to being courted by him, Vinson began to go his own way. His would-be mentor became quite unhappy when he learned that the chief did not always vote his way. Eventually, perhaps because Frankfurter realized his own influence was declining, the relationship between him and Vinson became extremely strained.

Because of his personality, Frankfurter, although blessed with an imposing intellect, could not lead even a Court composed primarily of justices who shared his preference for judicial deference to the legislative and executive branches. Although well suited to the temper of the times just after World War II, his brand of judicial restraint had become an anachronism by the time he died in 1965. In large part because of its emphasis on what courts should not do, although Frankfurter's creed was the focal point of debate among judges, lawyers, and constitutional scholars from the 1940s to the 1960s, he left a meager doctrinal legacy. In the opinion of biographer Michael Parrish, his greatest contribution to U.S. law was one made behind the scenes: helping Chief Justice Warren forge a unanimous Court to strike down school desegregation in *Brown v. Board of Education.* "There is now," as Parrish reports, "almost universal scholarly consensus that Frankfurter, the justice, was a failure" (Parrish 1994, 177).

## William Orville Douglas

Although better regarded by liberal scholars than Frankfurter, William O. Douglas (1898–1980) was a controversial figure during his thirty-six years on the Supreme Court. While serving longer than any other justice in history, the fiercely independent Douglas exhibited disdain for the collegial aspects of appellate judging and an aversion to writing carefully crafted opinions. A nonconformist, he conceived novel solutions to legal problems but outraged critics with his writings, his extrajudicial activities, and his lecherous personal life.

Although he had gone east as a young man, Douglas was a product of the West. Born in Maine, Minnesota, on October 16, 1898, he grew up in Yakima, Washington, where an impoverished single mother raised him alone after his father, a Presbyterian minister, died when he was six. As a boy, he washed windows, swept floors, and picked fruit alongside itinerant laborers. Although perhaps not really surviving a childhood bout with polio, as he claimed later, Douglas was a sickly youth, who overcame physical frailty by hiking in the mountains. He also starred in the classroom, becoming valedictorian of his high school class and winning a scholarship to little Whitman College. There he served in the Student Army Training Corps during World War I. After graduation, Douglas taught high school English for two years.

Then, bent on becoming an attorney, he headed east for Columbia Law School, riding freight cars and earning money to help pay for the trip by tending 2,000 head of sheep. His first wife's salary as a teacher and his earnings from tutoring financed his legal education. Douglas did well at Columbia, earning a position on the law review and graduating second in his class. His performance earned him a position with New York's prestigious Cravath firm, where he specialized in corporate

*William Orville Douglas (Harris and Ewing, Collection of the Supreme Court of the United States)*

bankruptcy and reorganization. Douglas left that position to try practicing in Yakima, but after eight months there, he returned to Cravath.

He left again in 1927 to accept a teaching position at Columbia, which was then beset by turmoil over what would become known as Legal Realism. Realists argued that in order to understand law and the behavior of legal institutions, one had to look at individual behavior and use the insights and methodologies of the social sciences. Douglas sided with some of the founding fathers of Realism in a nasty fight over the deanship and proposals to fundamentally restructure Columbia's curriculum. After one year, he followed other Realists to Yale, where he cultivated his expertise in corporate law and finance and became a chaired professor.

Restless and attracted by the dynamism of the New Deal, in 1934 Douglas secured an assignment from the new Securities and Exchange Commission (SEC) to study the protective committees used by stockholders to safeguard their interests during bankruptcy reorganizations. While commuting between New Haven and Washington, he attracted the attention of the SEC's head, Joseph P. Kennedy, who arranged to have him appointed to the commission in 1935. Two years later, President Roosevelt made Douglas its chair. A sociable individual who partied well, he developed friendships with numerous prominent New Dealers, became part of Roosevelt's inner circle, and even played in FDR's weekly White House poker games.

When Louis Brandeis retired from the Supreme Court in 1939, Douglas sought his seat. While he sent copies of speeches he had given to the president, friends promoted his candidacy. Aware that Roosevelt thought the position should go to a Westerner, they downplayed his Eastern residency and emphasized his Yakima roots. Impressed by those, as well as by Douglas's quick mind, his commitment to the New Deal, and the fact that he was a personal friend, Roosevelt nominated him on March 19. Less than a month later the Senate confirmed the forty-year-old Douglas by a margin of 62–4, making him the second youngest Supreme Court justice ever.

For Douglas, joining the Court did not mean leaving politics. He received serious consideration for the Democratic vice presidential nomination in 1940. In 1941 Roosevelt suggested that he resign from the Court to take charge of the War Production Board. When FDR dumped Henry Wallace as his running mate in 1944, he wanted Douglas to replace him. The president left the choice up to the Democratic National Convention, however, and it chose Harry Truman instead. After Truman became president, he offered to make Douglas secretary of the interior. He also asked him to be his running mate in 1948. Convinced that Truman would lose, Douglas chose to remain on the Court. In the 1950s he turned away from electoral politics, but not from dabbling in political affairs. During the 1960s Douglas tried to end the Vietnam War by developing back-channel communications between his old friend, President Lyndon Johnson, and the North Vietnamese. Johnson spurned his initiative, however.

That initiative represented an attempt to exploit his extensive foreign contacts. After World War II Douglas traveled extensively during Court recesses, visiting the Soviet Union, China, Burma, India, and other remote parts of the world. He published books and popular magazine articles about his travels. These represented just a fraction of his voluminous writings. Douglas brought out a two-volume autobiography and twenty-nine other books on topics ranging from international travel through the environment to political freedom. Needing money for alimony payments, his numerous girlfriends, and to maintain his lifestyle, he produced nearly a book a year. Most of the research and a good deal of the writing was done by others, especially his law clerks, whom Douglas, unlike his colleagues, seldom used to draft his Supreme Court opinions. One of his books, *Points of Rebellion* (1970), excited considerable controversy, both because it urged youth to rise up against a repressive "establishment" and because Douglas serialized it in an erotic review called *Evergreen*.

Although less controversial than some of his writings, his promotion of environmental causes also attracted widespread attention. Indeed, one of his most impassioned books was *A Wilderness Bill of Rights* (1965). Douglas was an avid naturalist, conservationist, hiker, and horseback rider. He did so much to promote preservation of the C & O Canal that the national historic park established there in 1977 was named for him.

Douglas's off-the-bench activities sometimes overshadowed his work on the Supreme Court. Yet, he produced more than 1,200 opinions in his lengthy career as a justice. During some terms Douglas wrote a separate opinion in every case the Court decided. Many of these were of questionable quality. Douglas, who maintained that being a justice was a four-day-a-week job, hated to waste time. He performed other tasks while listening to oral argument, decided cases quickly, and wrote rapidly. Sometimes his opinions were not carefully reasoned, and often his conclusions lacked the support of citations to relevant case authority. Douglas once declared, "I would rather create a precedent than find one" (Urofsky 1993, 82). As far as he was concerned the purpose of judging was to resolve real-life problems. The reasons for a ruling mattered far less than the result. He had little interest in writing academic dissertations on legal doctrine and sometimes did not even bother to explain his reasons for resolving a case the way he did.

Frankfurter's disciples in the legal academic community ridiculed Douglas's result-oriented approach. Yet, he produced more opinions that profoundly altered the law than did their hero. The fundamental rights branch of equal protection law begins with Douglas's innovative invalidation of a law providing for the compulsory sterilization of habitual criminals in *Skinner v. Oklahoma* (1942). *Griswold v. Connecticut* (1965) created the right to privacy in intimate affairs relating to sex and procreation. In *Harper v. Virginia Board of Elections* (1966), while holding that poll taxes violate the Equal Protection Clause, Douglas announced that the poor could not be treated differently with respect to the exercise of the fundamental right to vote. These landmark decisions were rendered before and after the Vinson era. Most of Douglas's memorable opinions from the period 1946–1953 are dissents. In *Dennis*, for example, he ridiculed the idea that the tiny American Communist Party threatened the security of the United States and argued that the extent of freedom of speech should not be made dependent on the identity of the person doing the talking. Douglas's opinions advocated liberal democratic values, often in a rather oracular tone. Toward the end of his career many of them read like manifestos. As G. Edward White explains, Douglas "gave consistent attention to the political implications of constitutional cases, consistent attention to the ideological basis on which a particular political stance rested" (White 1988, 390). Believing that the judiciary had political responsibilities, he disdained the idea of avoiding divisive issues by, for example, holding that the litigants seeking to raise them lacked standing. Douglas was determined to do justice and write moral ideals into law. Approaching his job like a common law judge, he faced policy issues squarely and, rather than leaving lawmaking to legislators, sought to make law himself. In order to award compensation to a farmer whose land had been rendered unusable for chicken raising by overflights of military aircraft but not actually seized by the government, for example, Douglas expanded the meaning of the Fifth Amendment's Takings Clause.

Typically, that decision defended the weak against the powerful. In his early days on the Court, Douglas, like other New Deal justices, supported regulatory authority. He remained a strong supporter of environmental regulation, but over time he came to believe that regulatory agencies were exercising too much power. He feared the power of aggregated wealth even more. Douglas supported vigorous enforcement of the antitrust laws and also sought to protect investors and creditors from abuse by corporate directors, officers, and controlling shareholders.

Although generally favoring the government over big business, he joined the majority in *Youngstown*, arguing in a concurring opinion that Truman had violated the Constitution by seizing the nation's steel companies, because only the legislative branch could expropriate private property. During Roosevelt's presidency Douglas accepted national security justifications for a curfew on Japanese Americans and their forced relocation from the West Coast, but after FDR's death, he became increasingly distrustful of executive power. By the end of the Vietnam War he was an outspoken critic of presidential war making.

Although at one time willing to place the national interest ahead of individual rights, by the 1950s Douglas had become an outspoken individualist. "Our starting point has always been the individual, not the state," he declares in a 1958 book, *Right of the People*. All human beings were entitled to personal independence and equal treatment, Douglas believed. They also deserved to be left alone. Unlike some champions of privacy, Douglas considered government, rather than the news media, its greatest nemesis. He also distrusted governmental restrictions on expression. Like Black, Douglas assigned a preferred status to rights guaranteed by the First Amendment. Although he spoke for the Court in *Zorach v. Clauson* (1952) when it upheld a released-time program under which public school students received religious instruction off campus, he eventually became a strict separationist. He also adopted Black's absolutist position on freedom of expression.

During the Vinson years, Douglas and Black frequently dissented together in cases, such as *Dennis*, in which the Court upheld anticommunist restrictions on free speech. Douglas also joined Black (and Frankfurter) several times in voting to grant Communists Julius and Ethel Rosenberg, who had been convicted of spying for the Soviet Union, a hearing before the Supreme Court. He voted the opposite way on several other occasions, and critics have questioned his motives in this case. Douglas did, however, have the courage to grant the Rosenbergs a stay of execution, an action the full Court reversed.

That was the sort of lone wolf move for which he became famous. Douglas was too committed to his own principles to be willing to engage in the sort of trimming and compromising generally required to secure the backing of a majority of his colleagues, and thus the opportunity to speak for the Court in an important case. He had little interest in consensus building and did not even regard maintaining good personal relations with his colleagues as very important. He also abused and mistreated clerks and other Court employees. It is hardly surprising that Douglas was not well liked. His relationship with Frankfurter was especially unpleasant. As a freewheeling activist, Douglas embodied everything Frankfurter detested, and they voted together in only 35 percent of nonunanimous cases during the 1946–1948 terms and 40 percent during the 1949–1952 terms. The conflict between them went well beyond jurisprudential differences. It reminded one observer of "two third graders seeing how spiteful they could be to each other" (Urofsky 1988, 71). Black, on the other hand, generally agreed with Douglas on issues (they voted together 71 percent of the time in the 1946–1948 terms and 61 percent of the time in the 1949–1953 ones) and enjoyed his company.

Even Black eventually pulled away from Douglas, however. The reason was that Black felt ashamed of his longtime ally's personal behavior. Douglas was a notorious womanizer. The only member of the Court to divorce, Douglas did it three times. He married his fourth wife when he was sixty-seven and she was twenty-three. That marriage epitomized the disdain for the views of others and fierce independence that characterized Douglas during his thirty-six-year career on the bench that ended with his retirement from the Supreme Court on November 12, 1975.

## Frank Murphy

Although not a loner like Douglas, William Francis (Frank) Murphy (1890–1949) was even more liberal. Indeed, he may have been the most liberal justice ever to serve on the Supreme Court. Believing no one was outside the protection of the Constitution, Murphy sought to extend the rights it guaranteed to everyone, even enemies of the United States. The law was at its finest, he believed, when it overcame transitory emotions to protect the unpopular against discrimination and persecution. Opinions based on such sentiments led critics to accuse Murphy of voting with his heart rather than his head and of lacking legal competence.

Murphy's much-maligned judicial philosophy was a product of his upbringing. Born in Sand Beach, Michigan, on April 13, 1890, Murphy was the son and grandson of Irish radicals. Although he was raised in a predominantly Protestant community, his father, a small-town lawyer, was a freethinker, and his mother was a devout Catholic. Young Frank grew up imbued with his father's radicalism and his mother's faith. Although eschewing many Catholic practices, he shared his mother's belief that one could not remain silent in the face of wrong.

After an unremarkable small-town boyhood, Murphy attended the University of Michigan. There he joined a fraternity and was something of a campus orator, but compiled an unimpressive academic record. After earning a law degree in 1914, he practiced in Detroit for three years, then served in the army during World War I. Following the war, Murphy briefly studied law at Lincoln's Inn in London and Trinity College in Dublin.

In 1919 he became an assistant U.S. attorney for the Eastern District of Michigan. After a brief return to private practice, in 1923, Murphy was elected a judge of the Recorder's Court, the principal criminal court in Detroit. He promptly expressed the belief that the way to get rid of criminals was to eliminate the conditions that bred them. On the bench Murphy displayed an unusual sensitivity to the interests of racial minorities and the poor. They supported him when he ran successfully for mayor of Detroit in 1930, and he responded to the massive unemployment caused by the Great Depression with a local public assistance program. Murphy also supported Roosevelt for president.

Roosevelt rewarded him with an appointment as governor general of the Philippines. His administration was successful financially, and Murphy, an opponent of capital punishment, commuted every death sentence he reviewed. He also brought a minimum wage and maximum hours program to the islands. In 1936, by then the high-commissioner of a semi-independent commonwealth, he returned home to run successfully for governor of Michigan.

Murphy enjoyed less success in that position. Confronted with sit-down strikes in the automobile industry, he called out the National Guard to restore order, while working behind the scenes to resolve the dispute. Each side thought he had been too sympathetic to the other. When Murphy ran for reelection in 1938, he lost. Roosevelt then brought him to Washington as attorney general. In that capacity he aggressively protected the interests of organized labor and racial minorities, establishing a Civil

*Frank Murphy (Pach Brothers, Collection of the Supreme Court of the United States)*

Rights Section within the Department of Justice. Attorney General Murphy also insti-
tuted prosecutions of the Democratic boss of Kansas City and a corrupt federal judge,
improved U.S. attorneys' offices and federal prisons, and upgraded the quality of judicial appointments.

On January 4, 1940, President Roosevelt elevated him to the Supreme Court.
Murphy, who would have preferred to become secretary of war, thought a better
choice could be found. He recommended several alternatives before finally, reluctantly, accepting the appointment. "I am not happy about going on the Court," he
wrote to his old parish priest. "I fear that my work will be mediocre" (Irons 1994,
331). Despite his reservations about himself, Murphy was confirmed without
objection.

On the bench he aligned himself with the liberal activists, Black and Douglas.
During the three terms they served together on the Vinson Court, Murphy voted with
Douglas in 68 percent of nonunanimous cases and with Black in 78 percent. His closest ally, however, was Wiley Rutledge, with whom he aligned himself 82 percent of the
time.

Murphy and Rutledge were good friends, and they shared passionate commitments to liberalism and civil liberties. Murphy, who "began and ended his entire public career as a consistent, committed liberal," wrote opinions that "swept aside technical 'niceties' in a quest for justice and human dignity" (Irons 1994, 331). He
subscribed fully to the "preferred position" view that rights outranked other constitutional values. During his three years on the Vinson Court, Murphy participated in fifty-
six civil liberties cases decided by nonunanimous vote and supported the claimed
right fifty-three times. Rutledge did so on fifty-two occasions, Douglas on forty-seven,
and Black on thirty-nine.

Although so strongly committed to the national military effort in World War II
that he persuaded General George Marshall to let him go on active duty as a lieutenant
colonel in the infantry, Murphy protested what he viewed as a denial of due process to
a Japanese general accused of war crimes. Although reluctantly concurring when the
Court upheld the imposition of a curfew on Japanese Americans, he was the only justice to dissent publicly when it held that they could constitutionally be excluded from
the West Coast. Although he joined in a 1940 decision that Jehovah's Witnesses children could be forced to salute the flag, thereafter, he "showed his commitment to principle by consistently supporting the Jehovah's Witnesses, [even though they] bitterly
attacked his beloved Catholic Church" (Irons 1994, 333).

Murphy's highly principled opinions did not make much of an impact. Of the 199
he wrote, 68 were dissents. Most of the 131 cases in which he spoke for the majority
were comparatively insignificant. Stone, who was chief justice during Murphy's first
six and one-half years on the bench, neither liked nor respected Murphy. Believing he
depended too much on his clerks to write his opinions, he seldom gave him an

important case. Yet, ironically, most of his significant majority opinions were published during this period. Particularly important was *Thornhill v. Alabama* (1940), which held that peaceful picketing was communication protected by the First Amendment. In 1943 Murphy spoke for the Court when it overturned the denaturalization of a Communist Party leader on grounds that the case against him had not been proved by clear, unequivocal, and convincing evidence.

Because he was so out of step philosophically with a majority of the Vinson Court, Murphy seldom got the chance to do anything but dissent during those years. He did write what John Frank considers a well-crafted majority opinion in a rather obscure workers' compensation case, *Industrial Commission v. McMartin* (1947), and in *Trupiano v. United States* (1948), he limited somewhat the authority of police to conduct sweeping searches incident to arrest without getting a warrant. His most important search-and-seizure opinion, however, was his dissent in *Wolf v. Colorado*, arguing that the exclusionary rule should be applied to the states. Murphy also dissented in *United States v. United Mine Workers* (1947). Fittingly, his last opinion was a dissent, in which he opposed dismissing the pending appeal of Gerhart Eisler, an accused Soviet spy, who had fled the country. A few weeks after writing it, Murphy died of a heart attack on July 19, 1949. Despite his passionate commitment to many of the noblest principles embodied in the Constitution, he had not done much to shape constitutional law.

## *Robert Houghwout Jackson*

Unlike Murphy, Robert Houghton Jackson (1892–1954) produced opinions that were both masterfully written and of lasting legal significance. One defined the outer limits of congressional power under the Commerce Clause for more than half a century, and another still provides the analytical framework that judges use to evaluate separation-of-powers issues. Yet, Jackson regarded his work on the Supreme Court as less important than his service as a prosecutor at the Nuremberg war crimes trials, and he was the central figure in a famous feud that disrupted and embarrassed the Court. A jurisprudential maverick, he is, of all the members of the Vinson Court, the most difficult to categorize.

Among the things that differentiated Jackson from most of his colleagues was his lack of a law degree. Born on a farm in Spring Creek, Pennsylvania, on February 13, 1892, he never went to college, and while he attended Albany Law School for a year, he did not graduate. He learned his profession by "reading law" in the office of a Jamestown, New York, attorney. Jackson was the last Supreme Court justice to qualify as a lawyer in this nineteenth-century manner.

*Robert Houghwout Jackson (Harris and Ewing, Collection of the Supreme Court of the United States)*

After his admission to the bar, he practiced for more than two decades in Jamestown, where he represented businessmen, labor unions, and farmers. Active in local bar associations, he also became a leader in the struggle to democratize the unrepresentative American Bar Association. A politically active Democrat, Jackson met Franklin Roosevelt before World War I. They were in contact during the 1920s, and while he was governor of New York, Roosevelt offered Jackson a position on the New York Public Service Commission. He declined, and until age forty-two had held no public office other than acting corporation counsel of Jamestown.

Jackson was an adviser to Governor Roosevelt, however, and campaigned for him when he ran for president in 1932. Roosevelt brought him to Washington in 1934 as general counsel to the Bureau of Internal Revenue. After initiating successful tax evasion proceedings against former Secretary of the Treasury Andrew Mellon and winning a Supreme Court decision upholding the constitutionality of the Public Utility Holding Company Act while on special assignment with the Securities and Exchange Commission, Jackson moved on to the Department of Justice. There he headed the Tax and Antitrust divisions before becoming solicitor general in 1938. Two years later Roosevelt made him attorney general.

Jackson was considered a serious contender for the 1940 Democratic presidential nomination, but when FDR decided to run for a third term, that possibility evaporated. Like Murphy before him, Jackson moved up to the Supreme Court. When Chief Justice Charles Evans Hughes retired in the summer of 1941, Roosevelt promoted Stone to his position and offered Jackson Stone's old seat. The Judiciary Committee approved his choice unanimously, and the Senate confirmed Jackson with only one dissenting vote.

Within months after Jackson joined the Supreme Court, the United States entered World War II. He longed to be doing something more directly related to the war effort than deciding cases. That is probably why, when four years later, President Truman asked him to head up the U.S. team prosecuting major German war criminals at Nuremberg, Jackson, despite the objections of Chief Justice Stone, accepted. "To represent the government in an international trial, the first of its kind in history, was a challenge no man who loved advocacy would pass up willingly," he explained later (Kurland 1995, 1306). Jackson also told an interviewer, "I regard [the Nuremberg trials] as infinitely more important than my work on the Supreme Court" (Kurland 1995, 1305).

The trials interrupted Jackson's work on the Court for eighteen months, and Jackson's absence from Washington contributed to the development of a feud between him and Black. The two men had philosophical differences on a number of issues, and they had clashed sharply over Black's failure to disqualify himself in *Jewell Ridge Corp. v. Local 6167, United Mine Workers* (1945), a 5–4 decision in which one of the parties had been represented by an attorney who was once Black's law partner. While

Jackson was in Europe, Chief Justice Stone died suddenly. Jackson, expecting to succeed him, learned of media reports (which were untrue) that Black had threatened to resign if Truman made Jackson chief justice. After the president announced that he was nominating Vinson, Jackson fired off an angry cable to Truman, summarizing his ideological and ethical disagreements with Black and denouncing him for torpedoing his candidacy. Then he sent a splenetic telegram to the congressional judiciary committee, which he released to the press. Washington was shocked, and as Daniel Farber reports, "The repercussions of this ugly public fight between the justices poisoned Jackson's later years on the Court" (Farber 1994, 258).

After his return from Nuremberg, Jackson and Black managed to reestablish a civil relationship, but their philosophical differences persisted. On the Vinson Court they voted together in just 40 percent of nonunanimous cases. Only with Douglas did Jackson find common ground less often. On the other hand, he voted with his closest ally, Frankfurter, in 74 percent of cases during the 1946–1948 terms and in 69 percent during the 1949–1952 ones. Jackson also aligned himself with Reed and with Vinson and the other Truman appointees more than 60 percent of the time. His votes were not entirely predictable, however. As Farber observes, Jackson was "something of a maverick" (Farber, in Urofsky, ed. 1994, 257). Although he generally disagreed with Black and his allies in cases involving civil rights and civil liberties, for example, what many regard as his greatest opinion was a ringing defense of freedom of expression. In *West Virginia State Board of Education v. Barnette* (1943) Jackson declared, right in the middle of World War II, that Jehovah's Witnesses could not be forced to salute the flag.

Even more doctrinally significant than *Barnette* was *Wickard v. Filburn* (1942). Speaking for the Court in that case, Jackson declared that in the exercise of its power to regulate interstate commerce, Congress could limit the amount of grain a farmer grew for home consumption and use on his own land. Unable to define an outer limit to congressional authority that would spare Filburn from federal regulation, Jackson surrendered to the realities of an integrated national economy. No matter how local an activity seemed, he declared, if in combination with those of other people doing the same thing, it had a substantial economic effect on interstate commerce, Congress could regulate it. The practical effect of this decision was to make the Commerce Clause for more than half a century an essentially limitless source of congressional power. Believing that clause mandated a national market, in *H. P. Hood and Sons, Inc. v. Dumond* (1949), Jackson used it negatively to prevent Massachusetts from excluding New York milk from the Boston market.

He did even more to shape separation of powers doctrine than Commerce Clause law. In a concurring opinion in *Youngstown Sheet and Tube Company v. Sawyer* (1952), Jackson argued that matters with respect to which the president might seek to act fell into three categories: those where he was authorized to act by Congress, those in which he acted in opposition to the expressed will of Congress, and those with respect to which Congress had remained silent. His power was greatest when he had congressional authorization. With respect to matters concerning which Congress had remained silent, the president had concurrent power, which he could exercise unless and until Congress spoke. His authority was most limited when he attempted to act in opposition to the expressed will of Congress. Jackson thought Truman had done that when he seized the steel mills and hence considered that action unconstitutional. Later judges found his three categories useful for resolving other disputes over the extent of presidential power, and his *Youngstown* opinion has been the basis of most decisions in this area since 1952.

Although exercising a positive influence on the development of separation of powers doctrine, Jackson generally took a negative stance toward the First Amendment. Although *Barnette* was a ringing defense of the rights of an unpopular minority, in another 1943 case he argued in a dissenting opinion that municipalities might limit door-to-door solicitation by Jehovah's Witnesses in order to protect the privacy of their residents. In *Terminello v. Chicago* (1949) he protested a decision overturning the conviction of an anti-Catholic and anti-Semitic speaker for using words that aroused public anger and dispute. Concurring in *Dennis v. United States* Jackson argued that Communists were not entitled to the protection of established First Amendment doctrine because the Communist Party was a conspiracy.

Perhaps, as some have suggested, his novel approach to the Communist case was influenced by what he had learned at Nuremberg about the tactics of totalitarian movements. Jackson's almost eccentric opinion in *Dennis* was typical, however. He was brilliant and could be highly creative. Ever the maverick, though, he continued to confound friend and foe alike until his death on October 9, 1954. His last important action as a justice was to silently go along with the majority in *Brown v. Board of Education*, although he had earlier drafted an opinion expressing profound reservations about what the Court was doing in that case.

## Wiley Blount Rutledge

Unlike Jackson, Roosevelt's last Supreme Court nominee, Wiley Blount Rutledge (1894–1949), was a friend and ally of Frank Murphy. He shared Murphy's liberalism and his passion for civil liberties, and like him, on the Vinson Court he was generally part of a losing minority. Indeed, Rutledge accomplished even less than his ally, for death felled him after only six years as a justice. A life that ended prematurely had begun in Cleveport, Kentucky. Rutledge's mother died when he was a boy, and his father, a fundamentalist Baptist preacher, moved the family from place to place around the South before finally settling down in little Marysville, Tennessee. Young Wiley regularly accompanied him to camp meetings, and although Wiley later became

*Wiley Blount Rutledge (Harris and Ewing, Collection of the Supreme Court of the United States)*

a Unitarian, "his father's fervor was reflected in his zeal for justice and right" (Israel 1995, 1314).

At sixteen Rutledge entered the preparatory department of Marysville College, where he studied ancient languages and met and courted a young Greek instructor, whom he later married. At the end of his third year, he transferred to the University of Wisconsin. Rutledge, who received a B.A. from the University of Wisconsin in 1914, planned to attend its law school, but financial difficulties forced him to take a job as a high school teacher in Bloomington, Indiana, instead. While teaching, he attended the Indiana University Law School. The physical strain of doing both led to a collapse that put him in a sanatorium. After recovering from tuberculosis, Rutledge took a teaching job in Albuquerque, New Mexico, where he also acted as secretary to the school board. In 1920 he moved to Boulder, Colorado, where he again studied law while also teaching. He received his LL.B. degree from the University of Colorado in 1922.

Rutledge then took a job with a Boulder law firm. After just two years in practice, he accepted an appointment to the University of Colorado law faculty. He spent the next fifteen years as a legal academician, teaching at the University of Colorado in Boulder and Washington University in St. Louis and serving as dean at Washington University and at the University of Iowa College of Law. His scholarly output was modest, and he was not a pedagogical innovator. Dean Rutledge did become known as an inspiring teacher, however, as well as an outspoken defender of the underdog. An ardent New Dealer, he publicly condemned conservative Supreme Court decisions and supported Roosevelt's "Court-packing" proposal.

Roosevelt considered appointing Rutledge to the Court in 1939 and, after choosing Frankfurter and Douglas instead, named Rutledge to the U.S. Court of Appeals for the District of Columbia, where he sat with Fred Vinson. During his four years at the Court of Appeals, Rutledge wrote 118 opinions. These generally reflected New Deal attitudes. He was favorable toward the increasing power of administrative agencies and consistently ruled in favor of the National Labor Relations Board and unions. Although unwilling to free convicted criminals on technicalities, Rutledge was not afraid to do so to avoid injustice. "With world events running as they have been," he wrote in *United States v. Woods* (1942), "there is a special reason at this time for not relaxing the old personal freedoms."

After Justice James Byrnes resigned from the Supreme Court in October 1942, Roosevelt elevated Rutledge. Attorney General Francis Biddle favored giving him the seat, and he possessed the judicial experience Chief Justice Stone wanted in Byrnes's successor. Both his service on the Court of Appeals and his academic background impressed the president, as did the fact that he was from west of the Mississippi River. Western senators were demanding a justice from their region. Rutledge was confirmed by a voice vote on February 8, 1943.

Once on the Court, he joined a liberal bloc that already included Black, Douglas, Murphy, and the chief justice. When death put Vinson in Stone's place, Rutledge had a personal friend in the center seat. The two men did not become Supreme Court allies, however. During their three terms together, Vinson agreed with Rutledge less frequently than with any other justice. They voted together in only 44 percent of nonunanimous cases. In contrast, Rutledge sided with Douglas, Black, and Murphy 66, 76, and 82 percent of the time, respectively. The reason was that Rutledge had a judicial philosophy that was far closer to theirs than to Vinson's. Like the chief, Rutledge supported the regulatory authority of the federal government. Unlike Vinson, he was highly suspicious of governmental power when it impinged on individual rights. Rutledge adhered to the "preferred position" concept and, along with Murphy, went beyond Black's incorporation doctrine. They maintained that the Due Process Clause required states not only to obey the Bill of Rights but to afford other substantive protections as well. Next to Murphy, Rutledge was the Court's most consistent supporter of individual rights claims. He accepted those made by criminal defendants 91 percent of the time and found constitutional violations in 79 percent of First Amendment cases.

Rutledge was also a defender of organized labor. Thus, when the Court upheld an injunction against a coal strike in *United States v. United Mine Workers* (1947), he dissented, arguing that it violated the Norris-LaGuardia Act. Fittingly, the most significant majority opinion he wrote, in *Thomas v. Collins* (1945), protected both organized labor and free speech. It struck down as a violation of the First Amendment a Texas law that required union organizers to obtain an "organizers card" from the state before soliciting members.

What made *Thomas v. Collins* unusual was that Rutledge seldom spoke for the Court in civil liberties cases. The 171 opinions that he wrote were almost evenly divided among majority opinions, concurrences, and dissents. Most of those in which he announced the decision of the Court, however, involved mundane matters. Rutledge was often part of the majority in admiralty and tax cases. He spoke for the Court eleven times on Commerce Clause questions and dissented only once. The most notable of these decisions was *Bob-Lo Excursion v. Michigan* (1948), which rejected the claim that, as applied to a boat operating between Detroit and an Ontario amusement park, a Michigan antidiscrimination statute impermissibly interfered with federal control of foreign commerce.

Although pragmatic on many matters, where civil liberties were concerned, Rutledge was unyielding. His "opinions rank him among the foremost defenders of liberty in the Court's history" (Israel 1995, 1319). The most memorable was his stirring dissent in *In re Yamashita* (1946), which argued that the United States should comply with its own Constitution in trying a Japanese general accused of committing atrocities in the

Philippines. Rutledge's dissents in Vinson Court criminal procedure cases anticipated later rulings of the Warren Court. With respect to equality, he was even further ahead of his time, urging a Court that was just beginning to attack racial segregation to use the Equal Protection Clause against gender discrimination as well. Dissenting in *Goesaert v. Cleary* (1948), Rutledge maintained that treating men and women differently violated that constitutional provision, a position a majority of the Court did not reach until 1971.

By then Rutledge, who died of a cerebral hemorrhage on September 10, 1949, had been dead for more than two decades. Had he outlived his friend, Fred Vinson, he might have become part of the liberal majority that rewrote constitutional law during the chief justiceship of Earl Warren. By dying prematurely, Rutledge became, to use A. E. Kier Nash's apt analogy, a judicial John Kennedy, a judge whose unfulfilled promise will forever outshine his actual accomplishments.

## *Harold Hitz Burton*

Unlike Rutledge and all of the other members of the Vinson Court, Harold Hitz Burton (1888–1964) was a Republican. His views and voting record resembled those of the chief justice and the other Democrats appointed by President Truman, however. When the 1945 retirement of Justice Owen Roberts left Chief Justice Stone (who had been elevated to his position by Democrat Franklin Roosevelt) as the only Republican on the Court, Truman found himself under pressure to avoid exacerbating the existing partisan imbalance. Seeking to build good relations with the opposition by nominating someone from the GOP, the new president turned to an old friend from the Senate. As Ohio's junior senator, Burton had been a key member of the so-called Truman Committee, that investigated profiteering and fraud in government contracts during World War II. The president's choice pleased Republican Senator Arthur Vandenberg, who wrote to him, "I think you have made a magnificent choice in your selection of a nominee for the Supreme Court" (Kirkendall 1995, 1324).

The man Truman nominated to replace Roberts was the forty-seven-year-old son of an MIT professor and dean, who had been born in a Boston suburb. He attended school in Switzerland, was fluent in French, and held degrees from Bowdin College and Harvard Law School. After completing his legal education, he migrated to Cleveland. From there, Burton moved west to Salt Lake City. After heading the legal department of the Idaho Power Company and serving as an army officer in France during World War I, he returned to Cleveland. There, Burton practiced corporate law and also taught it at Western Reserve University. In addition, he became active in veterans' affairs and local politics. In 1927 he was elected to the East Cleveland School Board and in 1928 won a seat in the Ohio House of Representatives. Burton served for three

*Harold Hitz Burton (Harris and Ewing, Collection of the Supreme Court of the United States)*

years as Cleveland's chief legal officer and also chaired a commission that drafted a new charter for the city. In 1934 the people of Cleveland elected him mayor, and six years later Ohio voters sent him to the U.S. Senate.

Burton was, according to his biographer, "a middle-of-the-roader with a conservative slant" (Berry 1978, 13). An internationalist, he sometimes voted with Senate Democrats on important issues. His moderation and political pragmatism made him appealing to Truman, suggesting that as a judge he would be neither highly partisan nor intensely ideological. The fact that he was one of them made Burton appealing to his fellow senators, who confirmed him unanimously the day after he was nominated.

On the bench Burton proved to be very much what Truman had expected. Eschewing the liberal activism of Black, Douglas, Murphy, and Rutledge, Burton generally aligned himself with Reed and the chief justice. Although he dissented somewhat more frequently than they did, his rate of dissent was substantially below that of all other members of the Court. Burton lacked a firm philosophical commitment to judicial restraint, but his political views made him more likely to vote with Frankfurter and Jackson than with the members of the liberal bloc.

Those views also made him likely to support the government's position on economic issues. He upheld its power to renegotiate wartime contracts in order to curb fraud and profiteering. Burton also endorsed the Justice Department's efforts to regulate business under federal antitrust statutes and joined the majority in a decision limiting the operation of state law in areas regulated by the Taft-Hartley Act. He did, however, desert Vinson, Reed, and the Truman administration in *Youngstown Sheet and Tube Company v. Sawyer*, voting with the 6–3 majority that held that the president had acted illegally in seizing the nation's steel mills.

Burton sometimes deserted Vinson on civil liberties issues as well. Inclined to reject claims that First Amendment rights had been violated, he generally joined the chief justice in voting to uphold statutes and regulations adopted to combat espionage and subversion against claims that these violated the First Amendment. Burton was part of Vinson's majority in both *Dennis v. United States* and *American Communications Association v. Douds*. He also voted to support the operations of the federal loyalty-security program in *Bailey v. Richardson* (1951). In another 1951 case, however, Burton joined Black and Douglas in dissenting from a decision upholding a municipal ordinance requiring city employees to take an oath that they had not, and would not in the future, advocate or teach the violent overthrow of the government or affiliate with any organization that did so. In *Joint Anti-Fascist Refugee Committee v. McGrath* (1951), he spoke for a 5–4 majority that ruled in favor of three organizations seeking to have their names removed from the attorney general's list of subversive organizations.

That ruling rested on narrow procedural grounds. Burton also took a cautious approach in two other areas where he compiled a moderately liberal record. One of these was criminal justice. Although he generally supported law enforcement, "some of

Burton's most libertarian opinions involved criminal cases" (Rise 1994, 79). When he dissented from a ruling allowing a state to send a condemned man to the electric chair for a second time after its first attempt to execute him failed, however, Burton eschewed any criticism of the death penalty itself and indicated that if state law had authorized what prison officials wanted to do, he would not have objected. A similar caution characterized his civil rights record. Burton was a trustee of a black choir and a member of the NAACP, who supported an anti–poll tax amendment and legislation to create a permanent Fair Employment Practices Commission. Perhaps his most important opinion was the one he wrote for the Court in *Henderson v. United States* (1951), holding the segregation of railroad dining cars unlawful. Yet, five years earlier he had refused to join an otherwise unanimous opinion invalidating a Virginia statute that required segregation of public transportation, and he based the *Henderson* decision on the Commerce Clause, rather than on the Equal Protection Clause.

    Justice Burton was neither very bold nor very productive. Although the charges of columnist Drew Pearson that excessive party going kept him from getting his work done are without foundation, he was, at least initially, a painfully slow opinion writer and was never a profound or innovative one. During the 1954 term the Court's clerks voted Burton its best justice, but little in the record he left behind supports their assessment. He brought a sense of stability to what had been before his arrival a troubled tribunal. But Harold Burton was a plodding pragmatist, a moderate who practiced judicial restraint less out of conviction than because he supported the laws he voted to uphold.

## Tom Campbell Clark

Tom Campbell Clark (1899–1977), the second of President Truman's rather undistinguished appointees to the Supreme Court, resembled Burton in many ways, but unlike him, he was a Democrat. Like Burton, Clark was conservative, and although supportive of African American civil rights, he did little to protect civil liberties. He backed the chief justice even more consistently than did his Republican colleague.

    Born into a family of lawyers in Dallas, Texas, on September 23, 1899, Clark attended the public schools there. After a year at the Virginia Military Institute and service in the army during World War I, he returned to his native state to complete his education at the University of Texas, from which he received a B.A. in 1921 and an LL.B. in 1922. Then Clark joined his father's law firm. Achieving success in private practice, he also served as civil district attorney of Dallas County from 1927 to 1933.

    In 1937, through the influence of Senator Tom Connally, Clark secured a position with the United States Department of Justice. Starting in its War Risk Litigation Section, he moved on to the Anti-Trust Division. Following the Pearl Harbor attack, President

*Tom Campbell Clark (Harris and Ewing, Collection of the Supreme Court of the United States)*

Roosevelt appointed Clark Civilian Coordinator of the Western Defense Command. In that capacity Clark handled legal aspects of the relocation and internment of Japanese Americans. Next, he became the head of the War Frauds Unit of the Anti-Trust Division. That job brought him into close contact with Harry Truman, then the chairman of a Senate committee that was investigating waste and corruption in defense industries. Clark moved up to head of the Anti-Trust Division and later became the assistant attorney general in charge of the Criminal Division. He remained in contact with Truman, however, even assisting him in obtaining the 1944 vice presidential nomination.

After becoming president in 1945, Truman made Clark attorney general. As head of the Justice Department, the Texan continued to enforce the antitrust laws vigorously. He also took an interest in civil rights, pressuring the FBI to investigate lynchings and having his department file an amicus curiae brief in a case attacking the constitutionality of racially restrictive covenants. At the same time, however, Clark was playing a large role in the development of the Truman administration's internal security policies. Under his leadership the Justice Department created the first attorney general's list and secured authorization for the FBI to make greater use of wiretaps. In 1948, with the Truman administration under intense political pressure from Republicans for failing to do more to combat domestic communism, Clark personally authorized the prosecution of the top leaders of the American Communist Party under the Smith Act, despite the weakness of the evidence against them.

When he was nominated to succeed Justice Murphy, liberals and radicals protested loudly the selection of someone they viewed as a red-baiter. Truman himself is reputed later to have characterized the Clark nomination as the biggest mistake he made as president. If he actually said that, the assessment was unfair. By the time Clark retired from the Court, he had authored its landmark decision in *Mapp v. Ohio* (1961), applying the exclusionary rule to the states, and written opinions upholding the public accommodations provisions of the Civil Rights Act of 1964. In addition, in the late 1960s and early 1970s he led a productive campaign within the legal profession to improve the administration of justice. Clark spoke and wrote extensively on this subject between his 1967 retirement from the Court and his death a decade later on June 13, 1977.

During the Vinson years, however, the most notable thing about Clark was his consistent support for the chief justice. Truman had hoped that appointing Clark would strengthen the chief's position within the Court, and Clark quickly demonstrated that Vinson had been right in urging the president to name Clark. During the four terms that they served together, Clark agreed with Vinson in 83 percent of cases decided by nonunanimous opinions. By contrast, during this same period, Clark agreed with Douglas in only 40 percent of such cases. More contented than any other member of the Vinson Court with the direction it was taking, during the period

1949–1953, Clark hardly ever dissented. During his first term, he did not write a single dissenting opinion, and his total for the next three terms was only fifteen.

Consistent support for the chief justice meant consistent opposition to civil liberties. During the four years that they served together, Vinson rejected civil liberties claims 86 percent of the time, and Clark, at 76 percent, was not far behind him. Because of his earlier involvement in the case, he did not participate in the *Dennis* decision. Like Vinson, however, Clark generally supported anticommunist loyalty-security programs. Thus, in *Garner v. Board of Public Works* (1951), he spoke for the 5–4 majority that upheld a Los Angeles ordinance requiring city employees to file affidavits affirming that they were not then, and never had been, members of the Communist Party and to execute loyalty oaths that involved swearing they had not taught or advocated the violent overthrow of the government.

Despite such opinions, John Frank, although a liberal, rejects the characterization of Clark as an ardent red-baiter. *Wieman v. Updegraf* (1951) provides support for his position. In that case, the Court unanimously struck down an Oklahoma law that required government employees to swear they had not been members of any organization on the attorney general's list during the past five years. Clark wrote the opinion. In it he condemned the challenged statute for penalizing even those who had joined such groups without knowledge of their character.

Clark was less negative toward civil liberties claims than Vinson—but not much less. He normally supported the chief. Most of the opinions that have given his record a liberal tinge were written after Earl Warren assumed the center seat. As Richard Kirkendall has pointed out, Clark rarely disagreed with Vinson, "and thus a new era began for the Texan when the Vinson Court became the Warren Court" (Kirkendall 1995, 1352).

## Sherman Minton

Sherman Minton (1890–1965) was another consistent Vinson supporter. The last of Truman's four appointees, he brought to the Supreme Court more judicial experience than any of the others. Yet, he compiled a similarly undistinguished record. Even more surprising to many commentators was Justice Minton's conservatism, which seemed at odds with his history as one of Roosevelt's most loyal, and liberal, political lieutenants.

Minton rose to political prominence from humble origins. The son of poor and uneducated parents, he was born in a refurbished log cabin on a farm near the hamlet of Georgetown, Indiana. His family moved to Fort Worth, Texas, when he was a teenager, but a year later, "Shay" Minton used money he had saved to buy a ticket back to Indiana, where he finished high school in New Albany. He then attended Indiana University, supporting himself with a variety of odd jobs, while also starring in

*Sherman Minton (Harris and Ewing, Collection of the Supreme Court of the United States)*

baseball, playing football and basketball, and debating. After two fairly undistin-guished years as an undergraduate, Minton entered the Indiana University Law School, where he ranked first in his class when he received his LL.B. in 1915. His outstanding record earned Minton a $500 scholarship to the Yale Law School. There he studied under future Chief Justice William Howard Taft and earned an LL.M.

Minton returned to New Albany in the fall of 1916 to open his own law office. World War I soon interrupted his fledgling legal career. He enlisted in the Reserve Corps, receiving a commission and serving as a staff officer under General Pershing. He also used the opportunity afforded by a stay in France to take special law courses at the Sorbonne.

After the war, Minton joined an established firm in New Albany. He left it to move to Miami in 1925 but returned in 1928. Using involvement in the American Legion as a springboard, he plunged into Indiana politics, playing a large role in Democrat Paul V. McNutt's 1932 gubernatorial campaign. The victorious McNutt appointed Minton pub-lic counsel of the newly created Public Service Commission.

In 1934 he ran successfully for the U.S. Senate. An enthusiastic New Dealer, Minton voted against the Roosevelt administration only twice in six years. He became assistant majority whip in 1937 and moved up to whip in 1938. When Roosevelt intro-duced his "Court-packing" bill, Minton, whose first Senate speech had been an attack on the Supreme Court's decision invalidating the Agricultural Adjustment Act, strongly endorsed it. At FDR's request, he gave a national radio address in support of the pres-ident's plan.

When Minton lost his bid for reelection in 1940, Roosevelt made him a White House assistant. Then in 1941 he appointed him to the United States Court of Appeals for the Seventh Circuit. As an appellate judge, Minton proved reluctant to overturn the decisions of lower courts or to substitute his views for those of the legislators who had passed the laws he was asked to enforce. In cases involving alleged unfair business practices, he almost always sided with the public interest against the alleged monop-olizer, and in disputes arising under the National Labor Relations Act and the Fair Labor Standards Act, in which he wrote opinions, he ruled for the workers twenty out of thirty-four times. On the other hand, Minton decided against litigants claiming vio-lations of the Bill of Rights almost 85 percent of the time.

Patterns established on the Court of Appeals persisted after he joined the Supreme Court in 1949. Minton had been a leading contender for the seat that went to Black in 1937, but Roosevelt told his majority whip he needed him more in the Senate. In August 1945, soon after Truman, an old buddy who had occupied the adjacent seat in the Sen-ate, replaced FDR, Minton visited him, seeking an appointment to the Court. After Roberts's death later that year, Black, another of his Senate chums, urged the president to give that seat to Minton. The president appointed Burton instead. Just five days after Rutledge died, however, Truman at last nominated his old friend to the Supreme Court.

Liberals praised the nomination, whereas conservatives, still upset about Minton's support for the Court-packing plan, objected. The Republican-controlled Senate Judiciary Committee invited Minton to appear before it to explain his present views on Roosevelt's proposal and a controversial statement he had made on the hustings that "You can't eat the Constitution." Relying on a precedent set by Frankfurter, Minton declined to testify. The committee nevertheless approved his nomination, and the Senate confirmed him 48–16.

Rather than joining the liberal bloc, as many had anticipated, Justice Minton aligned himself with Vinson, Reed, Burton, and Clark. They formed a conservative majority that dominated the Court for the next four years, a period during which Minton agreed with Vinson in 81 percent of nonunanimous opinions. He hardly ever dissented. The proportion of cases per term in which he did so ranged from a low of 5 percent to a high of 18 percent.

Although Minton and Black were old political allies, Minton found his friend's activism less appealing than Frankfurter's judicial self-restraint. Despite not being a legal theorist, Minton usually voted in conformity with his conception of the judicial role, rather than following his policy preferences. Consistent with the position he had taken as a spokesman for the New Deal, Minton maintained that it was beyond the Court's prerogative to question the wisdom of legislation or executive actions. The Court might invalidate what the political branches had done only on those rare occasions when they violated explicit constitutional limitation, he believed. As David Atkinson observes, "Minton was receptive to Frankfurter's overtures in large part because the two Justices were in basic agreement on the proper role of the Supreme Court" (Atkinson 1975, 361). Along with a preference for restraint, Minton exhibited a fondness for stability, acquired from Taft, that made him extremely reluctant to depart from precedent. Together, these predilections turned a political liberal into a judicial conservative.

Minton was most comfortable when upholding exercises of governmental power. Thus, he joined Vinson's dissent in the steel seizure case. Only where discrimination against racial and religious minorities was involved was he likely to oppose the government. Although unwilling to join his colleagues in holding that a private club that helped select candidates for public office could not discriminate on the basis of race, Minton spoke for the Court in *Barrows v. Jackson* (1953), in which it ruled that the Equal Protection Clause prohibited a state court from awarding damages to neighbors of a property owner who had violated a racially restrictive covenant. He also cast one of the four votes that enabled the Court to hear and decide *Brown v. Board of Education*.

In criminal procedure cases, he afforded the government wide latitude. Minton interpreted restrictively the right to counsel, the privilege against self-incrimination, and the power of federal courts to grant habeas corpus relief to state prisoners. He also overturned a recent precedent requiring that, when practicable, police obtain a warrant before searching a suspect. His propensity to validate governmental action also led him to join the conservative majority in upholding initiatives allegedly required to save the country from subversion. Unlike Black and Douglas, Minton did not believe that judges had any special responsibility to preserve liberty. It was the people and the officials they elected who must do that. "If an agency of government had the power to restrict liberty, then he, as a judge, had to tolerate the restriction even though as a person he regarded it as unwise" (Kirkendall 1995, 1367). Consequently, no member of the Vinson Court had a less liberal voting record. Like the chief justice, Minton supported libertarian claims in less than 15 percent of civil liberties cases.

He was part of the majority in two cases upholding the procedures of the federal loyalty-security program, and he signed Vinson's opinion in *Dennis*. A year before that 1951 decision, Minton had spoken for the Court in another case involving American Communist Party leader Eugene Dennis, rejecting his contention that, because of the loyalty-security program, when tried in the District of Columbia for contempt of Congress, he should have been allowed to challenge for bias all potential jurors who were federal employees. Minton realized that Dennis, who had been accused of refusing to appear before the House Un-American Activities Committee, was actually being prosecuted for being a Communist. Nevertheless, Minton rejected Dennis's contention that fear of losing their jobs would necessarily make government workers less than impartial jurors. Minton also wrote the opinion of the Court in *Adler v. Board of Education* (1950), in which it upheld by a 5–4 majority a state law providing for the removal from their jobs of disloyal public school teachers and accepting membership in certain organizations as proof of disloyalty.

Such antilibertarian rulings should perhaps have been expected from a justice who had once introduced in the Senate a bill to make it a felony for a newspaper to publish a falsehood. The rulings seemed inconsistent with Minton's ultraliberal image, however, and have served to tarnish a judicial reputation that would be modest even in their absence. Minton's deference to the political branches, combined with the simplicity of his approach to judging, kept him from producing opinions of lasting significance. As Richard Kirkendall observes with considerable understatement, Shay Minton "did not become a distinguished member of the Court" (Kirkendall, in Friedman and Israel, eds. 1995, 1371).

## Conclusion

Minton, however, was not much less distinguished than Burton, Clark, and Chief Justice Vinson. President Truman stocked the Supreme Court with mediocrities, and along with the lackluster Stanley Reed, his appointees gave it a mediocre majority. Not all of the men who served on the Vinson Court were so undistinguished. Black was one of the greatest justices in the history of the Court, and although Douglas was eccentric, Jackson was unpredictable, and Frankfurter never fulfilled his promise, all of them were brilliant jurists who made major contributions to the jurisprudential debates that shaped constitutional law during the 1940s and 1950s. Nor were all of the members of the Vinson Court as conservative as Reed and the Truman appointees. Murphy and Rutledge were among the most liberal justices ever, and even after they passed away, Black and Douglas continued to emulate their liberal values and defend civil liberties. These were not, however, the judges who determined the outcome of controversial cases or wrote the opinions deciding them. Vinson and his allies did those things. They were the ones who gave the Vinson Court its reputation for conservative mediocrity, a reputation it richly deserved.

## References and Further Reading

Atkinson, David A. 1975. "From New Liberal to Supreme Court Conservative." *Washington University Law Quarterly*: 361.

Berry, Mary Francis. 1978. *Stability, Security, and Continuity: Mr. Justice Burton and Decision-Making in the Supreme Court, 1945–1958*. Westport, CN: Greenwood Press.

Breen, Daniel L. 1994. "Stanely Forman Reed." In *The Supreme Court Justices: A Biographical Dictionary*, ed. Melvin I. Urofsky. New York: Garland Publishing.

Farber, Daniel A. 1994. "Robert Houghwout Jackson." In *The Supreme Court Justices: A Biographical Dictionary*, ed. Melvin I. Urofsky. New York: Garland Publishing.

Frank, John P., and Vern Countryman. 1995. "William O. Douglas." In *The Justices of the Supreme Court, 1789–1995*, ed. Leon Friedman and Fred L. Israel. New York: Chelsea House.

Freyer, Tony Allan. 1990. *Hugo L. Black and the Dilemma of American Liberalism*. Glenville, IL: Scott Foresman/Little, Brown Higher Education.

Friedman, Leon, and Fred L. Israel, eds. 1995. *The Justices of the United States Supreme Court: Their Lives and Major Opinions*. New York: Chelsea House.

Glancy, Dorothy J. 1994. "William Orville Douglas." In *The Supreme Court Justices: A Biographical Dictionary*, ed. Melvin I. Urofksy. New York: Garland Publishing.

Irons, Peter. 1994. "Francis (Frank) William Murphy." In *The Supreme Court Justices: A Biographical Dictionary*, ed. Melvin I. Urofsky. New York: Garland Publishing.

Israel, Fred L. 1995. "Wiley Rutledge." In *The Justices of the Supreme Court, 1789–1995*, ed. Leon Friedman and Fred L. Israel. New York: Chelsea House.

Kirkendall, Richard. 1995. "Fred Vinson." In *The Justices of the Supreme Court, 1789–1995*, ed. Leon Friedman and Fred L. Israel. New York: Chelsea House.

———. 1995. "Harold Burton." In *The Justices of the Supreme Court, 1789–1995*, ed. Leon Friedman and Fred L. Israel. New York: Chelsea House.

———. 1995. "Sherman Minton." In *The Justices of the Supreme Court, 1789–1995*, ed. Leon Friedman and Fred L. Israel. New York: Chelsea House.

———. 1995. "Tom Clark." In *The Justices of the Supreme Court, 1789–1995*, ed. Leon Friedman and Fred L. Israel. New York: Chelsea House.

Kurland, Philip B. 1995. "Robert H. Jackson." In *The Justices of the Supreme Court, 1789–1995*, ed. Leon Friedman and Fred L. Israel. New York: Chelsea House.

Newman, Roger K. 1994. *Hugo Black: A Biography*. New York: Pantheon.

Parrish, Michael E. 1982. *Felix Frankfurter and His Times*. New York: Free Press.

———. 1994. "Felix Frankfurter." In *The Supreme Court Justices: A Biographical Dictionary*, ed. Melvin I. Urofsky. New York: Garland Publishing.

Rise, Eric W. 1994. "Harold Hitz Burton." In *The Supreme Court Justices: A Biographical Dictionary*, ed. Melvin I. Urofsky. New York: Garland Publishing.

Simon, James F. 1989. *The Antagonists: Hugo Black, Felix Frankfurter and Civil Liberties in Modern America*. New York: Simon and Schuster.

St. Clair, James E., and Linda C. Gurgin. 2002. *Chief Justice Fred Vinson of Kentucky: A Political Biography*. Lexington: University Press of Kentucky.

Urofsky, Melvin I. 1988. "Conflict among the Brethren: Felix Frankfurter, William O. Douglas and the Clash of Personalities and Philosophies on the United States Supreme Court." *Duke Law Journal* (1988): 71.

———. 1991. *The Continuity of Change: The Supreme Court and Individual Liberties, 1953–1986*. Belmont, CA: Wadsworth Publishing.

———. 1993. "William O. Douglas as Common Law Judge." In *The Warren Court in Historical Perspective*, ed. Mark Tushnet. Charlottesville: University of Virginia Press, p. 64.

———. 1997. *Division and Discord: The Supreme Court under Stone and Vinson, 1941–1953*. Columbia: University of South Carolina Press.

———. 2001. *The Warren Court: Justices, Rulings, and Legacy*. Santa Barbara, CA: ABC-CLIO.

Urofsky, Melvin, ed. 1994. *The Supreme Court Justices: A Biographical Dictionary*. New York: Garland.

White, G. Edward. 1988. *The American Judicial Tradition: Profiles of Leading American Judges*. Expanded ed. New York: Oxford University Press.

Yarbrough, Tinsley E. 1988. *Mr. Justice Black and His Critics*. Durham, NC: Duke University Press.

# 3

## *Major Decisions*

T he Vinson Court rendered only a few memorable decisions. That is perhaps not surprising, for it lasted a mere seven years. Perhaps had Fred Vinson lived longer, his Court would have accomplished more. During his brief tenure, the Supreme Court did hand down decisions in some areas, most notably civil rights, that foreshadowed landmark rulings that would transform U.S. law during the chief justiceship of Earl Warren (1953–1969). Had Vinson not died in 1953, he would be remembered as the man who headed the Court that decided *Brown v. Board of Education* (1954). Instead, mention of the Vinson Court most often calls to mind Cold War rulings restricting civil liberties.

Most of those rulings articulated doctrinal principles that were swept aside in the years that followed. The Vinson Court decided only one case of truly lasting significance. Half a century after it handed down its decision in *Youngstown Sheet and Tube Company v. Sawyer* (1952), that ruling remains the most important one ever rendered on the subject of the separation of powers between the president and Congress. *Youngstown* is the starting point for all legal discussions about the scope of the president's inherent authority to take the actions he considers necessary to deal with national emergencies. Perhaps appropriately, the *Youngstown* opinion that became the foundation for most of the law in this area is a concurrence, written by Associate Justice Robert Jackson. Chief Justice Vinson dissented in the case.

Vinson's best-known opinion is the one he wrote for the Court in *Dennis v. United States* (1951). In it he radically altered the established interpretation of the First Amendment in order to uphold a conviction of leaders of the Communist Party of the United States for teaching and advocating the violent overthrow of the government. *Dennis* reflects the Vinson Court's persistent insensitivity to civil liberties claims. It also exemplifies the way the international Cold War and the spasm of hysterical anticommunism that it triggered within the United States affected that Court's decision making. If there is any one ruling that epitomizes the jurisprudence of the Vinson Court, it is *Dennis*.

Yet, the anxious anticommunism and hostility toward civil liberties that *Dennis* exemplifies are perhaps not the most important attributes of the Supreme Court that

Fred Vinson headed. As Melvin Urofsky has suggested, this was above all a transition Court. When Vinson became chief justice, the United States was still demobilizing from its massive military effort in World War II. The Vinson Court had to deal with legal problems arising out of the transition from war to peace. It also had to face the challenges posed by changing racial attitudes and by the NAACP's litigation campaign against racial discrimination. The Vinson Court's rulings against the enforcement of racially restrictive covenants in housing and against segregation in transportation and higher education did not reject outright the separate-but-equal doctrine that had governed U.S. race relations since *Plessy v. Ferguson* (1896). They did, however, help to move both the law and the country in that direction, paving the way for the Warren Court's landmark ruling in *Brown v. Board of Education* (1954), as well as for the civil rights movement that defeated Jim Crow during the 1960s.

Although compiling a rather negative record in the field of civil liberties, the Vinson Court helped prepare the way for an explosive expansion of individual rights during the Warren era. The years of Vinson's chief justiceship witnessed intense debates within the Court over such fundamental issues as whether the Bill of Rights applied to the states, what the judiciary could and should do about legislative malapportionment, and how much cooperation between government and religion the Constitution would permit. Often, these debates pitted Justice Frankfurter against Justice Black, with Frankfurter generally taking the side least favorable to civil liberties claims. He usually prevailed during those years, but during the Warren era, Black and his supporters gained the upper hand. The ideas they wrote into constitutional law in the 1960s were not new, however. Most of them had been advanced in dissenting opinions published while Vinson was chief justice. For that reason the cases decided during those years, despite the transitory character of many of the legal rules they announced, are of considerable significance. They represent steps toward the future taken by a transition Court.

## *Aftermath of World War II*

By the time Fred Vinson became chief justice on June 24, 1946, more than a year had passed since the surrender of Japan ended the fighting in World War II. Six months after he took office, on December 31, 1946, President Truman issued a proclamation officially terminating hostilities. Yet, perhaps appropriately, in view of what an important role the new chief justice had played in the war effort, during Vinson's early years on the bench the Supreme Court continued to devote substantial attention to cases arising out of the recently concluded military conflict. It had to address, for example, the question of how long after the conclusion of hostilities Congress could continue to draw on its war power as a source of legislative authority. Curtailment of civilian construction during the war had created a severe housing shortage, which the demobilization of millions of veterans exacerbated. Congress responded with the Housing and Rent Act of 1947, but that law did not go into effect until July 31 of the year in which it was enacted, seven months after Truman proclaimed hostilities officially over. The Court upheld the law nonetheless, taking the position that Congress could legislate even after the cessation of hostilities to remedy evils arising out of a military conflict. Speaking for his colleagues, Justice Douglas acknowledged that under modern conditions the effects of a war might be felt in the economy for years after it ended, and that if the war power could be used in days of peace to treat all of the wounds that an armed conflict had inflicted on society, it might well swallow up all the other powers of Congress. In a concurring opinion, Justice Jackson expressed even greater concern about possible future abuses of this source of congressional authority, which he feared could become a threat to liberty. Despite such concerns, the Court unanimously upheld the Housing and Rent Act in *Woods v. Cloyd W. Miller Company* (1948).

Besides wrestling with the thorny issue of how long Congress could continue to use its war power, the Vinson Court also had to answer some difficult questions about the reach of U.S. military justice. In February 1946, a few months before Vinson became chief justice, the Court had decided *Duncan v. Kahanamoku* (1946), a challenge to the legality of the military courts that had been used to try civilians for ordinary crimes committed in Hawaii, following the imposition of martial law there on December 7, 1941. It declined to decide whether the Constitution prohibited Congress from authorizing the armed forces to try to punish persons from outside their own ranks, as they had continued to do in Hawaii until October 24, 1944. The Court did, however, hold that the statute governing the then-Territory of Hawaii, the Hawaiian Organic Act, had not empowered the military to substitute its version of justice for judicial trials at a time when the danger of enemy invasion of the islands had passed.

The same month that it decided *Duncan*, the Court, in *In re Yamashita* (1946), rejected a petition for a writ of habeas corpus, filed by the last Japanese commander in the Philippines. He contended that the U.S. military commission that had convicted him of war crimes and sentenced him to death lacked the power to do those things. The Supreme Court rejected the government's contention that it could not even entertain Yamashita's petition, but that was a hollow victory for the Japanese general. The Court went on to rule that the commission had jurisdiction to try him and that in exercising that jurisdiction it had—despite convicting him of crimes committed by his subordinates that he had not ordered and of which he may even have been unaware—not violated military, statutory, or constitutional law. Justices Murphy and Rutledge recorded powerful dissents, the latter accusing their colleagues of allowing a violation of "the basic standards of trial which, among other guarantees, the nation fought to keep" (*Yamashita* 1946, 42). One week later the two of them dissented again in *Homma v. Patterson* (1946), when the Court rejected a habeas corpus petition filed by another former Japanese commander in the Philippines, who was now a civilian. Homma's conviction was based in part on forced confessions, and as far as Murphy and Rutledge were concerned, the fact that he had been tried by a military commission did not excuse this violation of due process. "All those who act by virtue of the authority of the United States are bound to respect the principles of justice codified in our Constitution," Murphy insisted (*Homma* 1946, 760).

Murphy dissented without opinion two years later when the Court rejected that proposition in *Hirota v. MacArthur* (1948). The habeas corpus petitioners in that case were Japanese army officers and high-ranking officials of the Japanese government. Two of them had been prosecuted for war crimes and crimes against humanity and the rest for waging aggressive war and conspiring to do so. Unlike Yamashita and Homma, they had been tried and convicted by an International Military Tribunal that included judges from many countries that had fought against Japan, as well as from the United States. Because that body had been convened by a U.S. general—Douglas MacArthur—however, they contended, the U.S. Supreme Court had jurisdiction to review its judgments. The Court disagreed. It took the position that in setting up the International Military Tribunal, MacArthur had been acting as an agent of the Allied Powers, and consequently that U.S. courts had no authority to review or set aside the judgments that the tribunal had rendered or the sentences it had imposed.

The issue of whether U.S. judges could issue writs of habeas corpus to U.S. officials, who were illegally imprisoning someone in a foreign country then under U.S. control, arose again two years later in *Johnson v. Eisentrager* (1950). Justice Black argued that a U.S. court should be able to do this, but only Douglas and Burton agreed with him. A majority of the Court held that German nationals who had been convicted by a U.S. military commission sitting in China of continuing to fight alongside the Japanese after the surrender of Germany were not entitled to seek a writ of habeas corpus from a federal district court. This was so even though they were by then being held by a U.S. Army officer in a U.S. military prison in a part of Germany under the control of the United States. Speaking for the Court, Justice Jackson maintained that giving enemy aliens captured and imprisoned abroad standing to demand access to this country's courts would "hamper the war effort and bring aid and comfort to the enemy" (*Johnson* 1950, 779). The Court held that the Constitution did not confer immunity from U.S. military trial and punishment on alien enemies engaged in the hostile service of a government at war with the United States.

Nor did the Constitution, as construed by the Vinson Court, prevent punishing for treason U.S. citizens who gave aid and comfort to the enemy. In *Haupt v. United States* (1948), the Court interpreted an earlier Supreme Court decision that seemed likely to do that in a way that neutralized what had appeared to be a major impediment to successful treason prosecutions. Hans Max Haupt was a former German national, who was now a naturalized U.S. citizen. He had rendered assistance to his son, Herbert, also a naturalized citizen, after Herbert, following a brief return to their German homeland, had reentered the United States in 1942 on a sabotage mission for Germany. Hans sheltered his son, helped him purchase an automobile, and assisted him in obtaining employment in a factory that manufactured the Norden bombsite. Haupt argued that evidence of these actions did not satisfy the Constitution's requirement that treason be proved by the testimony of two witnesses to the same overt act, because they were commonplace activities, and someone who engaged in them was not necessarily doing so to aid the enemy. In *Cramer v. United States* (1945) the Stone Court had seemed to take the position that the two witnesses must establish not only that an accused traitor had done the acts alleged to satisfy the constitutional requirement but also that those acts were treasonous. Speaking for the Vinson Court, Jackson denied that *Cramer* had held that the two witnesses must attest to the treasonable intention with which the overt acts were performed as well as to the fact that the defendant had done them. He was less than clear, however, about what their testimony did have to show. In a concurring opinion, Douglas explained that if what the two witnesses' testimony proved the defendant had done was something that aided the enemy, other evidence could be used to establish his treasonous intent. Jackson did not dispute this interpretation of an opinion that, treason expert J. Willard Hurst believes, left the law on this vital point unclear. One thing about the *Haupt* decision was clear, however: It permitted the government to send the defendant to prison for the rest of his life. Only Murphy dissented, and he did so on the limited ground that, absent proof of treasonable intentions, merely giving shelter to one's son should not be considered an overt act of treason, even if it assisted the enemy. Although the precise meaning of *Haupt* was murky, it did seem to reduce significantly the burden of proof that prosecutors would have to meet in future treason cases.

## Presidential Power

*Haupt* was part of a pattern. Generally, the Vinson Court upheld whatever seemed likely to enhance national security. There was only one great departure from that pattern: *Youngstown Sheet and Tube Company v. Sawyer* (1952). That decision was exceptional in another respect as well: It limited presidential power. *Youngstown* came at the end of a period of tremendous expansion in the activity, influence, and prestige of the presidency, brought about by World War I, the New Deal, and World War II. The Supreme Court contributed to this development with its decision in *United States v. Curtiss-Wright Export Corporation* (1936). In that case the Hughes Court had both declared that in the field of international relations the authority of the national government extended beyond the powers granted to it by the Constitution and proclaimed that in the realm of foreign affairs the president was the sole organ of the nation.

The Vinson Court reaffirmed *Curtiss-Wright* when it refused, in *Chicago and Southern Air Lines, Inc. v. Waterman Steamship Corporation* (1948), to review an executive order concerning the involvement of U.S. citizens with foreign air transportation. Congress had authorized judicial review of some orders of the Civil Aeronautics Board (CAB), but the Court held that this mandate did not extend to those orders granting or denying applications by citizen carriers to engage in overseas and foreign transportation, which required the approval of the president. Judges were not permitted to review provisions of CAB orders that resulted from presidential directives, Jackson concluded. Besides being both the sole organ of the nation in foreign affairs and the commander in chief, he said, the president had available to him intelligence that judges lacked. Foreign policy decisions were political, not judicial, and the judiciary should leave all of them, including those involving air routes, to the political branches of the government. Justices Douglas, Black, Reed, and Rutledge believed the majority had misunderstood the statutory scheme created by Congress, which they did not think actually permitted judges to review presidential determinations. They agreed with the majority, however, that decisions of the president involving military matters and foreign relations could not be made subject to judicial review.

The deference to presidential decisions that the Vinson Court had displayed in *Waterman Steamship* made surprising its subsequent rejection of President Truman's claims concerning the inherent powers of his office in *Youngstown Sheet and Tube Company v. Sawyer. Youngstown* held that Truman had acted unlawfully when he seized the nation's steel mills in order to prevent a strike that threatened to disrupt production of a militarily vital commodity during the Korean War. As historian Maeva Marcus has written, "[T]he paramount importance of the *Steel Seizure* decision lies in the fact that it was made. . . . [B]y invalidating an action of the President, [it] helped to redress the balance of power among the three branches of government" (Marcus 1977, 228).

The case that produced this momentous result arose because of Truman's unwillingness to employ the Taft-Hartley Act, a statute that a Congress controlled by his Republican opponents had enacted over his veto. That law appeared to be designed to deal with the sort of situation that developed when the United Steel Workers of America threatened to go out on strike during the Korean War. The union and the steel manufacturers had agreed upon a wage increase, only to have implementation of their agreement thwarted by the Economic Stabilization Agency, a government bureau charged with preventing inflation, which effectively froze all wage and price increases. Fearing that a work stoppage in the steel industry would disrupt the war effort, Truman persuaded the steel workers to postpone their strike while he referred the matter to a Wage Stabilization Board, made up of representatives of labor, management, and the general public. The board recommended certain staggered wage increases and union benefits, but management rejected its proposals, and the union set an April 9,

1952, strike date. Truman could have delayed the walkout by invoking a provision of the Taft-Hartley Act, which authorized the government to secure an injunction imposing an eighty-day "cooling off period," during which the two sides in a labor dispute that threatened the national interest would continue to negotiate. That procedure was unacceptable to the Steelworkers, since it would freeze wages at present levels, and Truman had close ties to organized labor. Instead of resorting to the distasteful Taft-Hartley Act, a few hours before the strike was scheduled to begin, he issued an executive order, directing the secretary of commerce to take possession of most of the country's steel mills and keep them running. The companies, obeying the president's order only under protest, filed suit against him in federal district court.

Their case rocketed up to the Supreme Court. On April 30 a federal district judge issued a preliminary injunction against the seizure. A divided U.S. Court of Appeals for the District of Columbia granted a stay of his order while the government sought immediate review by the Supreme Court. Although neither of the courts below had rendered a final decision in *Youngstown*, the justices agreed to hear the case, with only Justices Frankfurter and Burton opposing the granting of a writ of certiorari. The Vinson Court has received considerable criticism for allowing the government to shortcut normal judicial procedures and for rendering a decision in *Youngstown* only two months after Truman seized the steel mills. That criticism seems justified. As Marcus points out (Marcus 1977, 147–148), shortly before the public announcement that the Court was going to take the case, negotiators for the two sides had reached a tentative settlement of the strike. Once news of its action broke, management, seeing a chance to avoid a government-mandated wage increase, refused to consummate the deal.

Steel company executives were about the only ones who thought that getting the Supreme Court to hear their case would do them any good. Few contemporary commentators believed they had much chance of winning. Truman, on the other hand, had plenty of reason for optimism. Not only had the political and judicial tides been running strongly in favor of presidential power for nearly two decades, but also, he had appointed four members of the Court that would decide the case. The president had based his decision to seize the mills in part on a memorandum prepared by Tom Clark, one of his appointees, when Clark was attorney general. Before issuing his order, Truman had met with his buddy, Chief Justice Vinson, who advised him on legal grounds to go ahead with the seizure.

Although the chief justice considered Truman's action legally justified, there was no statute authorizing him to do what he had done. Since he was not carrying out a law passed by Congress, his seizure of the steel mills could be lawful only if the Constitution itself empowered him to take such a drastic step to prevent a wartime steel strike. The government pointed to three clauses in Article I that, it contended, collectively gave him the necessary authority. One vests "the executive power" in the president. The second charges the chief executive to "take Care that the Laws be faithfully executed." The third declares that the president "shall be the Commander in Chief of the Army and Navy."

Most of the justices were not convinced that these constitutional provisions gave the president the power to do what he had done. Although they debated the case in their closed conference for four hours, a clear majority emerged fairly quickly for the view that Truman had overstepped the limits of his authority. Only Vinson, Reed, and Minton supported the president. Even two of his own appointees, Burton and Clark, deserted Truman. What prolonged the deliberations was disagreement among the six justices composing the majority over what the rationale for their decision should be. Although all believed Truman had exceeded the limitations on presidential power, they could not reach an accord on what those limitations were. Frankfurter suggested that in this case everyone should write his own opinion, and ultimately every member of the majority did so.

Because the chief justice was on the losing side, Black, as the senior member of the majority, got to decide who would write what was ostensibly the opinion of the Court. He gave the job to himself. In his opinion, "Black took a Jeffersonian position: if neither the Constitution nor an act of Congress specifically gave the executive power, then the president did not have the power" (Urofsky 1997a, 210). Not only was there no statute authorizing what Truman had done, but during its deliberations on the Taft-Hartley Act, Congress had rejected an amendment that would have authorized such governmental seizures in cases of emergency. "It is clear," Black asserted, "that if the President had authority to issue the order he did, it must be found in some provision of the Constitution" (*Youngstown* 1952, 587). Black did not think it was possible to sustain seizure of the steel industry as an exercise of the president's power as commander in chief of the armed forces, for while *theater of war* was an expanding concept, it was still the job of the nation's lawmakers, not its military authorities, to decide matters such as whether the government should take over private property in order to prevent a disruption of defense production. Nor could Truman's action be sustained under the constitutional provisions vesting the executive power in the president. What he had done was make law, not execute it. Lawmaking was a responsibility that the Constitution assigned to Congress, and in Black's opinion, it "did not subject this lawmaking power . . . to presidential or military supervision or control" (*Youngstown* 1952, 588). Black's *Youngstown* opinion was an example of his strict constructionism and constitutional literalism. As far as he was concerned, the Constitution gave some functions to Congress and some to the president. If one of them assumed a responsibility it assigned to the other, that branch was behaving unconstitutionally. Truman's seizure order was unlawful because it violated the separation of powers mandated by the Constitution.

Douglas agreed with Black that Truman had violated the Constitution by performing a function it assigned to the legislative branch. In a concurring opinion he argued that, in order for a seizure of private property, such as the one Truman had ordered, to be constitutional, the owners must be compensated. Since only Congress could appropriate the money needed to pay them, the president had to obtain its endorsement for such an action. By failing to do so, Truman had violated the separation of powers, making his seizure of the steel mills unconstitutional.

Although Douglas and Black viewed seizing the steel mills as something no president could ever do without congressional authorization, the other members of the majority believed that in some circumstances the president could lawfully take such an action on the basis of nothing more than the inherent powers of his office. The problem with what Truman had done, as far as they were concerned, was that it was something Congress had prohibited when it passed the Taft-Hartley Act. Frankfurter expressed not only his own views but also those of Jackson, Burton, and Clark when he wrote in his concurring opinion that by deciding not to authorize seizures, Congress had "expressed its will to withhold this power from the President as though it had said so in so many words" (*Youngstown* 1952, 602). It could not have more authoritatively and decisively expressed its purpose to disallow such a power in the president and to require him to request specific congressional authorization for any seizure he considered necessary had it written such a requirement into the text of the Taft-Hartley Act, Frankfurter believed. He also maintained, however, that "the legal enforcement of the principle of separation of powers [is] more complicated and flexible than may appear from what Mr. Justice Black has written" (*Youngstown* 1952, 589). If there was a tradition of the legislature silently going along with a particular kind of presidential action, Frankfurter maintained, that acquiescence added a "historical gloss" to the language of the Constitution, rendering constitutional what the text might suggest was unconstitutional. Although voting with Frankfurter to overturn Truman's seizure of the steel mills, Clark expressed the view that "the Constitution does grant the President extensive authority in times of grave and imperative national emergency" (*Youngstown* 1952, 662). Likewise, although agreeing that the president lacked the inherent power to seize private property under the present circumstances, Burton indicated that if Congress had not already acted, he would view the situation differently.

Although Jackson shared the views of Frankfurter, Clark, and Burton about why Truman's seizure of the steel mills had been illegal, in his concurring opinion he articulated an approach that could be used to analyze the validity of any allegedly unconstitutional presidential action. It was one that later judges would find compelling, and consequently Jackson's *Youngstown* concurrence has provided the analytical framework for most subsequent judicial analysis of separation-of-powers problems. According to Justice Jackson, the president's authority is greatest when he acts pursuant to an expressed or implied authorization from Congress, for then he can rely not only on those powers inherent in his office but also on those that Congress has delegated to him. The fact that Congress has not spoken on a matter does not necessarily mean that the president is powerless to act, Jackson maintained, for there is "a zone of twilight in which he and Congress may have concurrent authority, or in which its distribution is uncertain" (*Youngstown* 1952, 637). In that realm, congressional inertia, indifference, or quiescence might make it permissible for the president to act on his own if the situation required him to do so. His power is at its lowest ebb when he takes actions incompatible with the expressed or implied will of Congress, for all he can draw on then is "his own constitutional powers minus any constitutional powers of Congress over the matter" (*Youngstown* 1952, 637). Jackson believed that Truman's seizure of the steel mills fell into this third category and that neither the Commander-in-Chief Clause nor the other provisions in Article II that the government had cited as justification for his action empowered the president to do such a thing on his own. As a justice, he repudiated claims for inherent and unrestricted presidential emergency powers that he had made earlier as Roosevelt's attorney general.

Although Jackson disclaimed in the steel seizure case the expansive conception of executive power that he had championed during World War II, Chief Justice Vinson did not. In a dissenting opinion in which he spoke also for Reed and Minton, Vinson filled more than twenty pages with historical examples of situations in which presidents had taken action to deal with national emergencies, whether or not they had explicit statutory authorization to do so. "The absence of a specific statute authorizing seizure of the steel mills as a mode of executing the laws . . . has not until today been thought to prevent the President from executing the laws," he observed (*Youngstown* 1952, 701). Vinson accused the majority of adopting a messenger-boy concept of the presidency. "Presidents have in the past, and any man worthy of the Office should be in the future, free to take at least interim action necessary to execute legislative programs essential to the survival of the Nation," the chief justice declared (*Youngstown* 1952, 709).

Normally, the Vinson Court exhibited the sort of judicial deference to executive authority for which its nominal leader argued in his *Youngstown* dissent. Only because this case involved a clear conflict between the president and Congress, a body to which this Court also generally deferred, did it overrule Truman's seizure of the steel mills. *Youngstown* was unusual in another respect as well: It rejected the constitutionality of an action the government sought to justify as essential for national security. Such arguments usually prevailed in the Vinson Court.

## The Rosenberg Case

The Vinson Court generally endorsed whatever measures other government agencies considered necessary to protect national security. As its handling of the Rosenberg case illustrates, the Court condoned dubious actions that government agencies considered necessary to protect the country from Communists. During the Vinson era anxiety about domestic communism, inspired by the Cold War between the United States and the Soviet Union, gripped the public. These fears began developing at about the time that Fred Vinson became chief justice. The Cold War dominated the docket of his Court and distorted its decision making. Among the victims of its preoccupation with protecting the country from communism were Julius and Ethel Rosenberg.

The Rosenbergs were American Communists, charged with violating the Espionage Act by passing atomic secrets to the Soviet Union. They were convicted in March 1951 and executed two years later. At one time many radicals and liberals considered them innocent victims of the anticommunist hysteria that gripped the United States during the early years of the Cold War. A substantial body of evidence that has become available in recent years establishes that, although Ethel was only peripherally involved in illegal activity and certainly did not deserve the harsh punishment she received, Julius was indeed an important Russian spy. But historians have also unearthed proof of improper conduct in the Rosenberg case by, among others, the trial judge, the director of the FBI, and the attorney general of the United States. The fact that Julius was guilty does not alter the fact that very serious violations of due process marred the Rosenberg proceedings. Nor does it affect the merits of the legal arguments advanced by their lawyers, which included contentions that the judge was biased against them and that Julius and Ethel were really tried for treason, but denied the procedural rights the Constitution guarantees to persons accused of that crime. Although there were substantial reasons for reviewing the Rosenbergs' convictions, and the Vinson Court was given at least six opportunities to do so between June 7, 1952, and June 18, 1953, it always declined.

Its failure to grant the Rosenbergs a hearing was not the fault of Black or Frankfurter. Despite their disagreements on other issues, they stood together on this one, voting at every opportunity to hear the Rosenberg case. Under the Supreme Court's rules, however, a writ of certiorari will be granted only if there are at least four votes to do so. Black and Frankfurter could never muster more than three. Had Murphy and Rutledge still been alive, they almost certainly would have joined them, but on the more conservative post-1949 Court, Black and Frankfurter could recruit only one ally. Frustratingly, the identity of that supporter kept changing, so that although four justices actually voted to hear the Rosenbergs' appeal, the necessary number never did so at any one time. Burton, impressed by how strongly the Court's senior justices felt about the necessity of reviewing this case before any death sentence was carried out, joined them on the first two votes. He deserted Frankfurter and Black in April 1953, however, when attorneys for the Rosenbergs sought to introduce new evidence, including claims that one witness had committed perjury and that the prosecutor had prejudiced the case with out-of-court statements. Burton's desertion angered Frankfurter and provoked him and Black to make public their disagreement with the majority's refusal to take the case. Frankfurter also circulated a memorandum to his colleagues in which he pleaded with them to reconsider what he described as "the most agonizing situation since I have been on the Court" (Urofsky 1997a, 180). The Rosenbergs had raised procedural questions whose validity deserved the attention of the Court, he argued, and by declining to hear their case, it was compromising cherished traditions of Anglo-American law and abandoning the field to demagogic exploiters of the Communist issue, such as Senator Joe McCarthy. Two days later Douglas informed the other members of the Court that after studying further the Rosenbergs' allegations of prosecutorial misconduct, he had decided to vote to review their case and would publish a dissent from the denial of a writ of certiorari on that issue that would condemn the behavior of the U.S. attorney. Although he had gained a vote for his position, Frankfurter was upset about the proposed public dissent, which he considered unethical because it seemed to prejudge the merits of the case. He also regarded it as an attempt by Douglas, through threatening to embarrass the Court publicly, to blackmail his colleagues into agreeing to hear the Rosenberg matter. Frankfurter sought to deprive Douglas of the opportunity to write a dissent by persuading Jackson, who was also furious about what he considered "the dirtiest, most shameful, most cynical performance that I have ever heard of" (Urofsky 1997a, 181) to agree to vote for certiorari, providing the fourth vote needed to grant it, and thereby leaving Douglas with no denial to protest. Saying he had not realized his planned dissent would embarrass anyone, Douglas then announced he was withdrawing it. His objective accomplished, Jackson returned to his original position, leaving only Black, Frankfurter, and Douglas voting to grant review and ensuring that there would never be a Supreme Court hearing on the merits of the Rosenberg case. Historian Michael Parrish finds extremely disturbing the fact that Jackson "killed the opportunity for review less out of concern for the Court's reputation than out of hostility both to Justice Douglas and to the Rosenbergs" (Parrish 2000, 614).

Jackson fought other battles with Douglas over the Rosenbergs. Their lawyers tried to win a stay of execution for the convicted Communists by bringing forth new evidence that perjury had been committed at the trial and by also seeking a rehearing on the denial of their second petition for a writ of certiorari. In a confusing series of votes on different issues, the Rosenbergs repeatedly came up short. Unlike a writ of certiorari, a stay is granted only if a majority of the nine justices vote to do so. Consequently, despite the fact that Black, Frankfurter, Burton, and Jackson favored granting the Rosenbergs a stay on the perjured testimony issue, they did not get one because Douglas failed to provide the crucial fifth vote. He did, however, support giving them a rehearing on the second certiorari petition and a stay of execution pending argument on that issue. Unfortunately for the Rosenbergs, only Black and Frankfurter agreed with him on those matters. Frankfurter believed Douglas really did not care about the Rosenbergs, but was just trying to score points with liberals. A cynical Jackson observed that Douglas "opposed a hearing in open Court and only when it was per-fectly clear that a particular application would not be granted did he take a position for granting it" (Parrish 2000, 615). That observation may be unfair to Douglas, but it was because of his inconsistency that the Rosenbergs were still seeking a stay of exe-cution when the Court adjourned for its summer recess.

As the justices were about to scatter, Fyke Farmer and Daniel Marshall, two lawyers representing a coalition of civil liberties and church groups, intervened in the case, claiming that the defendants should have been tried under the new Atomic Energy Act rather than the Espionage Act. This was a potentially decisive argument, for the Atomic Energy Act contained procedural requirements for the imposition of the death penalty that clearly had not been followed in the Rosenberg case. Farmer and Marshall took their argument to Douglas, who consulted Frankfurter and Vinson. The former thought the matter worth looking into, but the chief told him that the two lawyers did not even have standing to raise it. Nevertheless, Douglas acted. On June 17, two days before the Rosenbergs were scheduled to be put to death, he issued an order staying their execution, pending further proceedings in the district court on the applicability of the Atomic Energy Act. Douglas then left Washington for his vacation home in the Pacific Northwest. He did not know that the previous day Jackson had met secretly with Vinson and Attorney General Herbert Brownell and the three had agreed that if Douglas issued a stay, the chief justice would call a special session of the Court to vacate it. Vinson did that, and did it without making any effort to inform Douglas, who learned of the special session by hearing about it on his car radio. The Court assembled on June 18 and for the only time heard arguments in open court on the Rosenberg case. Those were restricted, however, to the issue of whether the Atomic Energy Act's death penalty provision raised sufficient questions to support a stay. Only Frankfurter and Black agreed with Douglas that it did. The Court quickly voted 6–3 to vacate the stay, and that evening the Rosenbergs died in the electric chair.

They went to their deaths without ever getting a full hearing on the merits of their case, despite the fact that at various times five different members of the Supreme Court had voted that they should have one. The Vinson Court's handling of the Rosen-berg case merits the severe criticism it has received. At a time when this country was struggling to demonstrate that its system of government was superior to that of the Soviet Union, the Court missed an opportunity to demonstrate that in the United States everyone receives due process of law. At a time when civil liberties were being threatened by the excesses of McCarthyism, the Court missed an opportunity to stand up for them in a way that would have conveyed a powerful message to a panicky pub-lic. Yet, had the Rosenbergs gotten the hearing the Court repeatedly refused to give them, it would probably only have delayed the inevitable. As Parrish concludes, "[I]t is unlikely, given the ideological composition of the Vinson Court in 1952–53 and the cli-mate of anticommunism that the judicial process could have saved the couple even had their case been fully reviewed by the high court on several occasions" (Parrish 2000, 620).

## *Loyalty of Government Employees*

The decisions of the Vinson Court in cases involving allegedly disloyal government employees suggest that Parrish is correct. It exhibited little enthusiasm for protecting the constitutional rights of those suspected of disloyalty. Alleged subversives who challenged the procedures used to exclude them from government service prevailed more often than one might have expected, given the temper of the times and the attitudes of most of the justices. On those occasions when the Vinson Court ruled in their favor, however, it did so on narrow and rather technical grounds. Not until the 1960s, long after Earl Warren had replaced Vinson as chief justice, did the Supreme Court hand down decisions repudiating for basic constitutional reasons the tactics to which states and the federal government had resorted to combat domestic communism at the height of the Cold War.

Those tactics included the loyalty-security program that the Truman administration developed after Republicans made the alleged presence of Communists in the federal government an issue during the 1946 congressional elections. In March 1947, the president issued an executive order that directed the FBI to investigate the loyalty of all federal workers and to forward any derogatory information that it found to loyalty boards to be established in all of the principal bureaus of the government. These panels would hold hearings to determine whether there were reasonable grounds to believe that accused individuals were disloyal. In those proceedings such a belief could be established by showing that the employee was a member of one of a number of organizations designated by the attorney general as totalitarian, Fascist, Communist, or subversive. A suspect employee was not permitted to examine the FBI files on the basis of which a board had acted or even to be informed of the names of her accusers.

The Vinson Court's first encounter with this loyalty-security program came in *Bailey v. Richardson* (1951). That case involved an employee of the Federal Security Agency who had been barred by a loyalty board from government service for three years. Baily claimed that the board's action amounted to an unconstitutional bill of attainder, and the Court of Appeals for the District of Columbia agreed. It nevertheless upheld the board's action under a well-established principle that there was no constitutional right to federal employment, and that consequently, no due process was required to remove a government worker. Nor did the board's action violate the First Amendment, the Court of Appeals ruled, for it was also well established that the Constitution did not prohibit politically motivated removals from office. When the case reached the Supreme Court, Justice Clark, who had been the head of the Justice

Department when the proceedings against Bailey began, disqualified himself. This left the Court split 4–4. When that happens, the result below is affirmed without opinion. Thus, the Court upheld Bailey's exclusion from federal employment without explaining or justifying its decision.

It did, however, publish opinions in *Joint Anti-Fascist Refugee Committee v. McGrath* (1951), decided on the same day as *Bailey*. *McGrath* was a challenge to the attorney general's list of subversive organizations, brought by three groups that were seeking to have their names removed from that dishonor roll. The Joint Anti-Fascist Refugee Committee claimed it was just a charitable group that provided assistance to victims of the Spanish Civil War. The other two plaintiffs also denied they were Communist organizations or engaged in subversive activities. The Supreme Court ruled for them by a 5–3 margin (with Clark again not participating). The members of the majority could not agree on a rationale, however. Only Black and Douglas questioned even indirectly whether the government was allowed to regulate ideas by creating proscriptive lists. "Officially prepared and proclaimed governmental blacklists possess almost every quality of bills of attainder, the use of which was from the beginning forbidden to both national and state governments," Black declared in a strong concurring opinion (*McGrath* 1951, 143–144). Although he and Douglas insisted that the attorney general had no authority to draw up such lists, Frankfurter condemned only the procedures the Justice Department had employed. He insisted that these violated due process because the designated organizations had not been given notice and there were no criteria for inclusion. Jackson agreed with Frankfurter that the problem here was a due process one, emphasizing the failure of the government to give the organizations included on the list a hearing. In what was supposed to have been the opinion of the Court, Burton rested the decision on even narrower grounds. Although acknowledging that this case "bristled with constitutional issues," he avoided all of them, ruling for the plaintiffs on the ground that Truman's executive order creating the loyalty-security program did not authorize the attorney general arbitrarily to designate certain organizations as subversive. Only Douglas joined Burton's opinion announcing the judgment. Reed dissented for himself, Minton, and the chief justice. Small wonder that, although voting with the majority, Jackson decried as "unfortunate" the fact that the Court had "flounder[ed] in wordy disagreement over the validity and effect of [these] procedures" (*McGrath* 1951, 183).

The Court had fewer problems with the methods used by state and local governments to ensure the fealty of their employees, almost all of which it found acceptable. These governments relied heavily on loyalty oaths and denied employment to persons who belonged to certain designated organizations and/or advocated the violent overthrow of the government. A majority of the Vinson Court approved of such methods, as long as allegedly disloyal public employees were subjected to sanctions only for knowing membership in subversive organizations. The Court first disclosed where it stood on these state and local security measures with its decision in *Gerende v. Board of Supervisors* (1951). There, with a per curiam opinion, it upheld a Maryland law requiring candidates for public office to file affidavits disavowing both belief in the overthrow of the government and membership in any subversive organization. The Court affirmed the constitutionality of this statute only after being assured by Maryland's attorney general that it required disavowal only of "knowing" membership in groups of the prohibited type.

Clark's majority opinion in *Garner v. Board of Public Works* (1951), which the Court decided just a few weeks after *Gerende*, relied on this same distinction between knowing and innocent membership. In *Garner* the Court upheld a Los Angeles ordinance that required city employees to execute affidavits disavowing belief in the violent overthrow of the government and also to swear that they had not belonged to any subversive organizations for the past five years. Frankfurter dissented, in part because he did not think that this law distinguished adequately between knowing and innocent membership. Although he did not think that the retroactive character of the oath it required made it unconstitutional, Burton, Black, and Douglas did. They joined in condemning the Los Angeles ordinance as a bill of attainder.

Only Black and Douglas dissented, however, when the Court upheld New York's controversial Feinberg Law in *Adler v. Board of Education* (1952). That 1949 statute implemented an earlier provision of the state's Civil Service Law that prohibited the appointment as a teacher or public school employee of any person who taught or advocated the violent overthrow of the government. The Feinberg Law required the New York Board of Regents to publish, after notice and hearing, a list of all subversive organizations that advocated such overthrow. Subsequent membership in any group on the list would constitute prima facie evidence that an educator was guilty of the forbidden teaching and advocacy and would preclude her from being appointed or retained as a public school teacher. Speaking for the majority, Justice Minton reiterated the oft-repeated dicta that there was no constitutional right to government employment. He went on to declare that public school officials had both the right and the duty to screen teachers to ensure their fitness and maintain the integrity of the schools as part of an ordered society. Douglas dissented for himself and Black, condemning the Feinberg Law as a menace to academic freedom that would "inevitably turn the school system into a spying project" (*Adler* 1950, 509). He emphatically maintained that the Constitution guaranteed freedom of thought and expression to everyone and argued that states could not make public employees second-class citizens by denying them those rights.

A majority of the Vinson Court never accepted that position. In *Wieman v. Updegraf* (1951), however, it did for the first time invalidate a state loyalty oath. The Oklahoma statute at issue in *Wieman* required all state officers and employees to swear not only that they did not advocate the violent overthrow of the government or belong to any organization that did so, or to the Communist Party or any other subversive group, but that they had not been affiliated with any such organization for the past five years. This law went too far even for the Vinson Court. In an opinion written by Justice Clark, it rejected the generalization that there was no constitutionally protected right to public employment, as well as the notion that the mere act of membership in a subversive organization could disqualify someone from holding a government job. There was, Clark declared, a decisive distinction between this law and those upheld in *Garner*, *Adler*, and *Gerende:* Unlike them, it did not require that in order to be excluded from government employment, someone must have had knowledge of the subversive character of the group with which he was affiliated. "Indiscriminate classification of innocent with knowing activity must fall as an assertion of arbitrary power," he concluded (*Wieman* 1951, 190).

## The Communist Issue and Free Speech

In his *Wieman v. Updegraf* opinion Clark sought to distinguish the law struck down in that case not only from those the Court had upheld earlier in *Gerende*, *Garner*, and *Adler*, but also from the one it had found constitutional in *American Communications Association v. Douds* (1950). The Oklahoma law really was not all that different from those that had passed muster earlier, however. As Melvin Urofsky points out, since *Douds*, his colleagues had come "to feel uncomfortable . . . under Justice Black's constant dissents regarding freedom to think" (Urofsky 1997a, 163). In addition to the passage of time, what set *Wieman* apart from *Douds* was that the earlier case had involved a federal law. When an act of Congress was challenged, the predilection of Vinson and most of his colleagues was to endorse Congress, for the Court generally supported whatever the other branches of the national government did. When the challenged legislation was intended to protect the country from communism, their equally strong commitment to ensuring national security also came into play. In *Douds* and *Dennis v. United States* (1951), another case in which the Court upheld a federal law used to combat communism, such considerations overrode the concerns about freedom of thought and expression that animated Black. Consequently, the First Amendment suffered damage from those decisions.

At issue in *Douds* was the constitutionality of Section 9(h) of the Taft-Hartley Act, a law that required labor union officials to file affidavits disavowing membership in the Communist Party and belief in the violent overthrow of the government or have their unions denied access to the National Labor Relations Board. Attacking the constitutionality of this statute were the American Communications Association, an organization heavily infiltrated by the Communist Party of the United States (CPUSA), and the firmly anticommunist United Steel Workers of America. They contended that

Section 9(h) violated the First Amendment by denying union officers the liberty to hold whatever political views they chose and to associate with whatever political groups they wanted, as well as by depriving unions of the right to choose their own officers without interference from the government. Speaking for the Court, Vinson upheld the challenged law. He acknowledged that by enacting this statute, Congress had discouraged the exercise of political freedom, but justified what it had done with the observation that the legislative branch had determined this restriction was necessary to prevent disruptive politically motivated strikes. According to Vinson, Section 9(h) was constitutional because it was a valid exercise of the power of Congress to regulate interstate commerce. He used the Commerce Clause to evade the First Amendment issues in the case. Although concurring in the judgment, Frankfurter and Jackson did not find this case as easy as Vinson did. Jackson candidly acknowledged, "if the statute before us required labor union officers to forswear membership in the Republican Party, the Democratic Party, or the Socialist Party, I suppose all would agree that it was unconstitutional" (*Douds* 1950, 422). Black did not think that the fact that the target of Section 9(h) was the Communist Party made it valid. He found the constitutional justification Vinson had offered for that law utterly unpersuasive. "No case cited by the Court provides the least vestige of support for . . . holding that the Commerce Clause restricts the right to think," Black declared (*Douds* 1950, 446). "The problem with Vinson's opinion," as Urofsky perceptively observes, "lay not in his argument that rights could sometimes be abridged in return for government benefits. . . . Rather, he totally disregarded the First Amendment issues raised by Black, Frankfurter and Jackson and also ignored the overly broad sweep of the Taft-Hartley [Act]" (Urofsky 1997a, 161). The chief's reason for doing those things was his conviction that First Amendment freedoms were "dependent upon the power of constitutional government to . . . survive." Such a government could continue to exist, he believed, only if it had the power to protect itself, not just against illegal conduct but also "against incitements to commit unlawful acts" (*Douds* 1950, 394).

Like *Douds, Dennis v. United States* (1951) exemplifies what Frances Rudko calls Vinson's "zealous effort to maintain the authority of the national government" (Rudko 1988, 71). Decided one year after *Douds, Dennis* was another badly flawed attempt to reconcile the First Amendment with Cold War internal security concerns. It "constituted the final judicial validation of the government's loyalty-security program" (Urofsky 1997a, 169). In *Dennis*, legal scholar Harry Kalven laments, "the Court missed an opportunity to take advantage of great events to make a major contribution to the development of the First Amendment tradition" (Kalven 1988, 191). Historian Michal Belknap offers an even harsher assessment. "*Dennis*," he writes "served mainly to give the imprimatur of the Supreme Court to an assault upon freedom of expression and association that was the essence of McCarthyism" (Belknap 1993, 55).

The target of their criticism is a case that arose out of a notorious "political trial, inspired by the then intensifying Cold War between the United States and the Soviet Union" (Belknap 1994, 209). Despite its loyalty-security program, the Truman administration came under attack by Republicans in Congress for doing too little to combat domestic communism. Responding to this GOP pressure, in 1948 then–Attorney General Clark initiated a prosecution of the top leaders of the CPUSA. The government charged the twelve members of the party's national board with violating a 1940 sedition law, known as the Smith Act, by conspiring to teach and advocate the violent overthrow of the government and to set up the Communist Party to engage in such teaching and advocacy. One of the indicted Communists was not tried because he had a bad heart, but from January to October 1949 the other eleven stood trial before Judge Harold Medina in the federal courthouse on New York's Foley Square. This proceeding was as tumultuous as it was lengthy. Both the government and the CPUSA exploited the courtroom for propaganda purposes. The trial featured protest demonstrations by Communists and their supporters, designed to pressure the government into dropping the charges against the defendants, and endless wrangling between Judge Medina, who exhibited an obvious bias against the accused, and their combative attorneys, who made themselves instruments of a CPUSA propaganda campaign. It ended with the conviction of all eleven defendants. In addition, Medina held the defense attorneys, as well as defendant Eugene Dennis, who had represented himself, guilty of contempt, and sentenced them to jail for terms ranging from thirty days to six months.

Dennis and the lawyers appealed their contempt sentences to the Second Circuit Court of Appeals, which reversed some of the specifications but let stand both the convictions and the sentences. In *Sacher v. United States* (1952), the Supreme Court affirmed the Court of Appeals by a 5–3 vote, with Clark not participating. Jackson wrote the opinion. Black and Douglas dissented, along with Frankfurter, who objected strenuously that Medina should not "have combined in himself the functions of both accuser and judge" (*Sacher* 1952, 28). Besides being imprisoned for contempt, the Foley Square defense attorneys became targets of disciplinary actions by a number of bar associations. These proceedings generated a good deal of appellate litigation, including one case, *In re Isserman* (1953), which reached the Supreme Court while Vinson was still chief justice. After the Supreme Court of New Jersey ordered Abraham Isserman disbarred, he was required to show cause why he should not lose the right to practice before the U.S. Supreme Court itself. With the chief justice writing the opinion, the Court held that Isserman had failed to do that and ordered him disbarred.

Although the Foley Square Smith Act trial spawned other Supreme Court decisions, by far the most important ruling generated by that tumultuous proceeding was *Dennis v. United States*. In that case the Communist leaders contended that their conviction violated the First Amendment. For more than a decade the Court had been determining whether challenged governmental actions violated that constitutional guarantee by subjecting them to the so-called clear-and-present-danger test, developed by Justices Oliver Wendell Holmes Jr. and Louis Brandeis during the decade just after World War I. Under this test a restriction on speech violated the First Amendment unless there was a clear and immediate danger that the proscribed expression would bring about some serious substantive evil that Congress or a state legislature had a right to prohibit. The government could, of course, outlaw revolution or even attempting or conspiring to launch a revolt. In *Dennis*, however, the prosecution had offered no proof that the Communists were about to convert their advocacy into action, because it had no such evidence. Instead, prosecutors had introduced mountains of Marxist-Leninist literature, which showed at most that members of the CPUSA wanted capitalism replaced with communism as soon as possible and did not think the capitalists would give up their power without a fight. The government contended that, because Medina had instructed the jury that it could convict the Communist leaders only if it found that they had intended to overthrow the government as soon as the opportunity presented itself, this was enough to satisfy the First Amendment. Their lawyers disagreed, arguing that prosecutors had failed to establish the existence of a clear and present danger. Their clients, they contended, were being punished merely for advocating ideas, and doing that violated the First Amendment. Justice Department lawyers responded that, while *Douds* had acknowledged government might not censor political views, that decision had also recognized the permissibility of imposing incidental restrictions on expression in order to regulate dangerous conduct. The Communist leaders were being punished not for their speech but rather for forming fifth columns serving the aggressive purposes of the Soviet Union. Although the defendants had been prosecuted for conspiring to teach and advocate Marxism-Leninism, the Justice Department treated this as if it were a case about conspiring to overthrow the government.

So did the Supreme Court. It quickly and easily decided the case against the Communist leaders. The conference at which the justices discussed *Dennis* was devoid of acrimony. Indeed, according to Justice Douglas, who was on the losing side of a 6–2 vote (Clark abstained), it was largely pro forma. "[T]hose wanting to affirm had minds closed to argument or persuasion." He found that "amazing because of the drastic revision of the 'clear and present danger' test which affirmance requires" (Urofsky 1997a, 170).

Vinson gave himself the job of making the necessary revision. He accomplished it with a plurality opinion in which he spoke only for Reed, Burton, Minton, and himself. The job of affirming the convictions of the Communist leaders would have been easier had the chief justice simply eschewed the clear-and-present-danger test entirely and based the decision on *Gitlow v. New York* (1925), a case in which the Supreme Court had taken the position that the test did not apply when a legislative body had already determined that a particular kind of speech was dangerous. With respect to the teaching and advocacy of the violent overthrow of the government, Congress had made such a determination when it passed the Smith Act. Since *Gitlow* had never been overruled, Vinson could simply have relied on it as a precedent for upholding the *Dennis* convictions. The Court had abandoned *Gitlow*'s line of reasoning in the late 1930s, however, and the chief felt compelled to employ the clear-and-present-danger test that the Court had been using in recent years. The problem was that, since the Holmes-Brandeis rule required that the threatened evil be imminent, an honest application of that test would have required overturning the convictions of the Communist leaders as violations of the First Amendment.

In order to avoid that result, Vinson adopted what purported to be an explanation of the clear-and-present-danger test but was really a significant modification of it. In an opinion that he had written for the Second Circuit Court of Appeals upholding the *Dennis* convictions, Judge Learned Hand had analyzed the applicable precedents and concluded that the purpose of the rule was to give courts a way of dealing with utterances that combined appeals to the understanding with advocacy of illegal action. "In each case," he had written, "they must ask whether the gravity of the 'evil [advocated by a speaker],' discounted by its improbability, justifies such invasion of free speech as is necessary to avoid the danger." Hand added that he had "purposely substituted 'improbability' for 'remoteness'" (*Dennis* 1951, 212). Thus, he had read out of the clear-and-present-danger test one of its most crucial elements. As far as Brandeis was concerned, as long as there was time for those holding opposing views to counter a speaker's message, the First Amendment would not allow speech to be punished. Only the threat of immediate danger could justify suppressing expression. By reading the imminence requirement out of the clear-and-present-danger test, Hand had fundamentally altered it. Nevertheless, Vinson adopted his revised version, which he quoted verbatim.

The chief justice had no trouble finding that this prosecution passed Hand's test (often referred to as the grave-and-probable-danger test). The reason was the Cold War. Because of it, during the period covered by the indictment (1945–1948) a situation existed that was very different from anything Holmes and Brandeis had confronted. "The formation by [the top officials of the CPUSA] of such a highly organized conspiracy, with rigidly disciplined members subject to call when the leaders, these petitioners, felt that the time had come for action, coupled with the inflammable nature of world conditions, similar uprisings in other countries, and the touch-and-go nature of our relations with countries with whom petitioners were in the very least ideologically attuned, convinces us that their convictions were justified" (*Dennis* 1951, 510–511). Or as Justice Reed, who signed Vinson's opinion, put it in a letter to Justice Frankfurter, "[A] teaching of force and violence by such a group as this . . ., is enough at this period of the world's history to make the protection of the First Amendment inapplicable"

(Belknap 1977, 138). As far as Vinson was concerned, the constitutional guarantees of free expression did not protect even agreeing to teach and advocate the violent overthrow of the government in the future, for it was the Communist's conspiracy itself that created the danger.

Although Frankfurter and Jackson agreed with him that the defendants had been constitutionally convicted, they declined to endorse Vinson's reasoning. Frankfurter disapproved of the policy decisions embodied in the Smith Act, for he feared that such a law could be used to silence critics of the government who did not advocate its violent overthrow but were worried that the authorities might misinterpret their remarks. Although concluding that the challenged statute was constitutional on its face, he indicated he believed it could be applied in a manner that would violate the First Amendment. Indeed, a few years later Frankfurter would seek to restrain the Justice Department from using the Smith Act to wage all-out war on the CPUSA. Only his rigid devotion to judicial restraint enabled him to uphold this distasteful law in *Dennis*. "Free speech cases are not an exception to the principle that we are not legislators, that direct policymaking is not our province," he wrote in a concurring opinion (*Dennis* 1951, 539).

Jackson also concurred. Unable to accept what Hand and Vinson had done to the clear-and-present-danger test, he argued that it should not be used in this case. It had been designed for situations involving the speech of a few isolated individuals, he maintained, and should be reserved for cases of that type. Laws that punished advocating the violent overthrow of the government were designed for anarchists, and since violence was only one of many means that Communists used to reach their revolutionary ends, forcing prosecutors to prove a clear and present danger of armed revolt would make the CPUSA untouchable. As far as Jackson was concerned, the *Dennis* defendants had really been convicted of conspiring to overthrow the government, and their convictions should be sustained on that basis. His opinion was more honest than Vinson's, but it was legally flawed; the defendants had been charged with and convicted of conspiring to teach and advocate, not of conspiring to overthrow the government.

Unlike Jackson and Frankfurter, Black and Douglas rejected Vinson's conclusion as well as his reasoning. Dissenting, the Court's senior associate justice complained that in order to uphold the Smith Act and the convictions of eleven Communists, the chief justice had distorted the clear-and-present-danger test, thus constricting First Amendment rights. Black did not consider even that test sufficiently protective of freedom of expression. As far as he was concerned, any restriction on speech violated the First Amendment.

Douglas did not go that far, but he did insist that the clear-and-present-danger test had not been satisfied in this case. Whether a clear and present danger existed was a question of fact for a jury to decide, but one could do this only if presented with evidence that would support such a finding. There was none in this case. Douglas was not impressed by Vinson's efforts to establish the existence of a clear and present danger by taking judicial notice of the Cold War. The Court might as well say that the Communist leaders' speech was illegal because the Soviet Union was a threat to world peace, he remarked acidly. This case had been argued as though it involved the teaching of sabotage, espionage, street warfare, and the like, but the prosecution had presented no evidence of those things. Personally, Douglas considered the CPUSA "the most beset, and the least thriving of any fifth column in history" (*Dennis* 1951, 589). He faulted the majority for rendering freedom of speech dependent on the identity of the person doing the talking. Douglas found Jackson's opinion even more horrifying than Vinson's. Not until today, he observed, had anyone seriously suggested that conspiracy law could be used to turn speech into seditious conduct.

In 1951 Douglas and Black were voices crying in the wilderness. With the Cold War at its most frigid, most Americans feared the Soviet Union, reviled U.S. Communists, and found it impossible to distinguish these related but distinct entities from one another. Protecting national security seemed more important than protecting civil liberties. Unfortunately for the First Amendment, most members of the Supreme Court shared these popular attitudes. They believed that the Soviet Union posed a grave danger to the security of the United States, and in order to justify legal action against its ideological allies in this country, they altered the meaning of the First Amendment, reducing drastically the protection it afforded to anyone who seemed somehow related to the Soviet threat. "Beset by the same anxieties that gripped other Americans at the time, " writes legal historian William Wiecek, "most of the Justices of the Vinson Court acknowledged anticommunism as a legitimate expression of democratic politics, validating not only the national security state . . . but the domestic security state as well" (Wiecek 2002, 375).

## Local Government Restrictions on Speech

Although *Dennis* was by far the Vinson Court's most important First Amendment decision, it handed down a number of others that were doctrinally significant and helped to define the parameters of freedom of speech during the Cold War years. Generally, the Court sustained governmental restrictions on expression, but sometimes it invalidated them. It was skeptical about prior restraint and was more willing to strike down restrictions on expression imposed by local governments than to let the First Amendment thwart the implementation of federal policies, especially those with internal security implications. This was a conservative Court with a strong progovernment bias, but in the free speech area its decisions were not totally consistent.

Certainly, that was true of those involving loudspeakers. In *Saia v. New York* (1948) the Court by a 5–4 margin held unconstitutional a Lockport, New York, ordinance that required anyone wishing to use sound amplification equipment to secure the permission of the police chief. The defendant, a Jehovah's Witness, had obtained the required permit, but because some residents found the noise made by the loudspeaker with which he amplified his religious lectures annoying, the chief refused to renew it. The Court held the ordinance "unconstitutional on its face, [because] it establishes a previous restraint on the right of free speech in violation of the First Amendment" (*Saia* 1948, 559–560). Speaking for the majority, Justice Douglas acknowledged that the noise from loudspeakers could be a problem and conceded that a narrowly drawn statute regulating their volume and where and when they might be used would be permissible. He faulted the Lockport ordinance, however, for vesting standardless discretion in the chief. Frankfurter dissented for himself, Reed, and Burton, taking the position that this law was a reasonable means to prevent intrusions into the privacy of other users of the park. Justice Jackson wrote a somewhat more vigorous dissent, in which he characterized the holding of *Saia* as a perversion of the Constitution. This was not, as far as Jackson was concerned, a free speech case at all, but rather one about whether society could exercise some control over an "apparatus which, when put to unregulated proselytizing, propaganda, and commercial uses, can render life unbearable" (*Saia* 1948, 569).

Jackson was on the winning side the following year when the Court upheld a municipal ordinance prohibiting the use of sound trucks, loudspeakers, and amplifiers on the streets of Trenton, New Jersey, in *Kovacs v. Cooper* (1949). There was one significant difference between this law and the Lockport one: The Trenton law did not require a would-be speaker to get the permission of a public official before speaking. Thus, it did not impose a prior restraint on speech. As far as Reed was concerned, that made the Trenton measure a constitutional exercise of the police power, which did not abridge freedom of speech. In order to reach that conclusion, his "rather cloudy opinion" (Pritchett 1954, 45) treated this ordinance as applying only to amplifying devices that emitted "loud and raucous" noises, a very dubious reading of its language. Burton and the chief justice signed what Reed wrote, but Jackson and Frankfurter, who could see no difference between *Kovacs* and *Saia*, did not. Instead, each published a concurrence, in which he argued that the earlier case had been wrongly decided. Black, Douglas, Rutledge, and Murphy dissented. Jackson accurately summed up the effect of the two sound truck decisions when he commented that they would "pretty hopelessly confuse municipal authorities as to what they may or may not do" (*Kovacs* 1949, 98).

Their confusion could only have been increased by *Public Utilities Commission v. Pollak* (1952). The *Saia* dissenters and the *Kovacs* majority seemed to be animated by concern for the privacy rights of unwilling listeners, who had no way to avoid the messages that operators of sound amplification equipment blasted at them. In *Pollak*, however, the Court held that there had been no violation of the First Amendment when riders of Washington, D.C., streetcars were forced to listen to music and advertising played by the bus company. It was privately owned, but the District of Columbia's Public Utilities Commission had authorized the disputed practice. In a typical example of Vinson Court deference to legislative authority, the justices concluded that, although a legislature might prohibit raucous sounds in public places, the First Amendment did not itself protect unwilling audiences from having to listen to them. This was so even when those assaulting their privacy acted with the approval of the government.

Although erratic in the way it treated those who bombarded unwilling listeners with messages they did not want to hear, the Vinson Court was surprisingly consistent in affording constitutional protection to speakers prosecuted for expounding their views without first obtaining licenses from municipal authorities. Three years after *Saia*, the Court overturned another conviction of Jehovah's Witnesses in *Niemotko v. Maryland* (1951). The defendants in that case had been prosecuted for disorderly conduct after they held Bible talks in a public park without first securing the permission of the park commissioner. They had sought it, but he refused to give his authorization, and a review of the commissioner's decision by the city council was delayed. The Supreme Court believed the council had failed to approve the Witnesses' request because it objected to their refusal to salute the flag and their views on the Bible. Noting the lack of any evidence that the Jehovah's Witnesses had engaged in disorderly conduct, the Court unanimously reversed their convictions. Vinson concluded that Witnesses had a right to equal protection of the laws in the exercise of First Amendment rights that had "a firmer foundation than the whims or personal opinions of a local governing body" (*Niemotko* 1951, 272).

The chief justice also spoke for the Court in *Kunz v. New York* (1951), where it held unconstitutional a New York City ordinance that made it illegal to hold an outdoor public worship meeting without first obtaining a permit from the police commissioner. Kunz, an ordained Baptist minister, got a permit that entitled him to engage in outdoor preaching during calendar year 1946. The city revoked it in November of that year, however, after a hearing on evidence that he had ridiculed and denounced other religious beliefs during his meetings. New York rejected applications for permits that he filed in 1947 and 1948. On September 11, 1948, Kunz was arrested for speaking in Columbus Circle without one. He was convicted and fined $1,000. Chief Justice Vinson and most of his colleagues viewed this as another case of prior restraint by an administrator vested with standardless discretion to control the right of citizens to speak. Vinson did not think the fact that Kunz's religious meetings had caused disorder in the past justified this restriction, for there were appropriate remedies to which the authorities could resort if his speeches caused violence now. Jackson disagreed with the chief. He considered it reasonable that New York should protect the dignity of its people "against fanatics who take possession of its streets to hurl into its crowds defamatory epithets that hurt like rocks" (*Kunz* 1951, 313). By giving Kunz the right to launch verbal attacks on Jews and Catholics, the majority was letting him play with explosives in the public streets, Jackson maintained. As for its view that the community must "not only tolerate but aid him, I find no such doctrine in the Constitution" (*Kunz* 1951, 314).

Jackson's *Kunz* dissent reiterated concerns he had expressed earlier in his dissenting opinion in *Terminello v. Chicago* (1949). *Terminello* was the first of two major decisions by the Vinson Court addressing the difficult problem of the extent to which the First Amendment protects a speaker whose speech excites violence, not because he urges his listeners to commit it, but because his words outrage hostile members of the audience. Father Arthur Terminello, a defrocked Catholic priest, had attacked Jews and the Roosevelt administration during a 1946 speech before eight hundred sympathizers in Chicago. Outside, more than a thousand protesters rioted. They threw rocks and stink bombs through the windows, and the police were hard pressed to keep them from storming the hall. After managing to get Terminello and his supporters safely out of the building, officers arrested him on disorderly conduct charges. With Douglas writing the opinion, the Supreme Court reversed his conviction for that offense, because of what it maintained was an improper charge by the trial judge to the jury. This was an issue Terminello's attorneys had not even raised. "Douglas's opinion received wide notice in the press as proof of the high level of tolerance in America" (Urofsky 1997a, 167). It outraged Jackson, however. In a dissent joined by Frankfurter and Burton, he excoriated the majority for taking the position that the country must forego order in order to achieve liberty, faulting it for "fix[ing] its eyes on a conception of freedom of speech so rigid as to tolerate no concession to society's need for public order" (*Terminello* 1949, 14). Vinson dissented, too, although on narrower and more legalistic grounds.

Three years later he and Jackson were again on the same side in a hostile-audience case. *Feiner v. New York* (1951) was decided on the same day as *Kunz*. The petitioner, Irving Feiner, a procommunist college student, had angered some of those in a racially mixed audience of about seventy-five persons with a street-corner speech that included derogatory remarks about President Truman, the American Legion, the mayor of Syracuse, and other local officials. Feiner also urged African Americans to rise up and fight for equal rights. His speech excited the crowd, with some of those present indicating support for him and others voicing intense opposition. Several onlookers commented to the two policemen on the scene about their failure to control the crowd, and one of them threatened violence if the police did not act. Although one officer demanded that Feiner get down off the box from which he was speaking, Feiner twice refused to do so and kept on talking. With the crowd pressing closer, the police finally arrested him. Feiner was subsequently convicted of disorderly conduct. The Supreme Court affirmed his conviction 6–3. Speaking for the majority, Vinson took the position that the existence of a clear and present danger of riot, disorder, and interference with traffic justified the action the police had taken. In order to uphold the conviction in a hostile-audience case, the chief justice used a test designed for speech that incited those who heard it to engage in violence advocated by the speaker. Although he acknowledged that the objections of an unfriendly audience could not be allowed to silence someone, Vinson added that this did not mean the authorities were powerless to act to prevent a breach of the peace when a speaker "passes the bounds of argument and persuasion and undertakes incitement to riot" (*Feiner* 1951, 321). Melvin Urofsky justifiably accuses him of validating a "heckler's veto" (Urofsky 1997a, 168). Although expressing some concern that the majority's approach could enable those who wished to silence a speaker to accomplish their objective by creating a disturbance in the crowd, Frankfurter concurred. Jackson did not write an opinion, but he used his *Kunz* dissent to express his belief that the type of police control the Court had approved in *Feiner* was actually more dangerous than the permit system it had held unconstitutional in that case. Black dissented, joined predictably by Douglas and, unexpectedly, by Minton. "The balancing in this case," writes Urofsky, who shares their reservations about *Feiner*, "totally ignored the values of free speech" (Urofsky 1997a, 168).

## Group Libel

The values of free speech also received what Black and Douglas regarded as inadequate support in *Beauharnais v. Illinois* (1952). In that case Frankfurter developed the concept of "group libel," a creation Black and Douglas feared might stifle thought and speech. Joseph Beauharnais was the head of an organization called the White Circle League, which distributed on street corners antiblack leaflets, in the form of petitions to the mayor and city council. These asked that the police be used to halt further encroachment by African Americans into previously all-white neighborhoods. The leaflets referred to the need "to prevent the white race from becoming mongrelized by the negro" and to the "rapes, robberies, knives, guns and marijuana of the negro." They also appealed for people to join the White Circle League and for financial contributions. For distributing these leaflets, Beauharnais was prosecuted under an Illinois law making it unlawful to publish or exhibit any writing, picture, drama, or motion picture that "portrays depravity, criminality, unchastity, or lack of virtue of a class of citizens of any race, color, creed or religion . . . or exposes the citizens of any race, color, creed or religion to contempt, derision, or obloquy, or which is productive of breach of the peace or riots" (*Beauharnais* 1952, 251).

   The Supreme Court affirmed Beauharnais's conviction and the constitutionality of the statute by a 5–4 vote. Writing for the majority, Frankfurter observed that every state provided for the punishment of libels directed at individuals. Clearly, it was libelous falsely to accuse someone of being a rapist, a robber, a carrier of knives and guns, and a user of marijuana. The only question then, as far as Frankfurter was concerned, was whether the Fourteenth Amendment prevented states from punishing such libels when they were directed at "collectivities" and flagrantly disseminated. He did not think so. Frankfurter delved into the long history of racial tensions in Illinois, which seemed to him to show that "we would deny experience to say that the Illinois legislature was without reason in seeking ways to curb false or malicious defamation of racial and religious groups" (*Beauharnais* 1952, 261). The Court had to trust legislative judgments, he maintained, and to leave the states with some room to employ trial and error to determine the best policies for dealing with difficult social issues. If legislatures abused their discretion by passing under the guise of punishing group libel laws that encroached on freedom of utterance, the Supreme Court could nullify the offending statutes.

The very Illinois law at issue in this case encroached on the First Amendment right of citizens to petition the government for redress of grievances, Black believed. He was not impressed by Frankfurter's attempt to condone the censorship for which it provided by painstakingly analogizing this statute to the law of criminal libel. "[T]he sugar coating does not make the censorship less deadly," Black commented caustically (*Beauharnais* 1952, 271). Douglas joined his dissent and also wrote one of his own, which Reed joined. More surprising was Jackson's dissenting opinion. He agreed with his frequent ally, Frankfurter, that states had the power to pass group libel laws. Jackson believed, however, that the clear-and-present-danger test, of which he was normally quite critical, should be employed to determine the constitutionality of such laws. The leaflet at issue in this case had been held punishable without any showing of the probable consequences of its publication. Such a demonstration was necessary, Jackson believed, to make this sort of restriction on expression constitutional.

With a bare majority of the Court supporting Frankfurter, the group libel concept he had invented to justify the restrictions placed on Beauharnais's expression slipped into constitutional law with a less than impressive mandate. This decision did not generate much enthusiasm, and for a long time it seemed rather unimportant. *Beauharnais* would receive renewed attention in the 1990s, however, when the adoption by many colleges and universities of regulations prohibiting hate speech that attacked others on the basis of their gender, race, ethnicity, or sexual orientation would trigger heated debate about the constitutionality of laws prohibiting what amounted to the libeling of particular groups. This Vinson Court precedent would be offered up to justify laws that conservatives condemned for requiring what they characterized as "politically correct" speech.

## The First Amendment and Picketing

The Vinson Court tolerated not only the punishment of speech that derogated particular groups but also restrictions on labor union picketing. In cases such as *Senn v. Tile*

*Layers' Union* (1937), *Thornhill v. Alabama* (1940), and *American Federation of Labor v. Swing* (1941), the Hughes Court had taken the position that peaceful picketing was a form of communication, protected by the First Amendment. Although a Frankfurter opinion in *Carpenters and Joiners Union v. Ritter's Café* (1942) implied that it might involve something more, the Stone Court held in that case that a union could not be prohibited from engaging in peaceful picketing even in the absence of a normal type of labor dispute. The Vinson Court picked up the suggestion in Frankfurter's opinion, however, and turned it into constitutional doctrine.

In *Giboney v. Empire Storage* (1949) the Vinson Court upheld an injunction a Missouri court had issued, pursuant to a state law against restraint of trade, that prohibited a union from picketing an ice company in response to its refusal to enter into an agreement the union had signed with other wholesale ice distributors not to sell to nonunion retailers. When the Court first discussed the case, Black, Douglas, Reed, Murphy, and Rutledge all voted to reverse the state court. At that point Black remarked that an injunction against picketing differed little from one against a newspaper forbidding it to publish something that would violate a law; both were impermissible prior restraints on expression. Frankfurter argued, however, that picketing was more than speech, and eventually Black and the other members of what it had appeared would be a liberal majority to overturn the injunction came around to his point of view. Black wrote an opinion for a unanimous Court in which he asserted that the right to picket must be balanced against other social values. "Here the picketers [had done] more than just exercise their freedom of expression; they had attempted to use economic influence to coerce the employer in a manner contrary to state policy" (Urofsky 1997a, 198). Freedom of speech and press did not protect speaking and writing that were part of a course of conduct that violated a valid criminal law. Black offered assurances that in holding this, the Court was "mindful of the essential importance to our society of a vigilant protection of freedom of speech and press" (*Giboney* 1949, 501).

Nevertheless, *Giboney* marked the beginning of what Urofsky characterizes as "a new circumspection regarding picketing" (Urofsky 1997a, 200). In *International Brotherhood of Teamsters v. Hanke* (1950), for example, the Court held that a state might sometimes prohibit picketing even if the union's goal was legal. The objective of the Teamsters Union was to pressure two Seattle used car dealerships into becoming union shops, even though both were owner-operated and had no employees. If they did what the union wanted, the dealers contended, they would then have to close on nights and weekends in order to comply with a maximum hours limitation the union wanted to impose to protect its members, and that would force them out of business. State judges enjoined the Teamsters' picketing, and the Vinson Court affirmed their action by a 5–4 vote. Speaking for a plurality that also included Jackson, Burton, and Vinson, Frankfurter took the position that the injunction was justified because the State of

Washington was free to strike whatever balance it wanted between competing economic interests. His principal feat, according to C. Herman Pritchett, "was making the famous 1937 case of *Senn v. Tile Layers' Protective Union*, which had been favorable to picketing, support a conclusion . . . which restricted picketing" (Pritchett 1954, 56–57). Unlike Frankfurter, Black had not entirely abandoned labor unions and the protection of their right to engage in peaceful picketing. He dissented, along with Minton and Reed, who published an opinion expressing their belief that the Court's earlier decisions had established a "doctrine that 'peaceful picketing and truthful publicity' is protected by the constitutional guaranty of the right of free speech" (*Hanke* 1950, 484). That did not appear to be a view shared by a majority of the Vinson Court, however.

## The Vinson Court and Labor Rights

Picketing was only one of the areas in which the Vinson Court proved less protective of organized labor than its immediate predecessors had been. Since the start of the New Deal the federal government had been committed to safeguarding the right of workers to organize and bargain collectively. A number of legislative measures, such as the National Industrial Recovery Act of 1933 (NIRA) and the National Labor Relations (Wagner) Act of 1935, reflected the high priority given labor on the administration's policy agenda. The Wagner Act had created the National Labor Relations Board (NLRB) to administer the act and authorized it to umpire a broad range of questions involving the relationship of employers and employees.

The Hughes Court upheld that law. Following the so-called Court-packing episode in 1937, it used the "stream of commerce" and "effect on commerce" theories to justify government regulation of labor relations. For the first time, the Court saw the economy not as an infinite number of discrete, local events, but as a national, integrated whole. When industries "organize themselves on a national scale, making their relation to interstate commerce the dominant factor in their activities," Chief Justice Hughes said in *National Labor Relations Board v. Jones and Laughlin Steel Company* (1937), "how can it be maintained that their industrial labor relations constitute a forbidden field into which Congress may not enter when it is necessary to protect interstate commerce from the paralyzing consequences of industrial war?" (*Jones and Laughlin Steel* 1937, 41). *Jones and Laughlin Steel* and its companion case, *National Labor Relations Board v. Friedman-Harry Marks Clothing Company*, had "important and immediate consequences." The Wagner Act "had not only injected the federal government into a new field but had substantially changed the rules of the marketplace, giving more power to workers and their unions" (Urofsky 1997a, 185).

Labor also benefited from the Court's decisions dealing with the First Amendment's protection of speech. The changes in the Court's membership following 1937 prompted various groups and individuals to seek out a "broader interpretation of constitutionally protected rights." Organized labor, among others, initiated several cases testing the First Amendment's Speech Clause. In *Senn v. Tile Layers' Union* (1937), Justice Brandeis suggested that picketing, aside from its role in labor disputes, might also be a form of speech. Justice Murphy followed with an extremely broad interpretation of picketing as expression in *Thornhill v. Alabama* (1940), declaring that if free debate were to "fulfill its historic function, it must embrace all issues about which information is needed or appropriate" (*Thornhill* 1940, 102).

As the trade union movement gained strength during the New Deal period, it also sought other kinds of First Amendment protection from the courts. For example, in *Hague v. Congress of Industrial Organizations* (1939), the Congress of Industrial Organizations (CIO) successfully challenged a Jersey City ordinance requiring permits for public meetings. This ordinance had been used against union organizers on the ground that they were Communists. The Court concluded that it had been made an "instrument of arbitrary suppression of free expression" (*Hague* 1939, 516). Similarly, in *Thomas v. Collins* (1945), the Court voided a Texas statute that required labor union officials to secure an organizer's card before soliciting for members. Four members of the Court dissented, however, claiming that a state could regulate public meetings for the purpose of maintaining peace and order, provided it administered the rules in a neutral manner. Within two years the dissenters on the Stone Court would become the majority on the Vinson Court.

During World War II the Roosevelt administration subordinated all labor issues to maintaining wartime production requirements, and many union leaders became concerned that the government's defense needs could be detrimental to the labor movement. Officials in the Roosevelt administration attempted to protect the gains labor had made prior to the war in exchange for the support of union officials in meeting the needs of wartime. When the war ended, labor was effusively praised by administration spokespeople. Antilabor sentiment had increased during the war, however. Congress had created the National War Labor Board to manage controversies between employers and employees that might impact on war production, and while workdays lost to strikes decreased significantly, board actions "did not always sit well with particular groups of workers" (Urofsky 1997a, 189).

Despite the efforts of the War Labor Board, there were strikes during the war. The most serious of these was led by John L. Lewis, head of the United Mine Workers (UMW). When he took his men out on strike in April 1943, Roosevelt seized the coal mines and blamed Lewis for the stalemated contract negotiations. Although the president received some criticism for the way he handled the situation, most blamed Lewis for acting against national interest in the midst of a war emergency. As a result of the coal strikes, Congress passed the War Labor Disputes (Smith-Connally) Act of 1943. That law authorized the president to take control of industries critical to the war effort if other methods to resolve labor disputes failed. Among its provisions was one forbidding union contributions to political campaigns, a precursor of one of the elements in the Taft-Hartley Act of 1947 (Urofsky 1997a, 190).

The War Labor Board was largely successful in maintaining labor peace during the World War II, and there were no challenges to its authority. Hence, there were no Supreme Court decisions about the board. The equilibrium that existed during the war among labor, management, and the government deteriorated rapidly as the country began the postwar reconversion of the economy, however. Congress removed wage and production controls at the close of hostilities. Prices for virtually all goods skyrocketed immediately, and strikes erupted as workers demanded higher wages to enable them to pay inflated prices. Conservative politicians attributed the runaway inflation to the excessive demands of unions. At the same time, congressional opponents of organized labor began to work on scaling back the gains unions had secured through the Wagner Act. John L. Lewis, whose conduct had precipitated the Smith-Connally Act, fueled the antilabor sentiment in 1946, and this time his actions spawned a case that reached the Supreme Court.

On May 21, 1946, in order to end a costly strike, the federal government seized control of the country's bituminous coal mines. Soon after the seizure, Interior Secretary Julius Krug and Lewis reached an agreement and signed a contract covering the duration of government control. Over the next few months, Lewis concluded his miners deserved better, and he declared his intention to use provisions of the contract with the private coal operators to terminate the agreement with the government. On November 15, Lewis informed Krug that the contract would be terminated five days later. His announcement was the "equivalent of a strike order since his miners would not work without a contract" (Urofsky 1997a, 191). The Truman administration indicated it would renegotiate even though Secretary Krug believed the agreement reached the preceding May was still in effect. The government then sought a temporary restraining order to prevent the strike. An injunction was issued, but Lewis and the UMW ignored it, arguing that the Norris-LaGuardia Act of 1932, which "prohibited courts from issuing injunctions in private labor disputes, also applied to the federal government" (Urofsky 1997a, 191).

U.S. District Court Judge Alan Goldsborough rejected the UMW argument, made the temporary restraining order permanent, and fined both the UMW and Lewis for civil and criminal contempt. Three days after the contempt citations, Lewis ordered the miners to go back to work until the Supreme Court had an opportunity to hear arguments in the case. Although the government had prevailed with Judge Goldsborough, it asked the Supreme Court for expedited review. Even though Lewis ended the strike threat, the Court agreed to this request. It also consolidated the union's case with that of its president. The central issue seemingly could not have been clearer: Did the Norris-LaGuardia Act apply to the government as an employer? Several other questions stemmed from that one, including: What was the status of the contract between the UMW and the private operators? Could the union and Lewis be held in contempt? If so, could they be found in contempt in a joint proceeding? And had Judge Goldsborough imposed an excessive fine?

The Vinson Court justices shared, at least to a large degree, the generally held view that U.S. workers had performed admirably during the war. At the same time, they recognized the necessity to preserve the integrity of the judiciary. Judge Goldsborough might have been wrong in his decision, but a court order was a court order, and it had to be obeyed. Lewis had in effect "thumbed his nose" at the judge's order and at the federal courts more generally. His defiance of the restraining order simply could not be tolerated. The Court issued its decision on March 6, 1947, with "no fewer than seven separate questions divid[ing] the justices" (Urofsky 1997a, 193).

Five members of the Court—Vinson, Reed, Burton, Black, and Douglas—concluded that the Norris-LaGuardia Act did not apply to the government. As they read the language and legislative history of that law, Congress had intended it to apply only to private employers. This conclusion was somewhat dubious since Justice Frankfurter, who had participated in the writing of Norris-LaGuardia, adamantly dissented. These same five justices further determined that when the government seized the mines, it had become the proprietor, and the contract negotiated by Lewis and Secretary Krug superseded any contract between the miners and the private owners in existence at the time the seizure took place.

Jackson joined the majority in deciding that injunctive relief was available to the government in this situation, a conclusion that Frankfurter vigorously disputed. The War Labor Disputes Act of 1943 had provided statutory justification for seizure of the mines. The legislative history of that measure indicated that Congress had "specifically rejected the use of injunction as a remedy against interference with seized plants." As Frankfurter pointed out, "the whole course of legislation indicates that Congress withheld the remedy of injunction. The Court now holds that Congress authorized the injunction." If the government had become the private employer the Court judged it to be, then the Norris-LaGuardia Act applied to the government because it stood in the place of the private employer. As a result, the remedy of injunction was not available to it. If the government had not become the equivalent of a private employer, on the other hand, then the judgment made by Congress in passing the War Labor Disputes Act precluded recourse to injunction (Urofsky 1997a, 193–194).

With only Murphy and Rutledge dissenting, the Court affirmed the contempt convictions of Lewis and his union for ignoring the restraining order. This result was not unexpected. Most judges are of the view that the appropriate way to challenge a court order is to comply and then appeal. Lewis and the UMW did neither, but defied the order instead. In the Court's view, Judge Goldsborough was trying "to preserve existing conditions while [he] was determining [his] own authority to grant injunctive relief." The defendants, in making their "private determination of the law, acted at their peril," and their disobedience constituted criminal contempt (*United States v. United Mine Workers* 1947, 293). Even Frankfurter, so insistent that Judge Goldsborough could not enjoin the union, agreed that once a restraining order had been issued, Lewis and the union needed to comply with it. "The greater the power that defies law," Frankfurter argued, "the less tolerant can this Court be of defiance" (*United States v. United Mine Workers* 1947, 312).

The Court overlooked the joint trial of the union and Lewis for civil and criminal contempt, concluding that there had been no "substantial prejudice" to either party. Murphy and Rutledge disagreed on this point. According to Rutledge, the "idea that a criminal prosecution and a civil suit for damages or equitable relief could be hashed together in a single criminal-civil hodgepodge would be shocking to every American lawyer and to most citizens" (*United States v. United Mine Workers* 1947, 364). Finally, the Court decided that Judge Goldsborough's $3.5-million fine on the UMW was excessive and ordered the amount reduced to $700,000, with the remaining $2.8 million to be imposed only if the union failed to withdraw its November 15 strike notice. The $10,000 fine on Lewis was upheld.

The Vinson Court had to deal with labor-management issues in radio as well as the coal industry. In 1946 Congress had passed the Lea Act, commonly called the "anti-Petrillo Act," which made it illegal for the American Federation of Musicians (AFM), headed by James Petrillo, to bargain with radio broadcasters over such issues as hiring standby musicians and paying for rebroadcasts of live performances. The measure was aimed at curbing the "feather-bedding" practices of the union by which it pressured radio stations to employ large studio orchestras. The union challenged the law, and a federal district court found it impermissibly vague. The Vinson Court ruled against the AFM and its leader in *United States v. Petrillo* (1947), reversing the lower court's vagueness decision and remanding issues about free speech and involuntary servitude to the trial court.

Antilabor conservatives had a bigger target than union musicians. It was, of course, the Wagner Act. The initial proposal to change it, the Hatch-Burton-Ball bill, came in 1945 with the first wave of postwar strikes. That measure proposed to place all federal mediation and conciliation activities under a new agency, establish an unfair labor practices board to hear and rule on complaints by either labor or management, prohibit the closed shop (an arrangement in which only union members could be hired), require arbitration in certain circumstances, and make penalties applicable equally to unions and management. The bill never left committee, but a stronger version did. It provided for a federal mediation board and a sixty-day cooling-off period before any strike could be called, and also stipulated that workers who quit their jobs during the cooling-off period would lose their rights under the Wagner Act. The bill also proposed a ban on secondary boycotts and jurisdictional strikes and authorized courts to issue injunctions to prevent violence or disruptive picketing. Truman promptly vetoed the measure, and its supporters could not override him. Three months later Congress passed the Hobbs Act, which amended the Anti-Racketeering (Copeland) Act of 1934. The Copeland Act made extortion affecting commerce a crime. The original act had been aimed at organized crime and included an exemption for unions using lawful means to obtain their objectives. The Hobbs Act eliminated this exemption. All of these proposals laid the foundation for the Taft-Hartley Act of 1947.

The 80th Congress reflected a growing antiunion animus. Republicans as well as some conservative Democrats opposed the Wagner Act, and the disruptive strikes after the war strengthened their resolve to impose restrictions on labor unions. The Taft-Hartley Act gave management greater rights in labor disputes and curtailed some of organized labor's power. The statute prohibited the closed shop, secondary boycotts, and jurisdictional strikes. It made unions liable for breach of contract or for damages resulting from jurisdictional disputes. It provided for a "cooling-off" period before strikes and authorized the president to seek an injunction to delay for eighty days a work stoppage that would adversely affect the nation. Finally, the act prohibited political contributions by unions and excessive dues. Thirty states, taking advantage of Section 14b of the act, adopted laws restricting union power, the "most common being the so-called right to work statutes, which prohibited making union membership a condition of employment" (Urofsky and Finkelman 2002, 754–755).

The Wagner Act had designated a number of management practices as "unfair labor practices." The 80th Congress believed it had made federal policy far too favorable for unions. Consequently, Taft-Hartley established a comparable list of practices forbidden to labor. It also tightened procedural rules to reduce the discretion of administrative agencies, such as the NLRB. Senator Taft claimed, however, that the act was not intended to repeal the Wagner Act, only to correct its deficiencies. The new restrictions it placed upon the NLRB did not produce significant changes in the board's regulatory behavior, although its fact-finding processes did now more closely resemble a legal model. For organized labor the only real "take back" in the act was its rejection of the closed shop.

Like many postwar statutes, Taft-Hartley had "little regard for civil liberties," requiring union officials to swear they were not members of any subversive organizations. In some respects, this provision marked the beginning of the postwar Red Scare. It was the only section of Taft-Hartley to reach the Supreme Court, which upheld it in *American Communications Association v. Douds* (1950). Chief Justice Vinson, a "cold warrior from the start," could only "square the overly broad sweep of [this provision] with the First Amendment by ignoring it, and trying to ground the power [Congress had used] in the Commerce Clause" (Urofsky and Finkelman 2002, 755–756).

In the same antiunion vein was a unanimous 1949 decision upholding state laws prohibiting closed-shop labor agreements. Counsel for organized labor failed to convince the Court in *Lincoln Federal Labor Union v. Northwestern Iron and Metal Company* (and the companion case of *Whitaker v. North Carolina*) and *American Federation of Labor v. American Sash and Door Company* that the anti–closed shop provisions violated labor's rights to freedom of contract, free speech, and assembly. Speaking for the Court, Black tried to take some of the edge off the ruling by suggesting that it was only trying to remain consistent with its repudiation of substantive due process a decade earlier. He suggested that the unions were asking for a "return . . . to the due process philosophy that has been deliberately discarded." Although claiming constitutional protection from state laws discriminating against union members, the unions also "assert[ed] that the same Constitution forbids a state from providing the same protection for nonunion members" (*Lincoln Federal Labor Union v. Northwestern Iron and Metal Company* 1949, 537). The Court concluded that state law could act to protect those who did not belong to unions.

The Vinson Court also addressed several times the issue of labor's status under the federal antitrust laws. The problem was not a new one, having existed since the Sherman Act was passed in 1890. The Clayton Act of 1914 had ostensibly exempted labor from federal antitrust prohibitions, but the language of its Section 6 actually said only that the antitrust laws "should not be interpreted to prevent unions from unlawfully carrying out their legitimate goals." The conservative Taft Court "seized on this wording" and reiterated several times that the Clayton Act "had not freed unions from injunctive restraint by the courts when their actions so warranted, which meant that judges could continue to enjoin picketing and boycotts under the guise that these activities violated the antitrust laws" (Urofsky 1997a, 202). The Norris-LaGuardia Act of 1932 prevented federal courts from interfering in nonviolent labor disputes, and a number of states adopted similar statutes, applying to their courts. But questions about what union activities could come under federal antitrust regulations remained.

When employees seized a nonunion plant in Philadelphia and prevented the entry of plant managers and nonunion workers, the company filed a Sherman Act suit for triple damages. The Court held in *Apex Hosiery Company v. Leader* (1940) that, although some of the union actions might have been criminal under state law, they did not constitute the kind of interference with interstate commerce covered by the Sherman Act. In reaching this result, however, Justice Stone created some uncertainty about the test that should be applied in Sherman Act cases against unions. The following year, Justice Frankfurter said in *United States v. Hutcheson* (1941) that union activities were insulated from federal antitrust laws unless the union acted in concert with nonlabor groups to further its objectives. This appeared on the surface to be a clear-and-protective standard, but postwar circumstances would show that was not the case.

Following the war, the Vinson Court heard cases in which union activities went beyond traditional labor practices and affected commerce in ways that clearly impinged on antitrust policy. In *United Brotherhood of Carpenters and Joiners v. United States* (1947), for example, the Court reviewed a criminal prosecution of employers and unions for acting in concert to monopolize portions of the finished lumber business in the San Francisco area. The unions asserted that the Norris-LaGuardia Act protected their officers. There "was no doubt that the unions had engaged in anticompetitive and perhaps even criminal activity." A majority of the Vinson Court saw the "purpose and effect" of Norris-LaGuardia as restricting the "responsibility or liability in labor disputes of employer or employee associations . . . except upon clear proof" that the acts charged had been "expressly authorized, or necessarily followed from a granted authority, by the association" (*United Brotherhood* 1947, 406–407). Since the jury had not been instructed that liability was limited in this way, the Court reversed all the convictions. Frankfurter, Burton, and Vinson disagreed, concluding that the ruling had immunized "alert and powerful" unions as well as corporations involved in labor disputes from Sherman Act liability (*United Brotherhood* 1947, 422).

The Vinson Court's handling of labor picketing created substantial uncertainty about where the line was drawn between permissible and impermissible government regulation. The Vinson Court's picketing cases are discussed in more detail in the free speech section of this chapter. A few comments are appropriate here as well. Urofsky suggests that it is possible that had these cases come up a "decade or two later," after the Warren Court had "moved to a more protective position on speech and speech-related conduct, there might have been a more consistent pattern." But by the time the Vinson Court handed down the last of its picketing decisions, a "no-man's-land had been created that left the public, the unions, and the lower courts more than a little confused" (Urofsky 1997a, 201). Apparently, indiscriminate prohibitions of picketing were unconstitutional, but peaceful picketing could be regulated if a state determined that such restrictions served the public interest.

The conservative postwar political climate pushed the Court to the view that labor picketing was so inextricably bound up with considerations of restraint of trade, labor-management relations, and other socioeconomic problems that substantial regulatory discretion must be left to the states. In *Giboney v. Empire Storage* (1949), for example, the Vinson Court sustained a Missouri court's injunction prohibiting picketing that had been intended to coerce an employer into an agreement that violated the state's antitrust laws. Even for Justice Black, the right to picket had to be balanced against other societal interests. The First Amendment does not mean, Black argued, that "conduct otherwise unlawful is always immune from state regulation because an integral part of that conduct is carried on by display of placards by peaceful picketers" (*Giboney* 1949, 498).

The following year, the Vinson Court reiterated this point in *International Brotherhood of Teamsters v. Hanke* (1950). It ruled that a state might ban picketing, even where a union's objectives were lawful, when it might produce ends considered by the state to be socially undesirable. The Court's new "circumspection" regarding picketing appeared in other cases, such as *Building Services Employees Union v. Gazzam* (1950), *Hughes v. Superior Court of California* (1950), and *Local Union No. 10 v. Graham* (1953). Although its decisions "did not mark a return to the days before Norris-LaGuardia," they did indicate that "just as labor no longer enjoyed a privileged position with Congress, so too the courts believed that time had come to strike a balance" (Urofsky 1997a, 200).

Just before Vinson took the center chair, the Stone Court had decided *Hunt v. Crumboch* (1945), another Sherman Act case. The Court ruled that the union workers' collective decision to withhold their labor did not violate the federal antitrust law, so Justice Jackson wrote a powerful dissent that reflects the conflict that divided the Court. He declared that the labor movement

> has come full circle. The working man has struggled long, the fight has been filled with hatred, and conflict has been dangerous, but now workers may not be deprived of their livelihood merely because their employers opposed and they favor unions. Labor has won other rights as well, unemployment compensation, old-age benefits and, what is most important and the basis of all gains, the recognition than the opportunity to earn his support is not alone the concern of the individual but is the problem which all organized societies must contend with and conquer if they are to survive. This Court now sustains the claim of a union to the right to deny participation in the economic world to an employer simply because the union dislikes him. The Court permits to employees the same arbitrary dominance over the economic sphere which they control that labor so long, so bitterly and so rightly asserted should belong to no man. (*Hunt* 1995, 830–831)

The concern that labor had gotten too powerful, a perception that generalized beyond the Court, contributed to the passage of Taft-Hartley.

When the nation was threatened with a steel strike during the Korean War, Taft-Hartley provided President Truman with the means of dealing with this labor-management crisis. It included procedures whereby the government could invoke an eighty-day "cooling-off" period to at least postpone any strike that could adversely affect the public interest. But Truman did not want to use the Taft-Hartley Act, which had become law over his veto. Although it would not have provided a permanent solution, this statute "involved statutory justification and would have bought time in which a settlement might be reached—or, failing that, Congress could have imposed a solution through legislation." Truman chose not to invoke Taft-Hartley. Instead, he seized the steel mills, informed Congress of what he had done, and "invited its astounded members to take legislative action if they thought it necessary" (Urofsky and Finkelman 2002, 770). Since no statute authorized his action, the president based his executive order seizing the mills on the inherent powers of his office. The steel companies challenged it in court, but most experts expected the president would prevail in this litigation. To their surprise, the Vinson Court ruled against Truman. By a 6–3 vote it held in *Youngstown Sheet and Tube Company v. Sawyer* (1952), that the president had exceeded his constitutional authority. The *Youngstown* case is discussed in more detail elsewhere in this chapter, but brief mention is warranted here because of the labor conflict that precipitated Truman's seizure order. This case was one of many in which the president's political allies in organized labor fared badly before the Vinson Court.

## Incorporation

Civil liberties also fared badly in the Vinson Court. Yet, despite the antilibertarian tenor of those times, the Vinson era was a seminal period for one of the most important developments in this area of constitutional law, the "incorporation" of much of the Bill of Rights into the Due Process Clause of the Fourteenth Amendment. "Incorporation" became the focus of intense debate within the Vinson Court. The controversy concerned whether provisions of the federal Bill of Rights applied to actions of state governments, and its implications were substantial and readily apparent. Before 1868, the year in which the Fourteenth Amendment was added to the Constitution, the Bill of Rights placed constraints on the federal government exclusively. In 1833, Chief Justice John Marshall offered the definitive pre–Fourteenth Amendment analysis of their reach in *Barron v. Baltimore:* The Bill of Rights "constrain[s] only the government created by the document," the federal government (*Barron* 1833, 247). Put another way, the limits on state actions that might violate individual rights came exclusively from state law. The language of the Fourteenth Amendment made the *Barron* ruling a "dead letter," however, although not for several decades.

The Fourteenth Amendment provides in part that a state may not "deprive any person of life, liberty, or property, without due process of law." There have been a variety of views concerning how much the Fourteenth Amendment actually conveys Bill of Rights provisions to the states. In the decades immediately following 1868, the Supreme Court was reluctant to use it for that purpose. Rather, the Court largely maintained Marshall's interpretation. The Court eventually settled on a "selective" approach to incorporation, which applied to the states those rights that, according to Justice Benjamin Cardozo, are of the "very essence of a scheme or ordered liberty" (*Palko v. Connecticut* 1937, 325). Even prior to *Palko*, however, the Court had incorporated two clauses of the First Amendment. The Taft Court reached the conclusion that these applied to the states in *Gitlow v. New York* (1925), where Justice Sanford observed that "we may and do assume that freedom of speech and of the press—

which are protected by the First Amendment from abridgment by Congress—are among the fundamental personal rights and liberties protected by the due process clause of the Fourteenth Amendment from impairment by the states" (*Gitlow* 1925, 666). Extension of the free press protection to the states in *Gitlow* was reinforced by the Hughes Court in the prior restraint case of *Near v. Minnesota* (1931). *Palko* subsequently provided the theoretical framework for the incorporation of other civil liberties guarantees as well.

Following *Palko*, the Hughes Court incorporated the First Amendment provisions on assembly (*DeJonge v.* Oregon 1937) and free exercise of religion (*Cantwell v. Connecticut* 1940). The Stone Court, which followed it, incorporated no other Bill of Rights provisions, even though a number of its justices, including Black and Douglas, strongly supported further incorporation. But the Stone Court was able to consider First Amendment cases from state courts because it had already been determined that, with respect to freedom of expression, the states were subject to the same constitutional limitations that applied to the federal government. The significance of the fact that most of the First Amendment had been incorporated was magnified because of the "preferred position" doctrine. It posited a role for the Court suggested by Justice Harlan Fiske Stone in *United States v. Carolene Products Company* (1938), where he argued that the deference usually accorded legislative judgments in matters of economic regulation might not apply to cases arising under the Bill of Rights. Under the preferred position doctrine, the usual presumption of validity given to legislative judgments is overridden by the elevated or "preferred" position assigned to the freedoms secured by the Bill of Rights. The "preferred position" view was accepted by a majority of Supreme Court justices until Stone's death and his replacement by Vinson. The Vinson Court's contribution to the incorporation process will be discussed in the religious freedom and rights of the accused sections that follow.

## Free Exercise of Religion

Prior to the 1930s there had been practically no case law involving the religion clauses of the First Amendment. In 1879 a Mormon challenge to a federal law banning bigamy in the territories had been rejected by the Court, which clearly distinguished belief and action; belief was entitled to full protection, it said, whereas religious conduct or practices had to comply with generally applicable laws. Although nearly every state afforded some guarantee of religious freedom, nonmainstream sects often ran afoul of generally applicable secular laws. The Jehovah's Witnesses, for example, frequently encountered difficulties with state statutes and local ordinances. Beginning in the 1930s, the Witnesses challenged these laws on free exercise of religion grounds. A number of the early cases involved door-to-door solicitation or street-corner preaching. In these the Court often found for the Witnesses on free speech grounds.

The Hughes Court ruled for them in *Cantwell v. Connecticut* (1940), and in doing so extended the Free Exercise Clause to the states. It also adjusted the belief-action distinction to provide constitutional protection for some conduct of religious practitioners. This development would prove significant to evolving free exercise jurisprudence, but it was not crucial to the Vinson Court's only major free exercise case, *Kedroff v. St. Nicholas Cathedral* (1952). Following the Russian Revolution in 1917, members of the Russian Orthodox Church in the United States sought to separate themselves from the administrative control of the mother church in Russia. The New York legislature, wishing to free U.S. believers from the subversive influences of the Russian church, enacted the Religious Corporations Act, which required that all churches under the control of the Russian Church be governed instead by the ecclesiastical body of the U.S. separatist movement. This law gave rise to a dispute about the possession and use of the church building in New York City. The New York Court of Appeals upheld the validity of the statute against a free exercise challenge by the appointees of the mother church in Russia.

The Vinson Court, with Reed writing the opinion, reversed the New York court. It had declined to recognize the appointee of the Moscow Hierarchy of the Russian Orthodox Church under terms of the Religious Corporations Act. An enactment by a legislature, Reed said, "cannot validate [an] action which the Constitution prohibits." The statute transferred the control of Russian Orthodox churches in New York to the governing authorities of the Russian Church in the United States. Legislation that "regulates church administration, the operations of the churches [and] the appointment of clergy . . . prohibits the free exercise of religion." Although the Religious Corporations Act required New York churches to "in all other respects conform to, maintain and follow the faith, doctrine, ritual, communion, discipline, canon law, traditions and usages" of the Russian Orthodox Church, "their conformity is by legislative fiat and subject to legislative will" (*Kedroff* 1952, 107). In upholding the validity of the New York law, the state court apparently had assumed that the statute "does nothing more than permit the trustees of the Cathedral to use it for services consistent with the desires of the members of the Russian Church in America." The reach of the law, however, "goes far beyond that point," Reed suggested. By "fiat it displaced one church administrator with another." It passed control of "matters strictly ecclesiastical from one church to another." It thus "intrude[d] for the benefit of one segment of a church the power of a state into the forbidden area of religious freedom contrary to the principles of the First Amendment" (*Kedroff* 1952, 119). Ours is a government, Reed concluded, which "by the law of its being allows no statute, state or national, that prohibits the free exercise of religion." There were occasions when civil courts had to draw lines between the responsibilities of church and state for the "disposition or use of property." Even in those cases, however, when the property right "follows as an incident from decisions of the church custom or law on ecclesiastical issues, the church rule controls" (*Kedroff* 1952, 120).

## *Establishment of Religion*

*Kedroff* involved the Free Exercise Clause, but it had been assumed since the Court incorporated that guarantee in *Cantwell*, that the Establishment Clause would also apply to the states. It was a "very nearly forgotten and untested provision of the First Amendment," however, at least when compared with the Free Exercise Clause (Pritchett 1954, 11–12). It took center stage when the Vinson Court inquired into the highly sensitive area of public aid to private schools, particularly Catholic parochial ones. In 1930, the Hughes Court had unanimously upheld in *Cochran v. Louisiana State Board of Education* a Louisiana law providing free textbooks to pupils in both public and private schools. The theory underlying *Cochran* was that the aid was being given to the children and not to the school, and hence that the state was assisting them rather than religion. Most state courts embraced this reasoning, which came to be known as the "child benefit" doctrine.

The Vinson Court used this child benefit rationale in resolving its first establishment case, *Everson v. Board of Education of Ewing Township* (1947). There it reviewed a state law under which parents could be reimbursed for costs incurred in transporting their children to both public and private schools. Ewing Township, acting pursuant to this statute, authorized transportation reimbursements to parents of all children attending school in the township, including those enrolled in religious institutions. By a 5–4 vote (with Black, Douglas, Murphy, Vinson, and Reed in the majority), the Court held that this was simply a public welfare measure and that the First Amendment did not require exclusion of persons of any faith from receiving benefits under it.

Black, who wrote for the majority, suggested that it was "much too late to argue that legislation intended to facilitate the opportunity of children to get a secular education serves no public purpose." It was not the case that a law had "a private rather than a public purpose because it provides that tax-raised funds will be paid to reimburse individuals on account of money spent by them in a way which furthers a public program" (*Everson* 1947, 7). Black proceeded to declare that, like the Free Exercise Clause, the First Amendment's prohibition of the establishment of religion applied to the states through the due process language of the Fourteenth Amendment. The Establishment Clause, he announced, meant at least that neither a "state nor the Federal Government can set up a church." Neither could pass laws that "aid one religion, aid all religions, or prefer one religion over another." Neither could "force nor influence a person to go to or to remain away from church against his will or force him to profess a belief or disbelief in any religion." Further, no person could be punished for "entertaining or professing religious beliefs or disbeliefs, for church attendance or nonattendance." No tax in any amount could "be levied to support any religious activities or institutions, whatever they may be called, or whatever form they may adopt to teach or practice religion." Neither a state nor the federal government could "openly or secretly, participate in the affairs of any religious organizations or groups and vice versa." Borrowing Jefferson's language, Black proclaimed that the Establishment Clause had been intended to "erect a wall of separation between Church and State" (*Everson* 1947, 15–16).

"Measured by these standards," Black continued, the Court could not say that the First Amendment prohibited New Jersey from spending tax-raised funds to pay the bus fares of parochial school pupils as a part of a "general program under which it pays the fares of pupils attending public and other schools." He acknowledged that the reimbursement program helped get students to church schools, but compared the state's interest in safely transporting children to providing policemen to protect them from the "very real hazards of traffic." Similarly, parents might be reluctant to permit their children to attend schools that the "state had cut off from such general services as ordinary police and fire protection, connections for sewage disposal, public highways and sidewalks." Denying church schools such services "so separate and so indisputably marked off from the religious function," would make it difficult for religious schools to operate. That was "obviously not the purpose of the First Amendment." The Establishment Clause required government "to be neutral in its relations with groups of religious believers and nonbelievers; it does not require the state to be their adversary." The Constitution did not demand an adversary relationship between religion and government—state power was "no more to be used so as to handicap religions than . . . to favor them." The Court concluded that the New Jersey law under review in *Everson* did "no more than provide a general program to help parents get . . . children, regardless of their religion, safely and expeditiously to and from accredited schools" (*Everson* 1947, 17–18).

Initially, only Justices Frankfurter and Rutledge voted against upholding the New Jersey law. Frankfurter tried to find another vote against it by lobbying Frank Murphy, the only Catholic member of the Court. He urged him to follow his conscience and uphold the doctrine of separation of church and state. When Murphy refused to vote against the New Jersey law, Frankfurter "lambasted him for failing to live up to his responsibilities as a judge" and suggested that his biographers would have to "explain away how [he] had allowed his Catholicism to take precedence over his responsibilities as a justice on the high court" (Urofsky 1997a, 234).

Besides lobbying Murphy, Frankfurter pressured Rutledge to strengthen his dissent. After six revisions, Rutledge produced one of his best opinions. Like Black, he employed the "high wall of separation" metaphor. His conclusion, however, was the opposite of Black's—if one really believed in the strict separation of church and state, the New Jersey bus law could not be upheld. After examining Black's historical arguments, Rutledge reached the conclusion that "money taken by taxation from one is not to be used or given to support another's religious training or belief, or indeed one's own"; "the prohibition is absolute." Rutledge asked whether New Jersey's reimbursement program "furnishes support for religion by the use of the taxing power? . . . Certainly it does," he answered, "if the test remains undiluted as Jefferson and Madison made it" (*Everson* 1947, 44–45).

Aware of Frankfurter's efforts to draw other justices away from the majority, Black revised his own opinion, "bolstering the basic theme that the First Amendment required a high wall of separation—but still approving the reimbursement law." Frankfurter would later say it was "characteristic of [him] to utter noble sentiments and depart from them in practice" (Urofsky 1997a, 234). Certainly, the majority opinion did not provide a persuasive rebuttal to the dissenters' contention that paying for transportation to church schools constituted direct aid to religious education. Black's internally inconsistent opinion—beginning with a reference to the need to keep a high wall of separation between church and state and concluding by validating governmental assistance to church schools—inspired one of the greatest of all judicial epigrams: Jackson's comparison of Black's reasoning to Byron's Julia, who "whispering 'I will ne'er consent,'—consented" (*Everson* 1947, 19).

Jackson added that the prohibition against establishment of religion "cannot be circumvented by a subsidy, bonus or reimbursement of expense to individuals for receiving religious instruction and indoctrination" (*Everson* 1947, 24). The State "cannot make public business of religious worship or instruction, or of attendance at religious institutions of any character." The objective of the Establishment Clause was to "take every form of propagation of religion out of the realm of things which could directly or indirectly be made public business and thereby be supported in whole or in part at taxpayers' expense" (*Everson* 1947, 26). Religious teaching, Jackson continued, "cannot be a private affair when the state seeks to impose regulations which infringe on it indirectly, and a public affair when it comes to taxing citizens of one faith to aid another, or those of no faith to aid all." If the state could provide aid such as this to religious schools, it might also regulate them. Many groups have "sought aid from tax funds only to find that it carried political controls with it. Indeed this Court has declared that 'it is hardly lack of due process' for the Government to regulate that which it subsidizes" (*Everson* 1947, 27–28).

The ruling against which Jackson dissented so vigorously was controversial and brought a flood of mail to the Court. Its decision the following year in *McCollum v. Board of Education* (1948) provoked an even greater public response, however. *McCollum* was a challenge to a program of the Champaign, Illinois, school system, which had, like many districts across the country, set aside an hour out of the school week when clergy from a number of denominations could come into the schools to provide religious instruction to those students electing to receive it. The religious teachers were not paid by the schools, but they were under the supervision of the school superintendent. Also, attendance was compulsory for participants in the program.

The Court struck down the Champaign released-time program, with only Justice Reed dissenting. Black spoke for the eight-justice majority. Although only a year had passed since *Everson*, Black's Establishment Clause position had moved toward the view expressed by Rutledge in his dissent in that case. He wrote that the constitutional question posed by the released-time case "could not have been clearer." Black emphasized that the religious instructors, though not school employees, were "subject to the approval and supervision of the superintendent of schools." Students choosing not to take the religious instruction were required to leave their classrooms and go elsewhere in the building to continue their secular studies. Those excused from secular instruction "were required to be present at the religious classes. Reports of their presence or absence were to be made to their secular teachers." The state's compulsory education system "thus assists and is integrated with the program of religious instruction carried on by separate religious sects." As a result, the "tax-established and tax-supported public school system" was assisting religious groups in spreading their faith; this fell "squarely under the ban of the First Amendment (made applicable to the states by the Fourteenth) as we interpreted it in *Everson* (1947)" (*McCollum* 1948, 209–210). Black was emphatic that the Court's ruling did not "manifest a governmental hostility to religion or religious teachings." But, because the state's "tax-supported public school buildings were used for the dissemination of religious doctrines," the state was affording "sectarian groups an invaluable aid in that it help[ed] to provide pupils for their religious classes through the use of the state's compulsory public school machinery." That was, Black concluded, "not separation of Church and State" (*McCollum* 1948, 211–212).

Black and Frankfurter agreed that the released-time plan violated the Establishment Clause, but Black was not prepared to distance himself enough from his *Everson* opinion to satisfy his rival, who did not want *McCollum* in any way based on that opinion. Frankfurter and the other *Everson* dissenters agreed not to join Black's initial draft with its "approving references" to the earlier decision. Although Frankfurter refused to compromise, when Black agreed to omit certain references to *Everson*, Burton and Rutledge joined his opinion. Frankfurter was "furious," and although he would have preferred that others argue the point, he felt compelled to write his own concurring opinion (Urofsky 1997a, 235).

It began by noting that Frankfurter had dissented in *Everson* because he believed that "separation means separation, not something less." Although his language suggested categorical rejection of released-time programs, he said his remarks were only directed toward religious education that occurred in public school buildings. He saw public schools as an "Americanizing and unifying force," a place where children from all backgrounds "developed a common American outlook." Frankfurter feared that religious education in the schools would destroy that "most powerful agency for promoting cohesion among a heterogeneous democratic people." The public school, he believed, "must be kept scrupulously free from entanglement in the strife of sects" (Urofsky 1997a, 236).

The debate on released-time religious education did not end with *McCollum*. The Vinson Court revisited it in the 1952 case of *Zorach v. Clauson*. Following *McCollum*, a number of states, including New York, moved religious instruction off school property. Nonetheless, taxpayers challenged the New York program, contending it still involved state promotion of religion. The authority of the school, they argued, "supported participation in the program, public school teachers policed attendance, and normal classroom activities came to a halt so students in the program would not miss their secular education" (Urofsky 1997a, 236).

The primary difference between the New York plan and the one struck down in *McCollum* was that religious instruction did not take place on public school premises. This change was sufficient to gain it the support of three members of the *McCollum* majority who had voted to strike down the Champaign plan (Douglas, Vinson, and Burton), as well as two who had not been on the Court at the time of the earlier decision (Clark and Minton) and the lone *McCollum* dissenter (Reed). Black, Frankfurter, and Jackson, all in the *McCollum* majority, dissented in *Zorach*.

Douglas wrote for the six-justice majority. His opinion featured two themes. First, he sought to show that any system of rigid separation between church and state would be impossible. It would make government and religion adversaries—unfriendly and even hostile toward one another. Under such a regime, municipalities might be precluded from providing police or fire protection to religious groups. Douglas concluded, "that such a philosophy of hostility to religion could not be read into the Bill of Rights." He wanted not only to blunt the criticism directed at the Court following *McCollum*, but also to "find some grounds that would allow incidental benefits to religion yet would not create a situation in which tax dollars underwrote sectarian programs" (Urofsky 1997a, 237).

With that objective in mind, Douglas wrote, "We are a religious people whose institutions presuppose a Supreme Being." We foster an attitude on the part of government that "shows no partiality to any one group and that lets each flourish according to the zeal of its adherents and the appeal of its dogma." When the state "encourages religious instruction or cooperates with religious authorities . . .," Douglas continued, "it follows the best of our traditions" and it "respects the religious nature of our people and accommodates the public service to their spiritual needs." A contrary interpretation of the Establishment Clause would require that government show "a callous indifference to religious groups." Such a view would give preference to "those who believe in no religion over those who do believe." The Establishment Clause prohibited government from subsidizing religious groups, providing religious instruction, or using secular institutions to force one or some religion on any person. Douglas, however, found no constitutional requirement that "makes it necessary for government to be hostile to religion and to throw its weight against efforts to widen the effective scope of religious influence" (*Zorach* 1952, 313–314).

He disputed the contention that the released-time program involved the use of coercion to get public school students into religious classrooms. If there were any evidence in the record that the system was administered in a coercive manner or that teachers sought to persuade or force students to take religious instruction, then a "wholly different case would be presented," Douglas acknowledged. There was none, however. To the contrary, it would take "obtuse reasoning" to inject any free exercise issue into the released-time context. No one was "forced to go to the religious classroom and no religious exercise is brought to the classrooms of the public schools" (*Zorach* 1952, 311). The public schools merely accommodated their schedules to a program of outside religious instruction.

Black, Jackson, and Frankfurter all dissented. Jackson, who considered Douglas's opinion a "disaster," wrote to Frankfurter that "the battle for *separation* of Church and State is lost. From here on it is only a question of how far the intermixture will go." Frankfurter agreed with Jackson's views, but issued a separate dissent, in which he charged that the school system did not "close its doors" when some of its pupils went off to religious instruction. Yet, those who remained were "deprived of their opportunity for instruction since teachers did not plan substantive work, knowing a significant portion of their classes would be absent" (Urofsky 1997a, 237). Jackson seized on this same point. By compelling students not participating in the religious education program to attend other school activities, the state was clearly making "religious sects beneficiaries of its power to compel children to attend secular schools." As Jackson put it, the school "serves as a temporary jail for a pupil who will not go to church." This system, he continued, was clearly within the condemnation of the *McCollum* decision. Jackson condemned Douglas's attempt to distinguish the Illinois program from the New York one on the ground that the religious instruction took place outside the school building; he considered it "trivial, almost to the point of cynicism, magnifying . . . nonessential details and disparaging compulsion which was the underlying reason for invalidity" (*Zorach* 1952, 324–325).

Jackson observed further that the Constitution would not permit the state to require directly that "released time be spent under the control of a duly constituted religious body." Yet, the New York program accomplished that forbidden result by "indirection." The "greater effectiveness of this system" over voluntary attendance after school hours "is due to the truant officer who, if the youngster fails to go to the

Church school, dogs him back to the public schoolroom." Secular schooling was essentially suspended during the released time "so the nonreligious attendants will not forge ahead of the churchgoing absentees." The day that this country "ceases to be free for irreligion," Jackson concluded, "it will cease to be free for religion—except for the sect that can win political power." The same "epithetical jurisprudence used by the Court today to beat down those who oppose pressuring children into some religion can devise as good epithets tomorrow against those who object to pressuring them into a favored religion" (*Zorach* 1952, 325).

The opinion against which Jackson entered such a vigorous dissent suggests that the Court majority was "disposed to use any available method to quiet the storm caused by the *McCollum* decision." This impression is bolstered by the Court's ruling in the New Jersey Bible-reading case, *Doremus v. Board of Education*, decided a month prior to *Zorach*. In *Doremus* the Vinson Court avoided ruling on the constitutionality of a state statute providing for the reading of five verses of the Old Testament at the opening of each public school day. It resolved the case on the technical ground that the plaintiff lacked standing to sue. Douglas, Reed, and Burton, who were half of the majority in *Zorach*, dissented in *Doremus*, arguing that the Court should address the Bible-reading question. In any case, there "seem[ed] little doubt that additional controversies over the constitutional relation of church and state [would] continue to be pressed upon the Court." This was, political scientist C. Herman Pritchett believed, a "potentially explosive problem with which it will have to learn to live" (Pritchett 1954, 14). By softening the separationist tone of *McCollum*, however, *Zorach* did provide some underpinning for subsequent decisions, especially by the Burger Court, allowing government to take a position of "benevolent neutrality" toward religion.

## Adamson v. California *and the Incorporation Debate*

Although incorporating the Establishment Clause, the Vinson Court also engaged in a spirited internal debate over whether to apply the criminal justice provisions of the Bill of Rights to the states. The Truman appointees—Burton, Vinson, Minton, and Clark—generally followed Frankfurter's "call for judicial restraint and deference to the states," especially in the area of criminal procedure, where he "dominated the Court during the Vinson era." Justices who served between 1946 and 1953 "set the groundwork for the great due process revolution of the Warren era," but they did so "hesitatingly," and it was the positions taken by Black and Douglas in dissent that carried the day after Earl Warren became chief justice (Urofsky 1997a, 220).

During the Vinson years the debate over incorporation was about procedural due process. The pivotal question was not merely whether the framers of the Fourteenth Amendment intended to apply procedural protections from the Bill of Rights to the states, but about the meaning of due process itself. Both Black and Frankfurter had unconditionally rejected the use of substantive due process to nullify regulatory legislation. Procedural due process was another matter, however. Disputes about its meaning arose most often in criminal cases, and where the rights of the accused were concerned, there was substantial disagreement between Black and Frankfurter. Their divergent views "shaped the modern debate" (Urofsky 1997a, 220).

Frankfurter spoke of "canons of decency and fairness which express the notions of justice . . . even toward those charged with the most heinous offenses." The courts should not tolerate police tactics that "offend the community's sense of fair play and decency" or conduct that "shocks the conscience," he believed. Frankfurter saw due process as fundamental fairness and thought that, like beauty, it was a subjective concept. Black categorically rejected that view. If judges had the "discretion to determine fairness on the basis of what shocked them, then due process would vary from judge to judge and court to court." Black believed that constitutional protections were absolute in character. Frankfurter could not subscribe to such a rigid view of them. For him the Fourteenth Amendment's Due Process Clause itself provided a "sufficient limit on state abuse" (Urofsky 1997a, 221).

Black thought the Bill of Rights could give concrete content to the vague language of the Due Process Clause, but as far back as the 1880s the Court had rejected the argument that the Fourteenth Amendment had made the provisions of the first eight amendments applicable to the states. In *Twining v. New Jersey* (1908), it refused to invalidate a New Jersey law permitting a jury instruction that an unfavorable inference could be drawn from a defendant's unwillingness to take the stand in his own defense. The Fuller Court held that the Fifth Amendment privilege against self-incrimination did not extend to the states; thus it could not examine any specific practice claimed to abridge that privilege. Forty years later the Vinson Court revisited the issue *Twining* had decided in *Adamson v. California*. Admiral Dewey Adamson was an indigent African American who had twice been imprisoned for robbery. Seventeen years after his release from custody, he was arrested and charged with the murder of an elderly white woman. His fingerprints, which were found on a door in the woman's kitchen, constituted the only evidence linking him to the murder. At his trial, Adamson did not take the stand in his own defense, because his lawyer, wanting to keep the prosecutor from bringing up his prior criminal record, advised him not to. Under California law the state could suggest to the jury that it might draw an inference of guilt from a defendant's failure to testify. Following Adamson's conviction, his lawyer challenged this law, contending that it violated the Fourteenth Amendment. According to him, allowing comment on a defendant's failure to testify was equivalent to compelling the defendant to incriminate himself.

Frankfurter convinced a majority of his colleagues that *Twining* had already decided this issue. Reed's majority opinion acknowledged that such comment by a federal prosecutor would violate the Fifth Amendment. According to him, however, it was "settled law" that the privilege against self-incrimination was "not made effective against state action by the Fourteenth Amendment . . . right of national citizenship" (*Adamson* 1947, 51). Although the right to a fair trial was generally protected by the Fourteenth Amendment, it did "not draw all the rights of the federal Bill of Rights under its protection." That contention, Reed observed, had been "made and rejected" in *Palko v. Connecticut* (1937). *Palko* had held that those provisions of the Bill of Rights that were "'implicit in the concept of ordered liberty,' became secure from state interference by the [Due Process] clause. But it held nothing more" (*Adamson* 1947, 54). Reed deferred to the states to pursue their "own ideas of the most efficient administration of criminal justice." The purpose of due process, he continued, is "not to protect an accused against proper conviction but against unfair conviction." When evidence was before a jury that threatened conviction, it did "not seem unfair to require [the defendant] to choose between leaving the adverse evidence unexplained and subjecting himself to impeachment through disclosure of former crimes." A prosecutor's comment on failure to deny proven facts "does not tend to supply any missing element of proof of guilt." Rather, it "only directs attention to the strength of evidence for the prosecution or to the weakness of that for the defense" (*Adamson* 1947, 57–58). The Court remained convinced that the position *Twining* had taken was correct, because the Fifth Amendment protection against self-incrimination was simply not one of the fundamental rights inherent in "the concept of ordered liberty." "For a state to require testimony from an accused," Reed concluded, "is not necessarily a breach of a state's obligation to give a fair trial" (*Adamson* 1947, 54).

Black dissented, and after reviewing a draft of what he wrote in *Adamson*, Frankfurter, who had originally written only a brief concurrence, undertook a more extensive response to his rival. Frankfurter's interpretation of history indicated to him that the framers of the Fourteenth Amendment had not intended to subsume all of the Bill of Rights within it. He also sought to rebut Black's contention that the *Palko* formula was vague and left too much to judicial discretion—that "protection of rights relied on the mercy of individual subjectivity." The real issue, in Frankfurter's view, was not whether violation of a Bill of Rights provision was disclosed by the record of this case. Rather, the pivotal question was whether the trial had resulted in a conviction that deprived Adamson of due process. Review of that issue "inescapably imposes upon this Court an exercise of judgment upon the whole course of the proceedings in order to ascertain whether they offend those canons of decency and fairness which express the notions of justice." Such an application of the Due Process Clause did not mean that judges were "wholly at large," however. Judicial application of the Due Process Clause "must move within the limits of accepted notions of justice and is not to be based upon the idiosyncrasies of a merely personal judgment." An important safeguard against such individual judgment was an "alert deference to the judgment of the State court under review" (*Adamson* 1947, 67–68).

Frankfurter was responding to a Black dissent that has been called the "classic" argument for "total incorporation" of the first eight amendments into the Fourteenth. Black would later say that he considered his *Adamson* dissent the most important opinion of his judicial career. "There I laid it all out. . . . I didn't write until I came to the complete conclusion that I was reasonably sure of myself and my research." Just as the Bill of Rights applied "objective standards to the behavior of the federal government, so the application of the first eight amendments to the states would provide equally ascertainable criteria by which to judge state action." In a lengthy appendix he laid out his historical evidence, drawn largely from the congressional history of the Fourteenth Amendment (Urofsky 1997a, 214). As Roger Newman notes, however, "Black's was an advocate's history: he proved too much and ignored or swept away all doubtful evidence" (Newman 1994, 354).

Black rejected Cardozo's criteria as too vague because phrases like "civilized decency" and "fundamental liberty and justice" could be interpreted by judges to "mean many things." Such a natural law theory of the Constitution "degrade[s] the constitutional safeguards of the Bill of Rights and simultaneously appropriate[s] for this Court a broad power which we are not authorized by the Constitution to exercise," Black maintained. "The only way to avoid this abuse of judicial power was to carry out the original intent of the framers of the Fourteenth Amendment by applying all of the protections of the Bill of Rights to the states." For Black, total incorporation provided a way of objectively determining what were "the 'cannons of decency and fairness' that everyone accepted" (Urofsky 1997a, 216, 218). He called forcefully for the overruling of *Twining*, saying that he did not consider the Bill of Rights the "outworn 18th Century strait jacket" that opinion had called it. The provisions of the Bill of Rights might be considered "outdated abstractions by some," but the "ancient evils" they were designed to meet were "the same kind of human evils that have emerged . . . wherever excessive power is sought by the few at the expense of the many." Black feared to see the consequences of the Court's practice of "substituting its own concepts of decency and fundamental justice for the language of the Bill of Rights as a point of departure in interpreting and enforcing that Bill of Rights" (*Adamson* 1947, 89).

Douglas joined Black's opinion, but Murphy filed a separate dissent in which he attempted to synthesize the Frankfurter and Black positions. He wanted to incorporate the entirety of the Bill of Rights, as Black proposed, but he objected to what he saw as the "excessive rigidity" in Black's approach. There were times when a strict reading of the first eight amendments might not suffice to provide justice. In those instances Frankfurter's due process approach would allow judges to secure justice. Murphy argued for total incorporation and more. Occasions might arise where a proceeding "falls so short of conforming to fundamental standards of procedure as to warrant constitutional condemnation in terms of a lack of due process despite the absence of a specific provision in the Bill of Rights" (*Adamson* 1947, 124). As Melvin

Urofsky suggests, Murphy's approach, "almost ignored in the battle between Black and Frankfurter, prevailed, and it came into effect in the landmark 1965 case of *Griswold v. Connecticut*, which established a right to privacy that eventually came to be embedded in due process." Although the Court retained the Cardozo-Frankfurter approach of selective incorporation for the duration of the Vinson Court era, during the Warren years nearly all the first eight amendment guarantees were applied to the states (Urofsky 1997a, 219).

## Due Process Rights

The *Adamson* ruling, although important in the evolution of the incorporation debate, did not put the Vinson Court on a straight-line path on the rights of the accused. This Court seemed to swing between insisting on procedural fairness in state courts and deferring to the states' traditional role in administering justice. Less than a year after *Adamson*, it reviewed a Michigan case in which a trial judge had functioned as a one-man grand jury. The judge summarily indicted a suspect for contempt and convicted him in a secret trial at which the defendant had no opportunity to secure counsel, prepare a defense, call any witnesses of his own, or cross-examine grand jury witnesses. The Vinson Court, with only Justices Frankfurter and Jackson disagreeing, set aside the conviction in *In re Oliver* (1948).

Justice Black spoke for the majority. He asserted forcefully that the secrecy of the proceedings and the failure of the judge to afford Oliver a reasonable opportunity to defend himself violated the Due Process Clause of the Fourteenth Amendment. The traditional Anglo-American distrust of secret trials, Black observed, had been "variously ascribed to the use of this practice by the Spanish Inquisition," and to the "excesses of the English Court of Star Chamber." These institutions "symbolized a menace to liberty." In the hands of "despotic groups," they had become "an instrument for the suppression of political and religious heresies in ruthless disregard of the right of an accused to a fair trial" (*Oliver* 1948, 269–270). At a minimum, the Fourteenth Amendment entitled Oliver to a public trial, assistance of counsel, opportunity to cross-examine adverse witnesses, and the right to testify in his own behalf.

Rutledge dissented, pointing out that "much of the problem lay in the *Adamson* doctrine of allowing the states to experiment without hindrance." The *Oliver* case, he said, demonstrated how far the Court had "departed from our constitutional plan" when it permitted "selective departure" by the states from the "scheme of ordered personal liberty established by the Bill of Rights" (*Oliver* 1948, 280). Under the "guise" of permitting the states to experiment with improving the administration of justice, Rutledge believed the Court had left them free to substitute, "in spite of the absolutism of continental governments," their "ideas and processes of civil justice" for the old time-tried "principles and institutions of the common law" perpetuated in our Bill of Rights (*Oliver* 1948, 281).

As the *Adamson* ruling made evident, the Vinson Court was reluctant to extend any of the rights of the accused guarantees of the Bill of Rights to the states despite numerous opportunities to do so. Its lack of consensus about incorporation was reflected in an Eighth Amendment cruel-and-unusual-punishment case decided early in 1947. Willie Francis was to be electrocuted for murder in Louisiana. The electric chair failed to conduct enough electrical current to kill him. Before Louisiana could make a second attempt to execute him, Francis sought a writ of habeas corpus on the ground that to try again would constitute cruel and unusual punishment. The Vinson Court rejected this contention in *Louisiana ex rel. Francis v. Resweber* and sent Francis back to the electric chair. Four members of the majority declared that the Fourteenth Amendment's Due Process Clause would prohibit a state from executing someone in a cruel manner, but they did not indicate the Eighth Amendment's prohibition of cruel and unusual punishment extended to the states.

Reed suggested that the cruelty against which the Eighth Amendment protected someone who had been convicted was "cruelty inherent in the method of punishment, not the necessary suffering involved in any method employed to extinguish life humanely." That an "unforeseeable accident" had prevented the "prompt consummation of the sentence" could not "add an element of cruelty to a subsequent execution" (*Francis* 1947, 464). Francis's equal protection claim was rejected as well. Laws cannot "prevent accidents" nor can a law "equally protect against them all." So long as a law "applies to all alike," the requirements of equal protection were met. In Reed's view the Court could not assume that Louisiana "singled out Francis for a treatment other than that which has been or would generally be applied" (*Francis* 1947, 465).

Frankfurter concurred in a separate opinion. Although personally opposed to the death penalty, he declared that Louisiana's wish to make a second attempt to electrocute Francis did not "shock the conscience." In his view, the "penological policy of a state is not to be tested by the scope of the Eighth Amendment." According to Frankfurter, if he voted to deny Louisiana a second chance at executing Francis on due process grounds, he would be enforcing his private views, rather than the consensus of society, which was the standard that due process enjoined.

Several weeks after *Francis*, the Court set aside the conviction of a fifteen-year-old black youth who had been subjected to coercive police interrogation. The young man had been arrested about midnight on a charge of murder and questioned by "relays" of police from shortly after midnight until about 5 A.M., when he confessed. During the interrogation, he was not allowed to see a lawyer, friends, or even his family. The Court set aside his conviction even though he had been advised of his constitutional rights before signing a confession. Writing for the majority in *Haley v. Ohio* (1948), Douglas declared that what had "transpired would make us pause for careful inquiry if a mature man were involved." When a "mere child," who was an "easy victim of the law" was before the Court, "special care in scrutinizing the record must be used." A fifteen-year-old, when subjected to such process, was a "ready victim of the inquisition." Calling what had happened to the youth a "disregard of the standards of decency," Douglas said the Court could not "give any weight to recitals which merely formalize constitutional requirements." Formulas of respect for constitutional safeguards could not become "a cloak for inquisitorial practices and make an empty form of the due process of law which free men fought and died to obtain" (*Haley* 1948, 599–601).

## *The Fourth Amendment*

Unlike *Haley*, most of the defendants' rights cases decided by the Vinson Court involved Fourth Amendment issues. The first important one was *Harris v. United States* (1947). It began when FBI agents, in possession of an arrest warrant for Harris for sending forged checks through the mail, conducted a warrantless, five-hour search of his apartment. They did not locate the checks for which they were looking, but instead found four Selective Service classification cards in a bureau drawer. Following his conviction for possession of the cards, Harris challenged it on Fourth Amendment grounds. The Court found the search reasonable because the apartment had been under his "control," and his possession of the cards during the search meant the illegal possession offense was a continuing one, committed in the presence of the officers.

Chief Justice Vinson, writing for the 5–4 majority, pointed to the long-established principle that a search incident to arrest is lawful even in the absence of a search warrant. Such a search may extend to the "premises under [the] immediate control" of the defendant. In the Court's view, Harris had been in "exclusive possession" of the entire apartment; his control extended "quite as much to the bedroom in which the draft cards were found as to the living room in which he was arrested" (*Harris* 1947, 151). Furthermore, the cards were the property of the United States.

Frankfurter and Murphy issued dissents. As far as Frankfurter was concerned, protecting the Fourth Amendment was "not an outworn bit of Eighteenth Century romantic rationalism but an indispensable need for a democratic society" (*Harris* 1947, 161). He concluded his dissent by saying that after arresting a man in his house, to "rummage at will" among his papers in search of whatever will convict him appears . . . indistinguishable from what might be done under a general warrant (*Harris* 1947, 174). Murphy also saw the resemblance to a general warrant. The Court, he said, had "resurrected . . . the use of the odious general warrant . . . presumably outlawed forever from our society by the Fourth Amendment." The "mere fact" that someone was validly arrested "does not give the arresting officers untrammeled freedom to search every cranny and nook for anything that might have some relation . . . to any crime whatsoever" (*Harris* 1947, 183, 186). Rutledge and Jackson also dissented.

The Court seemed to move toward the views of the *Harris* dissenters in four 1948 cases. In *United States v. Di Re*, it reversed a conviction of a passenger arrested in a car in which the driver (and owner) and a government informer were also seated. The driver was under investigation for selling counterfeit gas ration coupons. When federal and state officers approached the car, the informant had coupons in his hand, which he said he had obtained from the driver. Without a warrant, police arrested Di Re and the driver and took them to the police station where they were searched. Counterfeit coupons were found in Di Re's possession, and he was convicted largely on the basis of that evidence. It was the unanimous view of the Vinson Court that the search of Di Re was unreasonable. A person "does not lose immunities from such a search by mere presence in a suspected vehicle," said Jackson (*Di Re* 1948, 587). A search "is not made legal by what turns up." In law, Jackson maintained, a search is "good or bad when it starts and does not change character from its success" (*Di Re* 1948, 595).

In *Johnson v. United States* federal narcotics agents, acting without a warrant, broke into a room that smelled of burning opium. The agents arrested the occupant and searched the room. They found both opium and an apparatus customarily used to smoke it. In a 5–4 ruling, the Supreme Court concluded that there was insufficient justification for a warrantless search even though it occurred incident to Johnson's lawful arrest. Jackson declared that when privacy rights are jeopardized, whether there is justification for a search must be determined by a judicial officer rather than a law enforcement agent. In this case, there were no exigent circumstances that would justify failure to obtain a warrant before making the search. The arresting officers did not have probable cause to take Johnson into custody until they entered the room and found her to be its only occupant. The government was attempting to "justify the arrest by the search and at the same time justify the search by the arrest. This will not do" (*Johnson* 1948, 16–17). "Any assumption," said Jackson, that evidence sufficient to "support a magistrate's disinterested determination" to issue a search warrant would justify the officers in making a search without a warrant "would reduce the [Fourth] Amendment to a nullity and leave the people's homes secure only in the discretion of the police" (*Johnson* 1948, 14).

In another case decided the same year as *Johnson*, *Trupiano v. United States* (1948), federal revenue agents had watched as an illegal still was constructed and put into operation. Over the course of a surveillance lasting several weeks, the agents could have obtained both search and arrest warrants, but they sought neither. When they finally moved in, one man was engaged in running the still. The Vinson Court sustained his warrantless arrest by a 5–4 margin. It went on to rule, however, that the warrantless seizure of the still was unreasonable since no exigency prevented the agents from obtaining a search warrant. Murphy indicated in his opinion that even though the still was contraband, a fact that undoubtedly would have supported the issuance of a search warrant, this did not "legalize the [warrantless] seizure." Furthermore, the "proximity" of the contraband property to the person arrested was a "fortuitous circumstance" inadequate by itself to sustain the seizure of the still (*Trupiano* 1948, 707–708).

The Vinson Court also held the search in *McDonald v. United States* unlawful. After a two-month surveillance of McDonald in connection with a numbers racket investigation, federal agents had entered his room, arrested him, and seized an adding machine and lottery paraphernalia. Without discussing the question of whether the arrest was lawful, in a 6–3 decision the Court held the search unreasonable. "Where, as here, officers are not responding to an emergency," Douglas said for the majority, there must be "compelling reasons to justify the absence of a search warrant. A search without a warrant demands exceptional circumstances." None were present here (*McDonald* 1948, 454).

The Fourth Amendment cases discussed above all involved federal law enforcement agents, which explains the Court's relatively aggressive enforcement of this Bill of Rights provision. The issue of whether state officers had to comply with the reasonableness requirements of the Fourth Amendment was not examined in these cases and remained unanswered until 1949 when the Vinson Court reviewed *Wolf v. Colorado*. Although the Court seemed to demand accountability from federal agents, it largely followed Frankfurter's lead when it came to state law enforcement officers. In assessing their conduct, it subscribed to Frankfurter's "shocks the conscience" test.

Furthermore, it did not impose upon them the exclusionary rule. The exclusionary rule prohibits the use of illegally seized evidence in criminal trials. The Fourth Amendment, however, does not mention this or any other means by which to enforce its ban against unreasonable searches and seizures. There has been considerable debate about the wisdom of this judge-made rule, but there is also general agreement that it is the only thing that makes the Fourth Amendment effective. If evidence will be excluded on a showing that the search that discovered it was unreasonable, law enforcement agents must be careful to make their searches and seizures reasonable so as not to risk the imposition of this drastic sanction. The White Court had attached the exclusionary rule to federal criminal trials in *Weeks v. United States* (1914). The Court explicitly held in *Weeks*, however, that it applied *only* to federal agents and federal trials. Over the next thirty years states exploited this double standard and largely ignored the commands of the Fourth Amendment.

This anomalous situation was reexamined by the Vinson Court in *Wolf v. Colorado* (1949). In *Wolf*, a deputy sheriff went to a doctor's office and, without a warrant, seized his appointment book and obtained from it the names of patients who were later interrogated. On the basis of evidence contained in the book and obtained from the patient interviews that followed, the district attorney initiated a prosecution against Wolf. The books were admitted into evidence at his trial, and he was convicted. The Supreme Court reached two incongruous conclusions in Wolf's case, and it was left to Justice Frankfurter to explain them. Using both his own view of due process and Justice Cardozo's standard from *Palko*, he partially applied the constitutional prohibition of unreasonable searches and seizures to the states. Noting that the incorporation thesis had been rejected by the Court "again and again," Frankfurter nonetheless declared that unreasonable searches and seizures by state agents violated the Constitution. This was not because the Fourteenth Amendment's Due Process Clause actually incorporated the Fourth Amendment but rather because unreasonable searches violated the *Palko* test for due process. Even though the essence of the Fourth Amendment now applied to the states, this did not mean the method used to enforce that right—the exclusionary rule—also applied to them. The exclusionary rule, effective as it might be, remained a judge-made doctrine and not a part of the Fourteenth Amendment. As a result, it was left to the states to develop their own methods to ensure compliance with this due process requirement. In other words, states could "ignore the Fourth Amendment even though it now applied to them, provided they did not act so unreasonably as to shock the conscience" (Urofsky 1997a, 229).

In his *Wolf* opinion Frankfurter spoke of the need for states to adhere to the mandate of the Fourth Amendment. The "security of one's privacy against arbitrary police intrusion by the police . . . is basic to a free society," he suggested, and it was implicit in the concept of "ordered liberty." The "knock at the door . . . as a prelude to a search, without authority of law but solely on the authority of the police" must be "condemned as inconsistent with the conception of human rights enshrined in the history and the basic constitutional documents of English-speaking peoples." Accordingly, Frankfurter did not hesitate to say that if a state were to sanction "police incursion into privacy" it would "run counter" to the protection afforded by the Fourth Amendment. How this protection was to be enforced was, however, a question of a "different order." The means by which the right should "be made effective" must be determined by the individual states (*Wolf* 1949, 27–28). A reasonable reading of Frankfurter's opinion is that he would have preferred that the states "maintain the same high standards as federal criminal procedure." He certainly hoped that extending the Fourth Amendment to the states would prompt them to establish high standards. If they did not, however, that would still "be acceptable because a federal system allowed diversity, and almost any practice that did not 'shock the conscience' would be permissible under this double standard." Despite the tone of Frankfurter's admonition, the ruling left the states free to decide whether or not they would adopt rules of procedure and evidence that were the equivalent of federal ones. As Paul Murphy notes, "it thus became a classic example of a basic right for which no judicial remedy was provided" (Murphy 1972, 270). Black concurred in the result. To his literalist way of thinking, the exclusionary rule was just a judicially created rule of evidence, not a commandment of the Fourth Amendment.

Justices Douglas, Murphy, and Rutledge all disagreed, and each dissented in *Wolf*. Douglas argued that evidence obtained in violation of the Fourth Amendment "*must* be excluded in state prosecutions" or the amendment "would have no effective sanction" (*Wolf* 1949, 40). Murphy wrote that the "conclusion is inescapable but one remedy exists to deter violations of the search and seizure clause. That is the rule which excludes illegally obtained evidence" (*Wolf* 1949, 44). Although Rutledge agreed with the Court's holding that the Fourth Amendment applied to the states, he rejected its "simultaneous conclusion" that the exclusionary rule did not. Without it, the protection of the amendment "might as well be stricken from the Constitution" (*Wolf* 1949, 47). Although Douglas, Murphy, and Rutledge could not command a majority in 1949, their position would prevail in 1961, when the Warren Court explicitly overruled *Wolf* in *Mapp v. Ohio*.

During the Vinson era, however, efforts to impose meaningful constitutional limitations on searches and seizures achieved only limited results. The Vinson Court, to be sure, did hold federal agents more accountable after *Harris v. United States* (1947). The position taken by the dissenters in *Harris* prevailed in subsequent cases such as *Di Re*, *Johnson*, *McDonald*, and *Trupiano*. The conservative Truman appointees "swung the pendulum back," however, and in *United States v. Rabinowitz* (1950), Minton "essentially allowed an extensive warrantless search at the time of proper arrest" (Urofsky 1997a, 227). In *Rabinowitz* the Court overruled *Trupiano*, which had been decided only twenty months earlier, at least to the extent that the earlier ruling required a search warrant on the basis of the practicability of procuring it rather than upon the reasonableness of a search following a lawful arrest. A warrant had been issued for the arrest of Rabinowitz on the charge of having sold fraudulently altered postage stamps. Incident to his arrest the officers searched his office and turned up additional altered stamps, the mere possession of which was a crime. Rabinowitz sought to have this evidence suppressed, but the trial court refused to do this. In a 5–3 decision, with Justice Douglas not participating, the Vinson Court agreed the evidence should not be suppressed.

Speaking for the majority, Minton observed that what constituted a reasonable search "is not to be determined by any fixed formula." The Constitution did not define an unreasonable search, and "regrettably, in our discipline we have no ready litmus-paper test." The Fourth Amendment, Minton suggested, "does not say that the right of the people to be secure in their persons should not be violated without a search warrant if it is practicable for officers to procure one." Rather, the amendment secured the people against unreasonable searches. The relevant test was not whether it was reasonable to obtain a warrant, but "whether the search was reasonable." Whether a search was reasonable depended on "facts and circumstances—the total atmosphere of the case" (*Rabinowitz* 1950, 63–66). In *Rabinowitz*, the search and seizure were reasonable because, among other reasons, they were incident to a lawful arrest, Rabinowitz's office was open to the public, it was small, and it was under the complete control of Rabinowitz himself. Black, Frankfurter, and Jackson, all of whom would have reaffirmed *Trupiano*, also suggested that a warrantless search incident to arrest was unreasonable if the arresting officers had time to secure a warrant and the need for conducting a search was clear before the arrest.

Following *Wolf*, the Vinson Court also heard additional Fourth Amendment cases where Frankfurter's flexible, due process approach determined the outcome. Thus, in *Rochin v. California* (1952), it reversed a conviction because the justices agreed unanimously that the conduct of the police "shocked the conscience." Having information that Rochin was selling narcotics, three sheriff's deputies went to his house and, finding the outside door open, entered, climbed the stairs, and forced open the door to Rochin's second-floor bedroom. Inside they found him sitting on the side of the bed. Visible to the deputies were two capsules lying on the nightstand beside the bed. When asked whose they were, Rochin grabbed the capsules and put them in his mouth. The officers subdued him and attempted to remove the capsules. Failing that, they handcuffed Rochin and took him to a hospital. There, at the direction of one of the officers, a doctor forced an emetic solution through a tube into Rochin's stomach. This stomach pumping brought up the two capsules, which were found to contain morphine. Rochin was convicted of possessing a controlled substance and sentenced to two months imprisonment. The Supreme Court unanimously concluded that the conduct of the police so "shocked the conscience" that the evidence obtained from the defendant's stomach should have been excluded from his trial.

*Rochin* demonstrated that Frankfurter's due process standard for measuring the rights of defendants remained the preferred approach of the Vinson Court. His opinion in that case contains Frankfurter's most compelling representation of his position. He suggested that the Court must be "deeply mindful" that the administration of justice was "predominantly committed to the care of the States." The concept of due process, he warned, "is not to be turned into a destructive dogma against the States." In reviewing state criminal cases, the Court was not left, as Black contended, "without adequate guides." Rather, it was to apply "historically settled" standards. The absence of "formal exactitude or want of fixity of meaning is not an unusual or even regrettable attribute of constitutional provisions," Frankfurter wrote. Words were symbols, he suggested, that "do not speak without a gloss." This gloss might be the "deposit of history, whereby a term gains technical content." But it did "not give them a fixed technical content." Rather, it "exacts a continuing process of application." When the gloss had not been fixed but was "a process of judgment, the judgment is bound to fall differently at different times and differently at the same time through different judges" (*Rochin* 1952, 169–170).

In Frankfurter's view, due process of law was "not to be derided as resorting to natural law." Here was a direct response to Black. Judicial exercise of judgment could not be avoided by "freezing due process of law." The notion that it could suggested that the "most important aspect of constitutional adjudication is a function for inanimate machines and not for judges." To exercise the "requisite detachment" in pursuit of objectivity demanded great self-discipline on the part of judges, but these were "precisely the presuppositions of our judicial process" and "precisely the qualities society has a right to expect from those entrusted with ultimate judicial power" (*Rochin* 1952, 171–172).

Black agreed with Frankfurter that Rochin's conviction must be overturned, but his reasoning was different. He saw the "search" of Rochin as compelled self-incrimination—incriminating evidence had been taken from him "by a contrivance of modern science." More importantly, Black's concurring opinion allowed him to reiterate his unwavering preference for fixed standards over formless due process. The effect of Frankfurter's opinion, he argued, was to empower the Court to nullify any state law that "shocks the conscience" or "runs counter to the decencies of civilized conduct" (*Rochin* 1952, 175). Black was dismayed that Frankfurter's approach vested the Court with "unlimited power to invalidate laws." He pointed to the ways in which the "evanescent standards" of this approach had been used to nullify state legislative programs enacted to "suppress evil economic practices." Of "graver concern" was the use of such a philosophy to "nullify the Bill of Rights." He had long ago concluded that the "accordion-like qualities" of such a philosophy "must inevitably imperil all the individual liberty safeguards" enumerated in the Bill of Rights. Unlike Frankfurter, he thought many constitutional provisions were stated in "absolute and unqualified language" (*Rochin* 1952, 176).

In part because of the disagreements between the justices, the Vinson Court era did not produce lasting doctrine regarding rights of the accused. The Warren Court, which followed, would undertake a comprehensive "revolution" in criminal rights jurisprudence. The passionately advanced exchanges between Frankfurter and Black not only dominated the Vinson era but also defined the debate in the Warren years that followed.

## Equal Protection Cases

The Vinson Court's comparatively liberal record in race discrimination cases stands in "sharp contrast to the generally antilibertarian trend of its decisions in other fields." A comparison of decisions from early and later in the Vinson era "reveals a progressively developing boldness in the handling of discrimination issues" (Pritchett 1954, 145).

## Transportation

In 1941, the Supreme Court upheld for the first time an African American's challenge to segregated transportation. Congressman Arthur Mitchell had been removed from a railroad car when the train of which it was a part crossed into Arkansas. Mitchell, a politically savvy plaintiff, first filed a complaint with the Interstate Commerce Commission (ICC), the federal agency with authority to regulate interstate carriers. The ICC found for the railroad, and Mitchell appealed to the Supreme Court. The Court upheld his claim in *Mitchell v. United States* (1941), but it did not directly confront the constitutionality of segregation in interstate commerce. Instead, the Court insisted that accommodations must be "substantially equal" to meet the "separate-but-equal" test. The ruling revealed a "changed temper" on the Court, one that might make it willing to take on "separate-but-equal" in transportation, given the appropriate occasion. Such an occasion came in *Morgan v. Virginia* (Pritchett 1954, 127).

The *Mitchell* decision encouraged the NAACP to press harder for reversing earlier rulings upholding segregation. The civil rights organization represented Irene Morgan when she challenged a Virginia law requiring her to take a seat in the back of an interstate bus. The African American woman argued that this statute could not apply to interstate passengers. In making that contention the NAACP relied on *Hall v. DeCuir* (1878), a case in which the Court had invalidated a Reconstruction Louisiana statute prohibiting discrimination on account of race on public conveyances. The Court believed that there must be a uniform national policy regarding railroads, which only Congress could provide. In the transportation cases that followed *DeCuir*, the Court validated the "separate-but-equal" doctrine, but did not "overrule *Hall v. DeCuir*'s holding regarding supremacy of Congress in interstate transportation" (Urofsky and Finkelman 2002, 774–775). In *Morgan*, the Court reiterated *DeCuir*'s reasoning to conclude that interstate rail and bus lines could not discriminate on the basis of race. Justice Reed made it clear, however, that the *Morgan* ruling did not affect state laws regulating intrastate commerce.

Two years later, the Vinson Court departed from the *Morgan* ruling in order to uphold a Michigan civil rights law even though it affected interstate and foreign commerce. A Detroit company operated steamboats between Detroit and Bois Blanc Island, which was located on the Canadian side of the Detroit River. The company refused to transport a black schoolgirl to the island on its boat with a number of her white classmates. Taking a page from the argument offered in the *Morgan* case, the company claimed that the Michigan Civil Rights Act could not be applied to foreign commerce. Writing for the Court in *Bob-Lo Excursion Company v. Michigan*, Rutledge disagreed. He acknowledged that the Court must be "watchful of state intrusion into intercourse between this country and one of its neighbors." At the same time, if "any segment" of foreign commerce "can be said to have a special local interest, . . . the transportation of [Bob-Lo Excursion's] patrons falls in that characterization." Except for a small portion reserved for a lighthouse and three cottage sites, the island was "economically and socially, though not politically, an amusement adjunct of the city of Detroit" (*Bob-Lo Excursion* 1948, 35). Rutledge distinguished *Morgan* by saying that it had not involved such a "locally insulated" situation. In a concurring opinion, Douglas offered an alternative rationale, suggesting the Equal Protection Clause would provide a "far more flexible tool and intimated that one could not square separate-but-equal with the constitutional mandate of equal protection" (Urofsky and Finkelman 2002, 775–776).

Jackson and the chief justice dissented. They were not in favor of insulating discrimination, but objected to permitting state power to reach foreign commerce. The Court admitted that the activity involved in this case was foreign commerce, Jackson said, but nevertheless was subjecting it to the police power of a state "on the ground that it is not very foreign." In doing so, it had failed "to lay down any standard by which we can judge when foreign commerce is foreign enough to become free of local regulation." Jackson was unable to distinguish the traffic across the Canadian and Mexican borders, "except perhaps in volume." Communities have "sprung up on either side, whose social and economic relations are interdependent, but are conducted with scrupulous regard for the international boundary" (*Bob-Lo Excursions* 1948, 44–45).

*Bob-Lo* illustrated the Vinson Court's problem in "attempting to achieve egalitarian goals through the cold-blooded and clumsy constitutional concept of commerce." *Henderson v. United States* (1951) provided it with an opportunity to "abandon the 'separate-but-equal' doctrine in favor of the clear-cut proposition that segregation, no matter how equal the facilities, is incompatible with the Constitution" (Pritchett 1954, 128). The case involved dining car service on the Southern Railway between Washington, D.C., and Atlanta. Ten tables in the dining car were reserved for white passengers, and one table, separated from the others by a curtain, for black passengers. Henderson, who had been traveling from Atlanta to Washington, D.C., in May 1942, wanted to eat dinner. Upon reaching the dining car, he found the "black" table was full, but the conductor refused to let him occupy an empty seat at one of the "white" ones.

Henderson filed a complaint with the Interstate Commerce Commission, but was unsuccessful in gaining relief. The ICC found that he had been subjected to "undue and unreasonable prejudice and disadvantage," but called the occurrence a "casual incident brought about by the bad judgment of an employee" (*Henderson* 1951, 820). As a result of this finding, the commission refused to enter a prospective order against Southern Railway to end the practice. The Vinson Court was reluctant to address segregation directly. Instead, it followed the *Mitchell* ruling. Although the Court struck down the dining car practice, it did so by finding that the discriminatory dining car arrangements "interfered with the equal access of passengers in violation, not of the

Constitution, but of the Interstate Commerce Act." Thus the case was disposed of without reaching the broader constitutional issue, and the "rule of 'separate-but-equal' escaped unscathed" (Pritchett 1954, 129).

Justice Burton spoke for the Court. His opinion indicated that Henderson had been denied a dining car seat that would have been available to him had he been white. He spoke of the entitlement of every person to be free from "unreasonable discriminations." Where a dining car was available to passengers holding tickets, each passenger was "equally entitled to its facilities." The curtains, partitions, and signs in the dining car "emphasize the artificiality of a difference in treatment which serves only to call attention to a racial classification of passengers holding identical tickets and using the same public dining facility." Here Burton's opinion took a cautious and narrow course. Because the Interstate Commerce Act invalidated the "rules and practices before us," he said, "we do not reach the constitutional or other issues suggested" (*Henderson* 1951, 825–826).

## Housing/Restrictive Covenants

Historically, two methods were used to accomplish residential segregation. The first was municipal ordinances mandating it. By the early 1900s, many cities had adopted such measures. One of these was reviewed by the White Court in 1917 in *Buchanan v. Warley*. There the Court struck down the ordinance from Louisville, Kentucky, on the ground that it was an "unconstitutional interference with the right of a property owner to dispose of his real estate." With municipal ordinances ruled constitutionally defective, the "field was thus left to the second protective device—restrictive covenants entered into by property owners binding themselves not to sell or lease their property to Negroes or other racial, national, or religious groups" (Pritchett 1954, 139).

The first restrictive covenant case, *Corrigan v. Buckley*, reached the Court in 1926. Buckley, a property owner and signatory to such a covenant, obtained a restraining order against Corrigan, another signatory, to prevent him from breaching the covenant. The Taft Court held that such agreements were wholly private and in no way constituted the "state action" that, ever since the *Civil Rights Cases* (1883), had been required to make the Fourteenth Amendment applicable.

In 1948 the Vinson Court reviewed two restrictive covenant cases. Although only six justices participated in *Shelley v. Kraemer*, they were unanimous in holding that the state action requirement had been met. Chief Justice Vinson argued, "among the civil rights intended to be protected from discriminatory state actions by the Fourteenth Amendment are the rights to acquire, enjoy, own, and dispose of property" (*Shelley* 1948, 10). It was clear to the Court that the restrictions on the right of occupancy of the kind embraced by the private covenants would violate the Fourteenth

Amendment if imposed by state statute or local ordinance. The amendment, however, "erects no shield against merely private conduct." Accordingly, the restrictive agreements "standing alone cannot be regarded as violative of any rights guaranteed to petitioners by the Fourteenth Amendment." But in this case, said Vinson, "there was more" (*Shelley* 1948, 13). Enter the state action linkage not found in earlier cases.

The purposes of the restrictive covenants, in the Court's view, "were secured only by judicial enforcement by state courts" (*Shelley* 1948, 13). That the action by state courts and judicial officers in their official capacities constituted state action for Fourteenth Amendment purposes was absolutely clear to Vinson. The Court was certain that there had been state action in these cases "in the full and complete sense of the phrase." The Shelleys were "willing purchasers" of the property. The property owners were "willing sellers," and the contracts of sale were "accordingly consummated." It was "clear that but for the active intervention of the state courts, supported by the full panoply of state power," the Shelleys "would have been free to occupy the property in question without restraint." Vinson concluded by saying that equal protection of the laws was "not achieved through indiscriminate imposition of inequalities" (*Shelley* 1948, 19, 22).

In a companion case, *Hurd v. Hodge*, he applied the *Shelley* holding to covenants in the District of Columbia. Although the Fourteenth Amendment does not apply to the national government, Vinson found that such covenants violated the 1866 Civil Rights Act. Indeed, the "explicit language employed by Congress to effectuate its purposes, leaves no doubt that judicial enforcement of the restrictive covenants by the court of the District . . . is prohibited by the Civil Rights Act" (*Hurd* 1948, 33–34). Furthermore, Vinson said, it was "not consistent" with the public policy of the United States to allow a federal court to "compel actions denied the state courts where such state action has been held to be violative of the guaranty of the equal protection of the laws." We cannot presume, Vinson concluded, that the public policy of the country "manifests a lesser concern for the protection of such basic rights against discriminatory action of federal courts than against such action taken by the courts of the States" (*Hurd* 1948, 35–36).

Since the Court had carefully preserved the legality of restrictive covenants, couldn't the signer of a restrictive covenant who breached its provisions be sued for damages by those with whom he had covenanted? The Vinson Court answered "no" to that question in *Barrows v. Jackson* (1953). A California property owner who had failed to comply with a covenant was sued by several neighbors on the ground that the value of their real estate had been substantially diminished when non-Caucasians took possession of what had been his property. The Court, through Justice Minton, announced it would not permit California to coerce a property owner into paying damages for failure to comply with an agreement that the state could not incorporate into a statute or enforce in equity.

The case was complicated by a standing problem. The party who allegedly "damaged" the property value of her neighbors argued that she could not be compelled to pay for that damage because the covenant discriminated against non-Caucasians. But she was not herself a non-Caucasian, and the Court typically does not permit a litigant to invoke someone else's constitutional rights. It relaxed the normal considerations of standing because of the "unique" character of the case and because it could not otherwise "close the gap to the use of this covenant, so universally condemned by the courts" (*Barrows* 1953, 259). In a rare dissent, Vinson said he could not see that this case was so "unique" that the Court should permit the defendant to "avail herself of the Fourteenth Amendment rights of total strangers" (*Barrows* 1953, 269).

## Discriminatory Unions/Employment

Near the end of the Vinson era, the Court indicated it would review more cases involving discrimination. Among these was *Brotherhood of Railroad Trainmen v. Howard* (1952). A union, the designated bargaining representative for white trainmen under terms of the Railway Labor Act, refused membership to African Americans and for years used its influence to eliminate the jobs of black trainmen. Under a strike threat, the union "persuaded" railroads to agree to keep black porters from also functioning as brakemen. Under the agreement between the railroad and the union, the railroads sought to discharge nonunion black porters and replace them with white union members. A group of porters, who for years had satisfactorily performed the duties of brakemen, filed a class-action suit seeking to nullify the agreement. The union argued that it was "merely using its bargaining power against other employees to protect its own members, not discriminating against minority members of its craft" (Pritchett 1954, 144). The Vinson Court disagreed.

The Court affirmed the lower federal courts' decision, accepting the complainant's allegations. The black employees had long been treated by both the union and the carriers as a "separate class for representation purposes." Here, train porters were threatened with loss of their jobs, said Justice Black, "because they are not white and for no other reason." The brotherhood had been designated as the representative of the trainmen through processes set out in the Railway Labor Act. Bargaining agents who "enjoy the advantages" of the act's provisions "must execute their trust without lawless invasions of the rights of other workers." The Court concluded that the brotherhood should be permanently enjoined from using the contract or "any other similar discriminatory bargaining device to oust the train porters from their jobs" (*Brotherhood of Railroad Trainmen* 1952, 773, 775).

Vinson, Minton, and Reed dissented in *Howard*. It was their view that the right of the brotherhood had existed prior to the passage of the Railway Labor Act. In addition, it "never purported to represent the train porters." Minton suggested that the Court had "reache[d] out" to invalidate the contract, not because the porters were brakemen entitled to representation by the brotherhood, "but because they are Negroes discriminated against by the carrier at the behest of the Brotherhood." Most important, the dissenters saw the union as private and did not agree with the majority that the Railway Labor Act, or any other federal law for that matter, barred race discrimination by private parties (*Brotherhood of Railroad Trainmen* 1952, 776–778).

The contract negotiated by the brotherhood was deemed illegal because it discriminated against the black porters. The central issue, of course, was whether federal law actually prohibited discriminatory acts by private parties. What the decision amounted to was that a private organization, "given privileges by federal legislation becomes subject to the limitations which would affect the federal government itself." Further, Black concluded, the Railway Labor Act contained an implicit code of fair employment practices. In Pritchett's view, this was a "piece of judicial legislation" (Pritchett 1954, 144–145).

## Equal Protection Based on Gender

The Vinson Court confined its equal rights decisions to cases involving race discrimination, with one exception. *Goesaert v. Cleary* (1948) addressed the unequal treatment of the sexes by a Michigan law that required all bartenders to be licensed and prohibited licensing women unless they were wives or daughters of the male bar owners. As *"beguiling"* as Frankfurter thought the issue was, "it need not detain us long." Michigan could, "beyond question," prohibit all women from working behind a bar, "despite the vast changes in the social and legal position of women." The Constitution, he observed, "does not require legislatures to reflect sociological insight, or shifting social standards" (*Goesaert* 1948, 465–466).

Frankfurter then addressed the exception for the wives and daughters of bar owners. Michigan, he said, cannot "play favorites among women without rhyme or reason." The Equal Protection Clause, however, only precluded "irrational discrimination"; it did not require that situations that were different "be treated in law as though they were the same." Michigan's legislature obviously believed that the "oversight assured through ownership of a bar by a barmaid's husband or father minimizes hazards that may confront a barmaid without such protecting oversight." The Court was not "in a position to gainsay such belief by the Michigan legislature." The state had not, Frankfurter concluded, "violated its duty to afford equal protection of the laws." Since the line the legislators had drawn was "not without a basis in reason, we cannot give ear to the suggestion that the real impulse behind this legislation was an unchivalrous desire of male bartenders to try to monopolize the calling" (*Goesaert* 1948, 466–467).

## Segregation in Higher Education

Although the Vinson Court's approach to gender discrimination reflected the attitudes of the past, its rulings in cases involving discrimination in public education looked to the future. The "separate-but-equal" doctrine had governed segregation of the races since *Plessy v. Ferguson* (1896). The first evidence that the Court might be rethinking that principle came in the late 1930s, when the Hughes Court took a tentative step against racial segregation in education. The case of *Missouri ex rel. Gaines v. Canada* (1938) arose out of the University of Missouri's refusal to admit an African American applicant to its law school. Missouri had no law school for racial minorities, but offered to cover Gaines's expenses at any law school in the region that would admit him. The Court ruled that its refusal to admit the African American applicant to its own law school violated the Fourteenth Amendment. At the same time, however, it retained the "separate-but-equal" doctrine. The Court would only go so far as to say that minority students had a right to be admitted to a "white" educational institution where no alternative institution existed for minorities. World War II diverted the Court's attention from this issue until the Vinson era. The Vinson Court expanded upon the *Gaines* ruling, but it proved unable or unwilling to take on directly the "separate-but-equal" doctrine itself. Its relatively few decisions in this area proved to be something of a transition, paving the way to the Warren Court's landmark ruling in *Brown v. Board of Education* (1954).

The Vinson Court's first case involved Ada Sipuel, who applied to the University of Oklahoma Law School, the only one the state had. As in *Gaines*, the school refused admission. Sipuel was told that a separate institution with "substantially equal" facilities would soon open. Represented by Thurgood Marshall, chief counsel for the NAACP, she sued for immediate admission. Just four days after oral arguments in her case, the Court issued a unanimous per curiam order in *Sipuel v. Board of Regents of the University of Oklahoma* (1948). It concluded that Sipuel was "entitled to secure legal education afforded by a state institution." Oklahoma was directed to provide her with one "in conformity with the equal protection clause . . . and provide it as soon as it does for applicants of any other group" (*Sipuel* 1948, 633). A makeshift law school was grudgingly created in the state capitol at Oklahoma City, with three teachers assigned to provide instruction to Sipuel and "similarly situated" others. When Marshall sought relief from the Supreme Court, only Justices Murphy and Rutledge were willing to consider whether the state had in fact established an equal facility.

Shortly after *Sipuel*, the Vinson Court took another case from Oklahoma, which was still trying to salvage "separate-but-equal." George McLaurin applied for admission to the University of Oklahoma's graduate program, hoping to earn his doctorate in education. Although he was admitted based on *Sipuel* (after having been denied admission initially), he had to "sit in the corridor outside the classroom, use a separate desk on the mezzanine of the library, and eat alone in a dingy alcove in the cafeteria." When this arrangement was challenged, the university reluctantly allowed McLaurin to sit in the classroom, but placed a rope bearing a sign saying "Reserved for Colored" around his seat (Urofsky and Finkelman 2002, 778).

The Vinson Court unanimously struck down the state's action in *McLaurin v. Oklahoma State Board of Regents* (1950). The state argued unsuccessfully that "the separations" imposed in this case were "in form merely nominal." The Court saw them as having "set McLaurin apart from other students" with the result that he was "handicapped in his pursuit of effective graduate instruction." The restrictions, Chief Justice Vinson said, "impair[ed] and inhibit[ed] his ability to study, to engage in discussions and exchange views with other students, and, in general, to learn his profession." Vinson suggested that as U.S. society "grows increasingly complex," the need for "trained leaders increases correspondingly." McLaurin's case represented the "epitome of that need" in that he was pursuing an advanced degree to become a "leader and trainer of others." Those who would eventually "come under his guidance and influence will be directly affected by the education he receives." The education and development of McLaurin's students would "necessarily suffer to the extent that his training is unequal to that of his classmates." The state-imposed restrictions on McLaurin's educational experience, which produced such inequalities, could not be sustained. Vinson acknowledged that removing the state restrictions would not necessarily "abate individual and group predilections, prejudices and choices." But at the very least, the chief justice concluded, the state would not be "depriving [McLaurin] of the opportunity to secure acceptance by his fellow students on his own merits" (*McLaurin* 1950, 641–642). As in *Sipuel*, the Court refused to overrule *Plessy*, but Vinson's opinion "provided a clue to the NAACP on how it might attack segregation in the future" (Urofsky and Finkelman 2002, 778).

The same day the Court decided *McLaurin*, it handed down its decision in the University of Texas Law School case, a decision that took it one step closer to overruling "separate-but-equal." Herman Sweatt had applied for admission to the law school in 1946. When he was denied admission, a federal district court gave the state six months to establish a law school for minority applicants. It hastily set up the School of Law of the Texas State University for Negroes. A makeshift classroom in an Austin basement was all that was provided initially, although a significant sum was subsequently appropriated to improve the institution (which eventually evolved into the Texas Southern University School of Law). Although the physical facilities and library had been expanded by the time the Vinson Court heard the case, Marshall and the NAACP were confident they could show that the library, faculty, and other "intangibles" at the minority law school were deficient when compared with those of the University of Texas Law School.

Again, Vinson spoke for a unanimous Court. They had been urged to address "broader issues" the chief justice reported, but he indicated they would not consider reversing *Plessy v. Ferguson*. Vinson then compared the two Texas law schools. The University of Texas Law School, from which Sweatt had been excluded, had sixteen full-time faculty members, some of whom were "nationally recognized." Its student body numbered 850, and its library contained more than 65,000 volumes. Among the "other facilities" available were a law review, moot court, scholarship funds, and an Order of the Coif chapter. The school's alumni "occupy the most distinguished positions in the private practice of the law and in the public life of the State." It was, in Vinson's view, "one of the nation's ranking law schools" (*Sweatt v. Painter* 1950, 632–633).

By comparison, the minority law school had no independent faculty or library. Instruction was to be provided by four members of the University of Texas Law School faculty, but their offices remained on its campus. Few of the ordered volumes for the library had arrived by the time the initial proceeding in the case took place, and there was no full-time librarian on staff. Most important, the school lacked accreditation. By the time the case was reviewed by the Vinson Court, the minority law school was "on the road to full accreditation," had a library of 16,500 volumes, a practice court, a legal aid association, and "one alumnus who ha[d] become a member of the Texas Bar." Nonetheless, the Court concluded that it could not find "substantial equality in the educational opportunities offered white and Negro law students by the State." By any measure, the University of Texas Law School was "superior." What was "more important," Vinson said, it "possesses to a far greater degree those qualities which are incapable of objective measurement but which make for greatness in a law school" (*Sweatt* 1950, 633–634).

Vinson characterized the legal profession as "intensely practical" as well as a "learned profession." Law school was the "proving ground for legal learning and practice," and it could not be effective "in isolation from the individuals and institutions with which the law interacts." Neither law students nor those who have practiced law "would choose to study in an academic vacuum." The minority law school excluded from its student body members of racial groups, "which number 85% of the population of the State" and included most of the "lawyers, witnesses, jurors, judges and other officials with whom [Sweatt] will inevitably be dealing when he becomes a member of the Texas Bar." With such a "substantial segment of society excluded," the education offered to Sweatt was not, the Court thought, "substantially equal" to that which he would have received at the University of Texas (*Sweatt* 1950, 634). The Supreme Court ordered him admitted to the Austin school, the first time it had ever ordered a black student admitted to a previously all-white educational institution on grounds that the state had failed to provide equal separate facilities. But despite the steps taken by the

Vinson Court in *Sipuel, McLaurin,* and *Sweatt,* the *Plessy* rule of "separate-but-equal" remained in force.

The justices had been anticipating a direct attack on the "separate-but-equal" doctrine after *McLaurin* and *Sweatt.* In June 1952, the Court announced that it would hear arguments later that year in cases challenging de jure school segregation in Delaware, Virginia, South Carolina, Kansas, and the District of Columbia. It had consolidated these cases, under the name of *Brown v. Board of Education,* with the Kansas appeal as the leading one, so that, according to Justice Clark, "the whole question would not smack of being a purely Southern one" (Urofsky and Finkelman 2002, 779). The justices were unable to reach agreement after the initial argument, however, and requested reargument of the cases in the fall of 1953. They asked counsel to address, among other questions, whether those proposing the Fourteenth Amendment had intended it to prohibit racial segregation in public schools. The Court also wanted counsel to discuss how desegregation should be implemented if the Court held state-mandated public school segregation unconstitutional.

Initially, the Court was deeply divided over whether to reverse *Plessy.* Justices Black, Douglas, Burton, and Minton wanted to explicitly overrule the 1896 decision. Chief Justice Vinson and Justice Reed, on the other hand, were reluctant to abandon "separate-but-equal." Justices Frankfurter and Jackson opposed racial segregation, but were apprehensive about judicial intervention in what had traditionally been a local matter. Finally, there was a realization that if the Court were going to take such a momentous step, it needed to present a united front to the country. Chief Justice Vinson appeared to be incapable of unifying all of his colleagues in support of a decision in the school segregation cases, but on September 9, 1953, Vinson died. By the time the Court heard reargument, Earl Warren had replaced him as chief justice. Only Reed continued to believe that state-mandated segregation was constitutional, and Warren, exhibiting the kind of leadership of which Vinson seemed incapable, managed to persuade him, for the good of the country, to make the inevitable decision unanimous. When *Brown* and the other cases were eventually decided in May 1954, Reed joined Warren's opinion, declaring that segregated schools were "inherently unequal."

## *Conclusion*

Because it was decided in 1954, rather than in 1953, *Brown v. Board of Education* became a Warren Court decision. It was, however, the Vinson Court that first wrestled with the issue that *Brown* decided. Its deliberations helped to forge the ruling of its more famous successor. In the field of school desegregation, as in so many other areas, Vinson's was a transition Court. With the exception of *Youngstown Sheet and Tube Company v. Sawyer,* its decisions were not particularly important, at least if importance is measured by lasting contributions to constitutional doctrine. The Vinson Court's internal debates over the cases it decided did make a substantial contribution to the development of the law, however. They entitle it to a far more important place in constitutional history than do its decisions themselves.

## *References and Further Reading*

Belknap, Michal R. 1977. *Cold War Political Justice: The Smith Act, the Communist Party, and American Civil Liberties.* Westport, CT: Greenwood Press.

———. 1993. "*Dennis v. United States:* Great Case or Cold War Relic." *Journal of Supreme Court History,* pp. 41–58.

———. 1994. "Cold War in the Courtroom: The Foley Square Communist Trial." In *American Political Trials,* ed. Michal R. Belknap. Rev. ed. Westport, CT: Greenwood Press, pp. 207–232.

Cortner, Richard C. 1981. *The Supreme Court and the Second Bill of Rights: The Fourteenth Amendment and the Nationalization of Civil Liberties.* Madison: University of Wisconsin Press.

Dubofsky, Melvin, and Warren Van Tine. 1986. *John L. Lewis: A Biography.* Urbana: University of Illinois Press.

Hurst, J. Willard. 1971. *The Law of Treason in the United States.* Westport, CT: Greenwood Press.

Kalven, Harry. 1988. *A Worthy Tradition: Freedom of Speech in America.* New York: Harper and Row.

Klugar, Richard. 1976. *Simple Justice: The History of* Brown v. Board of Education *and Black America's Struggle for Equality.* New York: Knopf.

Marcus, Maeva. 1977. *Truman and the Steel Seizure Case: The Limits of Presidential Power.* New York: Columbia University Press.

McCoy, Donald R. 1984. *The Presidency of Harry S. Truman.* Lawrence: University Press of Kansas.

Mendelson, Wallace. 1961. *Justices Black and Frankfurter: Conflict in the Court.* Chicago: University of Chicago Press.

Miller, Loren. 1966. *The Petitioners: The Story of the Supreme Court of the United States and the Negro.* New York: Pantheon Books.

Millis, Harry A., and Emily Clark Brown. 1950. *From the Wagner Act to Taft-Hartley.* Chicago: University of Chicago Press.

Murphy, Paul L. 1972. *The Constitution in Crisis Times, 1918–1969.* New York: Harper and Row.

Nelson, William E. 1988. *The Fourteenth Amendment: From Political Principle to Judicial Doctrine.* Cambridge, MA: Harvard University Press.

Newman, Roger. 1994. *Hugo Black: A Biography.* New York: Pantheon.

Parrish, Michael E. 2000. "The Rosenberg Atom Spy Case." *University of Missouri at Kansas City Law Review:* 601–621.

Pritchett, C. Herman. 1954. *Civil Liberties and the Vinson Court.* Chicago: University of Chicago Press.

Rudko, Frances Howell. 1988. *Truman's Court: A Study in Judicial Restraint.* Westport, CT: Greenwood Press.

Simon, James F. 1989. *The Antagonists: Hugo Black, Felix Frankfurter and Civil Liberties in Modern America.* New York: Simon and Schuster.

Tomlins, Christopher L. 1985. *The State and the Unions: Labor Relations Law and the Organized Labor Movement in America, 1880–1960.* Cambridge: Cambridge University Press.

Tushnet, Mark V. 1994. *Making Civil Rights Law: Thurgood Marshall and the Supreme Court, 1936–1961.* New York: Oxford University Press.

Urofsky, Melvin I. 1997a. *Division and Discord: The Supreme Court under Stone and Vinson, 1941–1953.* Columbia: University of South Carolina Press.

Urofsky, Melvin I., and Paul Finkelman. 2002. *A March of Liberty: A Constitutional History of the United States, Volume II: From 1877 to the Present.* 2d ed. New York: Oxford University Press.

Vose, Clement. 1959. *Caucasians Only: The Supreme Court, the NAACP, and the Restrictive Covenant Cases.* Berkeley: University of California Press.

Wiecek, William M. 2002. "The Legal Foundation of Domestic Anticommunism: The Background of *Dennis v. United States.*" *Supreme Court Review:* 375.

# 4

## *Legacy and Impact*

T ransition courts are not always well remembered by historians, and their decisions are often forgotten. Although the Vinson Court decided some important cases that pointed the way to the future, they are overshadowed by the greater steps taken by subsequent Courts. Similarly, transition courts in some instances are backward-looking, and thus are doubly condemned—too tied to the outmoded policies of the past and not wise or brave enough to march headlong into the future. Such is surely the case with the Vinson Court. Its decisions on free speech, for example, show the worst aspects of earlier Courts' uses of the clear-and-present-danger test, all of which would soon be abandoned, while the brave steps it took in the matter of race relations and segregation are lost because we shine the spotlight so prominently on the Warren Court's justly applauded decision in *Brown v. Board of Education* (1954) and its progeny.

Five justices who attended Fred Vinson's funeral were placed on the Court by President Franklin Roosevelt. They had been present when Harlan Fiske Stone took over the center chair from Charles Evans Hughes in 1941 and had attended Stone's funeral in 1946. It is not irrelevant to bring the Stone Court into the picture, because it, too, faced the same challenges that its successor did—the transition from the old classical jurisprudence with its emphasis on property rights to the new agenda, dealing with civil rights and civil liberties, questions of national security, and the manner and extent in which the Bill of Rights would be incorporated and applied against the states. Had at least two of the members of the Stone Court survived—Frank Murphy and Wiley Rutledge—it is very possible that the Vinson Court's record, especially in civil liberties, might well have been different. But the appalling mediocrity of the Truman appointees, and the lack of leadership qualities of Frederick Vinson, allowed Felix Frankfurter to hamstring the Court with his distorted notions of judicial restraint.

## *The Transformation of the Court*

Two of the men who sat on the Vinson Court would serve throughout the sixteen years that Earl Warren occupied the center chair: Hugo Black and William O. Douglas. In the end their ideas concerning free speech, incorporation, civil rights, and other matters would be adopted by a majority of the Court and would continue to influence the jurisprudence of those areas to this day.

The most important change in the Court's personnel came with the appointment of Warren. Like Vinson he could lay no claim to great skills in legal thought, but he did have a clear sense of what he wanted the Court to do—pursue justice. Furthermore, he was ready to abandon old ideas that obstructed that goal. Even more, Warren had what all great chief justices have: extraordinary political skills. One tends to forget that the Court, because it is the third branch of government, is by definition a political agency. It is not political in the partisan ways that Congress or the presidency are, and its members do not have to stand for periodic election. But it is political in the sense that politics is the art of governing, and that in order for its decisions to be accepted, the Court must ensure that they are handed down in a manner that will garner the greatest respect and obedience from the public.

Earl Warren had this trait, displayed most strikingly in his ability to bring the brethren together to speak in one voice in *Brown*. He knew how to get along with people, and although he found Felix Frankfurter a constant pain—as had Stone and Vinson before him—he was able to limit Frankfurter's effectiveness and circumvent him until, eventually, Frankfurter left the Court. Truman thought he saw some of these qualities in Vinson. The Court under Stone not only fractured on doctrinal issues, but there was conflict at a personal level as well. Truman selected Vinson with the hope that he could resolve the differences among the justices. Vinson was not equal to this task.

Warren had the great good fortune of having William Brennan Jr. join the Court shortly after he did. Despite the fact that both Warren and Brennan had been named by the conservative Dwight Eisenhower—whose views came much closer to those of Frankfurter than to those of Black and Douglas—both men shared a similar view of the role of the Court and the meaning of the Constitution. Beyond that, Brennan did have the intellectual ability to take Warren's intuitive conclusions, based on the chief's deeply ingrained sense of justice, and convert them into constitutional arguments. In no single controversy was this more apparent than in the matter of reapportionment. Although Warren wrote the ultimate opinion in *Reynolds v. Sims* (1964), in which he argued that people, not trees or farms, vote, it was Brennan who, in *Baker v. Carr* (1962), had come up with constitutional arguments to completely block Frankfurter's assertion that this was not a justiciable issue and should therefore be left to the legislatures and not to the courts.

Frankfurter himself was replaced first by Arthur Goldberg, who, under pressure from Lyndon Johnson, left the bench within a few years to be U.S. ambassador to the United Nations, and whose seat then went to Abe Fortas. With the appointment of Goldberg, then Fortas, and finally Thurgood Marshall, the liberals had a solid six-person block on the Court. The great achievements of the Warren Court in the area of civil liberties all date from the time Frankfurter left the bench in 1962.

Conservative thought was not, however, extinguished, and even in the late 1960s the Court split on a number of issues. John Marshall Harlan II, whom many considered one of the great judicial craftsmen of the twentieth century, picked up part of Frankfurter's load. Harlan was far more flexible than Frankfurter had ever been, however, and he believed that the Due Process Clause of the Fourteenth Amendment could be used, via the idea of substantive due process, to create new rights, such as privacy. Harlan occasionally would find allies in Potter Stewart and Byron White, but they also differed significantly from the men Truman had put on the Court, who tended to be bullied by Frankfurter and follow his lead. In matters of civil rights, White almost always joined with the liberals, as, for that matter, did Stewart and Harlan. But in matters of civil liberties, especially criminal procedure, he tended to be far more conservative. Harlan drew a sharp distinction between states and the federal government and proved the strongest champion of federalism on the Warren Court. No one has ever been able to classify Stewart in terms of liberal and conservative because he defies those descriptions. He was, as one of his clerks noted, a true common law judge who let the facts of the case guide him in his decision making. And in one area, the Press Clause, Stewart proved as liberal as any member of the Warren Court.

We tend to think of the Warren Court members as giants, and indeed many were. The jurisprudential legacies of Brennan, Black, Douglas, Harlan, and even Frankfurter have affected all subsequent Courts, and in the early part of the twenty-first century, the Court often looks at the precedents handed down not in the 1940s, but in the subsequent two decades. The stature of the Stone Court justices compares favorably with those of the Warren Court. Had the justices on the Court during the last three terms under Stone been able to remain for several more terms, the doctrinal "revolution" that occurred under Warren might have begun before there was a Warren Court. But that is not how events unfolded. Vinson replaced Stone, and he was joined by three other Truman nominees. None of these four is considered a giant. Rather, they were persons with extensive political experience, who reacted to the Cold War and Red Scare like other politicians of the period did. Even the "most levelheaded person could find much to worry about." In a short period of time, "one witnessed the Berlin blockade, the triumph of Mao Tse-tung and communists in China, the first Soviet atomic bomb, . . . the invasion of South Korea, and the exposure and subsequent conviction of the Rosenbergs." When the four Truman appointees joined Reed, Frankfurter, and Jackson, they gave the Vinson Court a "decidedly conservative slant compared to its more activist in the Stone years" (Urofsky 1997a, 158–159). The rulings of the Vinson Court were, in large part, a reflection of cautious and fearful times.

## Equal Protection

The record of the Warren Court in ending the judicial blessing given to racial segregation blinds us to the realities not only of what happened earlier, but of what came later as well. One has to give the Vinson Court some credit for cases like *Morgan v. Virginia* (1946), *Bob-Lo Excursion v. Michigan* (1948), *Shelley v. Kraemer* (1948), *Sipuel v. Board of Regents of the University of Oklahoma* (1948), *McLaurin v. Oklahoma State Board of Regents* (1950), *Terry v. Adams* (1953), and especially *Sweatt v. Painter* (1950). Those rulings paved the way to *Brown*. Moreover, the Vinson Court originally heard the arguments in the five school cases involved in *Brown* and set them down for reargument on the basis of specific questions that the justices wanted answered. Although it was long taken as truth that the Vinson Court was badly divided over segregation, common sense tells us that a Court with only one change—even if that change is the chief justice—would not make such a sweeping turn in only a few months. Earl Warren had the votes; what he did—and what Vinson could not do—was mass the Court and get everyone to sign onto a single opinion.

One should not, however, underestimate the contribution of the Vinson Court decisions in launching the great civil rights revolution of the mid-twentieth century. For decades, the "state action" requirement established in the *Civil Rights Cases* (1883) had made it virtually impossible for the Equal Protection Clause to apply to anything but the acts of state government. In *Shelley v. Kraemer* the Vinson Court began, albeit tentatively, to get around the "state action" barrier. It ruled in *Shelley* that the state furthered private discrimination if restrictive covenants, otherwise private contracts, were given effect through state courts. Similarly, in *Bob-Lo Excursion v. Michigan*, the Vinson Court ruled that a state civil rights law could reach discriminatory acts even if they occurred on a steamboat operating between the United States and Canada. The steamship company contended that the state law could not apply since the steamboat operated in foreign commerce and was thus insulated from state law. The Vinson Court concluded that although the commerce was technically foreign, the steamboat operations in this case were "highly local."

If one reads *Brown* carefully, one will note that Chief Justice Warren had precious few precedents to support his conclusion that racial segregation by itself violated the Equal Protection Clause and was therefore unconstitutional. The Vinson era cases began to move away from the separate-but-equal doctrine of *Plessy v. Ferguson* (1896) and lay the groundwork for its complete reversal. The Vinson Court found segregation to be unconstitutional in interstate travel, in graduate education, and in voting. It effectively nullified racially restrictive covenants by novel use of the state action doctrine, taking the position that because the state courts that enforced such covenants were state actors, the state was discriminating. The Warren Court would use a similar approach in cases such as *Burton v. Wilmington Parking Authority* (1961), when it found that the location of a wholly private segregated restaurant in a publicly owned parking garage constituted state action and thus required the restaurant to open its doors to all would-be diners.

Moreover, while the question of school segregation would certainly have reached the high court at some point, the fact is that it arose in the last term of the Vinson Court because of the decision handed down by that Court in the Texas law school case, *Sweatt v. Painter* (1950). There, the members of the Court openly acknowledged, for the first time, that in some circumstances separate could not be equal. If nothing else, the justices knew what made a good law school, and those elements could be found in the University of Texas Law School; they could not be, nor would they in the foreseeable future be, found at the alternative law school the state provided for black students. The Vinson Court recognized in *Sweatt* that there are "qualities which are incapable of objective measurement," qualities that are "intangible," which must be considered in the separate-but-equal calculus. As Thurgood Marshall, the chief tactician for the NAACP Legal Defense Fund noted, the *Sweatt* opinion was "replete with road markings telling us where to go next," and that arrow pointed to a frontal attack on *Plessy* (Urofsky 1997a, 256–257).

And it was the Vinson Court that accepted the four school cases and consolidated them into what would become *Brown v. Board of Education*, and which also took *Bolling v. Sharpe*, the challenge to segregation in the District of Columbia. Although scholars for a number of years believed that the Vinson Court was badly divided on the issue, recent scholarship as well as common sense tells us that the supposed divisions on the bench in 1953 could not have been that fundamental, since with the exception of one person, the Court that handed down the unanimous decision in *Brown* was the same Court that first heard the arguments in late fall of 1952. The Vinson Court, as it were, set the stage; the arrival of Earl Warren allowed the play to go forward as it did. Although Warren deserves much credit, his fellow justices at the time—all members of the Vinson Court the previous term—were ready to go there. They just needed someone to show them how (and, in the case of Stanley Reed, perhaps give a little push).

The new era of equal protection jurisprudence would not have been possible, or at least would have been long delayed, but for the decisions of the Stone and Vinson Courts. Those Courts did not set forth the new "jurisprudential path" in its entirety. Instead, the justices of the period 1941–1953 "began to accommodate themselves to a new agenda that looked primarily at civil rights and liberties rather than at property rights" (Urofsky 1997a, 262). In addition, the "great steps taken to protect civil rights and liberties" in the Warren and Burger Court eras would not have occurred "without the debates and explorations of their predecessors." As Urofsky points out, the conflict between Justices Black and Frankfurter "did much to define the constitutional parameters of that debate." Among other things, both justices believed that the Court "had the obligation to protect the rights of individuals." Their differences "helped their colleagues and the country determine how far the judiciary should go in this quest" (Urofsky 1997a, 263).

## Freedom of Speech

If the Vinson Court deserves much credit for moving to the brink of overturning *Plessy*, its record on freedom of speech has been completely repudiated. In fairness to Vinson and his colleagues, they had to operate in the context of a Cold War abroad and a national security witch-hunt at home, marked most infamously by the smear and fear tactics of Senator Joseph McCarthy. The Vinson Court's record in reviewing the loyalty cases that came before it shows that the judiciary, like the other branches of government, got caught up in the anticommunist hysteria of the times. Section 9(h) of the 1947 Taft-Hartley Act denied access to the National Labor Relations Board to those unions whose officers had refused to swear that they were not Communists. In *American Communications Association v. Douds* (1950), Chief Justice Vinson admitted that the law discouraged the lawful exercise of political freedom by requiring oaths related to individual political beliefs. For all practical purposes, Vinson and the majority ignored the Speech Clause of the First Amendment and the clear intent of the framers—that it serve as a shield against government infringement of free expression. The short-term consequences of *Douds* could be seen in a series of rulings that upheld regulations prohibiting alleged subversives from running for public office (*Gerende v. Board of Supervisors* [1951]), holding municipal jobs (*Garner v. Board of Public Works* [1951]), and teaching in public schools (*Adler v. Board of Education* [1952]).

It appeared for a while in the early 1950s that the Court would approve almost any infringement of free speech in the name of national security, and the full import of this trend can be seen in one of the most notorious cases of the Vinson years, *Dennis v. United States* (1951).

In fairness, the Supreme Court had entered the postwar era with relatively little Speech Clause jurisprudence aside from the "clear and present danger" test developed by Holmes and Brandeis in the early 1920s. From the beginning, critics had attacked the subjectivity of the test, which, in the hands of the conservative majority of the Taft Court, could always be used to stifle unpopular speech. Brandeis had refined the test with his opinion in *Whitney v. California* (1927), but the dearth of speech cases during the Roosevelt years did not give the Court much opportunity to develop and apply his ideas.

The Vinson Court had ample opportunity to consider the balance between free speech and other interests, but its rulings did little to clarify the issue. In *Terminello v. Chicago* (1949), the Court examined a disturbing-the-peace charge against a speaker whose words provoked riotous conduct by more than a thousand people protesting his speech. He was charged under an ordinance prohibiting "making any improper noise, riot, disturbance, breach of the peace, or diversion tending to a breach of the peace." The case provided what seemed an excellent opportunity to consider whether speech that tended to produce disruption was nonetheless protected by the First Amendment. Although the Vinson Court reversed the speaker's conviction, the majority supporting Terminello begged the First Amendment question and based its decision on the judge's improper charge to the jury. Two years later, the Vinson Court upheld the conviction of a speaker who was arrested for refusing to stop speaking before a potentially unruly crowd. It was the Vinson Court's view that the speaker could be convicted of disorderly conduct for the reaction he "engendered." In doing so, the Vinson Court validated the so-called heckler's veto.

In the Vinson speech cases, Black and Douglas became increasingly unhappy with "clear and present danger" and began to develop a new jurisprudence that viewed the First Amendment, especially the Speech Clause, as occupying a "preferred" position among constitutionally established rights. They also argued for an "absolutist" interpretation of the clause's prohibition against government abridgement of speech. But at least in the late 1940s and early 1950s, theirs were voices crying in the wilderness. Their dissents in *Dennis*, in which seven members of the Court upheld convictions of leaders of the American Communist Party for reading and thinking and discussing and teaching radical ideas—without any iota of actual action—were roundly denounced at the time. In the end, however, it was their ideas that would triumph. Indeed, the Douglas dissent was later seen as "one of the great defenses of free thought during the McCarthy era." In the end, Vinson Court Justices Douglas and Black would be "hailed as the true defenders of free thought in the postwar Red Scare." Vinson's majority opinion, derived from Learned Hand's reasoning at the court of appeals level, would turn out to have "no doctrinal significance" for several years (Urofsky 1997a, 175).

Scholars consider the Warren Court, unlike the one that Vinson headed, to be among the most speech-protective in the nation's history; parties that invoked free speech claims won nearly three-fourths of their cases before the Warren Court. But the Warren Court's contribution to speech jurisprudence lay less in the number of cases it decided than in the broad vision of the First Amendment that informed its decisions, a vision that differed markedly from the cramped view of the Vinson Court. A majority of the justices agreed with the Black-Douglas idea that free speech held a preferred position among constitutional values. They subscribed to Benjamin Cardozo's view that freedom of speech and thought "is the matrix, the indispensable condition, of nearly every other form of [freedom]" (*Palko v. Connecticut* 1937, 327). In addition, they saw that speech could be attacked not just directly, but indirectly, and that could not be allowed either. In *Bates v. City of Little Rock* (1960), the Court held that First Amendment freedoms "are protected not only against heavy-handed frontal attack, but also from being stifled by more subtle governmental interference" (*Bates* 1960, 253).

Even if one does not ascribe a preferred position to the First Amendment, it is clear that some of our most important rights are located in its clauses—freedoms of speech, press, religion, assembly, and petition. In the 1950s and 1960s, the Court expanded the concept of free expression in cases growing out of the civil rights movement, the protest against the Vietnam War, and the continuing problem of internal security. Rather than caving in to popular opinion, the Warren Court adhered to the notion of the First Amendment as a shield protecting free expression.

In *Brandenburg v. Ohio* (1969), the Warren Court responded to the criminal syndicalism statutes that Holmes and Brandeis had protested against in the 1920s. Brandenburg, the leader of a Ku Klux Klan group, had been convicted for advocating terrorism as a means of political reform. In the per curiam opinion, the Court voided the statute because its overly vague definition of criminal activities unduly restricted both advocacy and the right to assembly. *Brandenburg* has been described as combining the best of Holmes, Brandeis, and Learned Hand, in that it makes freedom the rule and restraint the exception, permits restriction only where a clear connection between speech and legitimately proscribed actions can be established, and requires that the government spell out its rules clearly and in the least restrictive manner. The problem with clear and present danger—that judges had to guess at the probability of danger— is replaced with a clearer and more easily ascertainable test: Will these words, in this context, incite action *now?* The so-called harmless inciter—one whose inflammatory words will not cause present action—is let alone.

Another concept that became a key idea informing the free speech decisions of the Courts that followed Vinson's was *overbreadth.* The overbreadth doctrine requires that governmental regulations of certain activity not reach anything that is constitutionally protected expression. Overbreadth refers to regulations that fail to distinguish adequately between those activities that may be restricted and those that may not. The doctrine acknowledges that speech and other First Amendment rights may be restricted, but requires the government to establish a compelling need to do so. Jurists may use the overbreadth test to keep governmental interference as minimal as possible. It provides justices who prefer the balancing approach with a means to achieve the goals of the absolutists, while at the same time retaining flexibility to meet emergency situations.

Overbreadth proved a useful doctrine in the various Vietnam protest cases. In *Bond v. Floyd* (1966), for example, the Court ruled that black activist Julian Bond's First Amendment rights had been violated by the Georgia House of Representatives, which had excluded him from membership because, it claimed, Bond could not conscientiously take the required oath to support the Constitution because of his antiwar sentiments. In a unanimous opinion, Chief Justice Warren ruled that neither public officials nor private persons could be punished for their opinions if they did not violate the law. Bond's statements, in which he expressed his admiration for those who opposed the draft, could not be construed as a violation of the federal law, which made it an offense to counsel, aid, or abet a person to refuse or evade registration for the draft. Warren assumed the legitimacy of that provision, but he held that it had to be interpreted narrowly. Expressing admiration for those who had the courage of their conviction did not constitute "counseling, aiding or abetting."

Speech may take several forms, and the Court consistently ruled that symbolic communication also comes under the First Amendment umbrella. In *Tinker v. Des Moines School District* (1969), the Court overturned the expulsion of three students for wearing black armbands to symbolize their opposition to the war. School officials claimed that the wearing of armbands interfered with proper discipline and might be disruptive. Justice Abe Fortas rejected this argument and held that students do not lose their constitutional rights when they enter the schoolhouse. School officials had shown no proof that any disruption had occurred. In fact, the record showed that the three students had been especially circumspect, explaining the armbands to those who asked without trying to impose their views on others. Fear that a disturbance might occur could not justify repression. "Our history says that it is this sort of hazardous freedom—this kind of openness—that is the basis of our national strength, and of the independence and vigor of Americans who grow up and live in this relatively permissive, often disputatious, society" (*Tinker* 1969, 508–509).

Symbolism had its limits, however, as the Court made clear in *United States v. O'Brien* (1968). David O'Brien and three others had burned their draft registration cards at an antiwar rally. They admitted they knew that the law prohibited mutilation or destruction of the cards, but they claimed protection under the First Amendment: The card burning symbolized their opposition to the Vietnam War. The Court, according to the chief justice, refused to accept "the view that an apparently limitless variety of conduct can be labeled 'speech' whenever the person engaging in the conduct intends thereby to express an idea" (*O'Brien* 1968, 367). The government had a legitimate interest in preserving the cards, since the draft played an important role in providing manpower for the nation's defense. Only Justice Douglas dissented, and he did not do so on First Amendment grounds; Douglas wanted the Court to deal with what he termed the underlying issue, "whether conscription is permissible in the absence of a declaration of war," a question that the Court consistently refused to hear (*O'Brien* 1968, 389).

Despite some whittling down during the 1970s, the overbreadth doctrine remains a core ingredient of First Amendment law; its importance lies not just in these few cases but also in its wider application. It is a present-oriented doctrine, requiring judges to look not at some horrid future possibility, but at what happened in a specific set of circumstances. Courts can also indicate to legislators whether certain restrictions might be valid if drafted more carefully and with the restrictions more tightly drawn. This satisfies those who believe that some restrictions may be valid in certain circumstances and that courts should give guidance in this area.

## Internal Security

The concerns with internal security did not end when Earl Warren became chief justice; as noted above, the men who constituted the Court in the early years of Warren's tenure were the same ones who had upheld the Truman administration's various internal security measures and who had voted to limit speech in *Dennis*. But it took a while to undo the work of the Vinson Court in this area.

The Court began to show greater sensitivity to free speech and security issues in subsequent Smith Act prosecutions. In *Yates v. United States* (1957), it set aside the convictions of fourteen middle-level Communist leaders. Justice Harlan ruled that the trial court had given too broad a meaning to the term *organize*, and he limited *Dennis*, in claiming that the Smith Act proscribed only advocacy "to do something, now or in the future, rather than merely to believe in something" (*Yates* 1957, 325). The Court sustained the part of the Smith Act that made membership in any organization advocating the overthrow of the government by force or violence a felony in *Scales v. United States* (1961). Yet in a companion case, *Noto v. United States*, Justice Harlan invalidated such a conviction on the grounds that the evidentiary test announced in *Scales* had not been met; the prosecution had failed to show that the Communist Party actually advocated forceful or violent overthrow of the government.

Commentators subsequently praised Harlan, a conservative Republican appointed by Eisenhower, for reinvigorating free speech protection and curtailing Smith Act prosecutions even though the Court had held the statute constitutional in *Dennis*. By "interpreting" *Dennis* and finding judicially manageable standards, he led the Court in a new direction; by imposing strict evidentiary criteria, Harlan in fact reestablished the Holmes test. It would have been politically troublesome to a Court already charged with being too liberal because of its civil rights decisions to have reversed *Dennis;* Harlan's approach avoided that danger while strengthening protection of speech. A similar pattern can be found in the Court's treatment of other anticommunist legislation of the period.

Congress had enacted the Internal Security Act (also known as the Subversive Activities Control Act, or McCarran Act), in the spring of 1950. Through a number of highly complicated provisions it required Communists and other "subversive" groups to register with the attorney general. To justify this admitted infringement on the First Amendment, Congress declared the existence of an international Communist conspiracy that constituted a clear and present danger to the United States. For enforcement of the law, Congress created a Subversive Activities Control Board which, despite broad administrative discretion, remained answerable for its decisions to the courts. President Truman vetoed the bill, calling it "the greatest danger to freedom of speech, press, and assembly since the Sedition Act of 1798" (Urofsky and Finkelman 2002, 763). But Congress, fearful of being considered soft on communism in an election year, promptly overrode the veto by large margins in both houses.

The Court, by a 5–4 vote, sustained the registration provision in *Communist Party v. Subversive Activities Control Board* (1961). Justice Frankfurter denied that the First Amendment prevented Congress from requiring registration of membership lists of "organizations substantially dominated or controlled by that foreign power controlling the world Communist movement." However, the Court did put aside convictions for refusing to register, on the grounds that the wording of board orders constituted a violation of the Fifth Amendment's prohibition against compelled self-incrimination (*Albertson v. Subversive Activities Control Board* 1965).

Since Section 6 of the act prohibited any member of a Communist organization from using a passport, the State Department now tried to revoke the passports of two party leaders. In *Aptheker v. Secretary of State* (1964), the Court invalidated that section because it "too broadly and indiscriminately restricts the right to travel and thereby abridges the liberty guaranteed by the Fifth Amendment" (*Aptheker* 1964, 505). Another section made it a criminal offense for a member of a Communist organization to work in any defense facility. In *United States v. Robel* (1967), the Court declared that section unconstitutionally overbroad as well, but this time because it violated the First Amendment right to freedom of association.

By the time Congress enacted the Communist Control Act of 1954, the Red Scare had ebbed considerably, and that statute's sweeping provisions had few practical consequences. Only one case ever reached the Supreme Court. In *Communist Party v. Catherwood* (1961), the Court gracefully sidestepped the constitutional questions by declaring that this particular case raised interesting questions of state law, which had to be resolved in state courts.

The Court's policy of upholding the antisubversion statutes in general, but then severely restricting their application, also allowed it to invalidate state efforts to penalize allegedly subversive activities. In *Pennsylvania v. Nelson* (1956), the Court overturned a conviction under a state law for conspiring to overthrow the government of the United States by force and violence. Chief Justice Warren held that the Smith Act, the McCarran Act, and the Communist Control Act had created a "pervasive" federal regulator scheme that allowed no room for state interference. The decision effectively nullified the use of laws in forty-two states against sedition and criminal anarchy to prosecute alleged Communist plots to overthrow the federal government; theoretically, states could still prosecute efforts to undermine state governments. A decade later, however, the Court ruled that a Louisiana subversive activities law was void because of vagueness. Finally, in *Brandenburg v. Ohio* (1969), the Court struck down all laws penalizing advocacy of ideas, no matter how radical, as contrary to the First Amendment's guarantee of free speech.

## *Freedom of Religion*

It would be difficult to overestimate the importance of the Vinson Court's decision in *Everson v. Board of Education of Ewing Township* (1947). In *Everson* the Court incorporated the Establishment Clause into the Fourteenth Amendment, making it applicable to the states. In addition, Justice Black set forth what is now considered the classic statement of strict separation jurisprudence. He suggested that the Establishment Clause means that government may not set up a church or pass laws that "aid one religion, aid all religions, or prefer one religion over another." Black concluded by using the words of Thomas Jefferson that the Establishment Clause was "intended to erect a 'wall of separation' between Church and State" (*Everson* 1947, 16). At the same time, the Court permitted the reimbursement of costs for transporting students to non-public schools. There is no question but that the Vinson Court bequeathed to future courts a clear statement that there should be an unbreachable wall of separation between church and state. But Black also fashioned the "child benefit" doctrine in *Everson:* the Establishment Clause does not permit the religion to benefit from actions of government, but it does not preclude individuals from benefiting from government programs. Consequently, so long as the student is the principal beneficiary of government aid, indirect benefit to religion is not forbidden. The Warren Court expanded on this Vinson Court ruling and in its Establishment Clause cases built upon Black's analysis in *Everson.*

The Vinson Court decided two cases involving so-called released-time programs, which set aside an hour a week when students were released from regular classes to get religious instruction. The first, *McCollum v. Board of Education* (1948), involved religious instruction on school premises, offered by clergy representing various denominations. With only one dissent, the Vinson Court disallowed such programs because public school buildings were used for the "dissemination of religious doctrines," and the state was affording "sectarian groups an invaluable aid in that it helps to provide pupils for their religious classes through the use of the state's compulsory public school machinery" (Urofsky 1997a, 235).

The Vinson Court's ruling in *McCollum* created a national furor among religious groups that offered some form of released-time instruction. Indeed, the reaction was so intense that the Court eventually modified its *McCollum* ruling. The released-time program under review in *Zorach v. Clauson* (1952) had moved the religious classes off school property. The program was challenged on the grounds that school authorities endorsed the program and monitored attendance at the religious classes and normal instruction was suspended during the hour of released-time classes. The Vinson Court's ruling in *Zorach* was the first so-called accommodationist outcome. Writing for the majority, Douglas said that the Establishment Clause did not require a total separation of church and state. That "could only lead to antagonism between the two, a result obviously not contemplated by the framers" (Urofsky 1997a, 237). Douglas would later require absolute separation of church and state, but in *Zorach* he pointed to a path of accommodation that would be embraced by the Burger and Rehnquist Courts.

In contrast, the Warren Court, in *Torcaso v. Watkins* (1961), upheld an individual's right not to believe in God, by striking down test oaths in Maryland. Nearly all states had had some form of test oath prior to the Civil War, requiring an affirmation of religious belief, but most had either been wiped off the books or allowed to stagnate in the late nineteenth century. Because the First Amendment had not applied to the states at that time, no cases testing such oaths had come before the Court prior to *Torcaso*. It in essence administered the coup de grâce to a moribund practice.

Prayer in public schools, however, was far from moribund when the Court declared the practice unconstitutional in *Engel v. Vitale* (1962). The New York Board of Regents had prepared, for use in public schools, a "nondenominational" prayer that read, "Almighty God, we acknowledge our dependence upon Thee, and we beg Thy blessings upon us, our parents, our teachers and our country." Many local school boards required that the prayer be recited daily in each class, but a number of parents challenged it as "contrary to the beliefs, religions, or religious practices of both themselves and their children" (*Engel* 1962, 423). The state's highest court upheld the rule so long as the schools did not compel students to join in the prayer when parents objected. By a 6–1 vote (with Frankfurter and White not participating), the Supreme Court held the practice "wholly inconsistent with the Establishment Clause." The prayer, according to Justice Black, could not be interpreted as anything but a religious activity, and the Establishment Clause "must at least mean that it is no part of the business of government to compose official prayers for any group of American people to recite as a part of a religious program carried on by government" (*Engel* 1962, 430–431).

Not since *Brown* had the Court come under as much public criticism as it did after *Engel*. Much of this stemmed from a misunderstanding of what the Court had said. Conservative religious leaders attacked the decision for promoting atheism and secularism. Southerners saw *Engel* as proof of judicial radicalism. "They put the Negroes in the schools," Representative George W. Andrews of Alabama lamented, and "now they have driven God out" (Urofsky 2001, 144). Senator Robert C. Byrd of West Virginia summed up the feelings of many when he complained, "someone is tampering with America's soul" (Urofsky and Finkelman 2002, 829).

The Court had its champions as well as its critics. Liberal Protestant and Jewish groups interpreted the decision as a significant move to divorce religion from meaningless public ritual and to protect its sincere practice. The National Council of Churches, a coalition of Protestant and Orthodox denominations, praised *Engel* for protecting "the religious rights of minorities," while the Anti-Defamation League, a Jewish organization, applauded the "splendid reaffirmation of a basic American principle" (Urofsky and Finkelman 2002, 829).

The justices did not oppose prayer or religion; the framers had gone to great lengths to protect individual freedom in this area. But to protect *individual* freedom, the state could not impose any sort of religious requirement, even an allegedly nonsectarian prayer. When the power and prestige of government is placed behind any particular belief, Black argued, "the inherent coercive pressure upon religious minorities to conform to the prevailing officially approved religion is plain." The Founding Fathers understood that "governmentally established religion and religious persecutions go hand in hand."

One year later the Court extended this reasoning in *Abington School District v. Schempp*, ruling that the Establishment Clause prohibited required reading of the Bible. A Pennsylvania law provided for the reading of at least ten verses of the Bible and the recitation in unison of the Lord's Prayer each day. The Schempp family, members of the Unitarian Church, challenged the law, claiming that the practice it required constituted a religious exercise.

Again, conservatives misinterpreted and attacked the Court's decision, claiming that the justices had now expelled the Bible along with God from school. The Reverend Billy Graham professed himself "shocked," and claimed that "prayers and Bible reading have been a part of American public school life since the Pilgrims landed at Plymouth Rock" (Powe 2000, 360). Justice Clark, however, had made it quite clear that classes could still study the Bible as literature or as a religious document; it just could not be used for proselytizing purposes or in any manner that partook of a religious exercise.

Prayer and Bible reading had been largely an Eastern and Southern experience; in the Midwest only about a third of the schools engaged in the practice, and only about a sixth of the schools in the West. After *Engle* and *Schempp*, religious practices vanished in the East and West, but continued in a more muted form in the Midwest. Opposition to the decisions centered in the South, where many school districts completely disregarded the rulings. The state superintendent of education in South Carolina told school boards to ignore *Schempp*, while Governor George Wallace of Alabama threatened to stage a "pray-in" at public schools. Critics of the Warren Court, especially in the South, objected to far more than the civil rights decisions.

Opponents of the prayer and Bible-reading decisions attempted to override the Court by amending the Constitution. From 1963 until the present, almost every session of Congress has seen the introduction of a proposed amendment to permit Bible reading or prayer in the public schools. In the early 1980s, resurgent Christian fundamentalists and President Ronald Reagan again called for prayer in the schools, only to discover that a majority of Americans still supported the Court's argument that religious freedom required the maintenance of the wall of separation.

A third Warren Court case following *Engel* and *Schempp* also aroused the ire of religious conservatives. The 1927 conviction of John Scopes for teaching Darwin's theory of evolution had not reached the Supreme Court on appeal because the Tennessee high court had dismissed the case on a technicality. As a result, the antievolution statutes in Tennessee and other states had never been subjected to constitutional scrutiny. Finally, in *Epperson v. Arkansas* (1968), a unanimous Court, speaking through Justice Fortas, found the Arkansas antievolution statute in conflict with the Establishment Clause. "Arkansas did not seek to excise from the curricula of its schools and universities all discussion of the origin of man. The law's effort was confined to an attempt to blot out a particular theory because of its supposed conflict with the Biblical account, literally read" (*Epperson* 1968, 109).

To say that the Burger and Rehnquist Courts have abandoned the strict separation test would be false; to say that they have attempted to forge more of an accommodation between religion and the state would be true. But although there have been some significant cases regarding public aid to parochial schools—the most significant being the approval of state-financed vouchers in Cleveland that could be used for public schools in *Zelman v. Simmons-Harris* (2002)—for the most part the basic premises of *Everson* remain, namely, that church and state should be separated and that neither ought to be able to control or influence the other.

## Incorporation

At least to a degree, the Vinson Court's record reflected the "changing of the so-called Old Court and the emergence of modern jurisprudential issues." The prime focus of the Supreme Court's postwar agenda was protection of civil liberties. Although the Warren Court was the principal contributor to this new agenda, the Vinson Court played a transitional role. The notion of the Court more closely scrutinizing government actions that affected protected rights had been introduced by Justice Harlan

Stone in *United States v. Carolene Products Company* (1938). Another aspect of the elevated concern for protected rights came in the incorporation debate. In the discussions that took place during the Vinson Court period, the "most important views are those of Hugo Black and Felix Frankfurter" (Urofsky 1997a, 213).

The debate over incorporation of the Bill of Rights had begun well before Fred Vinson took over the center chair, but during the Vinson years the majority followed Felix Frankfurter's views that incorporation should be selective and limited. The debate between the two views can best be seen in *Adamson v. California* (1947), in which both Frankfurter and Black, the arch-proponents of total incorporation, put forth their views. As noted in Chapter Three, *Adamson* resolved nothing.

The debate between the Cardozo-Frankfurter view of selective incorporation and the Black argument for total incorporation went on into the early 1960s, with Frankfurter, while he remained on the bench, able to fight off the liberals. Once he left, however, the Court's attitude changed significantly. Although never adopting Black's view of total incorporation, the Court used selective incorporation to bring practically all of the guarantees of the Bill of Rights into play against the states. The key to this development came from one of the more conservative members of the Warren Court, John Marshall Harlan, who developed his own ideas regarding what constituted fundamental fairness. One started by looking to the Bill of Rights, he reasoned, but courts had to remember that due process was a flexible concept. If the right was in fact fundamental, then the states were bound by it. States might, however, choose a variety of ways to apply a right, provided the methods they chose were themselves fair. This allowed the establishment of national norms, but still permitted the states to experiment within certain bounds. The Warren Court continued to use the language of "fundamental fairness," but incorporated more and more of the rights in the Fourth, Fifth, Sixth, and Eight Amendments, and insisted that once incorporated, these applied with equal vigor to the states as well as to the federal government.

## Rights of the Accused

During the Vinson years the Court, despite passionate appeals by Frankfurter, Black, and others, continued to allow states to engage in warrantless searches. Following the guidelines set forth in *Betts v. Brady* (1942), the Court refused to require that states provide counsel to defendants except in capital cases. Although the justices objected to coerced confessions, they adopted what has been called a "totality of the circumstances" approach to determine whether such a confession could be used. In regard to rights of the accused, the Vinson Court acted only when the circumstances were so egregious that no one could deny justice had been perverted. But they refused to incorporate any of the protections of the Fourth, Fifth, and Sixth Amendments. The incorporation issue was driven, at least in part, by considerations of federalism. The reluctance of the Vinson Court to incorporate any provisions of the Fourth, Fifth, and Sixth Amendments stemmed from the belief that states had a compelling claim on issues involving the administration of justice. Full incorporation of those amendments, the so-called revolution of due process, was the work of the Warren Court.

It would take far too long to go through all of the Warren Court's cases in this area (see Urofsky 2001, pp. 156–181). But by just highlighting the major cases, one can see how the Warren Court completely rejected the Vinson Court's approach.

The Fourth, Fifth, Sixth, and Eighth Amendments make up the bundle of rights afforded to persons accused of crime. The Fourth Amendment protects the security of individuals, both personally and in their homes, against search and seizure without proper authorization. It also proscribes the issuance of warrants without probable cause. The Fifth Amendment requires grand jury indictment and prohibits double jeopardy. Its most famous provision is a bar against forcing a person to testify against himself or herself. It also includes the guarantee that no one shall be deprived of life, liberty, or property without due process of law. The Sixth Amendment guarantees a speedy and public local trial, thus preventing the state from keeping an accused person incarcerated indefinitely or trying him or her in secret or at a place where the accused would face a jury of strangers. In order to ensure a fair trial, the Sixth Amendment guarantees the accused the right to know the charges, to confront his or her accusers, to compel witnesses to appear to testify, and most important, to have the assistance of counsel. These amendments, and the rights they encompass, are interrelated not only in their goal of protecting the rights of accused persons, but also in how they go about reaching that goal. The right to a fair trial often depends on whether the police acted within their prescribed limits, or whether the accused had access to a lawyer at an appropriate stage in the proceedings.

The Warren Court had, in this area as in its larger jurisprudence, two major aims. One involved a commitment to democracy, to making the guarantees of the Bill of Rights apply not only to the rich but to the poor as well. As Justice Douglas said in extending the right of counsel to appeals, "There can be no equal justice where the kind of appeal a man enjoys depends on the amount of money he has" (Urofsky 2001, 157). Clearly the Court could not give every person in the United States the resources to match those of the wealthy in defending against criminal prosecution. But it could require the government to provide the basic ingredients to ensure fair procedures, and it could try to educate people so that they knew their rights.

Secondly, the Warren Court wanted to make eighteenth-century notions of rights relevant and applicable in the middle of the twentieth century, to make the Constitution a "living" document. To do this the justices had to look past the wording of the Bill of Rights to discern the spirit of the framers. When wiretapping first came before the Court, Chief Justice Taft had dismissed the Fourth Amendment claim by noting there had been no actual entry; in his dissent, Justice Brandeis talked not about breaking and entering but about what the framers had intended: that people should be left alone by the government. This is the notion that Potter Stewart captured when he declared that the Fourth Amendment protects people not places. How to make that, and other parts of the Bill of Rights, living rights for those accused of crimes consumed a great deal of the Warren Court's energy.

## The Fourth Amendment: Search Warrants

The right of people to be secure in their homes and persons is the heart of the Fourth Amendment. Simply stated, that amendment prohibits the state from arbitrarily searching someone's home, office, or person or taking someone into custody without reason. For the police to search premises or arrest a suspect, they need—with certain exceptions—to convince a magistrate that they have probable cause, or at least reasonable suspicion, to believe that specific evidence can be found in a distinct place, or that a certain person did commit a particular crime. Prior to 1933 all a policeman had to do to get a warrant was intone a formula, "I have cause to suspect and I do believe that . . . ." Although courts normally assume that a policeman is telling the truth, the Supreme Court in *Nathanson v. United States* (1933) held that the Fourth Amendment required some proof to secure a warrant, that the magistrate needed facts, not just opinion, to justify the search. In *Harris v. United States* (1947), the Vinson Court ruled 5–4 that where police had a valid arrest warrant, they did not need a separate search warrant to make a lawful search. The following year the Court held invalid a warrantless search that preceded an arrest (*Johnson v. United States* 1948).

In 1961 the Supreme Court extended Fourth Amendment guarantees to the states in *Mapp v. Ohio*. Three years later, in *Aguilar v. Texas* (1964), the Court tried to give police, magistrates, and lower courts some guidelines as to what the Constitution required. The police needed, it said, to provide: (1) facts to justify probable cause, and (2) reasons that the magistrate should believe that probable cause existed.

If this had been all, few people would have been upset by the course of developing Fourth Amendment jurisprudence. Two cases in the final term of the Warren Court seemed to many people to be carrying the warrant requirements beyond reason, however. In *Spinelli v. United States* (1969), the Court tightened the guidelines considerably. Justice Harlan said that first, the magistrate must evaluate the truthfulness of the source of information, whether it comes from a police officer or an informant, and second, the magistrate must evaluate the adequacy of the facts to support probable cause. The Court in essence required police to corroborate their evidence in some way, so that the magistrate could rely on its truthfulness. As a practical matter, *Spinelli* would force police to tighten up their procedures for securing warrants. On the day Warren retired from the bench, the Court imposed a warrant requirement in situations where warrantless searches had previously been considered legitimate, namely, for searches incident to an arrest. In *Chimel v. California* (1969), Stewart held once police had satisfied themselves that the suspect had neither a weapon nor evidence on his person or within his immediate grasp, they must obtain a warrant in order to search further.

These rules now appear to be fairly commonsensical, if one is to give any credence to the Fourth Amendment. The outcry that greeted them must be seen in its historical context, namely, that state and local police had hardly bothered with warrants prior to the 1960s, and if they had (because required by some state constitutions to do so), they had been able to secure warrants from friendly magistrates with little more than an avowal of their suspicions. The Vinson Court had taken a somewhat erratic course during the 1940s as to what the Fourth Amendment required, but those cases had for the most part been ignored at the state and local levels. The Warren Court had not only attempted to lay down consistent Fourth Amendment rules, but more importantly, to apply them to the states as well.

## The Fourth Amendment: Wiretapping

In 1928 the Court began to deal with how modern technology affected the Fourth Amendment, when it ruled in *Olmstead v. United States* that wiretapping did not constitute an unauthorized search. In a highly formalistic opinion, Chief Justice Taft ignored the intent of the Fourth Amendment and claimed that there had been no actual entry, merely the use by police of an enhanced sense of hearing. To pay too much attention to "nice ethical conduct by government officials," he said, "would make society suffer and give criminals greater immunity than has been known heretofore" (*Olmstead v. United States* 1928). Taft's opinion was overruled by Congress in regard to federal law enforcement officials when it passed the 1934 Communications Act, but as late as 1952, the Vinson Court continued to allow states to conduct wiretaps without warrants.

One of the first decisions in this area by the Warren Court barred the use in federal courts of state-gathered wiretap evidence (*Benanti v. United States* 1957). Then in *Silverman v. United States* (1961), the Court unanimously overruled *Olmstead* and vindicated Brandeis's dissenting view. The justices were becoming aware of the pervasiveness of electronic surveillance as well as the scientific advances in the devices used. In 1928, Brandeis's law clerk had objected to the justice suggesting that in the future it would be possible to listen to conversations through walls and from far off. Less than thirty years later, a leading authority on privacy, Alan Westin of Columbia University, warned that "modern technology has breached at vital points the physical limits that once guarded individual and group privacy" (Urofsky 2001, 166). Physical trespass no longer made any sense as a demarcation between permissible and impermissible electronic surveillance, and the Court acknowledged this in 1967.

That year the Warren Court handed down its strongest decision yet in regard to electronic surveillance in *Katz v. United States* (1967). Justice Stewart's opinion merged many of the Fourth Amendment ideas the Court had been developing for more than a decade with the right to privacy it had recently announced in *Griswold v. Connecticut* (1965). Stewart admitted that the phrase "constitutionally protected area" failed to define the meaning and reach of the Fourth Amendment. In a notable phrase, he declared that "the Fourth Amendment protects people, not places." Where an action took place mattered less than whether a general expectation of privacy existed in that place; if so, then the individual's privacy would be protected there.

## The Exclusionary Rule

If the constitutional guarantee against unreasonable and unlawful searches is to have any significance, evidence seized in violation of the Fourth Amendment should be excluded from trial; otherwise it is a guarantee without meaning. Justice Day created just such an "exclusionary rule" in *Weeks v. United States* (1914), but it applied to only federal law enforcement officials. The Court had explicitly declared in *Weeks* that the rule did not apply to the states. Hence, for the next thirty years, state and federal authorities colluded in what came to be known as the "silver platter doctrine." Evidence obtained by state authorities in a manner that would be illegal if engaged in by federal agents could be admitted in federal court so long as there had been no federal participation in the search. In 1949 the Vinson Court took a step toward reining in warrantless state searches in *Wolf v. Colorado*, when Justice Frankfurter spoke for the majority in holding that unreasonable state searches and seizures violated the Fourteenth Amendment's Due Process Clause. Frankfurter, however, avoided the issue of remedies and in fact said that evidence so seized could be used in a state trial for a state crime. Since the exclusionary rule, effective as it might be in enforcing the provisions of the Fourth Amendment, was not itself a part of the amendment, its use was not required of the states. Instead, the Vinson Court left the issue of the enforcement of Fourth Amendment protections to the states. As Justice Murphy wrote in his dissent, "the conclusion is inescapable that but one remedy exists to deter violations of the search and seizure clause. That is the rule which excludes illegally obtained evidence" (*Wolf* 1949, 44).

In 1961, in *Mapp v. Ohio*, the Warren Court overruled *Wolf* 6–3, holding that the Fourteenth Amendment incorporated the Fourth Amendment and applied it to the states. The view of the *Wolf* dissenters on the exclusionary rule also emerged in *Mapp*.

Both the majority and minority in *Mapp* agreed that the police had acted egregiously. The three dissenters (Harlan, Frankfurter, and Whittaker) objected to imposing a federal judge-made rule on the states, but the majority argued, as had Justice Day a half-century earlier, that the only remedy to violation of the Fourth Amendment—the only way to ensure that police did not just ignore it—was to deprive them of the fruits of an illegal search. There is general agreement that for the Fourth Amendment to be effective, there must be some remedy for its violation. This seemingly obvious conclusion is clouded, however, by the public's failure to understand why evidence that clearly establishes guilt cannot be used and why, as Benjamin Cardozo once put it, "the criminal is to go free because the constable has blundered."

The exclusionary rule rests on several considerations. In *Mapp* the Court spelled out one of them, namely, that the only way to deter police from illegal searches is to deprive them of the evidence they obtain. Another was later described by Chief Justice Warren Burger as "the 'sporting contest' thesis that the government must 'play the game fairly' and cannot be allowed to profit from its own illegal acts" (*Bivens v. Six Unknown Named Agents of Federal Bureau of Narcotics* 1974, 414).

## The Sixth Amendment: The Right to Counsel

In *Betts v. Brady* (1942), the Court decided by a divided vote that counsel for indigents did not constitute a fundamental right "implicit in the concept of ordered liberty" or an essential of a fair trial. The accused, according to the Court, "was not helpless, but was a man forty-three years old, of ordinary intelligence, and ability to take care of his own interests" at the trial (*Betts* 1942, 272). The Court endorsed a case-by-case review with an emphasis on the totality of the circumstances. In situations involving illiterate defendants or complex legal questions, then due process required an attorney.

This approach proved enormously time consuming, and despite hearing dozens of cases over the next two decades, the Court never established clear criteria to guide state judges in determining when counsel had to be provided. Moreover, it found special circumstances present in so many instances that by 1962 it had for all practical purposes eroded the *Betts* rule. Finally the justices decided to review the situation and accepted an appeal filed by an indigent, Clarence Earl Gideon, who had requested and been denied counsel in a Florida breaking-and-entering case.

Not only had the *Betts* rule come under increasing criticism over the years, but also a number of states had voluntarily adopted the federal standard of providing counsel to indigents accused of felonies. By 1962, forty-five states provided counsel for all or nearly all indigent felony defendants. Only five states—Alabama, Florida, Mississippi, North Carolina, and South Carolina—did not, and even in those states some cities and counties assigned attorneys to poor persons charged with serious crimes. As the Court prepared to hear Gideon's case, only two states backed the Florida position that the Court ought to leave the rule alone; twenty-two filed amicus briefs condemning *Betts* as "an anachronism when handed down" and asking that it be overruled.

The Court agreed, and Justice Black, who twenty-one years earlier had dissented in *Betts*, spoke for a unanimous bench in *Gideon v. Wainwright*, holding that the case had been wrongly decided. Numerous cases in the intervening years had proven conclusively that one could not have a fair trial without assistance of counsel, and that it was, therefore, "implicit in the concept of ordered liberty." The importance of counsel meant that the Fourteenth Amendment's Due Process Clause incorporated the Sixth Amendment right, making it applicable to the states.

*Gideon* applied only to felony cases; not until 1972 did the Burger Court extend the right to misdemeanor trials as well in *Argersinger v. Hamlin*. The Warren Court, however, did expand the right to counsel in two 1967 cases. In response to growing criticism of shoddy and unreliable police identification methods, the Court extended the right back to the lineup and applied the right to have an attorney to the federal government in *United States v. Wade*, and on the same day to the states, in *Gilbert v. California*. As Justice Brennan explained, the Sixth Amendment requires counsel from the time the police shift their investigation from a general sifting of facts to accusing a particular person. By this time Brennan could say that the Court had developed a set of precedents that agreed on the fact that the Sixth Amendment came into play at "critical" stages of criminal proceedings.

The Court, through *Gideon*, opened the eyes of the country to the great truth that absence of counsel meant absence of justice. What the Court understood, but would have a great deal of difficulty explaining in a manner that caught the popular imagination, was that the trial was not the only stage of the criminal justice process where the accused needed the help of an attorney. Perhaps the greatest criticism of the Court in this area came not when it extended what had started as a trial right forward to appeals, but when it pushed that right back earlier to police confrontation with a suspect in custody. The Court's concern over providing accused persons with effective counsel at all critical stages of the proceedings carried over into its Fifth Amendment decisions.

## The Fifth Amendment: The Privilege against Self-Incrimination

The right against compulsory self-incrimination had been established as a tenet of English common law by the end of the seventeenth century. The origins of the privilege are somewhat murky, but in English common law, as historian Leonard Levy explains, "the initially vague maxim that no man is bound to accuse himself had come to mean that he was not required to answer against himself in any criminal cause or to any interrogatories that might tend to expose him to persecution" (Levy 1968, 330). At about the same time a rule also developed that forced confessions could not be used against a defendant because of their unreliability.

From 1936 to 1964, the Supreme Court dealt with the issue of coercion on the basis of the Due Process Clauses of the Fifth and Fourteenth Amendments. In its first major case, *Brown v. Mississippi* (1936), the Court summarily reversed convictions in a state court based on confessions obtained through whippings. The Court decided thirty-five confession cases between 1936 and 1964, moving from easy ones where confessions had been induced through physical coercion to the much harder issue of psychological coercion. The justices attempted to define appropriate limits on police behavior through a case-by-case process. In some of its early decisions, the Warren Court showed its sensitivity to such factors as illiteracy, limited education, mental retardation, incompetence, and unnecessary delay in bringing a suspect before a magistrate, moving toward a "totality of the circumstances" test to determine whether the confession had been voluntary and thus was admissible.

Some members of the Court found the case-by-case approach as unsatisfactory in Fifth Amendment confession cases as they had in the post-*Betts* right to counsel cases. They believed that the voluntariness test did not give police and lower courts sufficient guidance. The "totality of the circumstances" standard appeared very subjective and caused confusion among trial and lower appellate court judges. In 1959, four members of the Warren Court pointed to the next phase of the evolving standard on confessions.

Vincent Spano had been arrested for murder, and although he repeatedly asked to see his attorney, who was in the police station, officers refused his request and continued to interrogate him until he confessed. The Court unanimously threw out the confession as involuntary, on the grounds that Spano had been "overborne by official pressure." Douglas, joined by Justices Black, Brennan, and Stewart, concurred in the result, but suggested that the real issue had been that Spano had been unable to see his attorney. They raised the question of whether any confession given without proper legal advice could be considered voluntary (*Spano v. New York* 1959).

In *Massiah v. United States* (1964), the Court moved away from the due process, totality of the circumstances approach to confession, emphasizing in its place the Sixth Amendment right to counsel. The Warren Court reached what it sought in one of the most famous—or infamous—cases in its history, *Miranda v. Arizona* (1966). There it tried to provide a simple standard, namely, the famous "Miranda warnings." In essence, the *Miranda* majority identified coercion in any form as the chief problem in determining the validity of confessions. Rather than proceed on a case-by-case basis, attempting to evaluate the totality of the circumstances, the Court laid down definite rules to guide police and lower courts. If they had been obeyed and the suspect confessed, then his confession would be admissible as evidence. If police failed to obey the rules, then the confession would be thrown out.

The police had to inform a suspect in clear and unequivocal terms that he or she had a right to remain silent; that anything said could be used in court; that the accused had a right to a lawyer, and if he or she had no money, the state would provide an attorney for them. If the interrogation continued without the presence of a lawyer, "a heavy burden rests on the Government to demonstrate that the defendant knowingly and intelligently waives his privilege against self-incrimination and his right to retained or appointed counsel" *(Miranda* 1966, 475).

*Miranda* is a logical culmination of the Warren Court's journey in search of a workable method to deal with the issue of forced confessions. It started out with the premise of earlier courts, that physical coercion could not be allowed and that an evaluation of the totality of the circumstances would determine whether due process had been violated. At the same time, the Court had been developing a broader interpretation of the Sixth Amendment right to counsel. In *Miranda* these various strands came together in the belief that for rights to be meaningful, a suspect must know about them before being questioned, because during interrogation the physical and psychological advantage resided with the police. One could not even remotely conceive of the Vinson Court adopting such a broad prophylactic rule.

In *Miranda* the Warren Court tried to do two separate things. First, it wanted to establish a prophylactic rule to aid judicial review. Although it is still possible to have a tainted confession even if the warning is given, the failure to inform suspects of their rights is a clear indicator that the confession should not be admitted. Some state and local police departments, who had never paid scrupulous attention to constitutional protection, did run into methodological problems following the decision. Once they adopted the *Miranda* warning as part of their standard procedures, they discovered that it did not undermine their effectiveness; in many cases, the accused wanted to confess and could hardly wait for the police to finish reading them their rights.

The second aspect of the decision reflected the Warren Court majority's view that in a democracy, with rights embedded in a written Constitution, all people had to be aware of those rights so that, if faced by police interrogation, they could make voluntary and intelligent choices. One should recall that few secondary-school systems taught much in the way of law prior to 1966, and not many people knew what rights they had. This situation has changed considerably in the last two decades, with nearly all states adopting Constitution and law segments in their public school social studies guidelines.

Despite the initial uproar against the "procriminal decision," the public quickly internalized the *Miranda* decision. In 1967, the old police show *Dragnet* was brought back to the air, and Jack Webb, as Joe Friday, would give the requisite *Miranda* warning, although making it clear that he considered this a hindrance to good police work. In contrast the star of the 1970s show, *Hawaii Five-O*, treated *Miranda* just as Earl Warren would have wanted, as a means of making the police more professional. Everyone in the United States who watched a police show on television soon became aware of the warnings; little children playing cops-and-robbers knew the words. Since giving the warning did not seem to interfere with good police work, before long all but the most fanatic conservatives stopped looking at *Miranda* as in any way "handcuffing" the police. Thanks in large measure to the media, one could argue that in this area Warren had been successful in achieving his goal of equalizing knowledge, so that poverty would not be a bar to exercising one's rights.

## Criminal Procedure in the Burger and Rehnquist Courts

Although conservatives singled out the Warren Court's criminal procedure decisions for special criticism, and Presidents Richard Nixon, Ronald Reagan, and George Bush appointed justices supposedly friendlier to the police, no major decision of the Warren Court in this area has been overturned. The hard-and-fast rules applied in some Fourth Amendment areas have been relaxed a bit, to allow common sense to govern, and so to some extent there has been a return to the old "totality of the circumstances" rule. But it has been very limited and a far cry from how the Vinson Court used it.

Perhaps the signal case showing how the judicial system has adopted the Warren Court and turned its back on the Vinson decisions was *Dickerson v. United States* (2000). In 1968 Congress had attempted to reverse the Warren Court ruling in *Miranda* with Section 3501 of the Omnibus Crime Control and Safe Streets Act, by giving a very broad definition to "voluntary" confessions. Every administration since then, including those of Nixon and Reagan, has considered that section unconstitutional, and none had defended it in court. Dickerson, indicted for bank robbery and related federal crime, tried to suppress statements he had made to federal agents. The U.S. District Court granted his motion to suppress, but a conservative advocacy group managed to win friend-of-the-court status in the Fourth Circuit and convinced the appellate panel that Section 3501 and not *Miranda* ought to govern the admissibility of confessions. The Supreme Court reversed, however, and concluded that Congress had no authority to supercede the Court's decisions, such as *Miranda*, which establish constitutional rules. Chief Justice Rehnquist, once a critic of *Miranda*, now announced that the warning had constitutional status.

## *Apportionment*

During the interim between Harlan Fiske Stone's death and Fred Vinson's appointment, the Court decided a case that not only reflected the growing chasm between Frankfurter and Black, but would also have profound implications for the nation's political system. In March 1946 the Court heard arguments in *Colegrove v. Green.* Professor Kenneth Colegrove of Northwestern University attacked the state's antiquated apportionment system, which, despite massive population shifts, had not been revised since 1901. As a result, even though a majority of the state's population now lived in major urban centers such as Chicago, legislative power remained entrenched in rural districts. Efforts to secure reform through state judicial and political methods had failed, since neither state judges nor the rural-dominated legislature had any desire to change the status quo. Colegrove then appealed to the federal courts, arguing that the Illinois system, which affected the drawing of congressional district lines as well, violated the Fifteenth Amendment ban on abridging the right to vote as well as guarantees in Article I (regarding apportionment of congressmen) and Article IV, which decrees that the United States "shall guarantee to every State in this Union a Republican Form of Government."

A "bob-tailed Court" of only seven justices handed down the decision; Stone had died, and Robert H. Jackson was still in Germany prosecuting the war crimes trials. Although four justices apparently found against Colegrove, in fact, the real decision paved the way for one of the landmark cases in the Warren era.

Frankfurter, speaking for himself, Harold Burton, and Stanley Reed, held that it was beyond the Court's competence to decide what he termed a "political question." Legislative appointment was a "non-justiciable" issue that fell within a realm the Constitution left to the political branches. Political questions were not amenable to judicial remedy. Frankfurter got his fourth vote from Wiley Rutledge, who, although he disagreed with Frankfurter on the justiciability issue, voted to dismiss the suit because, with the next election so close, it would be impossible to implement any workable remedy.

Black, Douglas, and Murphy dissented, on the grounds that a clear constitutional violation existed and that whenever that happened, the issues could be taken to federal courts for relief. No one, Black asserted in his dissent, "would deny that the equal protection clause would also prohibit a law that would expressly give certain citizens a half-vote and others a full vote" (*Colgrove* 1946, 569). What many observers failed to note was that although Colegrove lost the case, a majority of those who heard the argument—four of the seven justices—agreed on the justiciability of the matter.

Many states, of course, did reapportion every ten years in order to reflect changing population trends, and during the 1950s, three-fifths of all the states reapportioned one or both of their legislative chambers. Twelve states, however, had not redrawn their district lines for more than thirty years. Tennessee and Alabama had not redrawn theirs since 1901, and Delaware had not redrawn its since 1897. Within some states discrepancies of enormous magnitude existed; in Vermont, for example, the most populous assembly district had 33,000 persons, and the smallest had 238, yet each had one seat. Distortions also appeared in many state senates, which often followed geographical boundaries. In eleven state senates a voting majority could be elected by less than one-fifth of the population. In California, where 11 percent of the voters could elect a majority of the state senate, the senatorial district comprising Los Angeles had 6 million people, whereas a more sparsely populated district had only 14,000. In all of the states that had not reapportioned, as well as in many that had reapportioned but without using strict population criteria, the results magnified the power of the older rural areas while undervaluing ballots cast in new urban and suburban districts. Needless to say, the rural minorities who controlled the state houses had no incentive to reform, since doing so would dissipate their power.

Ironically, the first hint of change came in an opinion written by Frankfurter, who nonetheless continued to insist that courts should stay out of this political morass. In 1960 the high court struck down a flagrant gerrymandering scheme in Tuskegee, Alabama, which effectively disenfranchised nearly all of the city's African Americans. Frankfurter's opinion in *Gomillion v. Lightfoot* relied entirely on the Fifteenth Amendment, and he carefully avoided any intimation that the ruling might apply to other districting imbalances. Whatever Frankfurter's intentions, reformers believed they now had a foot in the courthouse door; two years later, over Frankfurter's objections, the Court accepted a suit brought by urban voters in Tennessee, where there had been no redistricting in sixty years.

*Baker v. Carr*, handed down late in 1962, took the Court away from the position Frankfurter had so vigorously defended in *Colegrove*. In one of his best and most scholarly opinions, Brennan, speaking for a 6–2 majority, held that issues such as alleged malapportionment could be litigated in federal court. He prescribed no particular solution, but sent the case back to district court for a full hearing; the high court would not deal with a remedy until the matter had been fully litigated and a final decree entered.

Despite strenuous and predictable dissents from Justices Harlan and Frankfurter, both of whom urged judicial restraint and deference to the political process, it is easy to see why the majority of the Court agreed to consider the apportionment cases. Frankfurter's dissent, as a matter of fact, gives us a clear understanding of exactly what the majority had in mind. He accused the majority of risking the Court's prestige in an area that should be left to the political process. "In a democratic society like ours, relief must come through an aroused popular conscience that sears the conscience of the people's representatives" (*Baker* 1962, 270). Although Harlan thought the system might be better, he found nothing in the Constitution to prevent a state "acting not irrationally, from choosing any electoral structure it thinks best suited to the interests, tempers and customs of the people" (*Baker* 1962, 334).

Both men ignored the heart of the issue—the political process had been stymied and perverted, so that the majority of the people could not adopt that system "best suited" to their needs because an entrenched minority blocked any and all change. The Court on a number of occasions had declared that not all issues could be resolved through litigation, and that in questions of public policy, change would have to come through the political process and not through the courts. In those cases, however, there had always been an assumption that the process would be amenable to majoritarian decision making, that all voters would have a say in the matter.

One month after delivering his dissent in *Baker v. Carr,* Frankfurter suffered a stroke; soon afterward, he retired. With the appointment of Arthur Goldberg, the liberals now held the balance of power on the bench. The reapportionment cases provide the clearest example of the great change that took place in the Warren Court and are key to understanding its commitment to democracy. Its members placed a high value on the integrity of the political process, since for all the debate about judicial activism and policymaking, the Court always looked to that process to resolve most of the public questions of the day. The whole rationale for judicial restraint and deference to the legislative will had been based on the belief that the legislature truly and accurately reflected the will of the people. For the majority of the Warren Court, depriving people of the full value of their ballots meant depriving them of the equal protection of the law, whether that deprivation came about because of race, poverty, or residence in an urban area.

Despite Frankfurter's dire warnings that the Court would do immeasurable harm to itself through entanglement in the "political thicket," in the end the Warren Court found not only a clear standard but one that quickly won the support of a majority of Americans. Following *Baker v. Carr,* the Court handed down decisions invalidating the Georgia county unit system as well as the state's congressional districting plan. *Gray v. Sanders* technically dealt with voting rights rather than apportionment, but given the gist of *Baker,* it was an easy case. Attorney General Robert F. Kennedy chose it as his maiden appearance in any court and argued the United States's amicus position against the Georgia unit system. Kennedy had memorized the facts of the case well, but most important, in his argument he uttered the words—"one man, one vote"—that would give the Court the key to overcoming Frankfurter's claim that there could be no judicially manageable relief. Justice Douglas applied an equal protection analysis, and then, borrowing Kennedy's phrase, articulated the formula that not only provided judicial guidance but also caught the popular imagination—"one person, one vote." Who could object to assuring every person that his or her vote counted equally with those of others? Support for the formula equated with support for democracy and the Constitution; opposition seemed undemocratic and petty.

Following *Baker* many legislatures had voluntarily redistricted one or both of their legislative chambers, but they did not know exactly what criteria the Court would apply to measure the fairness of their plans. In some states rural minorities blocked any effort at reform, and in Colorado the electorate, by a 2–1 margin, approved a plan that apportioned the lower house on a population basis, but gave rural areas additional, although not a controlling, weight in the upper house. In states where reapportionment had occurred as well as in states where it had been blocked, reformers launched dozens of suits seeking redress under the Equal Protection Clause.

In June 1964 Chief Justice Warren handed down the Court's decision in six representative cases. The leading suit, *Reynolds v. Sims*, attacked malapportionment of the Alabama legislature, which, despite a constitutional requirement for representation based on population and a decennial reapportionment, remained apportioned on the basis of the 1900 census. Lower courts had found this scheme, as well as two proposed "reforms," violated the Equal Protection Clause and had ordered a temporary reapportionment plan that combined features from the new proposals. Both sides in the lower court case then appealed. Warren built upon the analyses in the two Georgia cases and adopted Douglas's "one man, one vote" formulation as the constitutional standard. The chief justice dismissed all formulas that attempted to weigh factors other than population:

> To the extent that a citizen's right to vote is debased, he is that much less a citizen.
> . . . the weight of a citizen's vote cannot be made to depend on where he lives. . . .
> A citizen, a qualified voter, is no more or no less so because he lives in the city or
> on the farm. This is the clear and strong command of our Constitution's Equal Pro-
> tection Clause. (Lucas 1964, 567)

In the Colorado case, *Lucas v. Forty-Fourth General Assembly of Colorado*, the state contended that a majority of its voters, by a 2–1 margin, had voluntarily diluted their voting power to protect the rural minority. Warren rejected the argument out of hand; the Court dealt here not with the rights of minorities but with the rights of individuals. "It is a precept of American law," he declared, "that certain rights exist which a citizen cannot trade, barter, or even give away" (*Lucas* 1964, 736–737). An individual's constitutional rights could not be infringed because a majority of the people voted to do so.

Despite the uproar from rural-dominated legislatures and their allies in Congress that greeted these decisions, the opposition soon faded as new legislatures, elected under court-ordered plans, took control of the state houses. Moreover, influential citizen's groups, such as the League of Women Voters, endorsed *Reynolds* and the one-person, one-vote concept, and conducted educational campaigns to explain the rulings. And once implemented, reapportionment faced little opposition, as formerly dominant minorities could no longer block the majority will. No state, once reapportioned, sought to revive the old system.

Although the one-person, one-vote rule provided a clear and judicially manageable standard, some questions did remain, such as the level of exactitude as well as the reach of the decision. In *Swann v. Adams* (1967), the Court invalidated a Florida plan that had only minor deviations from the formula. Justice White agreed that the Constitution did not require absolute precision, but in this case the statute had failed to provide adequate justification for certain important deviations. As with other equal protection cases, the Court would employ a strict set of standards, so that states would have to show a compelling reason for any significant deviation. The following year in *Avery v. Midland County*, the Court brought city and county governments under the one-person, one-vote rule; remaining questions, and there were many, would be decided by the Burger Court.

The apportionment cases seemed a fitting climax to the Warren Court's so-called equal protection revolution. What had been the "last resort of constitutional arguments" had become, in a little more than a dozen years, a powerful tool to protect the civil rights and liberties of individuals. In some ways the apportionment cases constitute the Warren Court's most "radical" decisions. Unlike the desegregation cases, in which the Court had chipped away at the separate-but-equal doctrine for many years, apportionment had been a stranger in the courts. Conservatives later seized upon Frankfurter's argument in *Colegrove* as the proper standard for judicial restraint. That argument had never enjoyed support from a majority of his colleagues, however. Four of the seven justices who heard the case thought it justiciable, but they lacked any idea of how to develop a clear and manageable judicial standard. The Warren Court would develop such a standard in the 1960s.

By the time the Court agreed on the justiciability of apportionment in *Baker v. Carr* in 1962, it had had the experience of the desegregation cases and had learned several valuable lessons. First, the political process cannot always be relied on to remedy even a clear violation of constitutionally protected rights. Second, if courts intervene to protect such rights, then they must act boldly and set out clear rules. Third, new standards must be implemented without delay. The apportionment decisions showed the wisdom of these lessons; despite some vocal opposition from rural groups who would now lose power, the country quickly accepted the rationale of the decisions and the rightness of the solution.

There could hardly be a greater contrast between the philosophy of the Vinson Court and that of its successor than in their positions on the reapportionment issue. The Vinson Court, dominated by Frankfurter's philosophy, would ignore inequalities whenever possible, believing the judiciary should defer to legislative judgment on nearly all matters. What had become clear by 1953, as the Vinson justices themselves recognized in the school desegregation cases, was that as much as they would have preferred to avoid some issues, the Constitution demanded that they act. If, as some critics charge, the Warren Court carried judicial activism too far, at least in this area the wisdom of the Court fulfilling its responsibilities as protector of the rights guaranteed under the Constitution cannot be denied.

## The Steel Seizure Case

One would not think that *Youngstown Sheet and Tube Company v. Sawyer* (1952) would be the type of case by which one could measure a legacy. Unlike the racial desegregation decisions that led directly to *Brown*, and thus were adopted and expanded on by future Courts, or the decisions in the area of civil liberties that were later rejected outright, the steel seizure case occupies a curious yet important place in modern constitutional jurisprudence.

It involved the rights of labor, but the greater significance of the case lies in what it said about presidential power. As the Vinson Court struck down President Harry Truman's seizure of the steel mills, it rejected the arguments for inherent or aggregate executive authority, at least as asserted by the Truman administration. Each of the six justices who voted against Truman offered his own opinion. The Court thought that seizing private property was within the authority of Congress but not the president, even a president drawing on his powers as commander in chief. The Court was troubled by the seeming lack of limits that might apply to the inherent power the president was claiming. Most of the Vinson Court justices expressed their individual views on the nature of executive power. Perhaps the most valuable opinion came from Justice Robert Jackson. Presidential authority, he suggested, is greatest when a president acts at the "direct or implied command of Congress." In circumstances where Congress has not acted, the president may act in reliance on his own powers, in a "twilight zone" where it is unclear whether Congress or the president had the "ultimate responsibility." Presidential authority is weakest, Jackson concluded, when the executive acts in "defiance of either express or implied legislative intent" (Urofsky 1997a, 211). Jackson's analysis, as well as the thoughts of several other Vinson Court justices, continues to inform separation of power jurisprudence today.

In *Marbury v. Madison* (1803), Chief Justice John Marshall established that the Supreme Court would be the ultimate interpreter of the Constitution. It would not only be the court of last resort on constitutional issues and decide what specific provisions meant, but it would also decide when and if the other branches of government had responsibility for constitutional decision making. In *Youngstown*, albeit by a fractured vote, the Court in essence reaffirmed that authority, by deciding that although the Congress indeed had power to seize private property during a war emergency, the president lacked the authority to do so in 1952 in the absence of congressional delegation.

The Warren Court reaffirmed its role as constitutional arbiter in two cases. In *Cooper v. Aaron* (1958), it chastised the State of Arkansas for claiming that because it had not been a party to *Brown* it was not bound by the ruling ending racial segregation in public schools. In a unique opinion formally signed by all nine justices, the Court made quite clear that when it delivered a constitutional statement, all states (indeed it implied all citizens) were bound by its ruling. More than a decade later, in one of its last decisions, *Powell v. McCormack* (1969), the Warren Court reprimanded the House of Representatives for expelling Adam Clayton Powell Jr. and told the lower house of Congress that it had incorrectly read those provisions of Article I giving the House authority over its own membership. The Court, and only the Court, could say what the Constitution meant.

A little more than two decades later Congress, unhappy with a string of Court decisions on religious accommodation, passed the Religious Freedom Restoration Act (1993), designed specifically to overturn what religious leaders believed to be the excessively restrictive provisions of cases such as *Lyng v. Northwest Indian Cemetery Protective Association* (1988) and particularly *Employment Division, Oregon Department of Human Resources v. Smith* (1990). The law and its accompanying legislative history could not have been blunter in their statements that the Supreme Court had been wrong in eliminating the requirement that governments justify burdens on religious exercise imposed by laws neutral on their surface and that a better rule would be that government had to make reasonable accommodation to religious practices.

In *City of Boerne v. Flores* (1997), the Court denied that Congress had power under any section of the Constitution to impose upon the courts any particular interpretation of a constitutional provision. Justice Anthony Kennedy sternly read a civics lesson to the Congress. "When the political branches of the Government act against the background of a judicial interpretation of the Constitution already issued, it must understand that in later cases and controversies the Court will treat its precedents with the respect due them under settled principles" (*Flores* 1997, 436). The Court's views, and not those of Congress, would determine the meaning of specific constitutional provisions. As in the *Youngstown* case, the Court once again affirmed its primacy in constitutional interpretation.

## *Conclusion*

The Vinson Court in its seven years dealt with a number of important issues. Because Vinson's was a transition Court, however, it is not surprising that so few of the opinions it handed down have withstood the test of time. It should be lauded for the steps it took regarding the shameful treatment of people of color, and while the Warren Court decided *Brown* and its progeny, it is unlikely that the case could have been decided that way in 1954 without the earlier decisions of the late 1940s and early 1950s.

Perhaps one should not blame the Vinson justices for giving in to the Cold War mentality that gripped the nation; other courts in wartime have also found it more expedient to bend before the popular patriotism of the time than to attempt to thwart it because of constitutional principles. Several of the justices who voted to intern Japanese Americans during World War II also voted to restrict civil liberties, especially speech, during the postwar Red Scare. The Warren Court rode out the rest of the Red Scare, and starting in the 1960s managed to undo nearly all of the speech and internal security decisions of its predecessor. Free speech has been zealously guarded by the Burger and Rehnquist Courts as well.

The debate over incorporation that so gripped the Court in the 1940s no longer interests us except as history. Although occasionally a lower court judge will declare that the Bill of Rights does not apply to the states, he is always and quickly slapped down by the high court. The debate is over, and all but one or two of the articles of the Bill of Rights (incorporation has not been applied to quartering of troops, civil jury trials, or the right to keep and bear arms) are now incorporated. Black's vision—if not his rationale—is victorious. The cramped view of constitutional rights that Felix Frankfurter espoused is gone, replaced by the broader vision of Black and Douglas. If modern conservative courts occasionally use a restrictive interpretation, it is usually fact-specific and not intended as a general rule. The major rulings of the Warren Court wiping out the Vinson Court decisions in civil liberties and apportionment have been upheld and even expanded by its successors.

In one area the Vinson Court's view of the Constitution remains strong. That is the role of the Court as the ultimate arbiter of the nation's governing document. That is its most enduring legacy.

# References and Further Reading

Belknap, Michal R. 1977. *Cold War Political Justice: The Smith Act, the Communist Party, and American Civil Liberties.* Westport, CT: Greenwood Press.

Levy, Leonard. 1968. *Origins of the Fifth Amendment.* New York: Oxford University Press.

Powe, Lucas A., Jr. 2000. *The Warren Court and American Politics.* Cambridge, MA: Harvard University Press.

Schwartz, Bernard, ed. 1998. *The Burger Court: Counter-Revolution or Confirmation?* New York: Oxford University Press.

Tushnet, Mark V. 1994. *Making Civil Rights Law: Thurgood Marshall and the Supreme Court, 1936–1961.* New York: Oxford University Press.

Urofsky, Melvin I. 1991. *The Continuity of Change: The Supreme Court and Individual Liberties, 1953–1986.* Belmont, CA: Wadsworth Publishing.

————. 1997a. *Division and Discord: The Supreme Court under Stone and Vinson, 1941–1953.* Columbia: University of South Carolina Press.

————. 2001. *The Warren Court: Justices, Rulings, and Legacy.* Santa Barbara, CA: ABC-CLIO.

Urofsky, Melvin I., and Paul Finkelman. 2002. *A March of Liberty: A Constitutional History of the United States, Volume II: From 1877 to the Present.* 2d ed. New York: Oxford University Press.

Westin, Alan F. 1958. *The Anatomy of a Constitutional Law Case.* New York: Macmillan.

Yarbrough, Tinsley E. 2000. *The Rehnquist Court and the Constitution.* New York: Oxford University Press.

# PART TWO

## *Reference Materials*

# Key People, Laws, and Events

## Alien Registration (Smith) Act of 1940

The Alien Registration Act, more commonly known as the Smith Act, required aliens living in the United States to register with the federal government. Any alien associated with a subversive organization could be deported. The statute also placed severe restrictions on certain kinds of political expression by aliens or U.S. citizens. The Smith Act prohibited advocacy of the violent overthrow of the government, the publication of materials espousing forcible overthrow, and the organizing of a group dedicated to using violence as a means of achieving its objectives.

The Vinson Court upheld the Smith Act in *Dennis v. United States* (1951). Dennis was a leader of the Communist Party of the United States. He and other Communist Party leaders were convicted of illegal advocacy and conspiracy, and the Vinson Court upheld the convictions. In doing so, Chief Justice Vinson reshaped the clear-and-present danger test and suggested that in cases such as these courts must ask whether the "gravity of the evil, discounted by its improbability, justifies . . . invasion of free speech." This so-called sliding scale standard had been crafted by Court of Appeals judge Learned Hand. Vinson said the severity of the danger in this case was great enough that it need not be imminent. Regarding imminence, Vinson suggested, obviously, the words of the test could not mean that before the Government might act, "it must wait until the putsch is about to be executed, the plans have been laid, and the signal is awaited." Not only is governmental response allowed in such a situation, it is required if the government is "aware that a group aiming at its overthrow is attempting to indoctrinate its members and to commit them to a course whereby they will strike when the leaders feel the circumstances permit." The likelihood that the threat will succeed is not required either. An attempt to overthrow the government by force, even though doomed from the outset, is a "sufficient evil for Congress to prevent it" (*Dennis* 1951, 509–510).

## Brownell, Herbert, Jr.

Herbert Brownell Jr. was born in Peru, Nebraska, on February 20, 1904. He earned a bachelor's degree from the University of Nebraska in 1924 and received his legal education from Yale University Law School. He graduated in 1927 and was admitted to the New York bar that same year. He practiced law with the firm of Root, Clark, Buckner and Ballantine from 1927 to 1953. He became active in Republican Party politics and was elected to two terms in the state legislature. He chaired the Republican National Committee for three years beginning in 1944. He managed Thomas E. Dewey's successful campaign for the New York governorship (1942) as well as Dewey's unsuccessful presidential bids in 1944 and 1948. He was appointed attorney general of the United States by President Dwight Eisenhower on January 21, 1953, and held that office until November 8, 1957. He served as one of Eisenhower's key advisers and strongly urged the nomination of Earl Warren as chief justice of the U.S. Supreme Court. He also counseled that Eisenhower appoint lower court judges who favored racial integration in the South. Brownell was a strong anticommunist and advised Eisenhower not to grant clemency in the cases of Ethel and Julius Rosenberg. This, of course, pleased political conservatives. His support for civil rights, on the other hand, angered the same constituency and many Southern members of Congress. He left the Department of Justice in 1957 and returned to his private practice in New York. Brownell died in 1996.

## Cold War

Term used to describe the struggle that developed after World War II between the so-called Eastern bloc of nations headed by the Soviet Union and the Western bloc led by the United States. The conflict was called the Cold War because it was not "hot"; it did not involve actual fighting. The Cold War was the product of mutual distrust and suspicion by the United States, the Soviet Union, and their respective allies. The Western bloc believed the Soviet Union was seeking to expand communism throughout the world. The Eastern bloc believed the United States was engaged in practicing imperialism and attempting to stop the Communist revolution initiated by the Soviet Union. The Cold War began at the end of World War II, although relations between the two nations had been strained since the Russian Revolution in 1917. The United States and the Soviet Union were allies during World War II, and some believed the state of cooperation would survive the war. Major differences remained, however, particularly with regard to Eastern Europe. As a result, the Western bloc adopted a "get tough" policy toward the Soviet Union. The Soviets responded by accusing the United States and its capitalist allies of seeking to encircle it and overthrow its Communist economy and government.

Eastern and Western bloc relations deteriorated quickly after the February 1945 Yalta Conference. At Yalta, the Allied leaders agreed to set up occupation zones that would partition postwar Germany. Following Roosevelt's death in April 1945, Germany surrendered. The Allies met for the final time at Potsdam in July 1945. During the remainder of 1945 and early 1946, the Soviets cut off all contact with the West and occupied territories of Eastern Europe. In March 1946, British Prime Minister Winston Churchill said that an "iron curtain" had descended across Europe. In March 1947, Truman announced that the United States would assist any nation resisting Communist aggression. The Truman Doctrine developed into a broad policy of containing Communist expansion. Failure to find a way to end the occupation of Germany convinced U.S. Secretary of State George Marshall that the U.S.S.R. would not help Europe recover from World War II. Marshall proposed giving aid to European nations to foster their economic recovery. This proposal became his European Recovery Program, also known as the Marshall Plan. In June 1948, the Western Allies announced plans to unify their German occupation zones and establish the West German Federal Republic. The Soviets answered with a blockade of Berlin. For the next eleven months, West Berlin was supplied with food and fuel entirely by plane. The U.S.S.R. lifted the blockade in May 1949, and the Allies ended the airlift the following September. During the blockade, the United States pledged continuing military aid to Western Europe. The North Atlantic Treaty Organization (NATO), a mutual defense pact among the United States, Canada, and ten Western European nations, was the device developed for this purpose.

North Korean troops invaded South Korea on June 25, 1950. President Truman sent U.S. forces to aid South Korea. The Korean War was the first war in which troops of a world organization, the United Nations, fought an aggressor nation. Some historians believe the Korean War was a major turning point in the Cold War. It extended the Containment Policy to the Far East. It also introduced limited warfare to the East-West conflict as a substitute for nuclear war. The death of Soviet Premier Joseph Stalin changed the character of the Cold War. The new Soviet rulers softened their policies toward the Soviet satellites and the West. The arms race continued, however, and military alliances were strengthened on both sides. After the Cuban missile crisis in 1963, Cold War tensions eased. There was a loosening of ties among members of both the Communist and Western blocs during the 1960s. Cold War tensions heightened again in the early 1980s as a result of the Soviet intervention in Afghanistan. The growing military power of the Soviet Union led the United States to increase its defense budget. Many feared a full-scale resumption of the arms race. This did not occur, because Communist rule ended in a number of East European countries, Germany was reunified, and the Soviet Union dissolved in 1991. The following year, Russian President Boris Yeltsin and U.S. President George Bush formally declared that their respective countries did not regard each other as potential enemies. These events marked the end of the Cold War.

## Dennis, Eugene

Eugene Dennis was an American Communist Party leader born in Seattle, Washington, on August 10, 1905. His name from birth until 1935 was Francis X. Waldron Jr. Dennis attended the University of Washington, but dropped out after only one semester to support himself. He identified with the objectives of the Industrial Workers of the World (IWW). The Communist Party, which was created in 1919, embraced the revolutionary militancy of the IWW Dennis admired, and he joined the party in 1926. The next year Dennis moved to Los Angeles where he became the party's educational director for southern California. As an organizer for the Trade Union Unity League, Dennis helped organize a strike of 10,000 Mexican and Filipino lettuce pickers in California's Imperial Valley in January 1930. In April Dennis and others were indicted by a grand jury for "criminal syndicalism" for their role in the strike. Dennis fled to the Soviet Union to avoid prosecution. For the next five years Dennis worked for the Communist International, serving as an underground courier in the Philippines. In 1935 Dennis and his wife returned to the United States. It was on his return to the United States in 1935 that Francis Waldron changed his named to Eugene Dennis.

Dennis became state secretary of the Wisconsin Communist Party. After six months in Moscow in 1937 as the U.S. representative to the Communist International, Dennis returned to the United States and became a member of the party's ruling political committee in New York City. Dennis was a close ally of party General Secretary Earl Browder and supported his Popular Front. The Popular Front deemphasized the party's revolutionary ideology and worked instead to create coalitions among all groups willing to oppose the spread of fascism. In 1945 Browder was denounced by the Communists on orders from Moscow for his wartime "revisionism." Despite his close association with Browder, Dennis was appointed to the post of general secretary. In the end Dennis embraced party Chairman William Z. Foster's more militant style.

The Cold War brought a series of legal attacks on the Communist Party and its members. Dennis was a prominent target. He was convicted for contempt of Congress for refusing to answer questions before the House Un-American Activities Committee and in 1948 was one of the top party leaders indicted for violation of the Smith Act. After a highly visible trial, Dennis and the others were convicted. The case, *Dennis v. United States*, was taken to the Supreme Court, which upheld the verdict. Dennis was sent to the Atlanta penitentiary, where he served a five-year sentence. After his release, Dennis resumed party leadership and urged extensive reforms. Soviet Premier Nikita Khrushchev's denunciation of previous Premier Joseph Stalin bolstered the reform cause, but Soviet suppression of the Hungarian revolution in November 1956 swung the balance against the reformers. The party was badly damaged by these events and its membership was diminished to a few thousand members. Dennis was replaced as general secretary in 1959 but retained the largely honorary post of party chairman until his death in New York City in January 1961.

## Dewey, Thomas E.

Thomas E. Dewey was a governor of New York and was twice the Republican presidential candidate. Dewey was born in Owasso, Michigan, on March 24, 1902. He received his B.A. from the University of Michigan in 1923 and graduated from Columbia Law School in 1925. Dewey practiced law with two Wall Street law firms and became active in Republican politics. He met Herbert Brownell, who would later manage Dewey's presidential campaigns and serve as his closest political confidant. In 1931, Dewey became U.S. attorney for the Southern District of New York. During this period, he played a major role in prosecuting organized crime figures and members of the Tammany Hall political machine. His record as a prosecutor prompted New York Governor Herbert Lehman to appoint Dewey special prosecutor to prosecute racketeers. Dewey's success in this role made him a national hero and launched his career in state and national politics. In 1937 he ran for district attorney in Manhattan and overcame a 5–1 Democratic advantage in voter registration to become the first Republican to win that office in twenty-five years. In 1938, Dewey challenged Lehman for the governorship, but lost by 1 percent of the vote. Despite this political loss, Dewey arrived at the 1940 Republican nominating convention as a leading contender for the presidential nomination. The nomination went to Wendell Willkie, however. Nonetheless, Dewey consolidated his position at the forefront of the GOP by winning the New York governorship in 1942. Reelected for two additional terms, Dewey created an impressive record of achievement. He followed in the tradition of Theodore Roosevelt and the Republican progressives earlier in the century. He established the New York State university system and was a strong advocate of civil rights for blacks.

Dewey was the leading figure in the GOP during the 1940s. With Brownell's help, he built a formidable organization that secured the Republican presidential nominations in 1944 and 1948. Dewey and Brownell were also instrumental in securing the nomination for Dwight Eisenhower in 1952. Dewey's New York base and internationalist views on foreign policy also earned him strong support from Wall Street and the party's eastern establishment. In 1944 Dewey was a substantial underdog against President Franklin Roosevelt. Nonetheless, he waged a determined campaign and turned in the best Republican presidential performance since the 1920s, and as a result, he was the front-runner for the nomination in 1948. Dewey prevailed over Taft and Harold Stassen on the third ballot at the Republican convention. He and running mate, California Governor Earl Warren, appeared certain to win against President Harry Truman and a divided Democratic Party. Dewey was not as appealing a campaigner as Truman and was saddled with the do-nothing record of the Republican 80th Congress. Although the polls predicted a Dewey win, Truman won, and the Democrats regained control of Congress. Despite the defeat, Dewey remained a major force in the party. When it became apparent that Senator Taft was the front-runner for the 1952 nomination, Dewey felt it necessary to deny him the nomination. He persuaded General Dwight Eisenhower to run and offered the service of his political organization. Dewey's longtime political associate Herbert Brownell became attorney general in Eisenhower's administration. Dewey retired from the New York governorship at the end of his third term in 1955 and resumed his legal practice. He remained active in the party and served as an occasional adviser to Presidents Eisenhower and Nixon. In 1968 he declined Nixon's offer of nomination as chief justice of the Supreme Court. He died in Bal Harbor, Florida, in 1971.

## Eisenhower, Dwight D.

Dwight D. Eisenhower was a U.S. Army general and thirty-fourth president of the United States. Eisenhower was born in Denison, Texas, on October 14, 1890. He graduated from the U.S. Military Academy at West Point in 1915 and was commissioned a second lieutenant. His service during World War I was confined to the United States. After the war he held a number of staff positions. His military career did not develop quickly, and he expected forced retirement by 1940. Instead, Chief of Staff George Marshall called upon him to head the War Plans Division (later the Operations Division). In 1942 Marshall put Eisenhower in command of U.S. forces in Great Britain. When the United States needed to provide the supreme commander for the invasions of North Africa and France, Marshall again called on Eisenhower. Following the successful campaign in North Africa, Eisenhower was promoted to four-star general, and President Roosevelt made him supreme commander of the Allied Expeditionary Forces for the invasion of France in mid-1944. In February 1948 Eisenhower left the army to become president of Columbia University. Both political parties sought to persuade Eisenhower to run for president in 1948. President Truman even offered to accept a vice presidential nomination if Eisenhower became the Democratic candidate. Eisenhower declined, and Truman defeated New York Governor Thomas Dewey in the general election. In January 1951, Truman asked Eisenhower to become the first supreme commander of the Allied forces in Europe and began building a NATO armed force. In 1952 a group of Eastern "establishment" Republicans persuaded Eisenhower to seek the presidency. He agreed to run, but did not get the nomination without a protracted struggle with Ohio Senator Robert A. Taft. Once the nomination was secured, Eisenhower chose Senator Richard Nixon of California as his running mate, and together they defeated Illinois Governor Adlai Stevenson.

Eisenhower's first objective as president was to conclude the Korean War. In addition, he pledged to rid the government of political subversives and stop the advance of communism. In 1953 he directed the Central Intelligence Agency (CIA) to overthrow the governments in both Iran and Guatemala. When French Indo-China was about to fall to the Communists, Eisenhower was counseled to intervene there as well. He refused. At the 1954 Geneva Conference Eisenhower and Secretary of State John Foster Dulles agreed to a division of Vietnam and the creation of the South East Asia Treaty Organization (SEATO). It was under the auspices of SEATO that the United States agreed to defend South Vietnam. Three years into his first term Eisenhower suffered a heart attack. He recovered sufficiently to seek reelection in 1956. Stevenson was again the Democratic candidate, but could not overcome Eisenhower's popularity. The enthusiasm for Eisenhower did not transfer to the Republicans generally—the Republicans lost control of both the House and Senate. During Eisenhower's second term, he was faced with a number of domestic political challenges, including implementation of *Brown v. Board of Education* (1954). There were international challenges as well. In addition to the Soviet Union's successful launch of a space satellite, the Middle East became dangerously unstable. Eisenhower promised U.S. support to Middle East governments threatened by communism. Early in 1959, Fidel Castro took control of Cuba. Eisenhower had the CIA plan an invasion with a force of Cuban exiles. The plan called for a landing at the Bay of Pigs. Eisenhower chose not to implement the plan. In his farewell address he warned against "inordinate and unjustifiable influence" of the "military-industrial complex." Shortly after Nixon's inauguration as president in 1969, Eisenhower died at Walter Reed Hospital in Washington, D.C.

## Fair Deal

Name given to President Harry Truman's domestic program. The term *Fair Deal* was first introduced on January 5, 1949, although it generally refers to Truman's domestic initiatives over his entire presidency. Included in the Fair Deal were a full employment law, a national health insurance plan, extended Social Security, aid to education, civil rights legislation, public housing, universal military training, and an increase in the minimum wage. The Fair Deal was Truman's attempt to codify Franklin Roosevelt's vision of a complete economic constitutional order. It was, in his words, a "reminder to the Democratic party, to the country, and to the Congress, that progress in government lies along the road to reform in our private enterprise system and that progressive democracy has to continue to keep pace with changing conditions" (Milkis and Nelson 1994, 296).

Congressional Republicans were unwilling to support anything that sounded like an extension of Roosevelt's policies, and once the Republicans captured both houses of Congress in the 1946 midterm elections, Truman's domestic agenda was put on hold for two years. In 1948, Truman sought reelection despite public opinion polls indicating that he had no chance. After a vigorous campaign, however, Truman prevailed over the Republican nominee, Governor Thomas Dewey of New York. The Democrats regained control of Congress in 1948, and some components of the Fair Deal were enacted into law, including the Housing Act of 1949, which was the first to provide federal funds for urban renewal; the Fair Labor Standards Act Amendments of 1949, which raised the minimum wage; and the Social Security Act Amendments of 1950, which increased Social Security benefits and extended their coverage to include an additional 10 million persons, including agricultural and domestic workers, state and local government employees, and self-employed persons. Congress refused to create a national health care program and did little to reform education (with the exception of the G.I. Bill), however.

## Hand, Learned

Learned Hand was a federal judge born in Albany, New York, on January 27, 1872. Hand, originally named Billings Learned Hand, came from a family of lawyers, including his two uncles and his paternal grandfather. His father specialized in arguing before the New York Court of Appeals, on which he served briefly as a judge. After attending the Albany Academy, Hand entered Harvard College in 1889. After receiving his B.A. and M.A. degrees in 1893, Hand would have preferred to undertake graduate study in philosophy but fell prey to family pressures and entered Harvard Law School. After graduation in 1896, Hand dropped the use of the name Billings and though unsure of himself, returned to Albany to practice law. In November 1902 he moved to New York City. Although he found the practice of law dull and uninspiring, he was drawn to the subject intellectually and began to contribute to legal journals. The principal benefit that New York offered to Hand was acceptance among the city's intellectual elite, an involvement that, as his reputation as a civic reformer grew, led him into a judicial career. In 1909, after spending only a dozen years in private practice, and at the relatively young age of thirty-seven, Hand was named a district judge by President William Howard Taft. He had failed for two years to get a federal judgeship, but he had his supporters, in this case New York reformer Charles C. Burlingham, who, aware that Attorney General George W. Wickersham was counseling the new president to improve the quality of the federal bench, urged him to select Hand.

In his early years as a judge Hand remained actively engaged in public policy and political issues, to a degree that in the late twentieth century would have raised serious issues of propriety. Hand became an enthusiastic supporter of and participant in Roosevelt's Bull Moose Progressive movement, contributing to the "social and industrial" planks of the party's platform in 1912 and agreeing to be the party's candidate for chief judge of New York's highest court in 1913. With the conclusion of World War I, however, he decided to heed U.S. Supreme Court Justice Oliver Wendell Holmes's private advice and began to avoid public involvement in heated public disputes that were unrelated to his position on the bench. Hand adhered to this policy until his last decade of life, when his hostility to the spread of McCarthyism prompted him to speak out repeatedly, forcefully, eloquently, and earlier than almost any other establishment figure. In 1924 President Calvin Coolidge promoted Hand to the Court of Appeals for the Second Circuit. Hand became the court's chief judge in 1939 and served in that capacity until 1951 when he retired from active service.

Hand sat on the bench for more than fifty years and wrote nearly 4,000 opinions. He is counted among the leading judges of the twentieth century. In the early 1920s, Justice Holmes included Hand on his ideal Supreme Court, but he had no chance during the conservative Harding and Coolidge administrations, in part because ex-president Taft, then the chief justice, exerted his influence to block any consideration, undoubtedly still bitter over Hand's support for the insurgent Bull Moose movement that turned Taft into a one-term president in 1912. Hand's major contribution was to delineate an approach that sought to avoid the twin dangers of, on the one hand, reading laws too literally, so that the legislative purpose might be obscured, and interpreting them so broadly, on the other, that judges had too much discretion in imposing their personal views, which would undermine the meaning of the words used by Congress. Hand's most important and controversial constitutional contribution was his decision in *The Masses Publishing Company v. Patten* (1917), a ruling that safeguarded the right of *The Masses*, a left-wing magazine, to publish and distribute its pacifist, socialist views, however great their perceived threat to the prevailing national sentiment favoring the war. He is also known for diluting the clear-and-present danger standard in *Dennis v. United States* (1951), a decision upholding the conviction of American Communist leaders, including Eugene Dennis, for violating the Smith Act. He consciously recast the standard in a less speech-protective way, thereby reflecting both his growing skepticism of judicial enforcement of individual rights and his long-maintained obedience to Supreme Court doctrine. His primary achievement, however, was bringing a skeptical, analytical approach to bear in dealing with thousands of everyday cases involving virtually every facet of the law and rendering opinions that were characterized by cogent, clear expression. Hand died on August 18, 1961.

## Hiss, Alger

Alger Hiss was born in Baltimore, Maryland, on November 11, 1904. He received his B.A. degree from Johns Hopkins in 1926 and his law degree from Harvard in 1929. He served as a law clerk for Supreme Court Justice Oliver Wendell Holmes before beginning private practice in Boston. He was on the legal staff of the Department of Agriculture for three years starting in 1933 before moving to the State Department. In 1939 Hiss was assistant to the State Department's adviser on Far Eastern politics and in 1943 became special assistant to the director of the newly created Office of Far Eastern Affairs. He was executive secretary of the Dumbarton Oaks UN Conference in 1944 and the next year was promoted to deputy director of the Office of Special Political Affairs. He attended the Yalta Conference in 1945 as an adviser to President Franklin Roosevelt and served as temporary secretary-general of the United Nations at its inception. He headed the Carnegie Endowment for International Peace from 1946 to 1949. In 1948, Whittaker Chambers, a former Communist, testified before the House Un-American Activities Committee that Hiss had been a member of a Communist organization from 1934 to 1938 and that he belonged to a spy ring that had delivered State Department secrets to the Soviets. Hiss denied the charges but was indicted for perjury—the statute of limitations prevented a more serious charge. His first trial ended in a hung jury in 1949. The following year he was convicted in the second trial. He served more than three years in the federal prison at Lewisburg, Pennsylvania. Hiss maintained his innocence after his release and never returned to public life. The Hiss case ushered in the McCarthy era and brought the spotlight to Senator Richard Nixon as a congressional investigator. His case stimulated the development of the Red Scare, helping to elevate it to national prominence. Hiss practiced law in New York for many years before his death on November 15, 1996.

## Internal Security (McCarran) Act

Congress enacted the Internal Security Act, also known as the Subversive Activities Control Act, or McCarran Act, in the spring of 1950, which required Communists and other "subversive" groups to register with the attorney general. To justify this infringement on the First Amendment, Congress declared the existence of an international Communist conspiracy that constituted a clear and present danger to the United States. For enforcement of the law, Congress created a Subversive Activities Control Board, which, despite broad administrative discretion, remained answerable for its decisions to the courts. President Harry Truman vetoed the bill, calling it "the greatest danger to freedom of speech, press and assembly since the Sedition Act of 1798." But Congress, fearful of being considered soft on communism in an election year, promptly overrode the veto by large margins in both houses. The Court, by a 5–4 vote, sustained the registration process in *Communist Party v. Subversive Activities Control Board* (1961). The Court did put aside convictions for refusing to register, on the grounds that the wording of board orders constituted a violation of the Fifth Amendment's prohibition against self-incrimination (*Albertson v. Subversive Activities Control Board* [1965]). Since Section 6 of the act prohibited any member of a Communist organization from using a passport, the State Department tried to revoke the passports of two party leaders. In *Aptheker v. Secretary of State* (1964), the Court invalidated that section because "it too broadly and indiscriminately restricts the right to travel and thereby abridges the liberty guaranteed by the Fifth Amendment." Another section made it a criminal offense for a member of a Communist organization to work for any defense facility. In *United States v. Robel* (1967), the Court declared that section unconstitutionally overbroad as well, but this time because it violated the First Amendment right of association.

## Jehovah's Witnesses

The Jehovah's Witnesses are a religious sect begun by Charles Taze Russell in 1872. Today the society has upwards of a million members in the United States and more than 4 million members worldwide. The sect is also known by its corporate name, the Watchtower Bible and Tract Society. The term *Jehovah's Witnesses*, a name the sect took in 1931, is based on the view that their basic task is to witness on behalf of Jehovah.

The Witnesses are "fiercely evangelistic and publicly so." They "persistently solicit and proselytize." Their aggressive approach often put Witnesses at odds with state and local regulations. These regulations covered such matters as leaflet distribution, parade permits, license taxes, flag salutes, and the military draft. Typically, the Witnesses claimed such regulations impaired their First Amendment right to freely exercise religion. Between the mid-1930s and the end of the 1950s, the Witnesses brought more than fifty cases to the Supreme Court. Their chief legal counsel was Hayden C. Covington, and under his guidance, the Witnesses prevailed in more than 90 percent of these cases during the Stone and Vinson Court eras (Abraham 1998, 236–237).

## Jim Crow Laws

Jim Crow laws, which made racial segregation legal in the South, were enacted by states and municipalities beginning in the 1880s. The name Jim Crow is believed to come from a character in an antebellum minstrel song.

During the post–Civil War Reconstruction years in the late 1860s and the 1870s, blacks and whites often rode together in the same railway cars, ate in the same restaurants, and used the same public facilities, but did not interact as equals. Toward the end of the nineteenth century, the emergence of a significant black labor force in factories and large urban black communities presented a new challenge to white southerners. They could not control these new "freedmen" in the same informal ways they had been able to control rural sharecroppers, who were more directly dependent on white landowners and merchants than their urban counterparts. In the city, blacks and whites were in more direct contact than they had been in the countryside, and there was more social mixing. The Jim Crow laws were a way that white supremacists could institutionalize their desire to retain dominance over the black population. What had been maintained by custom in the rural South was to be maintained by law in the urban South. Railways and streetcars, public waiting rooms, restaurants, boardinghouses, theaters, and public parks were segregated; separate schools, hospitals, and other public institutions, generally of inferior quality, were designated for blacks.

Although blacks petitioned for redress under the Civil Rights Act of 1875, which required equal access to public accommodations, in 1883, the Supreme Court ruled the act unconstitutional. In this and other cases it wiped out most of the gains made by blacks during Reconstruction. The Court ruled that the Fourteenth Amendment prohibited state governments from discriminating against people because of race but did not restrict private organizations or individuals from doing so. Hence, it did not give Congress the authority to prohibit railroads, hotels, and theaters from practicing segregation. Eventually, the Court validated state legislation that discriminated against blacks. In 1896, in *Plessy v. Ferguson*, the Court held that separate accommodations did not violate the Equal Protection Clause of the Fourteenth Amendment if the accommodations were equal, legitimizing the principle of "separate but equal." In 1899, it went even further, declaring in *Cumming v. County Board of Education* that laws establishing separate schools for whites were valid even if there were no comparable schools for blacks.

The High Court rulings led to a profusion of Jim Crow laws. Signs marked "Whites Only" and "Colored" showed up everywhere. By 1914 every southern state had passed laws that created two separate societies—one black, the other white. Blacks were denied access to the vast majority of public accommodations. South Carolina prohibited blacks and whites from working together in the same room in textile plants, and from using the same entryways, exits, or lavatories. Mississippi statutes required segregation in hospitals, a practice soon adopted by other states. The state even forbade white nurses from attending black patients. Hundreds of Jim Crow laws existed on the books, but even the legal record did not provide an adequate gauge of the extent of segregation and its accompanying discrimination in southern life at the turn of the century. The laws established minimal requirements; in practice, segregation often went beyond what the statutes required. Institutionalized segregation bred further hatred and distrust among both whites and blacks.

Beginning in 1915, blacks began to win victories in the Court that chipped away at the Jim Crow laws. In *Guinn v. United States* (1915), the Court invalidated Oklahoma's grandfather clause, which permitted whites whose grandfathers had been able to vote prior to 1866, when no black person could, to vote even though they were unable to pass a literacy test designed to disenfranchise blacks. Southern whites also tried to deprive blacks of political power by creating the "white-only primary." In 1927 in *Nixon v. Herndon*, the Court rendered the white primary unconstitutional. In *Buchanan v. Warley* (1917), the Court struck down a Louisville, Kentucky, law requiring residential segregation. But by this time, even places of employment were segregated, and it was not until after World War II that the attempt to dismantle the Jim Crow system in the South really made headway.

A major blow against the Jim Crow system of racial segregation was struck in 1950, when the Supreme Court ruled that the University of Texas Law School must admit a black man, Heman Sweatt, because the separate law school the state had created did not provide an equal education. This was followed in 1954 by the Supreme Court's famous decision in *Brown v. Board of Education,* argued before the Court by Thurgood Marshall, which declared that segregated public schools were inherently unequal and therefore unconstitutional.

Blacks in the South, with the help of the National Association for the Advancement of Colored People (NAACP), the Southern Christian Leadership Conference (SCLC), and the Student Nonviolent Coordinating Committee (SNCC) used lawsuits, mass sit-ins, and boycotts to hasten desegregation. A march on Washington by more than 200,000 in 1963, at which Martin Luther King, Jr., delivered his well-known "I Have a Dream" speech, dramatized the civil rights movement to end racial discrimination. Southern whites often responded with violence to such demonstrations, and federal troops were needed to preserve order and protect blacks, notably at Little Rock, Arkansas (1957), Oxford, Mississippi (1962), and Selma, Alabama (1965). The Civil Rights Act of 1964, the Voting Rights Act of 1965, and the Fair Housing Act of 1968 finally ended the legal sanctions of Jim Crow. However, the attitudes Jim Crow laws reflected continued to exist in many places in the United States, and even in the year 2000 in the state of Florida, many black voters were, in practice, disenfranchised.

## The Korean War

A war between North and South Korea, which broke out on June 25, 1950, when North Korean forces invaded South Korea at several points across the 38th parallel. North Korea denied its invasion, insisting that the South Koreans had initiated the war. Evidence demonstrates that it was North Korea that launched a major assault on South Korea to oust the South Korean government in power at the time. In the initial weeks of the war, North Korea almost succeeded in its goal. Its aggression, however, encountered U.S. intervention and was condemned by the United Nations who created UN forces to assist South Korea. These forces were made up mostly of U.S. troops, but also included troops from Great Britain, France, Australia, Belgium, Canada, and a number of other nations. When the UN forces pursued North Korean forces deeply into North Korea to the Korean and Chinese border (the Yalu River), China dispatched its "volunteer" forces to fight in aid of North Korea. The UN forces were forced to retreat to the south of Seoul, the South Korean capital, but were eventually successful in repelling Chinese forces across the 38th parallel. This UN action was interpreted by the South Korean government as a precursor to a forceful reunification of the country, but in reality the UN forces were only authorized to take limited action to stop the aggression. A cease-fire was finally negotiated in 1953 along the current demilitarized zone, which is drawn along the initial 38th parallel division between North and South Korea, and which was regarded as topographically more defensible by the UN forces.

The Korean War was more than a war between North and South Korea. It occasioned the first UN action against an armed invasion. Though the price of this action was high, both sides paying heavily in terms of casualties and destruction of properties, it was successful in frustrating North Korea's attempt to forcibly reunify the country. The Soviet Union did not send troops, but it supplied North Korea with weapons. China's entry into the war on the side of North Korea was with the obvious blessing of the Soviet Union. For the United States, the Korean War was significant because in the course of the war, the concept of limited war was first applied, and political considerations were given priority, thus limiting the pursuit of ultimate military strategic necessities.

When World War II came to an end, the Red Army (U.S.S.R.) occupied Korea, north of the 38th parallel. In the south, the U.S. and Allied forces were in control. In 1948, when the UN introduced elections in Korea, the North Korean territory refused to hold them. After the elections in the south, the Republic of Korea was born under President Syngman Rhee. The U.S. troops withdrew from Korea in 1949. In 1950, the Communist forces in North Korea tried to invade the south. U.S. forces were sent immediately. The UN denounced the North Korean action. While the war between the Communist troops and the Americans, along with the South Korean army, was on, the Chinese army joined the war. China, which was a Communist nation, drove the UN troops back to the 38th parallel. The war dragged on without any concrete results.

The war in Korea and the one later in Vietnam had an adverse effect back home. As the war continued, public opinion went against the war. The United States, which had entered the war to "get rid of commies," was not very confident anymore, because of strong antiwar sentiments at home. A peace accord was signed in 1953, which brought one of the longest and the most tragic wars fought in U.S. history to an end. During the period after the Korean War, American people had to face a series of problems at home. Although the general prosperity in the country improved the standard of living for the people, economic recessions occurred regularly. Unemployment persisted in the industrial sector and other spheres. Moreover, farmers were not doing well economically either. There was a severe crisis in the various spheres of U.S. society, for example, education, the Black Power movement, that is, the civil rights movement, and urban development.

## MacArthur, Douglas

Douglas MacArthur was commander of U.S. forces in the Pacific during World War II, supreme allied commander in Japan during the occupation of Japan, and commander of U.S. and United Nations forces during the first year of the Korean War. MacArthur was born in Little Rock, Arkansas, on January 26, 1880. He graduated from West Point with highest honors in 1903. He served in the Philippines and Panama before joining the War Department in 1913. He distinguished himself in France during World War I and briefly commanded U.S. occupation forces in Germany at the end of the war. MacArthur served three years as superintendent at West Point before returning to the Philippines for several years. President Herbert Hoover appointed MacArthur army chief of staff in 1930, a position he held until 1935. He stepped down in 1935 to become adviser to the Philippine Commonwealth government led by his longtime friend Manuel Quezon. He retired from the military in 1937, but was called back into service by President Franklin Roosevelt, who was seeking to deter the aggressive actions of the Japanese. In March 1942, Roosevelt appointed MacArthur commander of one of the two Pacific war theaters. For the next thirty months, MacArthur devoted himself to retaking the Philippines. Conservative Republicans tried to get MacArthur to enter the 1944 presidential race, but the effort never materialized. Notwithstanding his politics, Roosevelt approved MacArthur's promotion to five-star general of the army. MacArthur became commander of U.S. forces in the Pacific the following spring. Retaking the Philippines took longer than expected—it did not occur until the Japanese surrender. Following the war, President Harry Truman, as a result of extensive political pressure from Republicans, designated MacArthur as occupation commander in Japan. Although the occupation was nominally an Allied effort, it was largely run by the United States. MacArthur tended to ignore direction from Washington and largely administered the occupation on his own terms. He was particularly pleased when he imposed a U.S.-written constitution in 1947. MacArthur decided to seek the Republican presidential nomination in 1948. The importance of Japan decreased with the Cold War and the ascendance of the Communists in China, and Washington attempted to reverse policy in Japan. MacArthur, seeing the policy change as an attempt to diminish his status, resisted. His bid for the nomination failed, and he relinquished influence on economic policy in Japan. MacArthur was critical of Truman's China policy and urged that Truman ensure the defense of Taiwan by withdrawing U.S. forces from South Korea. The outbreak of fighting in Korea prompted MacArthur to change his East Asian priorities. Despite criticism from MacArthur, Truman named him head of the United Nations military command. MacArthur increasingly came into conflict with Washington by advocating greater support of the Chinese Nationalists against the Communist Chinese. MacArthur eventually stalled out in his battlefield efforts in Korea. He blamed it on Washington's restrictions on attacking China. It became more evident that MacArthur was attempting to sabotage Truman's plans to obtain a ceasefire, and he was openly critical of Truman's policies generally. On April 11, 1951, Truman relieved MacArthur of his command. He tried to defend himself by making a number of speeches nationwide and renewed his quest for the Republican presidential nomination. When the nomination went to Eisenhower instead, MacArthur withdrew from politics. He lived a secluded life in New York City until his death in 1964.

## Marshall, George

George Marshall was born in Uniontown, Pennsylvania, on December 31, 1880. He graduated from Virginia Military Institute in 1901 and shortly thereafter was commissioned a second lieutenant in the U.S. Army. Marshall served on a number of military posts in the United States and the Philippines between 1902 and 1916. He was part of the force that landed in France in 1917. Over the next year, Marshall was instrumental in training U.S. forces for decisive initiatives against the Germans in 1918. He was assigned to the operations staff of General John J. Pershing, head of the American Expeditionary Forces. Marshall assumed principal responsibility for planning the decisive St. Mihiel and Meuse-Argonne offensives. By the time of the armistice, Marshall was chief of operations for the U.S. First Army. Marshall served as Pershing's executive officer until 1923 when he began four year's service in China. He returned to Washington in 1927 as an instructor at the National War College. He then became head of the Infantry School at Fort Benning, Georgia. After commanding army posts in Georgia and South Carolina, Marshall was recalled to Washington, D.C., to head the War Plans Division of the Army general staff. After Marshall served a brief period as deputy chief of staff, President Franklin Roosevelt chose to promote him to chief of staff.

When the Germans invaded Poland in September 1939, Marshall urged the buildup of the U.S. military. He advocated a "Europe first" approach to preparing for war against both Germany and Japan. Following Pearl Harbor, Marshall's responsibilities expanded greatly. He reorganized the War Department early in 1942 and became the central figure in the U.S. Joint Chiefs of Staff and Anglo-American Combined Chiefs of Staff. He emerged as Roosevelt's principal military adviser. Indeed, he became so indispensable that Roosevelt kept Marshall in Washington and selected his protégé, General Dwight Eisenhower, to command the Normandy invasion. In 1944 he was designated as general of the army and named *Time* magazine's "Man of the Year." Following the war, President Truman asked Marshall to attempt to prevent a civil war in China between the Nationalists and Communists. Despite his failure to avert that war, Marshall was recalled to Washington and named secretary of state early in 1947. For the next two years, he presided over one of the most important, creative, and controversial periods in U.S. foreign policy.

The period witnessed the emergence of the Cold War and the acceptance by the United States of a major role in international affairs. The main problem was European hunger. Although containment of the Soviet Union was important, economic assistance to Europe was the top priority. The European Recovery Program, commonly called the Marshall Plan, succeeded in reviving and integrating the nations of Western Europe.

The Marshall Plan also solidified the growing East-West split in Europe—most notably after the Communist coup in Czechoslovakia and the Soviet blockade of Berlin. The responses were to airlift supplies to Berlin and the creation of the North Atlantic Treaty Organization (NATO). Late in 1948 Marshall encountered serious health problems and resigned as secretary of state. He agreed to head the American Red Cross, but was nominated by President Truman to be secretary of defense. He was confirmed, but was subjected to serious criticism for his failure to fully support the Nationalist Chinese and for his support of the limited war strategy Truman undertook in Korea. In 1951 Marshall recommended and defended the removal of General Douglas MacArthur of his Far Eastern command. His European Recovery Program led to his winning the Nobel Peace Prize in 1953. He retired at the end of the Truman administration in 1953 and died in 1959. He is considered the architect and organizer of the Allied victory during World War II and of U.S. policies during the early years of the Cold War.

## Marshall, Thurgood

Thurgood Marshall was a civil rights lawyer and a Supreme Court justice. He was born in Baltimore, Maryland, on July 2, 1908. He graduated with honors from Lincoln University in Pennsylvania in 1930. Unable to get into the segregated University of Maryland Law School, Marshall enrolled in and commuted to Howard University Law School, where he became a protégé of the dean, Charles Hamilton Houston. After graduating first in his class from Howard in 1933, Marshall remained in Baltimore where he opened a private practice. Marshall was active in the Baltimore branch of the NAACP, and in 1936 Houston persuaded both the NAACP board and Marshall that Marshall ought to join him in New York as a staff lawyer for the NAACP. After Houston returned to Washington in 1938, Marshall remained and became the chief staff lawyer, a position he held until 1961. Early in his Baltimore practice Marshall decided to attack the policies that barred him from attending the University of Maryland. He won, and for the next fourteen years, Marshall pursued his challenge to segregated higher education through two main areas. In *Missouri ex rel. Gaines v. Canada* (1938), a case Houston developed and argued, the U.S. Supreme Court directed the University of Missouri to either admit Lloyd Gaines to its law school or open one for African Americans. The attack culminated in Marshall's case of *Sweatt v. Painter* (1950), in which the Court held that the law school Texas had opened for African Americans was not equal to the well-established law schools for whites. The cases that the Court decided under the name *Brown v. Board of Education* constituted Marshall's main efforts from 1950 to 1955. Marshall had his greatest triumph as a lawyer in *Brown*.

In the 1940s and 1950s he became a major civil rights leader. By the mid-1950s his role as a civil rights leader had superseded his work as an attorney and he had become a widely sought-after speaker and fund-raiser. In 1961 Marshall accepted an appointment to the U.S. Court of Appeals for the Second Circuit. Political maneuvering delayed his confirmation for nearly a year, after which he served on the Second Circuit for five years. In 1965 President Lyndon Johnson named Marshall U.S. solicitor general, the government's chief lawyer before the Supreme Court. Although neither said so explicitly, both Johnson and Marshall expected that Johnson would name Marshall to the U.S. Supreme Court as soon as possible. In 1967 Johnson manipulated Justice Tom Clark into resigning from the Court by naming his son Ramsey Clark attorney general, and that same year, saying it was "the right thing to do, the right time to do it, the right man and the right place," Johnson named Marshall to be the first African American Supreme Court justice.

Marshall joined a Court that was dominated by liberals, but within five years the Court's composition had changed dramatically following the retirement of Chief Justice Earl Warren and the deaths of Justice Hugo Black and Justice John Marshall Harlan. Instead of being active in the coalition that determined the Court's positions, Marshall found himself in a beleaguered minority that opposed the more conservative justices appointed by Richard Nixon and Ronald Reagan. Beyond his doctrinal contributions, Marshall provided a voice on the Court, and in the Court's internal deliberations, for black Americans and others with few champions. Feeling the effects of age, and having lost his closest ally on the Court when William Brennan retired in 1990, Marshall announced his retirement on June 27, 1991. He died on January 24, 1993, at Bethesda Naval Hospital in Maryland.

## McCarthy, Joseph

Joseph McCarthy was a U.S. senator from Wisconsin. He was born near Appleton, Wisconsin, on November 14, 1908. In 1930 he enrolled in Marquette University. He earned a law degree from Marquette in 1935 and moved back to the Appleton area to begin his political career. After an unsuccessful bid for district attorney, McCarthy was elected to a circuit judgeship. In 1942 McCarthy joined the marines. Though exempt from military service as a judge, he concluded that front-line action would be essential for political advancement once the fighting ended. He spent World War II as an intelligence officer in the Pacific. He embellished his record by portraying himself as a "tail-gunner" who flew dangerous missions against the Japanese. In 1946 McCarthy challenged Robert M. LaFollette Jr., the popular three-term incumbent, in Wisconsin's Republican senatorial primary. Overconfident, LaFollette did not campaign and McCarthy prevailed by 5,000 votes and then easily defeated his Democratic opponent.

McCarthy's early Senate years gave signs of trouble to come. He was sanctioned by Senate leaders for his conduct—they removed him from the Banking Committee and reassigned him to the lowly District of Columbia Committee. He needed an issue to salvage his political career. On the evening of February 7, 1950, he delivered a speech before a Republican woman's group in Wheeling, West Virginia, decrying "Communist influence" in the Truman administration. By then the subject was familiar. Indeed, he lifted large portions of his speech from an address by Congressman Richard Nixon. He added that he would not take the time to name all the men in the State Department who have been named as members of the Communist Party, but said he had a list of 205 names that were known to the secretary of state who were still working in the department. His charges commanded press attention, and the public was aroused. In the months before the Wheeling speech, Cold War tensions had reached a boil. China had recently fallen to the Communists in 1949, and the Russians had successfully tested an atomic bomb in August 1949. The Communists were winning the Cold War, said McCarthy, because of the actions of disloyal government officials. His allegations made him an instant celebrity.

Following the outbreak of the Korean War in 1950, with U.S. troops battling Communist forces in Asia, McCarthy's message took on special force. As the 1952 presidential campaign approached, he called Secretary of Defense George Marshall a traitor, mocked Secretary of State Dean Acheson as the "Red Dean of Fashion," and described President Truman as a drunkard, adding, "the son of a bitch should be impeached." Easily reelected in the Republican landslide of 1952, McCarthy became chairman of the Senate Committee on Government Operations and its Subcommittee on Investigations. With the authority to hire staffers, hold hearings, issue subpoenas, and publish final reports, the senator became a major force on Capitol Hill. For the key position of chief counsel, he selected Roy Cohn, an abrasive young attorney from Manhattan who had served as prosecutor in the Julius and Ethel Rosenberg spy trial. In 1953 Cohn and McCarthy held hearings on "Communist influence" throughout the federal government. Their targets included Voice of America, the Government Printing Office, and the Foreign Service. These hearings proved disastrous. Without uncovering any Communists, they served to undermine government morale, damage numerous reputations, and make the United States look sinister in the eyes of the world. Not surprisingly, Republican criticism of McCarthy began to build because McCarthy was now attacking a bureaucracy of his own party. Many expected Eisenhower to step in and silence McCarthy. Though Eisenhower despised McCarthy, he chose not to confront him. In the fall of 1953, however, McCarthy's subcommittee initiated fateful hearings into subversive activity in the U.S. Army. By 1954 Cohn and McCarthy were attacking the army for "coddling Communists" within its ranks. In April 1954 the Senate decided to investigate the feud between the army and McCarthy. At Eisenhower's insistence, Republican leaders agreed to televise the hearings. Eisenhower believed the cameras would capture the real McCarthy for the U.S. public. Lasting thirty-six days, the army-McCarthy hearings overshadowed events of greater importance, such as the Supreme Court's decision to end public school segregation and the French military defeat at Dien Bien Phu. Eisenhower's instincts proved correct. The American people did not like the McCarthy they saw on national television. At the conclusion of the hearings, a resolution calling for McCarthy's censure was introduced. In December 1954 the Senate voted to censure McCarthy for bringing the body "into dishonor and disrepute." The vote was 67–22, with only Republican conservatives opposed. Reporters and colleagues ignored him, and his influence disappeared. He spent his final days in the Senate a lonely figure, drinking heavily and railing against those who had deserted his cause. McCarthy died on May 2, 1957, at Bethesda Naval Hospital in Maryland of acute hepatitis caused by his alcoholism.

## McGranery, James Patrick

James Patrick McGranery was born in Philadelphia on July 8, 1895. He served in World War I as an observation pilot with the army air corps. He graduated from Temple University Law School in 1928 and was admitted to the bar the same year. McGranery was appointed chairman of the Registration Commission for the city of Philadelphia in 1934 by Governor Earle. He was a member of the House serving in the 75th through 78th Congress. In November 1943, he was appointed assistant to the attorney general and was responsible for supervising the Federal Bureau of Investigation, Immigration and Naturalization Service, Bureau of Prisons, and various divisions. Then he served as U.S. Federal Court judge for the Western District of Pennsylvania. In 1946 he was awarded the Medal of Merit by President Truman. On May 27, 1952, Truman appointed McGranery attorney general of the United States. He served in that capacity until January 20, 1953. He died on December 23, 1962.

## McGrath, James Howard

James Howard McGrath was born in Woonsocket, Rhode Island, on November 28, 1903. He received his Ph.B. from Providence College in 1926 and LL.B. from Boston University in 1929. He was admitted to the Rhode Island bar in 1929 and later was the recipient of numerous honorary degrees. From 1930 to 1934 he was city solicitor of Central Falls, Rhode Island. He served as United States district attorney from 1935 to 1940. From 1940 to 1945 he was governor of Rhode Island. McGrath served as solicitor general of the United States from 1945 to 1946. He was elected U.S. senator from Rhode Island in 1946. President Truman appointed McGrath attorney general of the United States on August 24, 1949. He resigned from that office on April 7, 1952, and entered private practice. He died on September 2, 1966.

## National Association for the
## Advancement of Colored People (NAACP)

The NAACP is the oldest and largest civil rights organization in the United States. It was founded in 1909 and by the end of the twentieth century had a membership of more than a half-million. In 1905, the noted civil rights activist W. E. B. DuBois indicated that he felt the time was right to establish an organization that believed in Negro freedom and growth. Du Bois's call resulted in the Niagara Movement, an organization of twenty-nine black businessmen, ministers, editors, and teachers. Four years later, in New York City, the Niagara Movement merged with a group of concerned whites—led by Southern journalist William English Walling and social worker Mary White Ovington, both of whom had been horrified by a bloody, antiblack rampage in Springfield, Illinois, in August 1908—to form the National Negro Committee. The name National Association for the Advancement of Colored People was adopted in 1910, and in 1911 the new organization was incorporated in New York State. Du Bois, who became director of publicity and research, founded the NAACP's communication arm, *The Crisis*, which he edited from 1910 to 1934. The African American cultural movement of the 1920s and 1930s, known as the Harlem Renaissance, found its most powerful voice in *The Crisis*. From its earliest days, the NAACP worked toward realizing its goals by means of legislation and the courts, and by educating the public about the ways that U.S. blacks were denied full citizenship. Its first major victory came in 1915 when the Supreme Court, in *Guinn v. United States*, held that "grandfather clauses," post–Civil War statutes aimed at disenfranchising blacks, were unconstitutional. The NAACP's struggle for full enfranchisement of blacks culminated in 1965 with the passage of the federal Voting Rights Act.

The NAACP's campaign against residential discrimination had its first success in 1917 with the Louisville, Kentucky, case of *Buchanan v. Warley*, in which the Court ruled that segregation ordinances were in violation of the Due Process Clause of the Fourteenth Amendment. Thirty-one years later, in *Shelley v. Kraemer* (1948), NAACP lawyers successfully argued that blacks were entitled to equality in the enjoyment of property rights. In 1946, the NAACP won the case of *Morgan v. Virginia*, where the Court banned states from having laws that sanction segregated facilities in interstate travel by train and bus. The NAACP achieved what many regard as its first important political victory in 1930, when its chief executive, Walter White, persuaded a majority of the U.S. Senate to vote against President Herbert Hoover's nomination of Judge John J. Parker—an opponent of black suffrage—to the U.S. Supreme Court. White headed the NAACP from 1931 to 1955 and campaigned vigorously for a federal law against the lynching of blacks by white mobs. The NAACP's drive to end segregation in public education began in the 1930s under the auspices of a legal team headed by

Arthur B. Springarn and Charles Hamilton Houston. Thurgood Marshall was the NAACP's chief legal counsel in 1954 when the Supreme Court, in the landmark decision *Brown v. Board of Education*, held school segregation unconstitutional because separate educational facilities were "inherently unequal." The NAACP was able to pressure President Harry Truman to sign an executive order banning discrimination by the federal government.

The NAACP Legal Defense and Education Fund, Inc. (LDEF) was founded in 1940 under the leadership of Thurgood Marshall. The LDEF was originally affiliated with the NAACP, but became an entirely separate organization in 1957. The LDEF has been involved in more cases before the Supreme Court than any organization except the U.S. Department of Justice. Although the LDEF has worked primarily through the courts, its strategies include advocacy, educational outreach, legislation monitoring, coalition building, and policy research. In addition to its landmark victory in *Brown*, during the 1950s the LDEF won many important cases that barred discrimination in housing, voting access, and jury selection and the use of forced confessions and denial of counsel. Since the 1950s, the LDEF has been engaged in a monumental effort to enforce the desegregation orders placed on numerous school districts throughout the country.

## North Atlantic Treaty Organization (NATO)

The North Atlantic Treaty Organization (NATO) is a military alliance established in 1949. NATO was a product of the Cold War—the rivalry between Communist countries, led by the Soviet Union, and noncommunist nations. NATO was primarily designed to deter aggression by the Soviet Union against nations in Western Europe. It also prompted the Communist nations to create their own military alliance called the Warsaw Pact. Each of the seventeen initial member nations agreed to respond to an attack on any other member country as an attack on itself. NATO is divided into a military and a civilian component. The civilian branch includes the North Atlantic Council, the highest authority in NATO. The council consists of the heads of government of the NATO members or their representatives. During the Cold War, NATO helped maintain peace in Europe through its policy of deterrence. NATO's headquarters was in Paris until 1967. When France withdrew its troops from the NATO military command, the headquarters was moved to Brussels, Belgium.

## Roosevelt, Franklin D.

Franklin D. Roosevelt passed the New York bar exam without completing his degree at Columbia Law School. He joined a practice with a prominent New York City law firm but spent a great deal of time at Hyde Park, the family home. He was urged to run for the New York Senate, and although he ran as a Democrat in a heavily Republican district, he won by a small margin. He was elected to a second term in 1912. He also worked on the presidential campaign of Woodrow Wilson in 1912 and later became assistant secretary of the navy in the Wilson administration. After a failed vice presidential campaign in 1920, he became vice president of the Fidelity and Deposit Company, a position he kept until 1928. Struck with infantile paralysis (polio) in 1921, Roosevelt was nevertheless elected governor of New York in 1928 and 1930 and two years later became the Democratic presidential nominee. As president, he surrounded himself with a number of economists, academics, and other experts, a group known as his "brain trust." He took office at a time when business was stagnant, millions were unemployed, and banks were failing. Congress was in session for 104 days in the spring of 1933, during which time fifteen major pieces of Roosevelt-sponsored legislation were enacted. Following the midterm elections of 1934, Roosevelt successfully pressed for adoption of additional social legislation. Congress passed the National Labor Relations Act, the Utility Holding Company Act, the Guffey-Snyder Bituminous Coal Act, the Social Security Act, and measures providing more aid to agriculture. In 1940 Roosevelt was elected to a third term, during which he took on the role of commander in chief. Roosevelt acquiesced to party leaders in 1944 and replaced Vice President Henry Wallace with Missouri Senator Harry Truman. Roosevelt died less than three months after he began his fourth term. Achievements of the Roosevelt administration rank among the most important of any presidency in U.S. history. Roosevelt's political coalition brought about a long-term realignment that produced Democratic majorities in the Congress, and he formed new agencies that significantly and permanently expanded the role of the federal government.

### Rosenberg, Ethel and Julius

Ethel Rosenberg was born in New York City on September 28, 1915. Julius was also born in New York City on May 12, 1918. Both were raised in poor, Orthodox Jewish families in the slum-ghetto that was New York's Lower East Side during World War I. Julius attended City College, was active in left-wing student circles, and studied electrical engineering, graduating with honors in February 1939. Ethel worked in a variety of clerical jobs and was active as an organizer in the trade union movement. Ethel and Julius met in 1936 and were married in 1939. In 1940 Julius received a position as a junior engineer for the Army Signal Corps, and they moved to a modest apartment in New York's Knickerbocker Village in the spring of 1942. In February 1945 Julius was removed from his position in the Signal Corps on the grounds that he had been a Communist. Soon thereafter, he started his own machine shop with Ethel's brother, David Greenglass, who, during World War II as an army recruit, had been assigned as a draftsman at the Los Alamos, New Mexico, atomic bomb project. On July 17, 1950, one month after arresting Greenglass for suspicious conduct and ten months after the

Soviets exploded a nuclear device, the FBI announced Julius Rosenberg's arrest. Government officials alleged that he had been at the center of a wartime Soviet spy ring that sent crucial information on the atomic bomb to the Soviet Union. On August 11, following her testimony before a federal grand jury investigating Soviet atomic espionage, Ethel was arrested by the FBI and made a codefendant with Julius. The Rosenbergs were indicted for participating in the conspiracy to steal the secrets of the atomic bomb. Their indictment occurred only weeks after the outbreak of the Korean War, which greatly accelerated both government and mass media campaigns against U.S. Communists.

At the trial, which began on March 6, 1951, Greenglass testified that he had made drawings of lens molds used in the development of the atomic bomb and passed them to a courier, Harry Gold. The password used was "I come from Julius." The Rosenbergs were represented by Emanuel Bloch, an undistinguished local attorney who failed to cross-examine Greenglass effectively or to cross-examine Gold at all. The Rosenbergs were convicted and sentenced to death by Judge Irving Kaufman on April 5, 1951. Following the convictions, the Rosenberg case acquired a different dimension, as many in the United States and throughout the world lobbied the Harry Truman and Dwight Eisenhower administrations to commute their sentences. This movement failed, given the anticommunist hysteria generated by the stalemated Korean War and the passage of the McCarran Internal Security Act (1950) and similar legislation aimed at politically segregating Communists and other radicals from the general population. Both the Truman and Eisenhower administrations refused to stay the executions, and on June 19, 1953, the Supreme Court vacated a stay given by Justice William O. Douglas on novel legal grounds. The Rosenbergs were executed in the electric chair at New York's Sing Sing prison that day. Many radicals and anti–Cold War liberals believed the Rosenberg case involving U.S. Jews, Communists, and nuclear espionage could lead to massive repression and perhaps a Fascist dictatorship. For conservatives and anticommunist, or Cold War, liberals, the case proved that U.S. Communists were foreign agents of the Soviet Union seeking to undermine the United States.

Since their execution, the case has remained subject to debate and reinterpretation. FBI documents secured through the Freedom of Information Act do not support Julius Rosenberg's innocence. They suggest, however, that Ethel Rosenberg had been brought into the case to force her husband to confess. Soviet documents obtained after the disintegration of the Soviet Union in the early 1990s seem to reinforce the conclusion that Julius Rosenberg was guilty.

## Stone, Harlan Fiske

Harlan Fiske Stone was President Calvin Coolidge's only nominee for the Supreme Court and the last justice appointed while Taft was chief justice. Stone was nominated to replace Justice Joseph McKenna, who left the Court in late 1924. Stone was nominated on January 25, 1925, and confirmed by a 71–6 vote of the Senate on February 5, 1925. Stone served on the Court until his death on April 22, 1946. His last five years on the Court were as its chief justice. In his twenty-one years on the Court, Stone produced 456 majority opinions. He also wrote 93 dissenting and 37 concurring opinions. Stone participated in just over half (835) of the Taft Court's decisions (51.73 percent). In the five years he served on that Court, Stone wrote 113 (7.0 percent) of its majority opinions and wrote or joined 35 dissents and 15 concurring opinions.

Stone was born in Chesterfield, New Hampshire, on November 11, 1872. He took his B.A. and M.A. degrees from Amherst College before completing his law degree at Columbia University in 1898. During his youth, he was a friend of Calvin Coolidge, and the two attended Amherst together. Stone was admitted to the New York bar and began a successful corporate law practice. During this period, Stone became a professor of law at Columbia. He later served thirteen years as dean of the Columbia Law School before returning to private practice in 1923. During this same period, Coolidge succeeded to the presidency upon the death of Warren Harding. He brought Stone to Washington in 1924 to replace U.S. Attorney General Harry Daugherty, whose tenure as head of the Justice Department was ended by corruption, including the Teapot Dome scandal. Coolidge not only wanted the scandal fully investigated, but wanted someone with a "squeaky clean" reputation. Stone met these needs. Although he held the position of attorney general for only a year, Stone was able to effect substantial organizational changes in the Justice Department.

Stone was the first Supreme Court nominee to actually appear before the Senate committee reviewing his nomination. Stone effectively responded to the questions posed by the committee's members and was subsequently confirmed by the full Senate on February 5, 1925. When Taft resigned in 1930, many expected Stone to succeed him. Taft, however, fearing that Stone would be unable to "mass" the Court—persuade the justices to join a single opinion—influenced Hoover to appoint Charles Evans Hughes instead. Stone served as an associate justice until June 12, 1941, when President Franklin Roosevelt nominated him to replace Hughes as chief justice. Stone was confirmed as chief justice in the Senate by voice vote on June 27, 1941, and he served in that capacity until his death on April 22, 1946.

Stone joined the Taft Court in 1925. Chief Justice Taft and the "Four Horsemen"—Justices Pierce Butler, James McReynolds, George Sutherland, and Willis Van Devanter—constituted an unyielding conservative majority through the decade of the 1920s. Many expected Stone to join this group, but almost immediately Stone became the third member of the Court's moderate-liberal minority, joining Oliver Wendell Holmes and Louis Brandeis. Throughout the remaining terms of the Taft Court, Stone's positions were typically represented in the opinions of Holmes and Brandeis, and it was not until the 1930s and the Hughes Court period that Stone became a spokesman for the moderate-liberal dissenters. Comparatively speaking, the Taft Court had a low dissent rate. Stone was the third most likely member of the Taft Court to dissent, ranking behind Holmes and Brandeis.

As a member of the Hughes Court, Stone was often found with Justices Brandeis and Benjamin Cardozo on the minority side in many significant economic regulation rulings. Like Holmes and Brandeis, Stone subscribed to the judicial self-restraint view. He believed that policy matters are the exclusive domain of the legislative branch, and Stone sought not to substitute his own policy preferences for those of elected legislators.

One of Stone's most powerful opinions was his dissent in *United States v. Butler*, a case that clearly reflected his philosophy of judicial self-restraint. To Stone, the majority in *Butler* read the Constitution too narrowly. In an emergency such as the economic depression, courts ought not question the means by which Congress exercises delegated powers into operation. The judicial function is to review legislative power to enact statutes, not determine whether the laws establish sound policy. Further, while executive and legislative actions are subject to judicial review, such review must be limited by the Court's self-imposed restraint. Stone remained on the minority side of most split decisions until the Court's doctrinal change of 1937. As a result of this change, Stone became part of the moderate-liberal majority for the remainder of the Hughes Court period.

During the infamous Court-packing controversy of 1937, Stone indicated to Roosevelt that he did not support changing the Court's size. At the same time, he understood Roosevelt's frustration with the Court and was active behind the scenes in urging the nomination of justices with the judicial philosophy of Justice Brandeis, Justice Cardozo, and himself. After 1937, the Court essentially deferred to economic regulation initiatives at both the federal and state levels. The Court's consensus on government power to regulate the economy did not generalize to all other constitutional issues, however. Cases containing civil liberties questions became more frequent as World War II approached, and these issues would prove to be even more divisive than economic issues. The Roosevelt appointees on the Court were more than willing to speak their minds on these matters, causing Stone to refer to justices such as Hugo Black, William Douglas, and Frank Murphy as "wild horses." Stone's relations with most of the Roosevelt-appointed justices, both before and after his elevation to chief justice, were strained at best.

During his first term as chief justice, Stone agreed with Justices Black and Douglas in only 25 percent and 23 percent of the Court's decisions, respectively. His highest agreement rate was 70 percent with Justice Roberts. In 1943, Stone's agreement percentage was highest with Justices Reed (78 percent) and Frankfurter (70 percent). Stone's agreement level with Roberts dropped to 49 percent and rose to more than 50 percent with the liberal-activist members of the Court in 1943. Justice Jackson was in Germany for the war trials during Stone's last term, and the Court functioned with only eight members. During this last term, Stone agreed most often with Justices Reed (80 percent) and Burton (78 percent). The agreement rate with the liberal-activist bloc was in the 40 percent range.

One of Stone's greatest contributions to U.S. law came in his majority opinion in *United States v. Carolene Products Company* (1938). The most significant aspect of this opinion was Footnote 4, where Stone suggested that the Court should subject statutes dealing with civil liberties and discrimination issues to more searching examinations than laws pertaining to economic matters. He called for a "double standard." It affirmed the economic self-restraint position that Stone so strongly endorsed, but paradoxically suggested that statutes that restrict individual rights should be subject to a closer scrutiny. In Stone's view, because the rights protection provisions of the Bill of Rights occupy a "preferred position" and require greater judicial vigilance, the doctrine still retains analytic value when the Court considers constitutional limits on government.

Stone's 1941 opinion in *United States v. Darby Lumber Company* examined the Fair Labor Standards Act of 1938, viewed by many as the last major piece of New Deal legislation passed by Congress. The ruling reversed *Hammer v. Dagenhart* (1916), and Stone's opinion abandoned the previously operative distinction between manufacturing and commerce. Stone concluded that the goods produced and marketed by the lumber company were part of a stream of commerce and thus could be regulated under the commerce power. The *Darby* opinion also rejected the doctrine of "dual federalism" from Tenth Amendment jurisprudence. Stone suggested that the Tenth Amendment "states but a truism that all is retained which has not been surrendered" (*Darby* 1940, 124).

One of Stone's most noteworthy civil liberties opinions was delivered in *Minersville School District v. Gobitis* (1940). The Court ruled in *Gobitis* that citizens, at least public school students, could be compelled to salute the flag. Jehovah's Witnesses challenged compulsory participation in the flag salute exercise on the grounds of free exercise of religion. Justice Frankfurter said for the majority that "conscientious scruples" cannot relieve citizens from obedience to "general law not aimed [at] the promotion or restriction of religious beliefs" (*Gobitis* 1940, 594). Stone was the only member of the Court to disagree. He concluded that if First Amendment guarantees are to "have any meaning they must be deemed to withhold from the state any authority to compel belief or expression of it where that expression violates religious convictions, whatever may be the legislative view of the desirability of such compulsion" (*Gobitis* 1940, 604). The position Stone advanced in *Gobitis* was sufficiently compelling that five other justices joined him when the Court overruled *Gobitis* less than three years later in *West Virginia State Board of Education v. Barnette* (1943).

As sensitive as Stone was to civil liberties, he failed to weigh in against the egregious internment of the Japanese during World War II. As an associate justice, Stone was one of the most significant contributors to U.S. law. His chief justiceship was strikingly unsuccessful by comparison. Although his appointment to head the Court was universally praised, he proved ineffective in the post. He disliked administrative work and lacked the skills necessary to unify his Court and keep differences under control. Stone's Court was the most frequently divided and openly quarrelsome in history. The conflict included personal sniping and bickering as well as substantive differences on issues. By the end of Stone's tenure, critics asserted that the divisiveness had caused a decline in the Court's dignity and authority.

In many ways, the chief justiceship was an unhappy ending to an otherwise illustrious public life. Part of Stone's difficulty as chief justice was his tolerance for disagreement. In the minds of some Court colleagues, he let conferences over pending cases and certiorari petitions continue far too long. The Stone Court did not generally observe the normal Court protocol of allowing the justices to speak in turn by ascending levels of seniority. As a result, the discussions went in many different directions. Another problem was that Stone did not have the ability or perhaps the inclination to indulge the egos of some of his colleagues. Jackson believed that Stone's problem was that he dreaded conflict and wished to avoid it even at high cost. His willingness to permit dissension to continue unintentionally abetted the already high degree of conflict that was inevitable, given the positions and personalities of the "wild horses" (Johnson 1994, 433).

Stone's performance as an associate justice led most scholars to rank him as one of the great justices to sit on the Court. His performance as chief justice was certainly less than that, but ought not obscure his otherwise outstanding tenure on the Court. He was incapable of applying the type of pressure that Taft and Hughes could exert in the conferences. He either could not or would not rely on comradeship or persuasiveness or political loyalties to bind his colleagues to him. He would not even seek to create this illusion for the public. Stone was almost sixty-nine when he succeeded Hughes in the center chair and served in that capacity less than five years. Those five years proved less satisfactory, less happy than his sixteen as associate justice. Even so, the experts ranked him as one of the great justices to sit on the Court.

## Taft, Robert

U.S. senator and son of President William Howard Taft, Robert Taft was born in Cincinnati, Ohio, on September 8, 1889. He graduated from Yale University in 1910 and received his law degree from Harvard Law School in 1913. He returned to Cincinnati in 1914 and moved to Washington, D.C., in 1917 to serve as legal assistant to Herbert

Hoover at the Food and Drug Administration. Taft won election to the Ohio House of Representatives in 1920. While serving six years in the state legislature, he demonstrated the intense partisanship that characterized the remainder of his political career. Retiring from the legislature in 1926, Taft resumed his legal career as a partner in a Cincinnati firm. He largely confined his political activities to local issues, although he served a single term in the Ohio State Senate from 1931 to 1932. Increasingly irritated by President Franklin D. Roosevelt's New Deal, Taft sought election to the U.S. Senate in 1938. Taft's intellect and ability were so evident that after barely a year, he mounted a serious challenge for the Republican presidential nomination. At the nominating convention, Taft and Thomas Dewey stalemated one another and the nomination went to Wendell Willkie. In the Senate Taft acquired a national reputation as the most eloquent defender of traditional U.S. "individualism" against the assaults of New Deal Democrats. Taft's consistent aversion to U.S. military intervention in Europe during the late 1930s also contributed to his "reactionary" reputation. Although not a Nazi sympathizer, Taft believed that the United States should intervene against Hitler only if directly attacked. He opposed measures—such as the proposed Lend-Lease Bill of 1941—that drew the United States closer to a military commitment on Britain's behalf. He also feared the further expansion of federal government and presidential power that would be required to win the war.

In 1944 Taft stood aside for Ohio's Governor John Bricker, but Bricker lost the Republican presidential nomination to Dewey. Because of President Harry Truman's unpopularity and the apparent exhaustion of the New Deal, the Republicans won control of both houses of Congress in the 1946 congressional elections. By far his most notable piece of legislation was the Labor-Management Relations Act of 1947, better known as the Taft-Hartley Act. Passed over Truman's veto in an atmosphere of widespread concern over indiscriminate strikes, Taft-Hartley outlawed secondary boycotts; allowed states to pass "right-to-work" laws that made it harder for labor unions to organize; authorized the president to order a "cooling-off" period to stop strikes; and required unions to register and file financial reports with the Department of Labor. In 1948 Taft again contended for the Republican presidential nomination, but despite the normal enthusiastic backing of the Midwestern stalwarts, his showings in the primary elections were indifferent. At the convention Taft's forces were outorganized and outmanuevered by the Eastern moderates, and the nomination went to Dewey. The Taft and Dewey forces blamed each other for the unexpected defeat by Truman, and Taft and Dewey supporters were irreconcilable thereafter.

Once again in the minority during Truman's second term, Taft assumed a leadership role in the debate over U.S. foreign policy, following Vandenberg's death in 1950. In 1949 Taft had opposed ratification of the NATO agreement, arguing that it would give the Russians the impression that we are ringing them with armies for the purpose of taking aggressive action when the time comes. Concurrently, Taft joined the so-called China Lobby and regularly denounced the Truman administration, first for "losing" China to communism and then for negligence in failing to avert the North Korean invasion of South Korea in June 1950. As the leading Republican in the Senate, Taft could not avoid association with the accusations of his fellow Republican Senator Joseph McCarthy that the State Department and the Truman administration were riddled with Communist agents. With Thomas Dewey discredited by successive defeats, Taft finally looked likely to succeed in his third attempt at the Republican nomination. To stop Taft, the Dewey forces turned to the only candidate who could defeat him, General Dwight Eisenhower. Ultimately in 1952, as in Taft's previous defeats, it was the organizational superiority and resources of Taft's moderate opponents and their grasp of the new technology of electoral campaigning that enabled them to succeed. Following his bitter defeat at the convention, Taft was reconciled with Eisenhower in a September meeting. Taft finally became majority leader by a one-vote margin in a Senate controlled by the Republicans. Taft was stricken in April 1953 with the fatal cancer that killed him three months later in New York City. To the "new right," Taft was a martyr and symbol of true conservative principle shunted aside in favor of a corrupt "me-too" Republicanism. Conservatives espousing Taft's views on limited government, such as Barry Goldwater and Ronald Reagan, ultimately won back the presidential GOP from the Eastern establishment. The Taft-Hartley Act also effectively restricted the growth of the labor movement in large sections of the United States and contributed to organized labor's long-term decline as a political power. Ironically, although unable to emulate his father by reaching the presidency, Taft had more long-term impact on the politics of his party and his country than his illustrious father.

## Truman, Harry S.

Harry S. Truman was the thirty-second president of the United States. He was a student of military history and obtained an appointment to West Point but was later rejected because of defective vision. He held a variety of jobs, spending twelve years as a farmer before being appointed postmaster of Grandview, Missouri. After military service overseas, he returned to Missouri to join the political machine of Tom Pendergast, a local politician in Kansas City. Pendergast was responsible for Truman's appointment to an administrative body comparable to a county board of commissioners. Eight years later, Truman was elected to the U.S. Senate from Missouri; he was reelected in 1940.

There was little doubt at the 1944 Democratic National Convention that Roosevelt would be nominated to run for a fourth term; interest at the convention centered on the selection of a running mate. Roosevelt replaced his third-term vice president, Henry Wallace, with Truman, who was to serve only eighty-three days before he succeeded to the presidency on Roosevelt's death. Truman presided over the conclu-sion of World War II and established himself as a strong advocate of U.S. postwar global involvement with a strong United Nations. Extensive erosion of his public approval ratings and Republican control of the House limited Truman's presidency. He vetoed the Taft-Hartley Act as damaging to the interests of labor, the only constituency still loyal to him. He fashioned the Truman Doctrine, a foreign policy designed to con-tain the spread of international communism; NATO was established as a component of the doctrine's objectives. After winning reelection in 1948 against seemingly over-whelming odds, Truman embarked on a domestic program called the Fair Deal. As the country became mired in the Korean War and the Cold War, however, attention and support for his Fair Deal proposals waned. He announced in March 1952 that he would not run for reelection and retired to his home in Independence, Missouri.

## Twenty-Second Amendment

The Twenty-Second Amendment term limits the office of president—no person shall be elected to the office more than twice. The amendment further provides that any person who has held the office of president or acted as president for more than two years of a term to which some other person was elected can be elected for only one more four-year term. It is the only amendment adopted since 1787 that, instead of expanding the power of the electorate, places limits on it. It was adopted in reaction to Franklin Roosevelt's election to four terms as president. The maximum period that a person can serve is ten years—two years by elevation to the office through death or disability of the elected president and two elected terms of four years each. In some cases, a person might be limited to six years since elevation for two years and a day through death, disability, or resignation of the elected president would make a person eligible for only one elected term of four years. The amendment was proposed March 24, 1947, by the Republican-dominated 80th Congress. It was certified as adopted on March 1, 1951. Once proposed by Congress, the amendment received a mixed response from the states. Only one other amendment to the Constitution has taken longer to ratify than the three years, eleven months required for the two-term limit. The amendment, although written in such a way as to exempt the incumbent Truman from its coverage, was a posthumous slap at Franklin Roosevelt, who had challenged the two-term tradition. Congress had never been fully satisfied with the original Con-stitution's provision for unrestricted presidential reeligibility. From 1789 to 1947, 270 resolutions to limit the president's tenure had been introduced in the House and Sen-ate. The Roosevelt years added a partisan dimension to this long-standing concern. Forty-one state legislatures ratified the amendment, although there was little discus-sion of its significance. What has been the effect of term limits on the influence of the president? Two-term presidents are necessarily lame ducks for the second term.

## Warren, Earl

Earl Warren was governor of California and chief justice of the U.S. Supreme Court. He was born in Los Angeles, California, on March 19, 1891. Both of his parents came to the United States as young children, his father from Norway and his mother from Sweden. They met and were married in Minneapolis, Minnesota, and moved to California in the 1880s. Warren moved from Bakersfield, California, in 1908 to attend college at the University of California at Berkeley. While an undergraduate, he worked in the gubernatorial campaign of Progressive Party candidate Hiram Johnson, and he remained a Progressive until the end of his political career. After graduation, Warren entered the university's law school and earned his degree in 1914. After law school, Warren practiced law until the United States entered World War I. He enlisted in the army and rose to the rank of first lieutenant before he was discharged in December 1918. The following year he became deputy city attorney in Oakland, California. In May 1920, he was hired as deputy district attorney by Alameda County. In 1925 Warren was appointed to fill the last year of the departing district attorney's term, and in 1926 he secured a full term in the position by winning his first election. He won reelection in 1930 and 1934. During his tenure as district attorney, Warren earned a national reputation for honesty, hard work, and scientific law enforcement by fighting crime and the political corruption that Prohibition, the excesses of the Roaring Twenties, and the Great Depression had exacerbated. By the mid-1930s, Warren was probably the best-known district attorney in the United States. In 1938 Warren ran for the office of attorney general of California. Cross-filing in the primaries, he won the Republican, Democratic, and Progressive Party nominations. Warren fashioned a distinguished record, but also supported the anticommunist witch-hunts led by Assemblyman Samuel Yorty. Warren also joined the post–Pearl Harbor hysteria, becoming a leading advocate of the internment of Japanese Americans. After he left the Court he urged the repeal of laws that allowed for the internment of civilians during national emergencies.

In 1942 Warren challenged Governor Culbert Olson in the November election. Warren won with 57 percent of the vote. In 1946 he won reelection by more than a two to one margin. In 1950, Warren won an unprecedented third term, defeating James Roosevelt, son of Franklin Roosevelt. Warren's policies were more Progressive than Republican. Warren soon gained a national reputation as a competent, Progressive Republican—bland of personality, but a good administrator and an ideal family man. His electoral success made him a potential presidential nominee. In 1948 he ran with Thomas Dewey as the Republican nominee for vice president. Although the ticket lost, Warren gained new national exposure and was regarded as a potential candidate in 1952. In the anticommunist period that followed World War II,

Warren adopted a more moderate position on challenging the rights of presumed radicals than he had before. He campaigned in some primaries, but by the time of the national convention, he was running a distant third behind Robert Taft and Dwight Eisenhower. Warren hoped to be a compromise candidate, but California Senator Richard Nixon worked for Eisenhower's nomination after pledging to support Warren. Despite his belief that Nixon was dishonest, Warren campaigned for the ticket. After the election Eisenhower discussed some cabinet positions with Warren and considered him for the Departments of Interior and Justice, but Warren was eventually promised the first vacancy on the Supreme Court. In July 1953, in preparation for that appointment, Eisenhower offered Warren the job of solicitor general. Warren was planning on taking the position when Chief Justice Fred M. Vinson died. In late September Eisenhower made Warren chief justice as an interim appointment.

In May 1954 Warren delivered a single opinion for a unanimous Court in *Brown v. Board of Education* and *Bolling v. Sharpe*. The *Brown* opinion is clearly Warren's most famous and most important. Warren's ability to bring unanimity to the decision in *Brown* was probably his greatest accomplishment and the key to the opinion's success. Warren's opinion in the case reveals his ability to see that the central issues of U.S. law are often social and political and that the Supreme Court must persuade not only lawyers and judges but the people of the nation as well. Its simplicity in declaring that segregation based on race is morally wrong and is particularly damaging to young children is both its great strength and its weakness. *Brown* elicited a widespread criticism that it was result-oriented and failed to have a basis in law. In *Brown* Warren displayed his ability to cut to the heart of the matter—that segregation was so fundamentally wrong that it could not be tolerated by the Constitution. In *Reynolds v. Sims* (1964), the second reapportionment case decided by his Court, Warren articulated the need for legislative districts based on population size, noting that "Legislators represent people, not trees or acres" (*Reynolds* 1964, 562). In *South Carolina v. Katzenbach* (1966), Warren wrote a strongly worded opinion upholding the Voting Rights Act of 1965.

On April 1, 1968, President Lyndon Johnson announced that he would not seek a second full term. Richard Nixon, Warren's lifelong political enemy, was to be the Republican candidate for president, and his chances of winning were dramatically improved following the assassination of Senator Robert Kennedy. Once convinced that Nixon would win, Warren notified Johnson of his plan to resign. Johnson nominated Abe Fortas to replace Warren, but scandal and a Senate filibuster prevented his confirmation. Warren remained chief justice until Nixon nominated his successor in 1969. In mid-1974, Warren suffered his third heart attack in six months. A week later, on July 9, 1974, Warren died in Georgetown University Hospital.

## *References and Further Reading*

Abraham, Henry J. 1998. *Freedom and the Court: Civil Rights and Liberties in the United States.* 7th ed. New York: Oxford University Press.

Belknap, Michal R. 1977. *Cold War Political Justice: The Smith Act, the Communist Party, and American Civil Liberties.* Westport, CT: Greenwood Press.

Blackman, John L., Jr. 1967. *Presidential Seizure in Labor Disputes.* Cambridge, MA: Harvard University Press.

Cochran, Bert. 1973. *Harry Truman and the Crisis Presidency.* New York: Funk & Wagnalls.

Johnson, John W. 1994. "Harlan Fiske Stone." In *The Supreme Court Justices: A Biographical Dictionary,* ed. Melvin I. Urofsky. New York: Garland.

Lacey, Michael J., ed. 1989. *The Truman Presidency.* New York: Cambridge University Press.

Leuchtenberg, William E. 2001. *In the Shadow of FDR: From Harry Truman to George W. Bush.* 3d ed. Ithaca, NY: Cornell University Press.

Lukacs, John. 1961. *A History of the Cold War.* Garden City, NY: Doubleday.

McCoy, Donald R. 1984. *The Presidency of Harry S. Truman.* Lawrence: University Press of Kansas.

Milkis, Sidney M., and Michael Nelson. 1994. *The American Presidency: Origins and Development, 1776–1993.* 2d ed. Washington, DC: CQ Press.

Morison, Samuel Eliot, Henry Steele Commager, and William Leuchtenberg. 1980. *The Growth of the American Republic.* 7th ed., vol. II. New York: Oxford University Press.

Phillips, Cabell. 1966. *The Truman Presidency: The History of a Triumphant Succession.* New York: Macmillan.

Urofsky, Melvin I. 1997a. *Division and Discord: The Supreme Court under Stone and Vinson, 1941–1953.* Columbia: University of South Carolina Press.

Woodward, C. Vann. 1974. *The Strange Career of Jim Crow.* 3d ed. New York: Oxford University Press.

# *Chronology*

**1945**    July 1  Tom Clark becomes U.S. attorney general.

July 17  President Truman participates in the first Potsdam Conference.

July 28  United Nations Treaty is approved by an 89–2 vote.

July 31  Justice Owen Roberts resigns from the Court.

August 6  Atomic bomb is dropped on Hiroshima, Japan.

August 9  Atomic bomb is dropped on Nagasaki, Japan.

August 14  Formal announcement of Japan surrender is made.

September 18  Justice Harold H. Burton replaces Justice Roberts.

**1946**    January 10  UN General Assembly convenes its first session in London.

January 14 *New York v. United States*—Court rules that sale of mineral water by the State of New York is a business, not a governmental function, and therefore is subject to federal taxes.

January 21  United Steel Workers Union strike closes the nation's steel mills.

February 4 *In re Yamashita*—Court rules that enemy commander may be tried in a military court on war crimes charges.

February 25 *Duncan v. Kahanamoku*—Court rules that trials before military tribunals in Hawaii are unconstitutional, as martial law cannot supplant civil law when civil courts are operating.

**1946,**
**cont.**

April 1  Four hundred thousand United Mine Workers strike.

April 22  *Girouard v. United States*—Court overrules *United States v. Schwimmer* (1931) and other previous decisions that conscientious objectors are ineligible for citizenship.

Chief Justice Stone dies.

April 25  Foreign ministers of Great Britain, France, the U.S.S.R., and the United States meet at the Paris Peace Conference.

June 3  *Morgan v. Virginia* invalidates a state law requiring racial segregation on public transportation that crosses state lines.

June 6  Truman nominates Fred Vinson to replace Stone as chief justice.

June 10  *Colegrove v. Green*—Court rules that courts ought not intervene in congressional apportionment cases.

In *Anderson v. Mt. Clemens Pottery Company*—another "portal-to-portal" case—Court holds that workers are entitled to receive pay for preparation time.

June 26  Frederick M. Vinson takes seat as chief justice of the Supreme Court.

July 4  President Truman declares Philippine independence.

August 1  President Truman signs the McMahon Act, creating the Atomic Energy Commission.

October 1  The International Military Tribunal in Nuremberg imposes the death penalty on twelve Nazi leaders.

**1947**

January 8  President Truman names George C. Marshall U.S. secretary of state.

February 10  Court upholds in *Everson v. Board of Education of Ewing Township* a state law permitting reimbursement for costs of transporting children to parochial schools.

Court refuses to rule on Hatch Act provisions in *United Public Workers v. Mitchell.*

March 6 Supreme Court upholds fine against John L. Lewis, head of the United Mine Workers Union, in *United States v. United Mine Workers.*

March 12 Truman announces Truman Doctrine to joint session of Congress.

March 24 Congress passes resolution proposing the Twenty-Second Amendment, which contains presidential term limits.

May 15 Congress approves Truman Doctrine aid to Greece and Turkey.

June 5 Secretary of State George Marshall proposes a plan for the economic recovery of Europe.

June 23 Congress overrides President Truman's veto of the Labor-Management Relations (Taft-Hartley) Act.

July 7 Hoover Commission is established to study the organization of the federal government's executive branch.

July 18 President Truman signs the Presidential Succession Act.

October 9 President Truman endorses a UN proposal for an autonomous Jewish state.

October 18 The House Un-American Activities Committee commences its investigation of the film industry.

Truman submits European Recovery Program, known as the Marshall Plan, to Congress.

**1948** February 16 Postwar rent control regulations upheld in *Woods v. Cloyd W. Miller Company.*

March 8 *Illinois ex rel. McCollum v. Board of Education* holds that religious education cannot take place in public school premises.

**1948,** April 3  Congress passes the Foreign Assistance Act (Marshall Plan) provid-
**cont.**  ing funds to rebuild war-devastated economies.

May 3  Court holds in *Shelley v. Kraemer* that state enforcement of racially
restrictive real estate covenants is unconstitutional.

May 14  Israel declares itself a sovereign nation. The United States is the first
to recognize its independence.

June 21  The Republican Party nominates Thomas E. Dewey of New York and
Earl Warren of California on its presidential ticket.

June 24  President Truman signs the Selective Service Act.

June 25  Congress relaxes immigration quotas to permit entry of displaced
persons (refugees) from Communist or former Axis countries.

July 12  The Democratic Party nominates President Truman for reelection.
Alben Barkley of Kentucky is named his running mate.

July 17  "Dixiecrats" form States Rights Party, which nominates Strom Thurmond as its presidential candidate.

July 23  The Progressive Party nominates Henry Wallace as its presidential
candidate.

July 26  An executive order bars segregation in the U.S. military.

November 2  President Truman is reelected president. Democrats gain control of both houses of Congress.

**1949**  January 3  Court rules that states have the authority to pass right-to-work laws
in *Lincoln Federal Labor Union v. Northwestern Iron and Metal Company.*

April 4  Representatives of the United States, Canada, and ten European
nations sign the North Atlantic Treaty, which sets the foundation for the
North Atlantic Treaty Organization (NATO).

May 16  An ordinance prohibiting breaches of peace stemming from provocative speech is struck down in *Terminello v. Chicago.*

June 27  Court refuses to require the exclusionary rule in state criminal trials in *Wolf v. Colorado.*

June 29  The United States removes its troops from Korea.

July 19  Justice Frank Murphy dies.

July 28  Tom C. Clark is nominated by President Truman to replace Justice Murphy.

August 10  President Truman signs the National Security Act, renaming the National Defense Establishment the Department of Defense.

September 9  Justice Wiley Rutledge dies.

October 15  Sherman Minton is nominated by President Truman to replace Justice Rutledge.

**1950**  February 20  Senator Joseph McCarthy challenges the loyalty of eighty U.S. State Department employees.

Court decides *United States v. Rabinowitz,* enabling police to seize property without a warrant.

May 8  Court rules in *American Communications Association v. Douds* that the anticommunist statement required under the Taft-Hartley Act is not unconstitutional.

June 5  President Truman signs the International Development Act.

Court rules in *Sweatt v. Painter* that state universities must admit African American students where segregated facilities are unequal.

Court rules in *McLaurin v. Oklahoma State Board of Regents* that segregation of minority university students is unconstitutional.

June 25  North Korea invades South Korea, prompting UN intervention.

July 8  General Douglas MacArthur appointed commander of the UN forces in Korea.

**1950,** September 23 Congress overrides President Truman's veto of the Internal
**cont.** Security Act, creating the Subversive Activities Control Board.

December 8 President Truman announces a trade ban on Communist China.

**1951** January 15 Court upholds conviction for inflammatory speech in *Feiner v.
New York.*

February 27 Twenty-Second Amendment establishing presidential term limits is ratified.

March 29 Julius and Ethel Rosenberg are convicted of espionage. They are
sentenced to death a week later.

April 11 General MacArthur is relieved of his command by President Truman.

June 4 Court upholds Smith Act convictions of Communist Party leaders in
*Dennis v. United States.*

September 8 Forty-nine nations sign the Japanese Peace Treaty.

**1952** January 2 Court reverses a narcotics conviction in *Rochin v. California*, in
which police officers pumped against his will the stomach of a defendant who
had swallowed morphine capsules.

March 3 Court rules in *Adler v. Board of Education* that persons found to be
subversives can be barred from public school employment.

March 30 President Truman announces he will not seek reelection.

April 8 President Truman orders federal takeover of the nation's steel mills in
an attempt to avert a steelworkers' strike.

April 28 Court upholds in *Zorach v. Clauson* a "released-time" religious education program conducted on private premises.

June 2 Court rules in *Youngstown Sheet and Tube Company v. Sawyer* that
President Truman does not have the authority to seize the steel mills; 600,000
steelworkers go out on strike.

June 27  Immigration and Naturalization Act, which retains immigration quotas, is adopted over President Truman's veto.

July 7  The Republican Party nominates Dwight D. Eisenhower of New York for president. Richard M. Nixon of California is named as his running mate.

July 21  The Democratic Party nominates Adlai E. Stevenson of Illinois and John J. Sparkman of Alabama on its presidential ticket.

July 24  The steelworkers' strike ends.

July 25  Puerto Rico becomes a U.S. commonwealth.

September 23  Richard Nixon, Republican vice presidential candidate, makes the so-called Checkers speech.

November 1  The United States explodes the first hydrogen bomb in the Marshall Islands.

November 4  Eisenhower is elected president.

**1953**  March 5  Joseph Stalin, premier of the Soviet Union, dies.

March 30  Congress creates the Department of Health, Education, and Welfare (HEW).

May 5  Congress votes to preserve state control over offshore oil reserves.

July 27  The Korean armistice is signed in Panmunjom.

September 9  Chief Justice Fred Vinson dies.

September 30  Earl Warren is appointed chief justice of the Supreme Court.

# Table of Cases

*Brown v. Board of Education*, 347 U.S. 483 (1954)

*Brown v. Mississippi*, 297 U.S. 278 (1936)

*Buchanan v. Warley*, 245 U.S. 60 (1917)

*Building Services Employees Union v. Gazzam*, 339 U.S. 532 (1950)

*Burton v. Wilmington Parking Authority*, 365 U.S. 715 (1961)

*Cantwell v. Connecticut*, 310 U.S. 296 (1940)

*Carpenters and Joiners Union v. Ritter's Café*, 315 U.S. 722 (1942)

*Chicago and Southern Air Lines, Inc. v. Waterman Steamship Corporation*, 333
    U.S. 103 (1948)

*Chimel v. California*, 395 U.S. 752 (1969)

*Civil Rights Cases*, 109 U.S. 3 (1883)

*Cochran v. Louisiana State Board of Education*, 281 U.S. 370 (1930)

*Colegrove v. Green*, 328 U.S. 549 (1946)

*Communist Party v. Catherwood*, 367 U.S. 389 (1961)

*Communist Party v. Subversive Activities Control Board*, 367 U.S. 1 (1961)

*Cooper v. Aaron*, 358 U.S. 1 (1958)

*Corrigan v. Buckley*, 271 U.S. 323 (1926)

*Cramer v. United States*, 325 U.S. 1 (1945)

*Cumming v. County Board of Education*, 175 U.S. 528 (1899)

*DeJonge v. Oregon*, 299 U.S. 353 (1937)

*Dennis v. United States*, 351 U.S. 494 (1951)

*Dickerson v. United States*, 530 U.S. 428 (2000)

*Doremus v. Board of Education*, 342 U.S. 429 (1952)

*Duncan v. Kahanamoku*, 327 U.S. 429 (1946)

*Employment Division, Oregon Department of Human Resources v. Smith*, 494
    U.S. 872 (1990)

*Engel v. Vitale*, 370 U.S. 421 (1962)

*Epperson v. Arkansas*, 393 U.S. 97 (1968)

*Everson v. Board of Education of Ewing Township*, 330 U.S. 1 (1947)

*Feiner v. New York*, 340 U.S. 315 (1951)

*Garner v. Board of Public Works*, 341 U.S. 716 (1951)

*Gerende v. Board of Supervisors*, 341 U.S. 56 (1951)

*Giboney v. Empire Storage*, 336 U.S. 490 (1949)

*Gideon v. Wainwright*, 372 U.S. 335 (1963)

*Gilbert v. California*, 388 U.S. 263 (1967)

*Girouard v. United States*, 328 U.S. 61 (1946)

*Gitlow v. New York*, 268 U.S. 562 (1925)

*Goesaert v. Cleary*, 335 U.S. 464 (1948)

*Gold Clause Cases*, 294 U.S. 240 (1935)

*Gomillion v. Lightfoot*, 364 U.S. 339 (1960)

*McDonald v. United States*, 335 U.S. 451 (1948)

*McLaurin v. Oklahoma State Board of Regents*, 339 U.S. 637 (1950)

*Minersville School District v. Gobitis*, 310 U.S. 586 (1940)

*Miranda v. Arizona*, 384 U.S. 436 (1966)

*Missouri ex rel. Gaines v. Canada*, 305 U.S. 337 (1938)

*Mitchell v. United States*, 313 U.S. 80 (1941)

*Morgan v. Virginia*, 328 U.S. 373 (1946)

*Nathanson v. United States*, 290 U.S. 41 (1933)

*National Labor Relations Board v. Friedman-Harry Marks Clothing Company*, 301 U.S. 58 (1937)

*National Labor Relations Board v. Jones and Laughlin Steel Company*, 301 U.S. 1 (1937)

*Near v. Minnesota*, 283 U.S. 697 (1931)

*New York v. United States*, 326 U.S. 572 (1946)

*Niemotko v. Maryland*, 340 U.S. 268 (1951)

*Noto v. United States*, 367 U.S. 290 (1961)

*Oliver, In re*, 333 U.S. 257 (1948)

*Olmstead v. United States*, 277 U.S. 438 (1928)

*Palko v. Connecticut*, 302 U.S. 319 (1937)

*Pennsylvania v. Nelson*, 350 U.S. 497 (1956)

*Plessy v. Ferguson*, 163 U.S. 537 (1896)

*Powell v. McCormack*, 395 U.S. 486 (1969)

*Public Utilities Commission v. Pollak*, 343 U.S. 451 (1952)

*Reynolds v. Sims*, 377 U.S. 533 (1964)

*Rochin v. California*, 342 U.S. 165 (1952)

*Rosenberg v. United States*, 344 U.S. 889 (1952)

*Sacher v. United States*, 343 U.S. 1 (1952)

*Saia v. New York*, 334 U.S. 558 (1948)

*Scales v. United States*, 367 U.S. 203 (1961)

*Senn v. Tile Layers' Union*, 301 U.S. 468 (1937)

*Shelley v. Kraemer*, 334 U.S. 1 (1948)

*Silverman v. United States*, 365 U.S. 505 (1961)

*Sipuel v. Board of Regents of the University of Oklahoma*, 332 U.S. 631 (1948)

*Skinner v. Oklahoma*, 316 U.S. 535 (1942)

*South Carolina v. Katzenbach*, 383 U.S. 301 (1966)

*Southern Air Lines, Inc. v. Waterman Steamship Corporation*, 333 U.S. 103 (1948)

*Spano v. New York*, 360 U.S. 315 (1959)

*Spinelli v. United States*, 393 U.S. 410 (1969)

*Swann v. Adams*, 385 U.S. 440 (1967)

*Sweatt v. Painter*, 339 U.S. 626 (1950)

# *Glossary*

**Adversary proceeding**  A legal process that involves a contest between two opposing parties. Formal notice is served on the party against whom an action has been filed to allow that party an opportunity to respond. This system is generally regarded as the most effective means for the evaluation of evidence.

**Advisory opinion**  An opinion of a court indicating how it would rule on an issue if the issue were presented in an actual case; an interpretation of law without binding effect. An advisory opinion offers a view on the legal effect of a law although no real case exists to present the legal question.

**Affirm**  An appellate court ruling that upholds the judgment of a lower court—that the judgment of the lower court is correct and should stand.

**Amicus curiae**  Latin meaning "friend of the court." A person or group, not a party to a case, that submits a brief detailing its views on a case. The purpose of an amicus brief is to direct a court's attention to an issue or argument that might not be developed in the same way by the parties themselves.

**Appeal**  A process by which a final judgment of a lower court ruling is reviewed by a higher court.

**Appellant**  The party who seeks review of a lower court ruling before a higher court; the party dissatisfied with a lower court ruling who appeals the case to a superior court for review.

**Appellate jurisdiction**  Authority of a superior court to review decisions of inferior courts. Appellate jurisdiction empowers a higher court to conduct such a review and affirm, modify, or reverse the lower court decision. Appellate jurisdiction is conveyed through constitutional or statutory mandate. Federal appellate jurisdiction is granted by Article III of the Constitution, which says that the Supreme Court possesses such jurisdiction "both as to law and fact, with such exceptions and under such regulations as the Congress shall make."

**Appellee**    The party that prevails in a lower court and against whom an appeal of the judgment is sought, in some situations called a "respondent."

**Assembly, right to**    A fundamental right provided by the First Amendment that the people are entitled to peaceably gather and petition the government for "redress of grievances." It includes the right to protest governmental policies as well as to advocate particular, even distasteful, views. The government can impose regulations on the time, place, and manner of assembly, provided that substantial interests, such as preventing threats to public order, can be shown.

**Balancing test**    A judicial decision-making approach where interests on one side are weighed or balanced against interests on another. This approach is used most frequently where courts are reviewing individual rights issues. An individual's free speech interests, for example, may be balanced against a societal interest for national security to determine if the speech is protected from regulation or not. Based on the traditional idea that individual freedoms and governmental authority must be kept in equilibrium.

**Brief**    A document containing arguments on a matter under consideration by a court. A brief submitted to a court by an attorney typically contains, among other things, points of law from previous rulings.

**Case**    A general term for an action, cause, suit, or controversy, at law.

**Case law**    Precedent created as courts resolve disputes. Case law is judge-made law, ruling on a specific set of facts.

**Case or controversy**    A constitutional requirement that disputes or controversies be definite and concrete and involve parties whose legal interests are truly adverse. This requirement is contained in Article III of the U.S. Constitution, and establishes a bona fide controversy as a precondition for adjudication by federal courts.

**Certification**    A process by which judges in one court state uncertainty about the rule of law to apply in a case and request instructions from a higher court.

**Certiorari**    Latin for "to be informed of, to be made certain in regard to." A writ or order to a court whose decision is being challenged on appeal to send up the records of the case to enable a higher court to review the case. The writ of certiorari is the primary means by which the U.S. Supreme Court reviews cases from lower courts.

**Citizenship**    A legal status that entitles a person to all the rights and privileges guaranteed and protected by the Constitution of the United States. All persons born in the United States or to parents who are U.S. citizens possess U.S. citizenship. Others may obtain citizenship through naturalization, a process established by Congress.

**Civil liberties**   Those liberties spelled out in a bill of rights or a constitution that guarantee the protection of persons, opinion, and property from the arbitrary interference of government officials. Civil liberties create immunities from certain governmental actions that interfere with an individual's protected rights.

**Civil rights**   Positive acts of government designed to protect persons against arbitrary and discriminatory treatment by government or individuals. Civil rights guarantees may be found in constitutions, but more frequently take the form of statutes.

**Class action**   A legal action in which one or more persons represent both themselves and others who are similarly situated persons. All members of a class must share a common legal interest and meet particular requirements in order to proceed as a class or collective action.

**Comity**   Legal principle that prompts a court to defer to the exercise of jurisdiction by another court. Comity is a rule of judicial courtesy rather than a firm requirement of law, and it suggests that a court that first asserts jurisdiction will not undergo interference by another court without its consent.

**Commerce Clause**   Provision found in Article I, Section 8 of the U.S. Constitution. The clause empowers Congress to "regulate commerce with foreign nations, and among the several states, and with the Indian tribes." Since the 1930s, the commerce power has been the basis for extensive federal regulation of the economy and, to a limited extent, federal criminal law.

**Common law**   A body of principles that derive their authority from court judgments that are grounded in common customs and usages. Common law consists of principles that do not have their origin in statute and, as such, is distinct from law created by legislative enactments.

**Concurrent jurisdiction**   Authority that is shared by different courts, and which may be exercised at the same time over the same subject matter.

**Concurring opinion**   An opinion by a judge that agrees with the decision of the majority, but disagrees with the majority's rationale; has arrived at the same conclusion, but for different reasons.

**Conference**   A meeting of Supreme Court justices in which the justices conduct all business associated with deciding cases. Conferences are closed to all but the justices, and it is where the Supreme Court determines which cases will be reviewed, discusses the merits of cases after oral argument, and decides by vote which party to a case will prevail.

**Constitutional court**    A federal court created by Congress under authority conveyed by Article III. Judges of constitutional courts serve for the duration of good behavior (life tenure) and are protected from having their salaries reduced by the legislature.

**De facto**    Latin for "in fact," actual.

**De jure**    A Latin word for "by right." A de jure action occurs as a result of law or official government action.

**Declaratory judgment**    A ruling of a court that clarifies rights of the parties or offers an opinion on a legal question and is invoked when a plaintiff seeks a declaration of his or her rights. It differs from a conventional action in that no specific order is issued and no relief or remedy granted.

**Decree**    A judgment or order of a court.

**Defendant**    The party who is sued in a civil action or charged in a criminal case; the party responding to a civil complaint. A defendant in a criminal case is the person(s) formally accused of criminal conduct.

**Demurrer**    An allegation by a defendant that even if the facts alleged were true, their legal consequences are not such as to require an answer or further proceedings in the cause. Under contemporary rules of civil procedure, a motion to dismiss a case for failure to establish a claim is more commonly used to accomplish the same objective.

**Dissenting opinion**    The opinion of a judge that disagrees with the result reached by the majority.

**Diversity jurisdiction**    Authority conveyed by Article III of the U.S. Constitution empowering federal courts to hear civil actions involving parties from different states.

**Due process**    Government procedures that follow principles of essential or fundamental fairness. Provisions designed to ensure that laws will be reasonable both in substance and in means of implementation are contained in two clauses of the Constitution of the United States. The Fifth Amendment prohibits deprivation of "life, liberty, or property, without due process of law." It sets a limit on arbitrary and unreasonable actions by the federal government. The Fourteenth Amendment contains parallel language aimed at the states. Due process requires that actions of government occur through ordered and regularized processes.

**En banc**    French for "in the bench." A proceeding in which all the judges of an appellate court participate as distinguished from a proceeding heard by a panel of three judges.

**Enjoin**    An order from a court that requires a party to perform or refrain from a specified action. A party is enjoined by a court issuing an injunction or a restraining order.

**Equity**    A system of remedial justice administered by certain courts empowered to order remedies based on principles and precedents developed by courts.

**Ex parte**    Latin for "only one side." Done for, in behalf of, or on the application of one party only.

**Exclusive power**    Authority that is assigned to either the national or state level of government, but not exercised by both.

**Executive order**    A regulation issued by the president, a state governor, or some other executive authority for the purpose of giving effect to a constitutional or statutory provision. An executive order has the force of law and is one means by which the executive branch implements laws.

**Federal question**    An issue arising out of provisions of the U.S. Constitution, federal statutes, or treaties. A federal court has authority to hear federal questions under powers conferred by Article III of the U.S. Constitution.

**Federalism**    A political system in which a number of sovereign political units join together forming a larger political unit that has authority to act on behalf of the whole. A federal system, or federation, preserves the political integrity of all the entities in the federation. Federal systems are regarded as "weak" if the central government has control over very few policy questions, and a "strong" system is one in which the central government possesses authority over most significant policy issues. Authority that is not exclusively assigned may be shared by the two levels and exercised concurrently. The Supremacy Clause of the U.S. Constitution requires that conflicts arising from the exercise of federal and state power be resolved in favor of the central government. Powers not assigned to the national government are "reserved" for the states by the Tenth Amendment.

**Grand jury**    A panel of 12–23 citizens who review prosecutorial evidence to determine if there are sufficient grounds to formally accuse an individual of criminal conduct. The charges a grand jury issues are contained in a document called an indictment.

**Habeas corpus**    Latin for "you have the body." Habeas corpus was a procedure in English law designed to prevent the improper detention of prisoners. The habeas process forced jailers to bring a detained person before a judge, who would examine the justification for his or her detention. If the court found the person was being improperly held, it could order the prisoner's release.

**Implied power**    Authority that is possessed by inference from expressed provisions of a constitution or statute. The intention is not manifested by explicit and direct words. The meaning is gathered by necessary deduction. Implied power is not conveyed by explicit language, but rather by implication or necessary deduction from circumstances, general language, or the conduct of parties.

**In camera**    Latin for "in chambers," in private. A hearing conducted with no spectators present.

**In re**    Latin for "in the matter of." The usual manner of entitling a judicial proceeding in which there are no adversary parties as such, but some issue requiring judicial action.

**Incorporation**    Refers to the question of whether the federal Bill of Rights extends as a limitation on state governments. The issue largely has been resolved, but several schools of thought on the matter have existed historically. The most sweeping position was that all of the Bill of Rights provisions connected to the states through the Due Process Clause of the Fourteenth Amendment. The clause prohibits a state from denying liberty without due process. Those advocating total incorporation viewed the term *liberty* as an all-inclusive shorthand for each of the rights enumerated in the Bill of Rights. A second opinion rejected any structural linkage of due process to the Bill of Rights and held simply that the Due Process Clause requires states to provide fundamental fairness. Due process is assessed under this standard by criteria of immutable principles of justice, or, as suggested by Justice Benjamin N. Cardozo in *Palko v. Connecticut* (1937), elements that are "implicit in the concept of ordered liberty." Application of such standards would occur on a case-by-case basis. The third opinion is a hybrid of the first two and is known as "selective" incorporation. The selective approach resembles the fundamental fairness position in that it does not view as identical those rights contained in the Bill of Rights and those rights fundamental to fairness. Unlike the fundamental fairness approach, however, the selective view holds that rights expressly contained in the Bill of Rights, if adjudged fundamental, are incorporated through the Fourteenth Amendment and are applicable at the state level regardless of the circumstances of a particular case.

**Indictment**    A written accusation presented by a grand jury to a court, charging that a person has done some act or omission that by law is a punishable offense.

**Injunction**    An order prohibiting a party from acting in a particular way or requiring a specific action by a party. An injunction allows a court to minimize injury to a person or group until the matter can otherwise be resolved, or it may prevent injury altogether. Failure to comply with an injunction constitutes a contempt of court. Once issued, an injunction may be annulled or quashed. An injunction may be temporary or permanent.

Temporary injunctions, known as interlocutory injunctions, are used to preserve a situation until the issue is resolved through normal processes of litigation. A permanent injunction may be issued upon completion of full legal proceedings.

**Judgment of the court**    The final conclusion reached by a court—the outcome as distinguished from the legal reasoning supporting the conclusion.

**Judicial activism**    An interventionist approach or role orientation for appellate decision making that has the appellate courts playing an affirmative policy role. Judicial activists are inclined to find more constitutional violations than those who see a more restrained role for courts; activists are more likely to invalidate legislative and executive policy initiatives. Judicial activism is seen by its critics as legislating by justices to achieve policy outcomes compatible with their own social priorities.

**Judicial notice**    The act by which a court recognizes the existence and truth of certain facts. These facts are recognized by the court's own initiative and not offered as evidence by either party.

**Judicial review**    The power of a court to examine the actions of the legislative and executive branches with the possibility that those actions could be declared unconstitutional. The power of judicial review was discussed extensively at the Constitutional Convention of 1787, but it was not included in the Constitution as an expressly delegated judicial function. The Supreme Court first asserted the power of judicial review in *Marbury v. Madison* (1803).

**Judicial self-restraint**    A role view of appellate court decision making that minimizes the extent to which judges apply their personal views to the legal judgments they render. Judicial self-restraint holds that courts should defer to the policy judgments made by the elected branches of government.

**Jurisdiction**    Jurisdiction defines the boundaries within which a particular court may exercise judicial power; it defines the power of a court to hear and decide cases. The jurisdiction of federal courts is provided in Article III of the Constitution in the case of the Supreme Court, and in acts of Congress in the case of the lower federal courts. Federal judicial power may extend to classes of cases defined in terms of substance and party as well as to cases in law and equity stemming directly from the federal Constitution, federal statutes, treaties, or those cases falling into the admiralty and maritime category. Federal judicial power also extends to cases involving specified parties. Regardless of the substance of the case, federal jurisdiction includes actions where the federal government itself is a party, between two or more states, between a state and a citizen of another state, between citizens of different states, between a state and an alien, between a citizen of a state and an alien, and where foreign ambassadors are involved. State constitutions and statutes define the jurisdiction of state courts.

**Jurisprudence**     A legal philosophy or the science of law. A term used to refer to the course or direction of judicial rulings. Jurisprudence draws on philosophical thought, historical and political analysis, sociological and behavioral evidence, and legal experience; it is grounded on the view that ideas about law evolve from critical thinking in a number of disciplines. Jurisprudence enables people to understand how law has ordered both social institutions and individual conduct.

***Jus belli***     Latin for the "law of war"; it applies directly to wartime. *Jus belli* addresses the rights and legal obligations of those nations engaged in warfare as well as the status of neutral nations.

**Justiciable**     A matter that may be appropriate for a court to hear and decide.

**Laissez-faire**     An economic theory that advocates the government ought not interfere with the dynamics of a free market economy—government should stay out of economic matters. Those subscribing to the laissez-faire view reject any form of government control or regulation of the economy. The decisions of the U.S. Supreme Court from the 1890s through 1937 frequently reflected laissez-faire values.

**Legislative court**     A court created by Congress under authority of Article I of the U.S. Constitution. Legislative courts may be assigned administrative functions in addition to or instead of judicial functions. Such courts facilitate development of some level of specialization in a court system. Judges of federal legislative courts may be granted life tenure by Congress, but do not have the same level of protection as judges of Article III or constitutional courts.

**Liberty of contract**     A laissez-faire doctrine used to free private agreements from governmental regulation. The liberty of contract concept holds that individuals have a right to assume contractual obligations affecting their personal affairs. This includes the right of employers and employees to agree about wages, hours, and conditions of work without government interference. The concept was a central element of substantive due process in which the courts closely examined the reasonableness of governmental regulations. The liberty of contract concept was used to strike down laws establishing minimum wages and maximum hours of work.

**Litigant**     A party to a lawsuit.

**Mandamus**     Latin for "we command." A writ issued by a court of superior jurisdiction to an inferior court or governmental official commanding the performance of an official act.

**Martial law**   Military government established over a civilian population during an emergency. Under martial law, military decrees supersede civilian laws and military tribunals replace civil courts. Martial law can be invoked by the president when necessary for the security of the nation. State governors, as commanders in chief of state militias, may declare martial law during an emergency occasioned by internal disorders or natural disasters.

**Moot**   The condition of a question presented in a lawsuit that cannot be answered by a court either because the issue has resolved itself or conditions have so changed that the court is unable to grant the requested relief.

**Motion**   A request made to a court for a certain ruling or action.

**Natural law**   Laws considered applicable to all persons because they are basic to human nature. Applies to all nations and people; contrasts with positive law.

**Naturalization**   Legal procedure by which an alien is granted citizenship. Congress is authorized by Article I, Section 8 of the Constitution to establish uniform rules for naturalization. An individual over eighteen years of age may be naturalized after meeting certain qualifications. These include 1) residence in the United States for five years; 2) ability to read, write, and speak English; 3) proof of good moral character; 4) approval by a judge or a federal court or a state court of record. The residence requirement is lowered for spouses of citizens and for aliens who serve in the armed services. Minors become citizens when their parents are naturalized.

**Obiter dictum**   Latin for "a remark by the way." Dicta are statements contained in a court's opinion that are incidental to the disposition of the case. Obiter dicta often are directed to issues upon which no formal arguments have been heard.

**Opinion of the court**   The statement of a court, which expresses the reasoning or *ratio decidendi* upon which a decision is based. The opinion summarizes the principles of law that apply in a given case and represents the views of the majority of a court's members.

**Order**   A written command issued by a judge.

**Original jurisdiction**   The authority of a court to hear and decide a legal question before any other court. Original jurisdiction typically is vested with trial courts rather than appellate courts, although Article III of the Constitution extends very limited original jurisdiction to the United States Supreme Court. Trial courts are assigned specific original jurisdiction defined in terms of subject matter or party.

**Per curiam opinion**   Latin for "by the court." An unsigned written opinion issued by a court.

**Petitioner**    A party seeking relief in court.

**Plaintiff**    The party who brings a legal action to court for resolution or remedy.

**Plurality opinion**    An opinion announcing a court's judgment and supporting reasoning in a case, but which is not endorsed by a majority of the justices hearing the case.

**Police power**    Authority that empowers government to regulate private behavior in the interest of public health, safety, and general welfare. In the U.S. constitutional system, police power resides with the state and not the federal government. The police power enables states and their respective local units of government to enact and enforce policies deemed appropriate to serve the public good. It is a comprehensive power, and substantial discretion is possessed by the states for its exercise. It is limited by various provisions of the U.S. Constitution and state constitutions, however, and must conform to the requirements of due process

**Political question**    An issue that is not justiciable, or that is not appropriate for judicial determination. A political question is one in which the substance of an issue is primarily political or involves a matter directed toward either the legislative or executive branch by constitutional language. The political question doctrine is sometimes invoked by the Supreme Court, not because the Court is without power or jurisdiction, but because the Court adjudges the question inappropriate for judicial response. In the Court's view, to intervene or respond would be to encroach on the functions and prerogatives of one of the other two branches of government.

**Preemption doctrine**    Holds that federal laws supersede or preempt state laws in certain policy areas. The preemption doctrine is grounded in the Supremacy Clause of Article VI and applies where the federal regulatory interest is so dominant or pervasive as to allow no reasonable inference that room is left for states to act. Congress may state explicitly such a preemptive interest, or the courts may interpret the intent of Congress fully to occupy the field.

**Preferred position doctrine**    Holds that legislative enactments that affect First Amendment rights must be scrutinized more carefully than legislation that does not. The preferred position doctrine says that certain legislative activity deserves priority consideration because it affects fundamental rights such as free speech. The burden is clearly on the state to demonstrate justification for limiting a preferred position freedom. The preferred position doctrine is attributed to Justice Harlan Fiske Stone, who said in a footnote to his opinion in *United States v. Carolene Products Company* (1938), that a lesser presumption of constitutionality exists when legislation "appears on its face to be within a specific prohibition such as those of the first ten amendments."

**Prior restraint**   A restriction placed on a publication before it can be published or circulated. Prior restraint typically occurs through a licensure or censorship process or by a full prohibition on publication. Censorship requirements involve a review of materials by the state for objectionable content. Prior restraint poses a greater threat to free expression than after-the-fact prosecution, because government restrictions are imposed in a manner that precludes public scrutiny, and the First Amendment prohibits prior restraint in most instances. Prior restraint may be justified, however, if the publication threatens national security, incites overthrow of the government, is obscene, or interferes with the private rights of others, but is otherwise heavily suspect.

**Procedural due process**   Fundamental fairness in the means by which governmental actions are executed. Procedural due process demands that before any deprivation of liberty or property can occur, a person must be formally notified and provided an opportunity for a fair hearing. Procedural due process must also be accorded persons accused of crimes and includes access to legal counsel, the ability to confront witnesses against the accused, and a trial by jury.

**Quash**   To annul, vacate, make void or totally do away with.

**Recusal**   The process by which a judge is disqualified from participating in the hearing or review of a case. Disqualification may be initiated by a party(ies) to a case or by the judge himself or herself when a judge's participation might be inappropriate because of self-interest or bias.

**Remand**   To send a case back to an inferior court for additional action. Appellate courts send cases back to lower courts with instructions to correct specified error.

**Removal jurisdiction**   The power to transfer a case, before trial or final hearing, from one court to another.

**Republicanism (Guaranty Clause)**   Government by representatives chosen by the people. A republic is distinguished from a pure democracy where the people make policy decisions themselves rather than through an elected representative. Article IV, Section 4 of the Constitution provides that the national government shall guarantee to each state a "republican form of government."

**Respondent**   The party against whom a legal action is filed.

**Reverse**   An action by an appellate court setting aside or changing a decision of a lower court. The opposite of affirm.

**Right**   A power or privilege to which a person is entitled. A right is legally conveyed by a constitution, statutes, or common law. A right may be absolute, such as one's right to believe, or it may be conditional so that the acting out of one's beliefs will not injure other members of a political community.

**Ripeness**    A condition in which a legal dispute has evolved to the point where the issue(s) it presents can be determined by a court. Ripeness is an issue that requires a court to consider whether a case has matured or developed into a controversy worthy of adjudication.

**Separation of powers**    The principle of dividing the powers of government among several coordinate branches to prevent excessive concentration of power. The principle of separation of powers is designed to limit abusive exercise of governmental authority by partitioning power and then assigning that power to several locations. The distribution of powers embodied in the U.S. Constitution functionally distinguishes between government and people, and between legislative, executive, and judicial branches. Although the Constitution creates three separate branches, it also assigns overlapping responsibilities that make the branches interdependent through the operation of a system of checks and balances.

**Sovereignty**    The supreme power of a state or independent nation free from external interference. Sovereignty is exercised by a government that has exclusive and absolute jurisdiction within its geographical boundaries.

**Standing**    The requirement that a real dispute exists between the prospective parties in a lawsuit before it can be heard by a court. As a result, courts typically are unable to respond to hypothetical questions. If a party does not have standing to sue, the matter is not justiciable.

**Stare decisis**    Latin for "let the decision stand." Stare decisis holds that once a principle of law is established for a particular fact situation, courts should adhere to that principle in similar cases in the future. The case in which the rule of law is established is called a precedent. Stare decisis creates and maintains stability and predictability in the law. Precedents may be modified or abandoned if circumstances require, but the expectation is that rules from previously adjudicated cases will prevail.

**State action**    An action taken by an agency or official of government. The state action concept is used to determine whether an action complained of has its source in state authority or policy. The concept is critically important in cases presenting allegations of discrimination. The Equal Protection Clause typically cannot be applied to private acts of discrimination. Rather, it requires conduct that occurs "under color" of governmental authority.

**Stay**    To stop, suspend, or hold in abeyance.

**Substantive due process**   Fundamental fairness in the content or substance of government policy. Substantive due process review requires courts to examine the reasonableness of legislative enactments—that laws be fair and reasonable in substance as well as application. Substantive due process is distinguished from procedural due process.

**Summary judgment**   A decision by a court made without a full hearing or without receiving briefs or oral arguments.

**Taxing power**   Article I, Section 8 of the U.S. Constitution permits Congress to "lay and collect taxes, duties, imposts and excises" and to provide for the "common defense and general welfare" of the United States. The scope of federal power to tax and spend has depended, at least in part, on the Court's interpretation of the "general welfare" phrase.

**Tenth Amendment**   Provision added to the U.S. Constitution in 1791 that retains or "reserves " for the states powers not assigned to the federal government. The Tenth Amendment has frequently been used to limit the actions of the federal government.

**Vacate**   To rescind, annul, or render void.

**Vested right**   A right that so completely applies to a person that it cannot be impaired by the act of another person. Such rights must be recognized and protected by the government.

**Warrant**   A judicial order authorizing an arrest or search and seizure.

**Writ**   A written order of a court commanding the recipient to perform certain specified acts.

# Annotated Bibliography

## Books

Abraham, Henry J. 1998. *Freedom and the Court: Civil Rights and Liberties in the United States*. 7th ed. New York: Oxford University Press.

Excellent narrative on the Supreme Court's role in defining constitutional rights. Provides insightful discussion of how Bill of Rights protections have been applied to state governments, the concept of due process of law, and the evolution of First Amendment and equal protection jurisprudence.

———. 1999. *Justices, Presidents, and Senators: A History of the U.S. Supreme Court Appointments from Washington to Clinton*. Rev. ed. Lanham, MD: Rowman and Littlefield.

Written by a preeminent constitutional scholar, this volume provides an analysis of the process used to select Supreme Court justices. Abraham discusses every nomination, successful or not, the motivations and expectations of the nominating president, and the Senate review and characterizes the on-bench performance of each justice.

Atkinson, David A. 1975. "From New Liberal to Supreme Court Conservative." *Washington University Law Quarterly:* 361.

Discussion of the incongruity between Sherman Minton's political liberalism preceding his appointment to the Court and the conservatism associated with his self-restraint jurisprudence.

Belknap, Michal R. 1977. *Cold War Political Justice: The Smith Act, the Communist Party, and American Civil Liberties*. Westport, CT: Greenwood Press.

An informative discussion of the Smith Act prosecutions of U.S. Communists during the Cold War period and the implications of these cases for political freedom in the United States.

————. 1993. *"Dennis v. United States:* Great Case or Cold War Relic." *Journal of Supreme Court History:* 41–58.

Insightful analysis of the Supreme Court's Smith Act ruling involving the national leadership of the American Communist Party.

————. 1994. "Cold War in the Courtroom: The Foley Square Communist Trial." In *American Political Trials*, ed. Michal R. Belknap. Rev. ed. Westport, CT: Greenwood Press, pp. 207–232.

Discussion of the Smith Act trial of eleven U.S. Communists for violation of the Smith Act.

Berry, Mary Francis. 1978. *Stability, Security, and Continuity: Mr. Justice Burton and Decision Making in the Supreme Court, 1945–1958*. Westport, CT: Greenwood Press.

The only extended discussion of Burton's thirteen years on the Court. With the exception of the first chapter, which is dedicated to representing Burton's pre-Court life, the remainder of the volume examines Burton's jurisprudence and his fit on the Stone, Vinson, and Warren Courts.

Blackman, John L., Jr. 1967. *Presidential Seizure in Labor Disputes*. Cambridge, MA: Harvard University Press.

Comprehensive examination of seizure as a response to labor disputes. Blackman studied seventy-one instances of presidential seizure of businesses and the effectiveness of seizure as an approach to addressing labor-management conflict. Extensive discussion of Truman's seizure of the steel industry in 1952.

Breen, Daniel L. 1994. "Stanley Forman Reed." In *The Supreme Court Justices: A Biographical Dictionary*, ed. Melvin I. Urofsky. New York: Garland Publishing, pp. 367–372.

Develops Reed's deference to federal power and decisions of the legislative and executive branches. Portrays Reed as a committed New Dealer, but not a judicial liberal who was reluctant to support claims of rights violations.

Cochran, Bert. 1973. *Harry Truman and the Crisis Presidency.* New York: Funk & Wagnalls.

A political biography of Truman, featuring the crises confronting his presidency—concluding World War II, the Cold War/arms race, containment, the Korean War, and McCarthyism among them.

Cortner, Richard C. 1981. *The Supreme Court and the Second Bill of Rights: The Fourteenth Amendment and the Nationalization of Civil Liberties.* Madison: University of Wisconsin Press.

Discussion of the impact of the Fourteenth Amendment on constitutional rights—how it enabled extension of Bill of Rights protections to the states.

Dubofsky, Melvin, and Warren Van Tine. 1986. *John L. Lewis: A Biography.* Urbana: University of Illinois Press.

Definitive biography on Lewis, his roots in trade unionism, and his rise to national prominence in the labor movement in the 1930s. Authoritative discussion of the strikes by his mineworkers during World War II and the litigation arising out of those actions.

Farber, Daniel A. 1994. "Robert Houghwout Jackson." In *The Supreme Court Justices: A Biographical Dictionary,* ed. Melvin I. Urofsky. New York: Garland Publishing, pp. 257–262.

Essay focuses on three of Jackson's most significant opinions—*Barnette, Wickard,* and *Youngstown.*

Frank, John P., and Vern Countryman. 1995. "William O. Douglas." In *The Justices of the Supreme Court, 1789–1995,* ed. Leon Friedman and Fred L. Israel. New York: Chelsea House Publishers, pp. 1219-1246.

Informative biographical discussion. Frank overviews Douglas's Court record and presents several cases to illustrate what he calls the "most important function" of Douglas during his almost four-decade tenure on the Court—his service as a "bridge from an old liberalism to a new."

Freyer, Tony Allan. 1990. *Hugo L. Black and the Dilemma of American Liberalism.* Glenville, IL: Scott Foresman/Little, Brown Higher Education.

Informative discussion of Black, his political background, and his positions on constitutional rights. Freyer focuses on the incongruity of Black's advocacy of applying

Bill of Rights provisions to actions of state governments and his literalism, which occasionally limited the scope of Bill of Rights protections.

Friedman, Leon, and Fred L. Israel, eds. 1995. *The Justices of the United States Supreme Court: Their Lives and Major Opinions.* New York: Chelsea House.

A superb five-volume set containing extended essays on all of the Supreme Court justices. Each essay provides biographical background information, but also includes substantial discussion of the justices' jurisprudence. An earlier edition of these volumes also contains a sample of two or three of each justice's major opinions.

Glancy, Dorothy J. 1994. "William Orville Douglas." In *The Supreme Court Justices: A Biographical Dictionary*, ed. Melvin I. Urofksy. New York: Garland Publishing, pp. 141–151.

The essay provides background discussion of Douglas followed by a concise examination of his jurisprudence, with particular attention directed toward his individual rights decisions.

Hurst, J. Willard. 1971. *The Law of Treason in the United States.* Westport, CT: Greenwood Press.

Authoritative discussion of the crime of treason and the evidence required to prove treasonous intent. Included is an appraisal of the Supreme Court's application of the law of treason in the *Cramer* and *Haupt* cases.

Irons, Peter. 1994. "Francis (Frank) William Murphy." In *The Supreme Court Justices: A Biographical Dictionary*, ed. Melvin I. Urofsky. New York: Garland Publishing, pp. 331–336.

Following biographical background, essay focuses on Murphy's apprehension about joining the Court and the impact of that apprehension on his first two terms. Irons also develops Murphy's commitment to individual rights and his zealous guardianship of constitutional rights.

Israel, Fred L. 1995. "Wiley Rutledge." In *The Justices of the Supreme Court, 1789–1995*, ed. Leon Friedman and Fred L. Israel. New York: Chelsea House, pp. 1312–1321.

A brief biographical essay that overviews Rutledge's route to the Court and a broad overview of his civil liberties jurisprudence.

Kalven, Harry. 1988. *A Worthy Tradition: Freedom of Speech in America*. New York: Harper and Row.

A detailed discussion of the U.S. constitutional experience under the First Amendment.

Kirkendall, Richard. 1995. "Fred Vinson." In *The Justices of the Supreme Court, 1789–1995*, ed. Leon Friedman and Fred L. Israel. New York: Chelsea House, pp. 1334–1345.

Essay traces Vinson's political background, Truman's objectives in naming him chief justice, and the impact of his seven-year tenure on the Supreme Court.

———. 1995. "Harold Burton." In *The Justices of the Supreme Court, 1789–1995*, ed. Leon Friedman and Fred L. Israel. New York: Chelsea House, pp. 1322–1333.

Essay features Burton's political background and his role on the badly divided Stone and Vinson Courts.

———. 1995. "Sherman Minton." In *The Justices of the Supreme Court, 1789–1995*, ed. Leon Friedman and Fred L. Israel. New York: Chelsea House, pp. 1361–1372.

Develops Minton's political association with President Truman and Minton's impact on the Vinson Court.

———. "Tom Clark." 1995. In *The Justices of the Supreme Court, 1789–1995*, ed. Leon Friedman and Fred L. Israel. New York: Chelsea House, pp. 1347–1360.

Essay features Clark's political background and how his joining the Vinson Court altered the ideological balance of the Court.

Klugar, Richard. 1976. *Simple Justice: The History of* Brown v. Board of Education *and Black America's Struggle for Equality*. New York: Knopf.

Definitive discussion of the *Brown v. Board of Education* case. Klugar describes the status of race relations in post–World War II United States, traces the litigation challenging segregated public education from the beginning, and examines the Supreme Court's three-year effort to resolve the issue.

Kurland, Philip B. 1995. "Robert H. Jackson." In *The Justices of the Supreme Court, 1789–1995*, ed. Leon Friedman and Fred L. Israel. New York: Chelsea House, pp. 1282–1311.

Extensive background on Jackson's political life, especially his involvement with the Roosevelt administration prior to his nomination to the Court. Develops Jackson's judicial philosophy and his contributions to constitutional law. Focuses on two reasons Jackson was dissatisfied with his Court service—his view that the Court's work was irrelevant when compared with the "struggle for freedom" taking place with the war and the level of conflict within the Court.

Lacey, Michael J., ed. 1989. *The Truman Presidency*. New York: Cambridge University Press.

Collection of essays on the Truman era, with sections on such domestic issues as labor and economic policy and social reform and such foreign policy issues as the Cold War, the arms race, and containment of communism.

Leuchtenberg, William E. 2001. *In the Shadow of FDR: From Harry Truman to George W. Bush*. 3d ed. Ithaca, NY: Cornell University Press.

A discussion of those presidents who followed Franklin Roosevelt through the administration of George W. Bush. The first chapter covers the presidency of Harry Truman.

Levy, Leonard, 1968. *Origins of the Fifth Amendment*. New York: Oxford University Press.

Traces the history of the self-incrimination protection from its English roots. Final two chapters are devoted to the experience in the United States following the ratification of the Fifth Amendment.

Lukacs, John. 1961. *A History of the Cold War*. Garden City, NY: Doubleday.

Examination of the origins of what Lukacs calls the "crystallization" of the Cold War from the end of World War II through the Eisenhower presidency.

Marcus, Maeva. 1977. *Truman and the Steel Seizure Case: The Limits of Presidential Power*. New York: Columbia University Press.

Excellent discussion of the economic and political context leading President Truman to seize the country's steel mills in 1952. Traces the litigation that followed and the Court's decision ending government management of the industry.

McCoy, Donald R. 1984. *The Presidency of Harry S. Truman*. Lawrence: University Press of Kansas.

A discussion of the political history of the United States from the time Truman succeeded to the presidency through his 1952 decision not to seek reelection. Thorough treatment of the conclusion to World War II, the Cold War, the Korean War, Truman's domestic initiatives, his unexpected reelection in 1948, seizure of the steel industry in 1952, and his decision not to seek reelection that same year.

Mendelson, Wallace. 1961. *Justices Black and Frankfurter: Conflict in the Court.* Chicago: University of Chicago Press.

A brief comparative examination of Justice Frankfurter's judicial restraint orientation and Justice Black's liberal activism across a number of constitutional issues, including separation of powers, federalism, and civil liberties.

Milkis, Sidney M., and Michael Nelson. 1994. *The American Presidency: Origins and Development, 1776–1993.* 2d ed. Washington, DC: CQ Press.

Traces the institutional evolution of the presidency beginning with the executive branch under the Articles of Confederation through to the modern presidency.

Miller, Loren. 1966. *The Petitioners: The Story of the Supreme Court of the United States and the Negro.* New York: Pantheon Books.

A detailed account of the Court's civil rights history beginning with the *Dred Scott* decision, to the ratification of the three post–Civil War amendments and the Court's decisions on those amendments through *Brown v. Board of Education.*

Millis, Harry A., and Emily Clark Brown. 1950. *From the Wagner Act to Taft-Hartley.* Chicago: University of Chicago Press.

Comprehensive discussion of the political dynamics leading to enactment of the Wagner Act in 1935. Covers the next ten years and the building pressure to counter the Wagner Act, which led to passage of the Taft-Hartley Act in 1947.

Morison, Samuel Eliot, Henry Steele Commager, and William Leuchtenberg. 1980. *The Growth of the American Republic.* 7th ed., vol. II. New York: Oxford University Press.

Excellent narrative discussion of the social and political development of the United States.

Murphy, Paul L. 1972. *The Constitution in Crisis Times, 1918–1969.* New York: Harper and Row.

An insightful discussion of the effects of the Supreme Court's decisions from the conclusion of World War I into the turbulent decade of the 1960s.

Nelson, William E. 1988. *The Fourteenth Amendment: From Political Principle to Judicial Doctrine*. Cambridge, MA: Harvard University Press.

Discussion of the history of the Fourteenth Amendment, including the views of liberty and equality preceding its adoption.

Newman, Roger. 1994. *Hugo Black: A Biography*. New York: Pantheon.

Traces Black's life from his early years in Alabama, to the U.S. Senate and his appointment to the Court. Divides Black's years on the Court into three periods—his first twelve years, the development of his absolutist views, and his final decade in which, in Newman's view, Black and his jurisprudence were "overtaken by events."

Parrish, Michael E. 1982. *Felix Frankfurter and His Times*. New York: Free Press.

A revealing discussion of Frankfurter's years on the Harvard Law School faculty, his "boys"—students who later made their marks in Washington after Harvard Law—and his role in Franklin Roosevelt's "inner circle."

———. 1994. "Felix Frankfurter." In *The Supreme Court Justices: A Biographical Dictionary*, ed. Melvin I. Urofsky. New York: Garland Publishing, pp. 171–181.

Effectively represents Justice Frankfurter and his self-restraint orientation throughout his Court years, but also develops Frankfurter's remarkable life prior to his appointment to the Court.

———. 2000. "The Rosenberg Atom Spy Case." *University of Missouri at Kansas City Law Review:* pp. 601–621.

Informative discussion of the Espionage Act convictions of Julius and Ethel Rosenberg for passing atomic secrets to the Soviet Union.

Phillips, Cabell. 1966. *The Truman Presidency: The History of a Triumphant Succession*. New York: Macmillan.

Narrative on the decade of the 1940s by a former *New York Times* journalist.

Powe, Lucas A., Jr. 2000. *The Warren Court and American Politics*. Cambridge, MA: Harvard University Press.

Divides the Warren Court era into four periods—the beginnings, the stalemates of the late 1950s, the liberal-activist period that followed for which the Court is best known, and the end of the era in 1969. Discussion features the *Brown* ruling and its aftermath and cases focusing on Cold War, civil rights, criminal justice, and legislative apportionment issues.

Pritchett, C. Herman. 1954. *Civil Liberties and the Vinson Court*. Chicago: University of Chicago Press.

A follow-up to his classic work on the Roosevelt Court, Pritchett examines the effect of judicial personality and values on the civil liberties' decision making of the Vinson Court.

Radcliff, William. 1996. *Sherman Minton: Indiana's Supreme Court Justice*. Indianapolis: Guild Press of Indiana.

One of the few useful discussions of one of the Vinson Court's less visible justices.

Rise, Eric W. 1994. "Harold Hitz Burton." In *The Supreme Court Justices: A Biographical Dictionary*, ed. Melvin I. Urofsky. New York: Garland Publishing, pp. 77–80.

Brief essay that overviews Burton's tenure on the Court. Suggests that Burton did not possess the well-developed judicial philosophy of many of his contemporaries, preferring instead to decide cases on narrow, fact-focused grounds.

Rudko, Frances Howell. 1988. *Truman's Court: A Study in Judicial Restraint*. Westport, CT: Greenwood Press.

An examination of the four Truman appointees—Justices Burton, Clark, Minton, and Vinson—and their respective judicial philosophies.

Schwartz, Bernard, ed. 1998. *The Burger Court: Counter-Revolution or Confirmation?* New York: Oxford University Press.

A collection of essays examining the historical legacy of the Burger Court and the extent to which it countered or modified the jurisprudence of the Warren Court.

Simon, James F. 1989. *The Antagonists: Hugo Black, Felix Frankfurter and Civil Liberties in Modern America*. New York: Simon and Schuster.

Justices Black and Frankfurter disagreed about whether federal Bill of Rights provisions ought to apply to the states and how considerations of procedural due process defined rights of those accused of crimes. Simon demonstrates how their divergent views shaped contemporary civil liberties jurisprudence.

St. Clair, James E., and Linda C. Gurgin. 2002. *Chief Justice Fred Vinson of Kentucky: A Political Biography.* Lexington: University Press of Kentucky.

A recent political biography on Vinson, whose pre-Court achievements were more substantial than his performance as chief justice. Probably the most informative source on Vinson.

Tomlins, Christopher L. 1985. *The State and the Unions: Labor Relations Law and the Organized Labor Movement in America, 1880–1960.* Cambridge: Cambridge University Press.

Thorough historical discussion of the labor movement from its origins in the late-nineteenth century through the New Deal and post–World War II eras.

Tushnet, Mark V. 1994. *Making Civil Rights Law: Thurgood Marshall and the Supreme Court, 1936–1961.* New York: Oxford University Press.

Excellent historical discussion of the activities of the NAACP in advancing civil rights in the United States between 1936 and 1961 and Thurgood Marshall's pivotal role in pursuing the organization's objectives. Tushnet examines the legal challenges to the "white primary" practice, segregation in higher education, and finally the historic *Brown v. Board of Education* ruling and the immediate responses to *Brown*.

Urofsky, Melvin I. 1988. "Conflict among the Brethren: Felix Frankfurter, William O. Douglas and the Clash of Personalities and Philosophies on the United States Supreme Court." *Duke Law Journal:* 71.

Urofsky examines the conflict within the Stone and Vinson Courts of the 1940s as a personality conflict of the Court's justices, particularly Douglas and Frankfurter, who both came to the Court as distinguished academics, members of Roosevelt's "inner circle," and dedicated to the New Deal.

———. 1991. *The Continuity of Change: The Supreme Court and Individual Liberties, 1953–1986.* Belmont, CA: Wadsworth Publishing.

Excellent narrative on the evolution of constitutional protection during the Warren and Burger Court eras. Traces the expansion of protections by the Warren Court and the limited revisionism of the Burger Court.

———. 1993. "William O. Douglas as Common Law Judge." In *The Warren Court in Historical Perspective*, ed. Mark Tushnet. Charlottesville: University of Virginia Press, p. 64.

Examines the criticism of Douglas's jurisprudence by approaching his contributions to U.S. constitutional development and focusing on Douglas as a common law judge sensitive to the needs of a rapidly changing society.

———. 1997a. *Division and Discord: The Supreme Court under Stone and Vinson, 1941–1953*. Columbia: University of South Carolina Press.

The Supreme Court had two chief justices during the period between the beginning of World War II and the Warren Court era. The chief justiceships of Harlan Fiske Stone and Fred Vinson lasted only twelve years, but were important "transitional" Courts in Urofsky's view. The unusually high level of division within these Courts is a carefully developed theme.

———. 1997b. *Felix Frankfurter: Judicial Restraint and Individual Liberties*. Boston: Twayne Publishers.

An insightfully developed discussion of Justice Frankfurter that features discussion of the origins of his judicial self-restraint philosophy and his application of this approach throughout his twenty-three years on the Supreme Court. Frankfurter came to the Court as a nationally prominent legal scholar, but was unable to effectively apply his great scholarship. Urofsky examines the failed expectations of Frankfurter's tenure on the Court and explains why this occurred.

———. 2001. *The Warren Court: Justices, Rulings, and Legacy*. Santa Barbara, CA: ABC-CLIO.

Part of ABC-CLIO's Supreme Court handbook series, Urofsky examines the political context of the Warren Court, its justices, its most significant rulings, and its unique legacy.

Urofsky, Melvin I., ed. 1994. *The Supreme Court Justices: A Biographical Dictionary*. New York: Garland.

A collection of essays about each of the 107 justices who have served on the U.S. Supreme Court. The essays contained in this volume were prepared by an extremely distinguished collection of authors and provide valuable analysis, albeit summarily, of the jurisprudence of the justices.

Urofsky, Melvin I., and Paul Finkelman. 2002. *A March of Liberty: A Constitutional History of the United States, Volume II; From 1877 to the Present.* 2d ed. New York: Oxford University Press.

A superb two-volume narrative on the history and development of the U.S. Constitution.

Vose, Clement. 1959. *Caucasians Only: The Supreme Court, the NAACP, and the Restrictive Covenant Cases.* Berkeley: University of California Press.

An excellent discussion of the use of restrictive covenants as a device for maintaining segregated neighborhoods, and the NAACP-sponsored litigation leading to the demise of the practice.

Westin, Alan F. 1958. *The Anatomy of a Constitutional Law Case.* New York: Macmillan.

A detailed case study of Truman and his seizure of the steel industry in 1952. Discussion features the reasons Truman chose seizure, the litigation that followed, the Supreme Court's ruling, and the political aftermath.

White, G. Edward. 1988. *The American Judicial Tradition: Profiles of Leading American Judges.* Expanded ed. Oxford, UK: Oxford University Press.

Volume contains a number of group and individual portraits of selected Supreme Court justices. Particularly valuable to an understanding of the Vinson Court are the chapters on Douglas and the members of the Warren Court.

Wiecek, William M. 2002. "The Legal Foundation of Domestic Anticommunism: The Background of *Dennis v. United States.*" *Supreme Court Review* 2002: 375.

Excellent essay on the Smith Act prosecution of the leaders of the American Communist Party in the late 1940s. Provides valuable insights on the lengthy trial and the Supreme Court's landmark ruling on political association.

Woodward, C. Vann. 1974. *The Strange Career of Jim Crow.* 3d ed. New York: Oxford University Press.

Examines the period following the Civil War, during which time racial segregation became public policy in most Southern states. Woodward discusses the eventual end of legal segregation and the vestiges of segregation that remain.

Yarbrough, Tinsley E. 1988. *Mr. Justice Black and His Critics.* Durham, NC: Duke University Press.

A systematic examination of and response to the most significant criticism of Justice Black's jurisprudence, which features both the academic critics as well as those with whom Black sat on the Supreme Court, in particular Justices Frankfurter, Jackson, and Harlan.

————. 2000. *The Rehnquist Court and the Constitution.* New York: Oxford University Press.

An authoritative examination of the Rehnquist Court—its justices and its doctrinal record on such issues as government power, federalism, individual rights, and equal protection. The volume focuses on the Rehnquist Court's preference for policymaking at the state and local, rather than the federal, level.

## *Internet Sources*

New Internet sites are introduced frequently. Readers who use the sites listed below are encouraged to explore the countless number of links to other sites that are provided in virtually every site you visit.

There are a number of excellent sites with information about the U.S. Supreme Court, some of which are listed below. The full text of Court decisions is available from some of these sites, but they are generally limited to cases decided since approximately 1900.

**Emory University School of Law** (two sites)
Electronic Reference Desk
http://www.law.emory.edu/LAW/refdesk/toc.html

Initial menu offers several useful categories of information, including federal and state laws in the United States and selected representation of laws from more than seventy other countries. This site contains a reference option as well as sections on law by subject, law schools, legal periodicals, legal career information, and selected law firms

**Federal Judicial Center**
http://www.fjc.gov/

Home page for the Federal Judicial Center, the research and education agency of the federal judicial system. Contains links to other courts, including the new Supreme

Court site and the newly added link to the History of the Federal Judiciary site that contains a biographical database of all federal judges since 1789, histories of the federal courts, and other historical materials related to the federal judicial branch.

### Federal Judiciary Home Page

http://www.uscourts.gov/

This page is maintained by the Administrative Office of the U.S. Courts and is a good source of information on the federal courts. The site contains a number of links to other valuable court/law-related sites. There is also a link that features recent developments regarding the federal courts, including the latest on the status of federal judicial vacancies.

### Federal Legal Information through Electronics (FLITE)

http://www.fedworld.gov/supcourt/index.htm

Site contains the full text of about 7,500 U.S. Supreme Court decisions from 1937 to 1975. Cases can be retrieved by case name or keyword. Links are provided to other sites such as the Cornell University site.

### Findlaw

http://www.findlaw.com/

Extraordinarily valuable and comprehensive site. Among other things, the site has federal and state cases and codes, U.S. and state resources, news and reference, a legal subject index, links to bar associations, lawyers, and law firms. Decisions of the U.S. Supreme Court back to 1893 can be accessed, as can decisions of federal courts and appeals rulings.

### Jurist: The Legal Education Network

http://jurist.law.pitt.edu/supremecourt.htm

Pittsburgh University Law School guide to the U.S. Supreme Court as an online introduction to the "jurisprudence, structure, history and Justices of America's highest court." Links the user to sites that contain Supreme Court decisions (e.g., Cornell, Findlaw), news about the Court, biographies of the Justices, the Court's procedures, and the latest media coverage of the Court.

### Legal Information Institute (LII)

http://www.law.cornell.edu/index.html

Cornell Law School site containing Supreme Court decisions since 1990, U.S. and state constitutions and codes, law by source or jurisdiction, including international law and "law about" pages providing summaries of various law topics. The site has a "current awareness" page that contains news about the Court. LII provides a free E-mail service that distributes syllabi of Supreme Court decisions within hours of their release.

## Lexis-Nexis Academic Universe

http://web.lexis-nexis.com/universe/

Lexis-Nexis is a subscription database that covers a wide range of news, business, and reference information. Free access can be obtained to Lexis-Nexis through Academic Universe, which is available through most educational institutions.

## National Center for State Courts

http://www.ncsc.dni.us

A comprehensive site with extensive information on state courts, state judges, and state court caseloads. Links are provided for information about federal courts and international courts.

## Oyez Project

http://oyez.nwu.edu/

Northwestern University multimedia database that allows users to hear oral arguments from selected cases, obtain summaries of more than 1,000 Court opinions, biographical information on all the justices who have served on the Court, and a virtual-reality tour of the Supreme Court building.

## Supreme Court

http://supremecourtus.gov/

A newly accessible site that overviews the Supreme Court as an institution, its functions, traditions, procedures, court rules, docket, and calendar. There is also information available on the justices and the Supreme Court building. "Plug in" capability is required to access information from this site.

## U.S. Federal Courts Finder

http://www.law.emory.edu/FEDCTS

Site links the user to all federal appellate courts. Supreme Court links connects the user to the LII site. Excellent source for U.S. Court of Appeals decisions. Click any of the circuits on the U.S. maps to access rulings covering the last several years.

### Westlaw

http://westlaw.com/

Westlaw is one of the largest and most comprehensive legal and business databases available on the Internet. Subscription is required for access, but prospective subscribers are able to fully explore the site on a trial basis.

### Yahoo Law

http://dir.yahoo.com/Government/Law/

Yahoo is a search engine with a separate and extensive listing of law-related sites. An easy-to-use and comprehensive searching device.

A number of newspapers provide good coverage of the U.S. Supreme Court. Among the best are the *New York Times* (http://www/nytimes.com) and the *Washington Post* (http://www.washpostco.com).

# *Index*